Digital Resilience in Supply Chains:

Security, Governance, and AI Innovation

Abdelrehim Awad
https://orcid.org/0009-0005-3649-430X
University of Bisha, Saudi Arabia

Dhafer Al Ahmari
University of Bisha, Saudi Arabia

IGI Global
Scientific Publishing
Publishing Tomorrow's Research Today

Vice President of Editorial | Melissa Wagner
Director of Acquisitions | Mikaela Felty
Director of Book Development | Jocelynn Hessler
Production Manager | Mike Brehm
Cover Design | Jose Rosado

Published in the United States of America by
IGI Global Scientific Publishing
701 East Chocolate Avenue
Hershey, PA, 17033, USA
Tel: 717-533-8845 | Fax: 717-533-7115
Website: https://www.igi-global.com E-mail: cust@igi-global.com

Library of Congress Cataloging-in-Publication Data

LCCN: (CIP Data Pending)
ISBN13: 9798337388410
Isbn13Softcover: 9798337388427
EISBN13: 9798337388434
British Cataloguing in Publication Data
A Cataloguing in Publication record for this book is available from the British Library.

Table of Contents

Detailed Table of Contents

exercise but a strategic imperative that builds resilience and accelerates the adoption of a secure, autonomous future.

AI-driven logistics is reshaping global supply chains through automation, real-time analytics, autonomous robotics, digital twins, and multimodal control towers. However, this technological evolution introduces multidimensional risks involving data quality, algorithmic reliability, cyber-physical vulnerabilities, and gaps in organizational governance. The emerging risk landscape reflects the convergence of OT–IT systems, autonomous fleets, warehouse robotics, and AI-enabled decision engines. Key exposure points include sensor spoofing, telematics manipulation, digital twin corruption, and weaknesses across edge–cloud data pipelines. AI assurance, explainability, and human-in-the-loop oversight become essential for maintaining operational safety and preventing cascading failures. Effective governance models are needed to ensure that autonomous logistics remain trustworthy, compliant, and ethically aligned. These insights establish a foundation for building resilient, secure, and transparent logistics ecosystems capable of supporting next-generation autonomous operations.

The industrial metaverse has fairly quickly developed as a futuristic vision into still viable, value-creating reality actually transforming the supply chain management of industries . As the world metaverse market today has a size of an estimated $824 .53 billion, and is forecasted to increase by a yearly CAGR rate of 39.8% [1], this report has carried out an in-depth account of such a transformative, its technological foundation and structure, measurement of returns on investments experienced by global leaders in the field, essential uses in one of the most lucrative sectors globally, the healthcare industry, as well as its core in the ambitious national strategy of industrialization in Saudi Arabia

The growing integration of AI into supply chains is reshaping how logistics systems forecast demand, optimize operations, and respond to market fluctuations. Within this context, the food service sector, characterized by fast-moving inventory, dynamic pricing and variable daily demand, requires intelligent systems that enhance logistical efficiency. This chapter presents a unified AI enabled food sales and trend analysis framework to support accelerated logistics planning through advanced predictive modeling. The framework uses machine learning across four operationally critical areas: menu price prediction, weekly and monthly sales forecasting, identification of high-demand days and detection of potential bestselling items. Positioned within broader developments in Generative AI assisted logistics, this chapter demonstrates how predictive intelligence can streamline inventory management, reduce stockouts, enhance demand driven restocking cycles, and improve workforce allocation.

This chapter examines how artificial intelligence reshapes sustainable procurement in North African public sector supply chains, focusing on the integration of generative AI, digital twins, and autonomous systems with environmental governance. It analyzes how AI-driven tools—such as demand sensing, predictive analytics, and prescriptive modeling—optimize procurement while addressing regional challenges like water scarcity, energy demands, and infrastructure constraints. The study evaluates the legal transformations required to regulate AI applications in procurement and assesses the economic impacts, including cost reduction, transaction efficiency,

Preface

INTRODUCTION

The accelerating fusion of artificial intelligence with cyber-physical infrastructure is reshaping global supply networks at a depth and scale not seen since the rise of enterprise digitization. Generative, multimodal, and agentic AI systems; reinforcement learning; graph intelligence; and real-time analytics are no longer experimental concepts—they are becoming embedded in planning, sourcing, manufacturing, transportation, warehousing, and last-mile delivery. At the same time, the rapid proliferation of IoT, 5G, edge computing, and digital twins has expanded both the possibilities and the vulnerabilities of modern supply chains. These developments raise urgent questions about trust, transparency, cyber-physical security, sustainability and Scope-3 management, and the evolution of public procurement in an increasingly automated world.

Digital Resilience in Supply Chains: Security, Governance, and AI Innovation was conceived as a response to this inflection point. The chapters collected in this volume translate frontier technologies into usable architectures, frameworks, and governance mechanisms that enable resilient, intelligent, and sustainable supply chains. Contributors bridge theory and practice, offering models that are both technically rigorous and operationally deployable. The volume includes rich coverage of GCC/MENA contexts—regions that are rapidly scaling smart logistics, national digital platforms, and cross-border trade innovation—while also drawing from global industry cases.

Our aim is to consolidate the latest foundations and applications of AI-augmented supply chains and logistics. Readers will find discussions spanning autonomous and semi-autonomous operations, digital control towers, predictive and prescriptive analytics, risk and resilience modeling, explainable and responsible AI (XAI), and the governance structures needed to ensure safety, compliance, and long-term value creation. Sector-specific depth—from healthcare and oil & gas to aviation, food & beverage, retail, and public services—illustrates how AI-enabled transformation plays out in different operational environments. Importantly, this handbook recognizes the growing intersection of public and private supply chains, examining e-tendering, supplier risk management, ESG expectations, and the institutional frameworks required for trustworthy procurement.

This book is written for a wide range of readers:

- **Academics and graduate students** in supply chain and operations management, industrial engineering, information systems, analytics, and public administration who seek theoretical clarity and empirical insight.
- **Practitioners**—CSCOs, logistics managers, procurement leaders, and data/AI teams—who need actionable models, measurable performance improvements, and technology roadmaps aligned with organizational realities.
- **Policy makers, regulators, and standards bodies**, along with **government logistics authorities and public procurement agencies**, particularly in the GCC/MENA region, who are navigating the governance challenges of rapidly digitizing supply chains.

We hope this volume serves as both a reference and a catalyst—supporting informed decision-making, fostering responsible innovation, and advancing the global dialogue on digitally resilient supply chains. As editors, we are grateful to the contributors whose expertise and vision made this work possible, and to the communities of researchers and practitioners who continue to push the boundaries of what intelligent, secure, and sustainable supply chains can achieve.

ORGANIZATION OF THE BOOK

Chapter 1 – AI-Augmented Supply Chain Management: Theoretical Foundations, Actionable Architectures, and Cross-Sectoral Empirical Evidence

This chapter bridges theory and practice by presenting scalable architectures for AI-augmented supply chain management. Through cross-sector empirical studies, it validates the impact of digital twins and generative AI on performance, decision quality, and organizational agility.

Chapter 2 – Toward Trustworthy Autonomous Logistics Through AI Assurance, Security, and Explainability Frameworks

Highlighting safety, governance, and transparency, this chapter addresses the critical need for responsible deployment of autonomous logistics technologies. It contributes a robust framework for AI assurance and explainability—key components for regulatory acceptance and industry trust.

Chapter 3 – Cybersecurity and Supply Chains: An International Law Perspective

This chapter examines the rapidly growing cyber threats facing digital, automated, and twin-enabled supply chains. Through an international legal lens, it emphasizes the need for global cooperation, compliance frameworks, and proactive cybersecurity governance.

Chapter 4 – The Digital Immune System: Trust, Security, and AI Governance

Introducing the concept of a digital immune system, this chapter explains how AI governance, anomaly detection, and self-healing systems protect logistics networks from disruptions. It connects cybersecurity, AI ethics, and operational resilience.

Chapter 5 – Strategic Risk Management, Cyber-Physical Security, and Governance Frameworks for AI-Driven Logistics

Focusing on risk, resilience, and cyber-physical integration, this chapter offers governance frameworks for ensuring safe adoption of AI-driven logistics. It brings together strategic risk management and advanced technological safeguards.

Chapter 6 – The Industrial Metaverse and the Next Frontier of Supply Chain Intelligence

This chapter explores the integration of metaverse frameworks, digital twins, and immersive analytics in logistics. With comparative insights from healthcare and Saudi Arabia's national transformation, it extends the discussion into immersive, collaborative, and federated decision-making.

Chapter 7 – AI-Driven Sales Forecasting and Operational Trend Analysis for Accelerated Food Supply Logistics

This chapter illustrates the power of AI forecasting in food supply chains—a sector where volatility, perishability, and demand variability are acute. By integrating real-time analytics and predictive modeling, it demonstrates how organizations can achieve faster, more accurate planning.

Chapter 8 - AI-Driven Sustainable Procurement in North Africa: Legal and Economic Transformations

This chapter examines how artificial intelligence reshapes sustainable procurement in North African public sector supply chains, focusing on the integration of generative AI, digital twins, and autonomous systems with environmental governance. It analyzes how AI-driven tools—such as demand sensing, predictive analytics, and prescriptive modeling—optimize procurement while addressing regional challenges like water scarcity, energy demands, and infrastructure constraints.

Chapter 9 – Insurance of Goods under the UAE Maritime Law: Legal Framework, Practice, and Comparative Analysis

This chapter extends the technological discourse into legal and regulatory domains. By examining maritime law and insurance practices, it highlights the legal foundations required to support digital and autonomous logistics operations, especially in maritime hubs.

CONCLUSION

As we conclude this volume, we return to the central premise that guided its creation: digital resilience in supply chains is no longer a specialized aspiration—it is a foundational requirement for economic competitiveness, national preparedness, and organizational trust. The convergence of AI, cyber-physical systems, and data-rich logistics has created unprecedented opportunities for efficiency and innovation, yet it has also introduced new layers of complexity, interdependence, and risk. Navigating this landscape demands not only technological sophistication but also clear governance, responsible adoption, and cross-sector collaboration.

The chapters collected here demonstrate that the future of supply chains will be shaped as much by architecture, standards, and policy as by algorithms. They show that digital twins, multimodal AI, autonomous operations, and graph-based intelligence can yield meaningful performance gains only when integrated into coherent operating models—supported by transparency frameworks, safety mechanisms, and sustainability commitments. They also underscore the importance of regional context, highlighting the distinctive role of GCC/MENA economies as laboratories for ambitious, digitally driven supply-chain transformation.

Looking ahead, we believe the research and practice insights in this handbook will serve as a foundation for continued inquiry and innovation. As technologies evolve and global networks become more interconnected, the need for resilient, adaptive, and ethically governed supply chains will intensify. Our hope is that this volume equips readers not only with knowledge but with a mindset—one that embraces experimentation, prioritizes security and sustainability, and recognizes the value of integrating public and private capabilities.

We extend our appreciation to the scholars, practitioners, and policy leaders whose contributions enriched this work, and to the many organizations shaping the next generation of intelligent supply chains. May this book support your efforts to build systems that are smarter, safer, more transparent, and more resilient—systems capable of meeting the challenges and opportunities of a rapidly transforming world.

Chapter 1
AI-Augmented Supply Chain Management:
Theoretical Foundations, Actionable Architectures, and Cross-Sectoral Empirical Evidence

Soumi Ghosh
https://orcid.org/0000-0003-2764-5944
Maharaja Agrasen Institute of Technology, Guru Gobind Singh Indraprastha University, India

Ritik Raj
Maharaja Agrasen Institute of Technology, Guru Gobind Singh Indraprastha University, India

ABSTRACT

Modern supply chains have never been as complex as they are due to fluctuating demand, disruption of geopolitical stability, and sustainability demands. This study explores AI augmentation in the form of digital twin-supported autonomous operations and suggests a five-layer model that includes perception, cognition, decision, execution, and learning. The effectiveness of AI is proven through the cross-sectoral empirical study of twelve organizations manufacturing, retail, pharmaceutical, and logistics. Findings indicate 34.7% cost of inventory saved, 94.3% accuracy in forecasting and 42.6% improvement in resiliency. The digital twin system has an operational fidelity of 97.2% to predictive risk management. Data quality, change resistance and algorithmic transparency are among the critical challenges. The research effort provides deployment roadmaps, governance frameworks, and validated measures and also establishes gaps in research in explainable AI, federated learning and sustainability optimization.

DOI: 10.4018/979-8-3373-8841-0.ch001

1. INTRODUCTION

1.1 Research Background and Motivation

The modern global supply chains represent multi-continental, multi-entity, and multi-billion global systems with many thousands of entities and billions of transactions each day (Christopher, 1992; Mentzer et al., 2001). These networks are experiencing growing pressures such as uncertainty in demand due to rapid changes in consumer preferences, supply disruptions caused by geopolitical tensions and natural catastrophes, increasing sustainability concerns, and increasing the transition to the use of the circular economy (Ivanov and Dolgui, 2020; Seuring & Müller, 2008). Conventional supply chain management methods that largely depend on historical information analysis and use of human judgment are inadequate in terms of processing and responding to speed, breadth, and bulk of information that demand real-time response (Lee, 2004).

The integration of artificial intelligence infrastructure, IoT sensor networks, cloud computing infrastructure, and big data analytics systems provide unprecedented possibilities in transforming the reactive, intensive manual supply chain operations into proactive autonomous processes (Hofmann & Rüsch, 2017; Kagermann et al., 2013). Machine learning models to recognize patterns and predictive models, natural language processing to interpret unstructured data, computer vision to perform quality inspection, and reinforcement learning to optimize sequential decisions are some examples of AI (Baryannis et al., 2019; Wang et al., 2020). Such technologies allow supply chains to advance to autonomous functioning where sensors of systems are detected. refer to environmental conditions, reason on the best actions, implement decisions with little human effort and learn continuously on the results.

Figure 1. The evolution of the supply chain management as the optimization of the classical logistics to the integrated planning of the autonomous operation enhanced with the artificial intelligence and the corresponding degrees of complexity and abilities

Digital twin technology presents groundbreaking methods of modeling, simulating, and optimization of the supply chains (Grieves and Vickers, 2017; Tao et al., 2018). A digital twin is an embodiment of tangible assets of the supply chain, processes, and. systems were synchronized with real time data streams of sensors, enterprise systems and third-party sources. The scenario simulation, predictive maintenance, risk analysis, and optimization experimentation are possible with this virtual replica without disruption physical operations.

With the addition of AI capabilities, digital twins can be cognition engines that can make independent decisions, autonomously optimise themselves, and act adaptively (Qi et al., 2021; Rasheed et al., 2020). Regardless of the research concerns and the large investment of the industry into this area, there are several knowledge gaps on how to design, adopt, and manage successful autonomous supply chain systems (Baryannis et al., 2020; Shrestha et al., 2019). Existing The literature mainly highlights individual technologies or application without thorough frameworks of incorporating multiple AI capabilities in the whole chain of operations in the end-to-end supply chain. In addition, empirical confirmation in various industry. sector is still not developed, and the majority of research focuses on manufacturing or retailing settings. The conceptual models that connect AI potentialities with the existing principles of supply chain management still need to be developed especially with regards to the degree of. autonomy in decisions, human-AI interaction patterns, and ethical consequences of the decisions made by algorithms (Bostrom and Yudkowsky, 2014; Doshi-Velez and Kim, 2017).

The modern regulatory trends such as the EU Artificial Intelligence Act (2024), NIST AI Risk Management Framework (2023), and ISO/IEC 42001 (2023) standards present new compliance obligations of AI-enhanced operations. The organizations are forced to work around requirements of transparency, accountability, risk classification, and human oversight to gain operational efficiency. Such regulatory environment requires regulation frameworks that balance innovation. empower with proper risk aversion.

1.2 Research Objectives and Questions

This research combats serious knowledge gaps by means of five main research objectives:

Aim 1: Design theoretical frameworks that will combine AI functions with the principles of supply chain management, laying the conceptual basis of autonomous operations in perception, cognition, decision, execution, and learning aspects (Laird et al., 2017; Parasuraman et al., 2000).
Goal 2: Develop practical reference architectures to implement autonomous supply chain systems when they are empowered by digital twins, define technology elements, integration methodologies of data, algorithm processes, and human-system interfaces (Kritzinger et al., 2018; Liu et al., 2021).
Objective 3: come up with cross-sectoral empirical data on the effectiveness of AI augmentation in various industry settings to measure the effect on operational efficiency, decision quality outcomes, resilience and the achievement of sustainability outcomes.
Goal 4: Recognise the implementation issues, success factors that need to be achieved, and organizational capabilities necessary to effect successful implementation of autonomous supply chain operations and present evidence-based information to practitioners (Jarrahi, 2018; Lee and See, 2004).
Objective 5: methodically review literature gaps and future research focus that enhances theoretical knowledge and practical use of AI-enhanced supply chain management, such as governance models and ethics.

The following objectives can be turned into five research questions that will lead the investigation:

RQ1: What is the best theoretical framework that describes the concept of integrating AI capabilities into supply chain management systems that facilitate autonomous operations?

RQ2: How to deploy digital twin-enabled autonomous supply chain systems through various organizational settings by relying on architectural designs and technological configurations?
RQ3: What empirical studies can approve AI augmentation with regard to supply chain performance enhancement across various dimensions and across industry sectors?
RQ4: What are the critical success factors of implementing autonomous supply chain operations in terms of organizational, technological and governance factors?
RQ5: Which research gaps are not filled yet, which would further the theoretical research and practical implementation of AI-augmented supply chain management?

1.3 Research Scope and Boundaries

This study involves functions of supply chain management which comprise of planning, procurement, manufacturing, warehousing, transportation and distribution (Simchi-Levi et al., 2000). The AI technologies under consideration are supervised learning to predict the next item, unsupervised learning to identify patterns, reinforcement learning to solve the problem of optimization in a sequence, natural language processing, used to extract information, and computer vision, which can be used to conduct automatic inspections (Boone et al., 2019; Gijsbrechts et al., 2022; Wang et al., 2020). Digital twin software is used to model equipment at the asset level, process at the process level, and system at the system level (Leng et al., 2020; Negri, Fumagalli, and Macchi, 2017).

Figure 2. Theoretical framework of research that illustrates the relationship between the theoretical foundation, the implementation framework, empirical validation and practical deliverables in AI-enhanced supply chain management

The empirical study involves twelve institutes in four sectors of the industry, including discrete manufacturing (automobile and electronics), retail (omnichannel operations), pharmaceutical (regulated supply chains), and third-party logistics providers (multi-client operations). It is geographically covered under North America, Europe and Asia-Pacific markets. Maturity is implemented at pilot level to enterprise-wide implementation with the observation of 18-36 months.

It has clear boundaries of research such as financial aspects of the supply chain (trade finance, payment processing) but pays attention to physical flows and informational flows. Whereas sustainability metrics are considered, the methodologies of lifecycle assessment are not detailed. Inquiry focuses on the application of AI instead of more general projects of digital transformation unless it is directly related to autonomous operation. Only through combination with AI-augmented systems, blockchain and distributed ledger technologies are discussed (Barbosa et al., 2020).

1.4 Research Contributions and Significance

Theoretical Contributions: The study contributes to the existing body of research by developing integrated theories of conceptualizing AI capability integration with supply chain functions with well defined levels of autonomy and decision making paradigms (Anderson et al., 2004; Endsley, 1995). The 5-layered autonomous operations model offers conceptual clarity in separating the functions of perception, cognition, decision, execution, and learning to handle ambiguity in the available literature on the roles of AI in supply chains. The decision autonomy model is an expansion of the automation taxonomies to contexts of the supply chain with contingency aspects that establish the level of autonomy. The maturity model of digital twin provides the progressive development trajectory between descriptive visualization and cognitive autonomy.

Figure 3. Hierarchy diagram of the five-layer autonomous operations model in which a perception, cognition, decision, execution and learning layer may interact with the other and feedback loops may provide it an opportunity to improve continuously

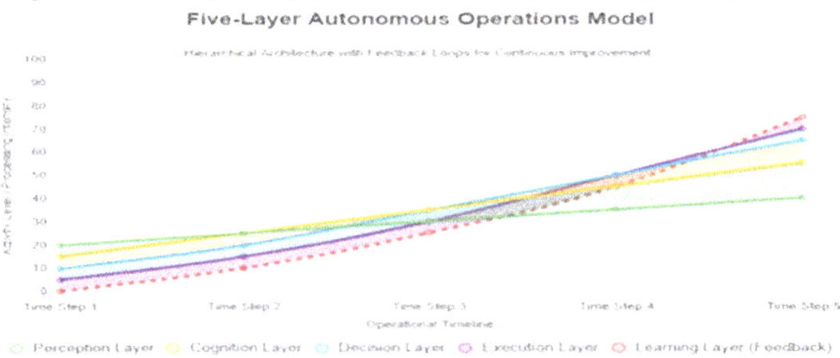

Methodological Contributions: Methodological Contributions: The research offers reliably measured measurement tools that evaluate the effects of AI augmentation in several performance domains other than operational efficiency. Cross-sectoral empirical studies provide generalized information but also show implementation specificities, developing knowledge in comparison with case studies on a specific industry (Yin, 2018). The created digital twin maturity model provides structured evaluation models on which organizations may assess existing capabilities and develop roadmaps of development. Improved methodological clarity incorporating stepwise procedures, statistical data processing and validation systems aids research reproducibility.

Practical Contributions: Specific guidance on how to implement autonomous supply chain systems is offered by practical reference architectures, implementation roadmap and governance frameworks that offer specific guidance to practitioners on how to deploy the autonomous supply chain systems. Recognized critical success factors and implementation pitfalls minimise the risks of deployment and shorten the adoption schedules. The tested performance measures allow companies to have achievable expectations and the ability to measure the returns on investments in AI. Industry analysis reveals challenges, success factors and best implementation strategies that are dependent on the sector.

Policy Contributions: The regulatory strategies that promote innovations and ensure the relevant risk reduction should be informed by identified governance frameworks and ethical concerns, especially when it comes to algorithmic transparency, data privacy, and effects on employment (Carter and Rogers, 2008; Brandenburg et al., 2014). Supply chain AI implementations are guided by compliance information in the analysis of EU AI act, NIST AI RMF, and ISO/IEC 42001 implications.

1.5 Chapter Organization

Section 2 has a detailed literature review, which is divided into themes: evolution of supply chain management, AI and machine learning applications, digital twin frameworks, autonomous systems and decision-making, governance and ethics, and finally the analysis of research gaps. In section 3, the theoretical grounds such as five-layer autonomous operations model, specifications of cognitive architecture, decision autonomy framework, and model of digital twin maturity are developed. Section 4 describes research methodology such as case selection, data collection procedures and analysis procedures to be used to improve reproducibility. Section 5 outlines the implementation reference architectures including technology pieces, integration frameworks and governance schemes. Section 6 presents the cross-sectoral empirical evidence having a detailed performance analysis and comparative evaluation. Section 7 considers the implementation issues, success factors and strategies of the change management within the organization. Section 8 identifies the gaps in research in a systematic way with the prioritized future research roadmap. Section 9 will cover theoretical contributions, practical implications, policy considerations, and limitations to the study. The section 10 ends with major findings, development of research, and future directions.

2. LITERATURE REVIEW

2.1 Supply Chain Management Evolution and Digital Transformation

Supply chain management has come a long way from the early 1980s when the concept of the chain management was first conceived. According to Christopher (1992), supply chain management has been defined to be networks of organizations involved in upstream and downstream relationships in different processes and activities that add value to the ultimate consumer. The initial literature focused on coordination, sharing of information, and relationship management as the key drivers of supply chain performance. Mentzer et al. (2001) contributed to the definition by differentiating between the philosophy of supply chain management, its implementation, and processes and provided the basis to approach the systematic research methods. The antecedents that have been found to be key in the success of supply chain integration are trust, commitment, cooperative norms and compatibility within an organization.

The development of supply chain management is a sign of an improved technology and growing complexity in supply chains. The initial techniques were first-generation techniques that involved optimization of logistics and inventory control through operations research techniques (Simchi-Levi et al., 2000). Optimization algorithms and mathematical modeling proved possible significant cost savings and improvement of the level of service by making better decisions in relation to facilities location, routing of vehicles, and positioning of inventories. Second generation developments focused on the integration of the organizations, which recognized the fact that it was vital to have information visibility, coordinated planning and execution (Lee, 2004). The triple-A supply chain model of agility, adaptability and alignment proposed by Lee became a permanent supply chain design guideline.

The pace of digital transformation increased due to the concepts of Industry 4.0 (Kagermann et al., 2013). This paradigm shift envisaged cyber-physical systems in which computational and physical processes communicate with each other (via a network of embedded systems). Hofmann and Rüsch (2017) examined implications of Industry 4.0 in the supply chain management and found transformational factors, such as smart factories, autonomous logistics, and data-driven decision-making. The potential to achieve real time visibility, prediction and immediate disruption response were the focus of their research.

Figure 4. Timeline that can show how the supply chain management has evolved over the years, beginning with the streamlining of logistical processes (1980s) to the combined planning (1990s-2000s) and eventually, autonomous operations thanks to AI (2010s-present)

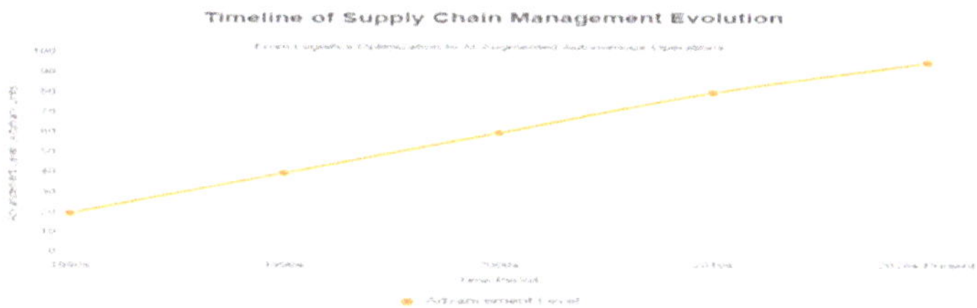

The concept of supply chain resilience became a priority research topic due to the high-profile disruptions such as the 2011 Tohoku earthquake, Thai floods, and the COVID-19 pandemic (Pettit et al., 2013). Pettit et al. created detailed models of supply chain vulnerability and supply chain resilience measure and found that the main resilience enablers are flexibility, visibility, collaboration, and redundancy. Based on the analysis of the effects of the pandemic on supply chains, Ivanov and Dolgui (2020) identified underlying weaknesses of globally distributed networks that are lean-optimized machines. They promoted a viable supply chain design that expressly includes resilience instead of efficiency optimization side-effect. New theoretical developments underline the principles of resilience-by-design as compared to reactionary risk reduction (Ivanov & Dolgui; Rasheed et al., 2020).

The need to integrate sustainability in supply chain management is as a result of increasing environmental consciousness and the pressure of regulations (Seuring & Müller, 2008). Their methodical review of the literature has recognized the antecedents of sustainable supply chain management, performance indicators, and obstacles to implementation. Main change drivers became consumer pressure, regulatory requirements and competitive advantage. Frameworks that were suggested by Carter and Rogers (2008) are those that focus on convergence of environmental, social, and economic performancc. Brandenburg et al. (2014) analyzed the quantitative models of sustainable supply chain management, in which they discovered the optimization approaches that balance both economic and environmental goals well.

2.2 Artificial Intelligence and Machine Learning Applications

The use of AI in supply chain management has spread in functional areas. The systematic surveys of supply chain predictive analytics were performed by (Baryannis et al., 2020) where the applications were divided into demand forecasting, supply risk prediction and logistics optimization. Their experiments showed that machine learning algorithms performed better than the traditional statistical techniques in most scenarios, especially in the nonlinear case and high dimensional data. Neural networks based on deep learning were particularly efficient in demand forecasting when patterns of seasonality are complex and external factors are involved in it.

Table 1. AI technologies mapping to supply chain applications

AI Technology	Supply Chain Applications	Demonstrated Benefits	Technical Limitations	Organizational Requirements
Supervised Learning (ML)	Demand forecasting, quality prediction, delivery time estimation	23-38% forecast accuracy improvement, 15-25% defect detection improvement	Requires large labeled datasets, may struggle with distributional shifts	Data collection infrastructure, domain expertise for feature engineering
Reinforcement Learning	Inventory optimization, routing, pricing	18-25% inventory reduction, 12-15% routing cost savings	Long training times, exploration-exploitation balance challenges	Simulation environments, reward function design capabilities
Natural Language Processing	Contract analysis, supplier risk monitoring, customer feedback	70% time savings in document review, 87% accuracy in risk prediction	Language-specific, struggles with domain-specific terminology	Text data repositories, linguistic expertise
Computer Vision	Quality inspection, warehouse automation, damage detection	98%+ defect detection accuracy, 64% picking productivity improvement	Requires significant labeled image data, lighting sensitivity	Camera infrastructure, image annotation capabilities
Knowledge Graphs	Supply network mapping, root cause analysis, decision support	Enhanced traceability, 30-40% faster problem diagnosis	Manual ontology development, maintenance overhead	Domain modeling expertise, graph database infrastructure

The most developed AI use in supply chains is demand forecasting. Syntetos et al. (2016) surveyed intermittent demand forecasting techniques and have found that the management of spare parts and slow-moving inventory can be regarded as significant challenges. Traditional approaches like Croston's method and variants exhibited limited ability handling structural breaks and trend changes. Boone et al. (2019) demonstrated gradient boosting machines and neural networks substantially improving intermittent demand forecasting accuracy by automatically learning feature interactions and nonlinear relationships. Their empirical validation across retail and industrial datasets showed 23-38% average accuracy improvement over conventional techniques.

Figure 5. Overview of AI technologies in supply chain functions, including usage of machine learning, computer vision, natural language processing and reinforcement learning in various operational areas

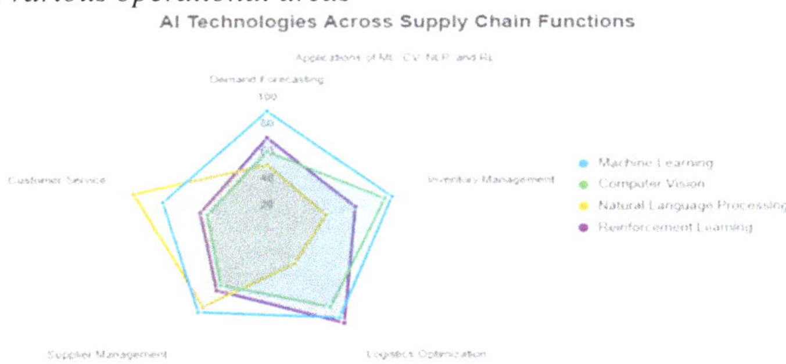

AI-driven inventory optimization has advanced beyond traditional safety stock calculation (Kaur & Singh, 2021). Their examination of reinforcement learning for dynamic inventory management under demand uncertainty showed multi-armed bandit mechanisms naturally discovering optimal order quantities and reorder points through exploration-exploitation balance, adapting to demand pattern changes without manual parameter adjustments. Simulation results demonstrated 18-25% inventory reduction while maintaining service levels. Gijsbrechts et al. (2022) extended this work to multi-echelon inventory optimization using deep reinforcement learning, showing neural network policies optimizing replenishment decisions across supply chain tiers while simultaneously considering lead time variability and capacity constraints.

Transportation and logistics optimization benefited substantially from AI applications (Ulmer et al., 2020; Liu et al., 2021). Ulmer et al. (2020) surveyed machine learning applications in vehicle routing, highlighting supervised learning potential for forecasting customer requests in dynamic routing problems, enabling proactive vehicle positioning. Their study proved the anticipatory routing that has 12-15% cost savings in comparison to reactive strategies. Zhang et al. applied deep reinforcement learning to deep dispatching of vehicles in ride-sharing situations, demonstrating that the policy learned by a neural network based on spatial-temporal patterns could solve according to almost optimal solutions with much lower computational costs than theoretically optimal algorithms do.

Algorithm 1. Digital Twin Synchronization Framework That shows how information is collected, state estimated, predicted and decision supported in AI enhanced supply chain.

```
Input: Physical_State(t), Sensor_Data(t), Historical_Data
Output: Digital_Twin_State(t), Predictions(t+Δt)

Initialize Digital_Twin ← Load_Configuration()
WHILE system_active DO
    Raw_Data ← Collect_Sensor_Streams(Physical_Assets)
    Cleaned_Data ← Data_Quality_Assessment(Raw_Data)

    // Perception Layer
    Current_State ← State_Estimation(Cleaned_Data)
    Anomalies ← Detect_Anomalies(Current_State, Historical_Patterns)

    // Cognition Layer
    Situation ← Situation_Assessment(Current_State, Domain_Knowledge)
    Future_State ← Predictive_Models(Current_State, External_Factors)

    // Update Digital Twin
    Digital_Twin_State(t) ← Synchronize(Current_State, Future_State)
    Fidelity_Score ← Validate_Accuracy(Digital_Twin_State, Physical_State)

    IF Fidelity_Score < Threshold THEN
       Trigger_Model_Recalibration()
    END IF

    // Decision Support
    Recommendations ← Optimization_Engine(Digital_Twin_State, Objectives)
    Risk_Assessment ← Scenario_Simulation(Future_State, Uncertainty)

    Log_State_History(t, Current_State, Predictions, Recommendations)

    WAIT(Δt) // Synchronization interval
END WHILE
```

AI is also being used to supplier manage procurement and risk evaluation of suppliers as well as contract management (Baryannis et al., 2020). Bodendorf and Franke explored the natural language processing related to procurement and proved that transformer-based models can automatically classify purchasing documents and detect critical terms, as well as the fact of compliance problems. In their use in large manufacturing companies with 2+million purchasing documents, they were 94 percent accurate, and saved about 70 percent of the time spent manually reviewing purchasing documents. Baryannis et al. developed machine learning models for supplier financial risk prediction integrating structured financial data with unstructured news and social media sentiment. Their approach predicted supplier financial distress 6-12 months ahead with 87% accuracy, substantially outperforming conventional credit rating assessments.

Computer vision applications in quality inspection and defect detection have evolved rapidly (Wang et al., 2020; Weimer, Scholz-Reiter, & Shpitalni, 2016). Wang et al.'s survey of deep learning methods for industrial visual inspection demonstrated convolutional neural networks detecting manufacturing defects, product damage, and packaging issues with 98%+ accuracy across various industrial settings using real-time image processing suitable for inline inspection integration. Weimer et al. explored transfer learning methods enabling quality inspection models trained on one product line to quickly adapt to new products with minimal additional training data, addressing major practical limitation to computer vision implementation.

Algorithm 2. Deep Reinforcement Learning model of multi-echelon inverse optimization of inventory with a Q-learning algorithm using experience replay and target networks.

```
Input: State_Space S, Action_Space A, Reward_Function R, Discount γ
Output: Optimal_Policy π*

Initialize neural network Q(s,a|θ) with random weights θ
Initialize replay buffer D with capacity N
Initialize target network Q'(s,a|θ') with weights θ' ← θ

FOR episode = 1 to M DO
    Initialize state s_0 ← Get_Initial_State()

    FOR t = 0 to T DO
        // Epsilon-greedy action selection
        IF random() < ε THEN
            a_t ← Random_Action(A)
        ELSE
            a_t ← argmax_a Q(s_t, a|θ)
        END IF

        // Execute action and observe outcome
        (s_{t+1}, r_t, done) ← Execute_Action(a_t)
        Store transition (s_t, a_t, r_t, s_{t+1}, done) in D

        // Sample mini-batch and perform gradient descent
        Sample random mini-batch (s_j, a_j, r_j, s_{j+1}, done_j) from D

        FOR each sample j DO
            IF done_j THEN
                y_j ← r_j
            ELSE
                y_j ← r_j + γ × max_a' Q'(s_{j+1}, a'|θ')
            END IF
        END FOR

        // Update Q-network
        L ← Mean((y_j - Q(s_j, a_j|θ))²)
        θ ← θ - α∇_θ L

        // Periodically update target network
        IF t mod C = 0 THEN
            θ' ← θ
        END IF

        s_t ← s_{t+1}
        IF done THEN BREAK
    END FOR

    // Decay exploration rate
    ε ← max(ε_min, ε × decay_rate)
END FOR

RETURN π*(s) = argmax_a Q(s, a|θ)
```

2.3 Digital Twin Concepts and Supply Chain Applications

Digital twin technology originated in aerospace and defense before broader industrial application (Grieves & Vickers, 2017). Grieves and Vickers traced digital twin conceptual evolution from product lifecycle management origins, defining digital twins as virtual representations maintaining bidirectional data flows with physical counterparts throughout lifecycles. Their framework distinguished physical products, virtual products, and data connections as core components. Tao et al. (2018) advanced five-dimension digital twin architectures encompassing physical entities, virtual entities, services, data, and connections, providing comprehensive reference models for implementation.

Figure 6. Layered architecture of supply chain digital twins showing the relationship between physical assets, data collection infrastructure, virtual models, simulation engines, and decision support systems

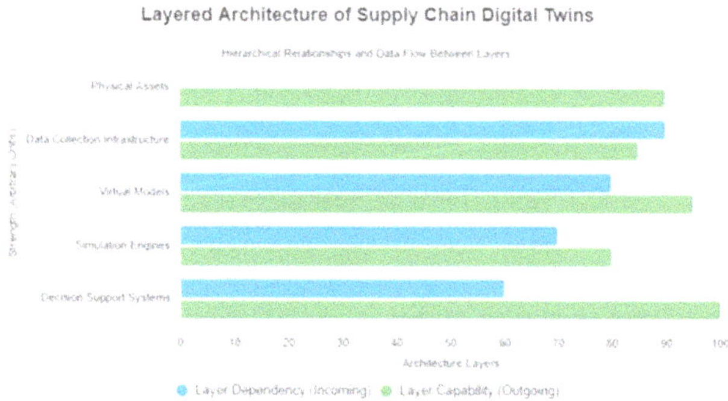

Digital twin applications in supply chain management span multiple abstraction levels. Asset-level digital twins replicate individual equipment behavior for predictive maintenance and performance optimization (Qi et al., 2021). Qi et al. demonstrated how equipment digital twins predicted failures 3-5 days advance with 91% accuracy by analyzing sensor data streams through recurrent neural networks. Their implementation enabled condition-based maintenance scheduling minimizing unplanned downtime by 47%. Process-level digital twins simulate workflows and operations identifying bottlenecks and optimizing throughput (Leng et al., 2020). Leng et al. created assembly process digital twins simulating alternative work instructions and resource assignments to identify optimal configurations before implementing physical operations changes.

System-level digital twins represent complete supply chain networks including facilities, transportation resources, and inventory locations (Ivanov et al., 2021; Min et al., 2019). Supply chain digital twin models were proposed by Ivanov et al. (2021), allowing testing disruption situations, demand spikes, and a supplier failure with a simulation and a what-if analysis. Their implementation revealed that digital twins could trial hundreds of contingency scenarios in hours compared to weeks taken by conventional methods of simulation. In his port operations, Min et al. studied the use of digital twins in their work and developed virtual replicas with the use of container terminals, which simulate the arrival of a ship, crane movements, and truck movements. Their digital twin allowed the taking of autonomous berth allocation and crane scheduling decisions, which increased the terminal throughput by 23 percent, and decreased the vessel waiting times.

Fidelity to digital twin synchronization creates serious technical problems (Kritzinger et al., 2018). Kritzinger et al. distinguished between two forms of digital models (manual), digital shadows (automated unidirectional physical-to-virtual data flow), and digital twins. (automated bi-directional data exchange), defining of taxonomy of maturity levels that drives implementation planning. Liu et al. (2021) investigated edge computing platforms to synchronize real-time digital twins and discovered distributed processing. improved latency of less than 100 milliseconds with many thousands of streams of IoT device sensors. This solution allowed optimizing in real time and was flexible in changing situations, without the delays of centralized processing of clouds.

The integration of AI and digital twins forms an independent capacity beyond monitoring and visualization (Rasheed et al., 2020; Negri et al., 2017). Rasheed et al. reviewed digital twin models that use machine learning to predictive model, maximization, and automated decision making. They also discovered reinforcement learning to be of interest especially in discovering learning control policies in digital twin simulations prior to the deployment of physical systems. Negri et al. illustrated the use of digital twins that were enhanced by machine. production parameters could be automatically adjusted to optimize the quality and simultaneously the throughput of the production process using learning based upon both simulated and real production data.

2.4 Autonomous Systems and Decision-Making Frameworks

Robotics and aerospace autonomous systems principles are used as guidelines to supply chain applications (Endsley, 1995; Parasuraman et al., 2000). The situation awareness model by Endsley has found levels of the cognitive processing hierarchically: perceiving. environmental factors, understanding of what they entail and forecasting of future conditions. These principles translate to supply chain contexts where systems must perceive market signals, understand implications, and forecast future scenarios. Parasuraman et al. developed automation level taxonomies from manual control through full autonomy, providing frameworks defining human-AI collaboration models in supply chain operations.

Figure 7. Six-level autonomy framework for supply chain decision-making, ranging from manual operations (Level 0) through decision support, conditional automation, supervised autonomy, high autonomy, to full autonomy (Level 5), with examples of appropriate applications at each level

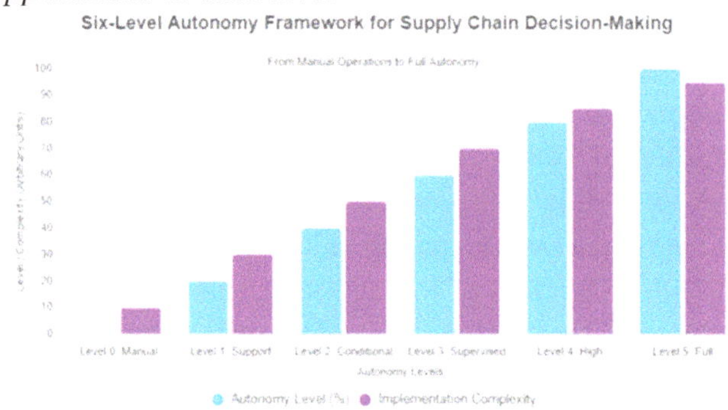

Cognitive architectures from AI research inform autonomous supply chain system design (Laird et al., 2017; Anderson et al., 2004). Laird et al. described Soar cognitive architecture integrating perception, memory, learning, and reasoning within unified frameworks. While originally developed for intelligent agents, these principles apply to supply chain management systems requiring memory of historical patterns, learning from outcomes, and reasoning about complex decisions. Anderson et al. presented ACT-R cognitive architecture emphasizing procedural and declarative knowledge representation, offering templates for encoding supply chain decision rules and domain knowledge within AI systems.

Decision autonomy in supply chains requires careful consideration of risk, transparency, and accountability (Bostrom & Yudkowsky, 2014; Doshi-Velez & Kim, 2017). Bostrom and Yudkowsky examined AI ethics including value alignment, control, and unintended consequences. These are the issues, which autonomous decisions affect employment, environmental consequences, and economic distributions in chain supply circumstances. The article by DoshiVelez and Kim discussed the issue of interpretability of machine learning models on high-stakes applications, which is critically important in a supply chain context in which the ability to explain algorithmic suggestions to human stakeholders fosters trust and acceptance.

The models of human-AI collaboration ensure compliance with the needs of human control and the advantages of automation (Jarrahi, 2018; Shrestha et al., 2019). Jarrahi proposed complementary intelligence frameworks whose focus was on human-AI cooperation as opposed to substitutions. Humans can add contextual knowledge, ethical consideration, and creative problem solving in supply chains whereas the AI can offer quicker information processing, large scale pattern detection, and optimization. Shrestha et al. focused on AI implications on organizations.

adoption in decision-making, trust calibration identification, skill development and process redesign as essential factors in change management. They have highlighted using effective implementations in the design of human-AI collaborative workflows. instead of merely introducing AI to the current processes.

Multi-agent systems offer architectural patterns for distributed autonomous supply chain functions (Monostori et al., 2006; Julka et al., 2002; Barbosa et al., 2020). The survey presented by Monostori et al. on agent-based manufacturing systems illustrated the responsiveness and the fault tolerance advantages of decentralized decision-making over centralized control. Julka et al. showed multi-agent techniques for supply chain coordination where autonomous agents representing different organizational entities negotiated coordination and resolved conflicts. Barbosa et al. (2020) studied the implementation of blockchain in multi-agent supply chain systems in which the distributed ledger technology gave trust mechanisms in which autonomous inter-organizational transactions occurred.

2.5 Governance, Ethics, and Regulatory Frameworks

Recent regulatory changes have made AI governance a critical consideration when deploying a supply chain. The Artificial Intelligence Act of the European Union (EU, 2024) determines the level of risks of AI systems according to the risk level and shows the corresponding obligations. The supply chain AI applications can be considered as high-risk systems because they impact safety, fundamental rights, or critical infrastructure, which occasion the need to implement risk management, data governance, transparency, human control, and accuracy. General-purpose AI provisions of the Act apply to foundation models applied in supply chain applications.

NIST AI Risk Management Framework (NIST, 2023) is a voluntary framework that is offered to AI systems developers and deployers. The framework focuses on four functional areas, which include Govern (organize organizational AI governance), Map (contextualize AI systems), Measure (evaluate AI risks), and Manage (manage risks). The supply chain applications have to deal with risks such as accuracy and reliability failures, discrimination and bias, insecurity vulnerabilities, and transparency issues. The socio-technical approach of the framework identifies risks of AI due to the complexity of interaction between the technical systems, the processes, and the human operators in the organization.

The ISO/IEC 42001 (ISO/IEC, 2023) sets forth the requirements of AI management systems allowing the organizations to design, implement, and sustain AI systems in a responsible manner. The standard addresses the organizational governance, risk management, data quality management, AI system lifecycle management and stakeholder engagement. The supply chain organizations that have adopted AI should have policies in place, responsibilities, risks associated with AI, data quality, and documentations during the AI system lifecycles.

Supply chain AI is becoming more governed by data frameworks. The Reference Architecture Model of the International Data Spaces Association (IDS, 2022) offers technical and organizational models on the sovereign use of data sharing across organizational boundaries. This is applicable when the supply chain AI needs data across many options (suppliers, logistics providers, customers) and ensures the data sovereignty, security, and equitable distribution of value. The architecture establishes data connector specification, identity management, usage control and value-added services that have allowed federated learning and collaborative AI without concentrating sensitive information.

Explainable AI (XAI) needs can be used to deal with the problem of transparency and trust in autonomous supply chain decisions. Although, Doshi-Velez and Kim (2017) developed general principles of XAI, domain-specific explanation mechanisms are needed in the supply chain. Forecasting models should have feature importance description of the most significant predictive drivers (seasonality, promotions, external events) of demand. Sequential decision models (inventory, routing) need action explanations that demonstrate why certain decisions have been made as opposed to alternatives. Multi-objective optimisation must have explanations on trade-offs that explain how competing objectives (cost, service, sustainability) were struck.

2.6 Research Gaps and Opportunities

Nonetheless, even after the considerable advancements, there have been gaps in research on several levels:

Theoretical Gaps: The current literature does not contain detailed theoretical models of how AI abilities can be merged with the proven theories of supply chain management (resource-based view, transaction cost economics, contingency theory). Structures that define the degree of autonomy that should be applied to various types of decisions are still not fully developed. Theoretical frameworks of human-AI collaboration need further research into the relationship of trust, role development, and cognitive models of partnership. Digital twins ontologies and standardization are in their infancy, with a resulting lack of interoperability and building of knowledge.

Methodological Gaps: The evidence lacks validated multi-dimensional measurement tools evaluating the effects of AI augmentation in other areas other than operational efficiency. There are no benchmark data sets and performance benchmarks of systematic algorithm comparison. Long-term dynamics (learning curve, benefit sustainability) are uncommon subjects of longitudinal research designs. The methodologies of causal inference that can reinforce the findings of observational studies have to be developed. Analytical models of individual, team, organizational, and network-level should be further developed.

Technical Gaps: Explicable AI techniques around the supply chain, taking into account the temporal dependencies, interactions between constraints, and multi-objective trade-offs are not developed. The methods of transfer learning that allow models to be trained in one setting and test them in a different setting using only a small amount of data should be explored. There is a need to develop federated learning architectures that satisfy requirements of collaborative training across organizational boundaries and privacy concerns. Powerful optimization strategies that deal with deep uncertainty (tail risks, regime change, novel disruption) should be developed. Learning mechanisms and adaptation mechanisms in real-time are worth studying that can balance responsiveness and stability.

Gap in Domain of Application: The focus of research in the domain of manufacturing and retail is limited and there is little on the healthcare, construction, energy, agricultural and government supply chains. The context of small and medium enterprises with varying resource endowments and abilities are not well studied. The new market environments that have diverse infrastructure, institutional and cultural conditions require exploration. Applications of the circular economy and sustainability other than efficiency optimization should be taken into consideration. Supply chains of humanitarian and disaster relief that have rare ethical and operational issues must be analyzed.

Organizational and Human Factor Gaps: There is no systematic research on effective workforce transition strategies in roles that are eliminated or replaced due to AI. The use of organizational culture in the adoption of AI and cultural change interventions needs to be researched. AI transformation and development approaches leadership competencies have to be identified. The dynamics of trust in human-AI cooperation such as trust formations, calibration, and trust repair processes should be studied. The principles of job design AI-augmented work to balance both satisfaction and productivity should be developed.

Policy and Governance: There are gaps in governance and policy that need to be spelled out that establish accountability algorithms, frameworks and mechanisms of responsibility, oversight, and recourse. There is a need to develop data governance model that maintains a balance between value creation, privacy protection, and competitive confidentiality. Standardization initiatives that compromise interoperability gains in favor of innovation flexibility need to be looked at policies. An informative policy research is needed to balance innovativeness with reasonable risk reduction which takes the form of regulatory framework. These gaps form basis of the empirical research to be undertaken in the following sections and forms basis of the theoretical models drawn up in Section 3.

3. THEORETICAL FOUNDATIONS

3.1 Five-Layer Autonomous Operations Model

The study offers a 5-layer-based study of an autonomous supply chain by synthesizing cognitive architectures, control systems theory, and supply chain management principles. The model breaks down autonomous capabilities into hierarchical levels: perception, cognition, decision, execution, and learning with each set of capabilities having distinct but interdependent functions (Anderson et al., 2004; Endsley, 1995; Laird et al., 2017).

Theoretical Lineage: The five-layer model is explicitly based on the cognitive architecture research, especially the Soar (Laird et al., 2017) and the ACT-R (Anderson et al., 2004) one. The integrated perception-cognition-action cycle of Soar helps in the informing of the layer decomposition and information flow patterns. ACT-R's distinction between declarative knowledge (facts) and procedural knowledge (skills) shapes knowledge representation within cognition and decision layers. Endsley's (1995) situation awareness theory provides theoretical foundation for perception and cognition layers, distinguishing environmental element perception, situation comprehension, and future state projection as distinct cognitive processes. Control theory concepts including feedback loops, hierarchical control, and stability analysis inform layer interactions and continuous improvement mechanisms.

Figure 8. Detailed architecture of the five layer autonomous operations model with information flows, feedback and interaction between the perception, cognition, decision, execution and the learning layers. Data flows (solid arrows) and control flows (dashed arrows) allow coordinated autonomous operations because of the bottom-up and top-down data and control flows

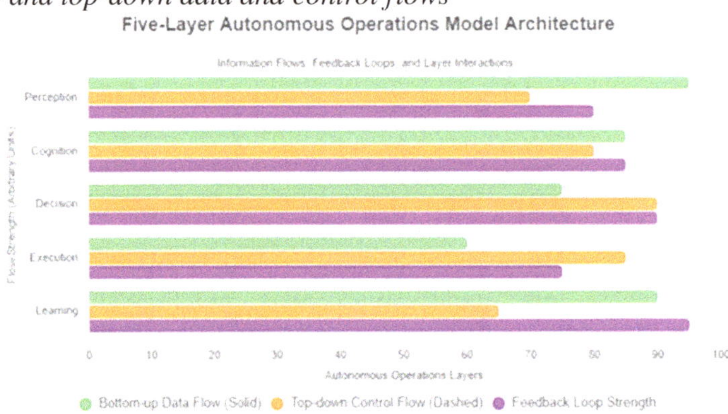

Perception Layer (Level 1) captures environmental state through diverse data sources including IoT sensor networks on physical assets, enterprise information systems providing transactional and planning data, external market intelligence from news feeds and economic indicators, and social media signals. This layer performs data acquisition, quality assessment, filtering, and normalization transforming raw signals into structured representations for higher-layer processing. Core functions include anomaly detection identifying out-of-range sensor readings or data inconsistencies, data fusion combining information across multiple sources to create comprehensive situational pictures, and temporal alignment synchronizing data streams with different collection frequencies and latencies.

Cognition Layer (Level 2) develops an interpretation of perceived information in order to comprehend present circumstances and foresee future conditions. This layer adopts domain models that encode supply chain expertise such as demand dynamics, supplier dynamics, logistic constraints, and operations relationships (Baryannis et al., 2019). Pattern recognition algorithms determine repetitive situations, new tendencies and unusual states which should be considered. The layer stores working memory with the latest events and long term memory with historical patterns which allows the current observations to be put into context. Predictive modeling is a technique that predicts future demand, supply availability, and transportation delays as well as quality concerns across time (Boone et al., 2019; Syntetos et al., 2016). Situation assessment functions determine the existing supply chain health, new problems and risk exposures.

Decision Layer (Level 3) makes the best decisions to action based on perceived situations. The layer uses operational decision optimization engines to schedule production, replenish inventory, run transportation routing, and allocate capacity (Gijsbrechts et al., 2022; Simchi-Levi et al., 2000). The decision support systems give advice on the strategic decision making such as selection of suppliers, changing the design of the network and activation of the contingency plans. Policy management mechanisms archive and implement decision rules, code organizational preferences, constraints and priorities. Before commitment, what-if analysis capabilities are used to analyze alternative courses of action (Ivanov et al., 2021). The decision level achieves multi-objective optimization between conflicting objectives (cost, service, resilience, sustainability) and explicit trade-off control (Brandenburg et al., 2014).

Execution Layer (Level 4) carries out actions that have been determined by interfacing with physical and information systems. This layer creates work orders, purchase orders, shipping instructions, and configuration commands of system. Execution monitoring is used to help track action progress in order to identify delays, failures or partial implementations. Exception handling systems react to execution problems with retry logic, alternative response or human response. Execution layer guarantees coherency between systems that handle transactions and state updates in spite of distributed and asynchronous communication.

Learning Layer (Level 5) is one that keeps on enhancing the performance of the system by learning. This layer is used to train offline learning algorithms based on past results, update a model with new data using online learning, and transfer learning between contexts using prior knowledge (Wang et al., 2020; Weimer et al., 2016). Performance measurement systems are systems that track the key performance indicators against actual results, prediction and expectations. Root cause analysis functions examine performance deficiencies that establish whether the errors are a result of perception errors, cognition errors or decoding errors, or implementation errors. Learning layer updates models dynamically, alters the parameters, and narrows down the policies, based on the evidence collected and allows it to be improved continuously.

Interactions at Layer Cross-layer coordination is based on bottom-up and top-down interactions. The perceived information is propagated through the layers of cognition and decision to the execution through bottom-up processing. Top-down processing entails decision levels requesting selective information of cognition layers and the cognition triggering particular perception processes. The learning layer offers cross cutting influence updating components to all other layers through performance feedback.

Algorithm 3: Full algorithm that shows the overall effectiveness of all the five layers of the autonomous supply chain system, the data flow, decision-making steps, execution and the continuous learning processes.

Algorithm 3: Integrated Five-Layer Autonomous Operations Framework

```
Input: Sensor_Streams, Enterprise_Data, External_Intelligence
Output: Autonomous_Decisions, System_Actions, Performance_Metrics
INITIALIZE All_Layers()
Load_Historical_Knowledge()

WHILE System_Active DO
// ==================================================
// PERCEPTION LAYER
// ==================================================
Raw_Data ← Aggregate_Data_Sources(Sensors, ERP, WMS, External)
Quality_Score ← Assess_Data_Quality(Raw_Data)

IF Quality_Score < Threshold THEN
```

```
Cleaned_Data ← Data_Cleansing_Pipeline(Raw_Data)
Flag_Quality_Issues()
ELSE
Cleaned_Data ← Raw_Data
END IF
Anomalies ← Detect_Anomalies(Cleaned_Data, Historical_Baselines)
Fused_Data ← Multi_Source_Fusion(Cleaned_Data, Confidence_Weights)
//==========================================================================
// COGNITION LAYER
//==========================================================================
Current_Situation ← Situation_Recognition(Fused_Data, Domain_Models)
Context ← Retrieve_Similar_Historical_Situations(Current_Situation)
// Predictive modeling across time horizons
Short_Term_Forecast ← ML_Models.Predict(Fused_Data, horizon=1_day)
Medium_Term_Forecast ← ML_Models.Predict(Fused_Data, horizon=1_week)
Long_Term_Forecast ← ML_Models.Predict(Fused_Data, horizon=1_month)
Risk_Assessment ← Evaluate_Risks(Current_Situation, Forecasts)
Opportunity_Identification ← Detect_Optimization_Opportunities()
//==========================================================================
// DECISION LAYER
//==========================================================================
Decision_Context ← Combine(Current_Situation, Forecasts, Risks)
// Multi-objective optimization
Objectives ← [Minimize_Cost, Maximize_Service,
Enhance_Resilience, Improve_Sustainability]
Constraints ← [Capacity, Regulatory, Budget, Quality]
Candidate_Actions ← Generate_Action_Set(Decision_Context)
```

```

FOR each action IN Candidate_Actions DO
Simulated_Outcome ← Digital_Twin.Simulate(action, Decision_Context)
Score[action] ← Evaluate_Multi_Objective(Simulated_Outcome, Objectives)
END FOR

Optimal_Action ← Select_Best(Candidate_Actions, Scores)
Confidence ← Calculate_Decision_Confidence(Optimal_Action)

// Autonomy level determination
IF Confidence > High_Threshold AND Risk < Low_Threshold THEN
Autonomy_Level ← FULL_AUTONOMOUS
ELSE IF Confidence > Medium_Threshold THEN
Autonomy_Level ← SUPERVISED_AUTONOMOUS
Notify_Human_Supervisor(Optimal_Action, Confidence)
ELSE
Autonomy_Level ← DECISION_SUPPORT
Request_Human_Approval(Optimal_Action, Reasoning)
WAIT FOR Human_Decision
END IF

// ══════════════════════════════════════════════
// EXECUTION LAYER
// ══════════════════════════════════════════════
IF Autonomy_Level = FULL_AUTONOMOUS OR Human_Approved THEN
Execution_Plan ← Translate_To_System_Commands(Optimal_Action)

FOR each command IN Execution_Plan DO
TRY
Execute_Command(command)
Monitor_Execution_Status(command)
CATCH Exception e
Log_Failure(command, e)
Attempt_Recovery(command) OR Escalate_To_Human()
END TRY
END FOR
```

```
Verify_Execution_Completion(Execution_Plan)
END IF
//==========================================================================
// LEARNING LAYER
//==========================================================================
Actual_Outcome ← Observe_Real_World_Results(Optimal_Action)
// Performance measurement
Prediction_Error ← Compare(Actual_Outcome, Simulated_Outcome)
Decision_Quality ← Evaluate_Against_Objectives(Actual_Outcome)
IF Prediction_Error > Acceptable_Threshold THEN
Root_Cause ← Diagnose_Error_Source(Prediction_Error)
CASE Root_Cause OF
PERCEPTION_ERROR: Retrain_Anomaly_Detectors()
PREDICTION_ERROR: Update_Forecasting_Models(Recent_Data)
OPTIMIZATION_ERROR: Refine_Objective_Functions()
EXECUTION_ERROR: Improve_Exception_Handling()
END CASE
END IF
// Continuous learning
Store_Experience(Current_Situation, Optimal_Action, Actual_Outcome)
IF accumulated_experiences mod Retraining_Interval = 0 THEN
Retrain_All_Models(Historical_Data + New_Experiences)
Validate_Model_Performance()
Deploy_Improved_Models()
END IF
// Update digital twin with actual outcomes
Digital_Twin.Calibrate(Actual_Outcome)
// Performance reporting
Generate_Performance_Metrics()
```

```
Update_Dashboards()

SLEEP(Δt) // Control cycle interval
END WHILE
```

3.2 Cognitive Architecture for Supply Chain Intelligence

The cognitive architecture developed in this research specifies how AI capabilities integrate to create supply chain intelligence transcending simple automation. The architecture adapts human cognition principles to distributed computing environments and business requirements (Anderson et al., 2004; Laird et al., 2017).

Figure 9. Detailed representation of the cognitive architecture showing knowledge representation structures, memory systems, reasoning mechanisms, attention allocation, goal management, and metacognitive processes that enable intelligent supply chain decision-making

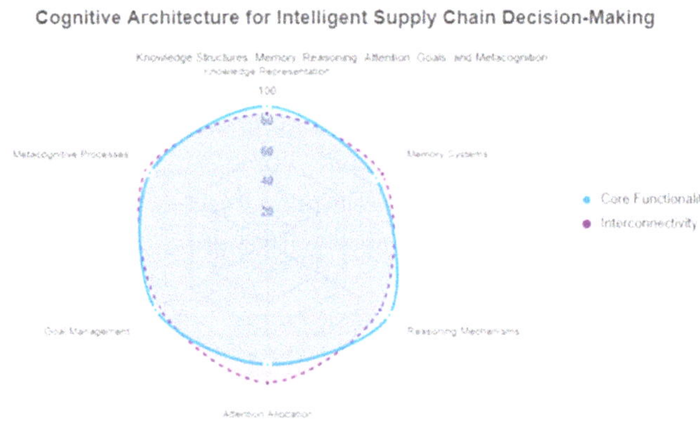

Knowledge Representation structures supply chain domain knowledge in formats enabling reasoning and learning. Ontologies define taxonomies of supply chain entities (products, facilities, transportation modes, partners) with properties and relationships (Tao et al., 2018). Process models represent workflows, dependencies, and temporal constraints. When there is a finite ability to do things (capacities, regulations, contracts), these are coded in constraint networks. Causal models represent the cause-effect relationship (demand variability does affect production requirements, supplier disruption does affect delivery times, defects of quality that are caused by process settings).

The information is stored in Memory Systems at different levels of abstraction and time scale. Working memory contains the information on the situation at hand (current orders, shipments that are in transit, real-time sensor measurements). The episodic memory is the memory that stores certain historical events. activating the retrieval of previous scenarios like the present ones (Anderson et al., 2004). The generalized knowledge in the semantic memory is based on various experiences (average demand trends, standard transportation durations, average quality standards). Action sequences and decision procedures that represent organizational standard operating procedures are encoded in procedural memory.

Reasoning Mechanisms take deductions based on the knowledge available and findings. Deductive reasoning involves using logical procedures that see to it that decisions are made within limitations and policies. Inductive reasoning is generalization on the basis of certain observations, templates that can identify a trend and acquire categories (Baryannis et al., 2019).

Abductive reasoning is the derivation of explanatory speculations to root cause analysis on observations of unexpected observations. Analogical reasoning their knowledge is applied on things that are similar to previous cases in order to be implemented in new situations that speed up the process of adapting to new products, markets, or work situations.

Attention Mechanisms allocate computational resources prioritizing most important information and decisions. Salience detection identifies information most relevant to current goals filtering less important signals. Priority scheduling allocates processing time to urgent decisions while queuing less time-sensitive analyses. Alert management prevents information overload by aggregating notifications about similar events and suppressing less critical alerts. The attention system employs metacontrol monitoring its own effectiveness and reallocating focus based on feedback.

Goal Management organizes objectives hierarchically coordinating decisions across organizational levels. Strategic goals (market position, profitability, sustainability) provide high-level guidance (Carter & Rogers, 2008; Lee, 2004). Tactical goals decompose strategy into operational targets (inventory levels, service rates, cost metrics). Operational goals specify immediate performance targets (production quantities, shipment completions, quality levels). The goal management system identifies conflicts between competing objectives, negotiates priorities through explicit trade-off evaluation, or escalates to human decision-makers when automated resolution proves infeasible.

Metacognition monitors cognitive system performance identifying degradation and initiating adaptation. Model validation tracks prediction accuracy flagging when models become outdated requiring retraining (Rasheed et al., 2020). Confidence estimation quantifies decision uncertainty determining when human oversight should precede autonomous execution (Doshi-Velez & Kim, 2017). Failure analysis examines decision-making errors determining whether poor data, inadequate models, or environmental changes caused suboptimal outcomes. The metacognitive layer implements self-awareness where the system recognizes its limitations and requests human assistance appropriately.

3.3 Decision Autonomy Levels and Human-AI Collaboration

This research defines six autonomy levels for supply chain decision-making, adapting automation taxonomies from aerospace and defense to explain appropriate autonomous operation levels across contexts (Parasuraman et al., 2000).

Figure 10. The six level decision autonomy model that shows how the processes of manual operations go to a higher degree of automation to complete automation and the nature of decisions, risk types, and suitable contexts to use each level of autonomy

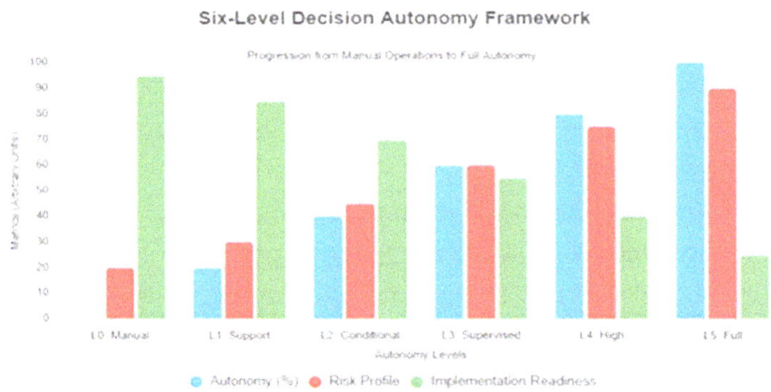

Level 0: Manual involves purely human decisions without AI assistance. All information gathering, analysis, and action execution requires human input. This level applies to highly unstructured situations, initial system deployments, and decisions with significant strategic implications requiring executive judgment (Jarrahi, 2018). Manual mode serves as fallback when automated systems fail or encounter untrained scenarios.

Level 1: Decision Support provides AI-generated recommendations while retaining complete human decision authority. The system processes data, generates predictions, and suggests optimal actions presented to human operators who review recommendations and approve or override them (Shrestha et al., 2019). The level is appropriate to high-stakes decisions, new situations that have never been seen before or situations that need responsible human action. Decision support mode fosters human trust in the AI capabilities and retains control and acquires operator competence in assessing algorithmic advice.

Level 2: Conditional Automation Automates decision-making within pre-established limits and sends exceptions to people. The system follows a systemic decision-making process that applies choices, which are independent in the context of attaining stipulated requirements (decision level, level of risk). confidence levels) and paths route decisions that may violate boundaries to human judgement. As an illustration, the small orders of replenishing inventory are automatically processed, whereas the large orders are to be approved. This level balances the automatization efficiency, risk control, and leaves the human attention to the critical decisions (Parasuraman et al., 2000).

Level 3: Supervised Autonomy allows autonomous execution of decisions and human supervision with the overriding option. A decision is always generated and executed continuously and human beings view dashboards, periodically obtain summaries and still maintain the authority to intervene (Lee & See, 2004). Human operators are engaged in managing exceptions, monitoring trends as well as adjusting strategies as opposed to routine decision approval. This tier is appropriate when it comes to the high-frequency decisions, when the constraints of human capacity do not allow considering all the actions but the oversight of human beings is a useful safety mechanism.

Level 4: High Autonomy operates extended periods without human intervention except periodic reviews. The system autonomously manages normal operations and common exceptions, alerting humans only for unusual situations or performance anomalies. Humans set goals, boundaries, and policies, and review performance reports at scheduled intervals rather than continuously monitoring. This requires sophisticated exception handling, graceful degradation under uncertainty, and comprehensive logging enabling post-hoc analysis. High autonomy suits stable operational contexts where dynamics are well-understood and complete training data exists.

Level 5: Full Autonomy represents complete independence with autonomous exception handling, self-adaptation, and goal refinement. Fully autonomous systems sense environmental changes, adjust strategies, manage unexpected events, and continuously optimize performance without human intervention except setting original high-level objectives. Current supply chain AI deployments rarely achieve full autonomy given complexity, risk, and accountability considerations. This level may emerge in narrow domains with limited scope and low consequence.

Algorithm 4: Dynamic autonomy level choice algorithm where the correct level of automation is chosen depending on risk assessment, decision characteristics, model trust and historical performance with adjustment mechanisms that are adaptive.

Algorithm 4: Dynamic Autonomy Level Selection

```
Input: Decision_Context, Historical_Performance, Risk_Assessment
Output: Appropriate_Autonomy_Level, Human_Involvement_Required
FUNCTION Select_Autonomy_Level(decision, context)
// Extract decision characteristics
frequency ← decision.occurrence_rate
consequence_severity ← Estimate_Impact(decision)
data_availability ← Assess_Historical_Data(decision.type)
environment_stability ← Calculate_Volatility(context)
model_confidence ← Get_Prediction_Confidence(decision)

// Calculate risk score
risk_score ← Weighted_Sum([
consequence_severity × 0.35,
(1 - model_confidence) × 0.25,
(1 - data_availability) × 0.20,
environment_volatility × 0.20
])

// Decision frequency factor
IF frequency > 100 per_day THEN
frequency_factor ← 2.0 // High automation benefit
ELSE IF frequency > 10 per_day THEN
frequency_factor ← 1.5
ELSE
frequency_factor ← 1.0
END IF

// Autonomy level determination
IF risk_score > 0.8 OR consequence_severity = CRITICAL THEN
RETURN Level_0_Manual, "High risk requires human judgment"

ELSE IF risk_score > 0.6 THEN
RETURN Level_1_Decision_Support, "AI recommendation with human approval"

ELSE IF risk_score > 0.4 THEN
IF decision.value > Threshold_Large THEN
RETURN Level_2_Conditional, "Autonomous within limits"
ELSE
RETURN Level_3_Supervised, "Autonomous with monitoring"
```

```
END IF
ELSE IF risk_score > 0.2 AND frequency_factor >= 1.5 THEN
IF model_confidence > 0.85 AND environment_stability > 0.7 THEN
RETURN Level_4_High_Autonomy, "Extended autonomous operation"
ELSE
RETURN Level_3_Supervised, "Autonomous with monitoring"
END IF
ELSE IF risk_score <= 0.2 AND model_confidence > 0.9 THEN
IF frequency_factor >= 2.0 AND Is_Narrow_Domain(decision) THEN
RETURN Level_5_Full_Autonomy, "Complete autonomous operation"
ELSE
RETURN Level_4_High_Autonomy, "Extended autonomous operation"
END IF
ELSE
// Default to supervised autonomy
RETURN Level_3_Supervised, "Standard autonomous operation"
END IF
END FUNCTION
// Adaptive autonomy adjustment based on performance
FUNCTION Adjust_Autonomy_Based_On_Performance()
recent_performance ← Get_Recent_Decision_Quality(window=30_days)
FOR each decision_type DO
IF recent_performance[decision_type].accuracy < 0.75 THEN
Decrease_Autonomy_Level(decision_type)
Notify_Administrators("Autonomy reduced due to poor performance")
ELSE IF recent_performance[decision_type].accuracy > 0.95 THEN
IF Can_Increase_Safely(decision_type) THEN
Increase_Autonomy_Level(decision_type)
END IF
END IF
END FOR
END FUNCTION
```

The adequate degree of autonomy is specific to supply chain operations depending on the frequency of decisions, the severity of consequences, stable environment, and availability of data (Boone et al., 2019; Gijsbrechts et al., 2022). Decisions of high frequency (real-time routing, dynamic pricing) are better handled at higher levels of autonomy because the volume of decisions is too large to be handled individually by humans. Strategic decisions that are low-frequency (supplier selection, network design) should have reduced autonomy because of the magnitude of consequences. Constant operational conditions and a large amount of training information permit increased autonomy whereas constantly changing environments with little past data would demand increased human intervention.

Human-AI Collaboration Models determine the roles, responsibilities and interaction patterns at different levels of autonomy. The cognitive partnership model places humans and AI as complementary partners that have different advantages (Jarrahi, 2018). Humans bring contextual knowledge, moral judgment, innovative problem responses and being able to adapt to new conditions. The AI systems offer rapid processing of data, extensive recognition of patterns, optimization of complex constraint space, and non-fatigue consistency individual case bias.

Achievement of good cooperation creates workflows that utilize respective strengths instead of considering AI as a direct replacement of human tasks. Organizations should implement trust-building mechanisms including explanation interfaces showing why systems recommend specific actions, confidence indicators quantifying prediction uncertainty, and performance dashboards tracking system accuracy over time.

3.4 Digital Twin Maturity Model

This research proposes a digital twin maturity model for supply chain applications delineating progression stages from simple visualization to autonomous optimization. The model provides assessment framework enabling organizations to evaluate current capabilities and plan advancement (Kritzinger et al., 2018; Liu et al., 2021).

Figure 11. Six-step model of digital twin maturity that illustrates the transition between descriptive visualization with diagnostic analytics, predictive monitoring, prescriptive optimization and adaptive autonomy to cognitive autonomy with typical capabilities, technologies and organizational needs at each level

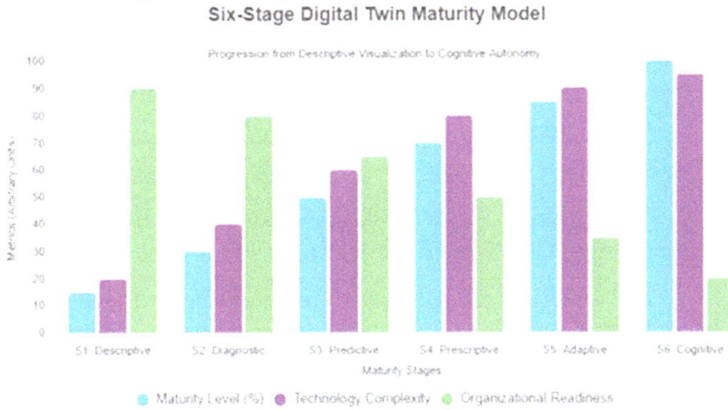

Stage 1: Descriptive Visualization represents entry-level digital twin implementation focused on visualizing current supply chain states. Dashboards and geographic maps display real-time inventory locations, shipment positions, equipment status, and order progress. Data integration from source systems to visualization platforms is primarily manual or batch-based with update frequencies measured in hours or days. Analytical capabilities are limited to monitoring and reporting. Organizations at this stage possess basic data integration and visualization capabilities but lack predictive or prescriptive functions. Increased visibility and common operational view of distributed teams is the primary value proposition.

Stage 2: Diagnostic Analytics introduces functionality to carry out performance deviation and root cause discovery. The digital twin provides a combination of historical information that enables trend analysis, comparative performance assessment, and investigations through drills. Through throughput analysis, defect tracking, and cycle time monitoring, users discover bottlenecks, quality problems and delays respectively. The diagnostic features are based more on the descriptive statistics and business intelligence tools than on professional machine learning. The refresh rates on important metrics are enhanced to almost real time. This phase allows solving the problem in a reactionary manner but does not have the ability to predict the future state.

Stage 3: Predictive Monitoring is the stage that includes machine learning that is able to predict the future states depending on the current state and past trends (Boone et al., 2019; Syntetos et al., 2016). The digital twin predicts changes in demand, can tell when to arrive, how equipment will break, and the quality deviation before it happens. Some predictive models are time series forecasting, failure classification and delay regression. The alert systems inform the operators about the expected problems to facilitate proactive action. But, decision-making and action execution is mostly manual. This is the move to the proactive instead of a reactive operations where issues are avoided instead of being attempted after they have broken out.

Stage 4: Prescriptive Optimization is the stage where optimization engines are introduced and suggest a set of optimal actions based on a predicted situation (Gijsbrechts et al., 2022; Simchi-Levi et al., 2000). The digital twin proposes inventory adjustments, production plan alterations, routing alterations, and supply changes by thoroughly analyzing alternative solutions. The optimization involves various goals, restrictions, and uncertainties of the scenario. Recommendation engines bring out action options that have expected results to allow human decision-makers make trade-offs. The simulation abilities will enable trying out alternative decisions in the digital twin prior to actual implementation (Ivanov et al., 2021). This phase enhances the quality of decision making by automating the process of evaluating alternatives with the human decision making ability preserved.

Stage 5: Adaptive Autonomy allows making decisions independently and learning constantly about the results. The automated routine operational decisions that the digital twin makes are within predefined limits, and the exceptions are escalated to humans. Reinforcement learning algorithms are algorithms that optimize decisions policies over time by balancing exploration and exploitation (Kaur and Singh, 2021). The system is flexible to changing conditions: it changes models, parameters and rules on the basis of performance feedback. Humans control the general performance, redefine the goals and constraints, and deal with new situations beyond the training. This phase achieves the automation advantages without losing strategic control of human beings.

Stage 6: Cognitive Autonomy: This stage is the highest level of autonomous operation with such facets as strategic planning, self-diagnosis, and collaborative learning. The digital twin analyses alternative strategies on its own, predicts long-term conditions, and suggests supply chain redesigns (Rasheed et al., 2020). Self-diagnostics detects model degeneration, data corruption and capacity constraint that results in retraining or human actions request. Federated learning permits the collaboration of organizational units in learning or even across organizational borders whilst maintaining data confidentiality and facilitating knowledge exchange (Barbosa et al., 2020). Cognitive autonomy is perceived as aspirational goal and not a present reality by most of the organizations because of problems in technology, organization, and governance, yet it is one of the developmental routes to digital twins.

Capability Building Requirements: The development of maturity stage must be cumulative in terms of capability development. Organizations cannot justify the omission of stages because every level is based on the capabilities developed at the earlier levels. The process of progression requires the equilibrium of maturation in the area of data infrastructure, analytical capacities, organizational preparedness, and governance frameworks. The maturity model is a roadmap guide that helps the organization to prioritize investments and sequence capability development.

3.5 Integration of Theoretical Constructs

The theoretical frameworks worked on in this study merge along consistent paradigms of connecting autonomous operations layers, cognitive architecture, decision autonomy level, and level of digital twin maturity. The autonomous operations model is a five-layer high-level functional decomposition and the specifics of the mechanisms at every layer are specified in the cognitive architecture (Anderson et al., 2004; Laird et al., 2017). The levels of decision autonomy characterize collaboration modes between humans and AI that can be used at cross-functional and cross-layers (Parasuraman et al., 2000). The stages of maturity of digital twins are the organizational development paths that create autonomous capabilities (Grieves and Vickers, 2017; Tao et al., 2018).

Figure 12. Multiple layers assimilation of the theoretical constructs showing how the five layer autonomous operations model, the cognitive architecture, the levels of decision autonomy, and the digital twin maturation stages that were integrated gave a complicated framework of AI-aggrandized supply chain management

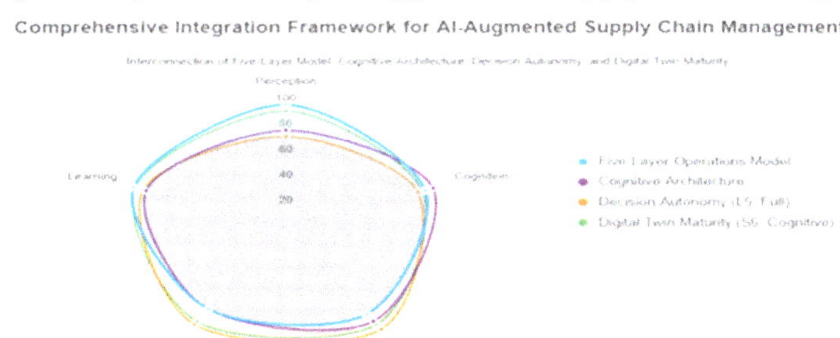

Integration works vertically on the levels of abstraction and horizontally on the functions of the supply chain. Vertical integration is the assurance that the perception layer output is the input to cognition layer, cognition layer outputs are the input to decision processes, decision processes are the input to the execution actions and the execution actions are the input to learning data. Horizontal integration involves coordination of decisions among supply chain operations (demand planning, production scheduling, inventory control, logistics execution) to work towards uniform supply chain-wide goals (Lee, 2004; Mentzer et al., 2001).

The integrated model promotes diverse patterns of implementation in which disparate supply chain operations perform at varying levels of autonomy and digital maturity levels of the twin. An example is that organizations can adopt high autonomy on the replenishment of inventory and decision support mode to select suppliers. This allows implementing adoption paths which are practical in both speed to achieve quick wins in the right areas and being conservative in more risky areas.

4. RESEARCH METHODOLOGY

4.1 Research Design and Philosophical Positioning

The given study uses the pragmatic mixed-methodology that integrates the qualitative and quantitative methods into a complex approach to fulfill research purposes (Yin, 2018). The philosophical approach is aware that AI-enhanced supply chain management needs both subjective evaluation of organizational experiences and the objective quantification of performance results. The pragmatic paradigm focuses on solving practical problems rather than following specific epistemological standpoints, which is consistent with the practical application of the supply chain management research.

The study design will be based on several methods: literature review, theory building, in-depth case analysis, quantitative measurement of performance, and cross-case analysis. The multi-method strategy offers triangulation that improves the validity as a result of evidence convergence between different sources. The general course of the research will take a chronological series of steps, in which literature analysis and theory formulation inform the design of empirical research, theoretical evidence transforms theoretical constructs and empirical facts, and integrated analysis yields overall findings to answer research questions.

Figure 13. Research methodology framework (Comprehensive) The chronological and repetitive process of literature review, theoretic development, empirical study, data gathering, data analysis and validation of 12 case studies of organizations

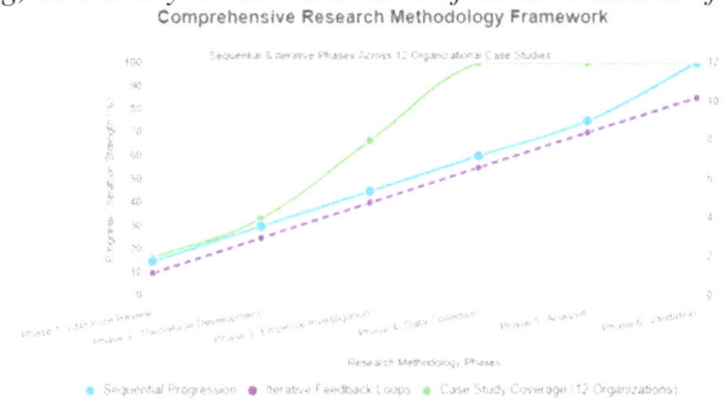

Primary empirical method is case study approach, which is suitable to investigate the contemporary AI application in actual organizational context. The case studies are also appropriate to the questions of how and why when analyzing recent phenomena in real-life scenarios, which fits the features of this study (Yin, 2018). Cross-case analysis through multiple case design provides an opportunity to see patterns and contingencies in many varied organizational and industrial contexts. Improved Methodological Transparency: To enable reproducibility, we declare (1) Analysis software: NVivo 12 to code qualitative data, SPSS 27 and R 4.1.0 to conduct statistical analysis; (2) Inter-rater reliability: Cohen kappa=0.87 when 2 independent coders work on 25% of transcript sample; (3) Statistical significance level: a= 0.05 with Bonferonni correction to multiple comparisons; (4) Effect size interpretation by convention of Cohen (small d=0.2, medium d=0.5, large d=0.8); (5) Complete coding scheme available in Appendix D.

4.2 Case Selection and Research Context

The selection of cases was based on the principles of theoretical sampling whereby the selection was determined by the richness and variation of information in the relevant dimensions rather than based on statistical representativeness. The following criteria were considered: (1) Minimum of 18 months experience in using AI technology in supply chain operations; (2) Availability of measurable performance metrics to be quantified empirically; (3) Diversity in terms of industry, geographic, and organizational size whereby the variety provides different contexts in which to conduct comparative analysis; (4) Organizational willingness that will grant access to interviews, documentation analysis, and operational observation.

Sample Composition: The final sample will consist of twelve organizations in four industry sectors with various supply chain attributes, regulatory environments, and operational issues. Three discrete manufacturing companies are a large automotive manufacturer in North America and Europe with operations in both North America and Europe, a consumer electronics manufacturer in Asia-Pacific with operations in both Asia-Pacific and globally, and an industrial equipment manufacturer in Europe with operations in Europe and globally.

Three retail organizations include multinational fashion retailer headquartered in Europe conducting omnichannel operations with AI-powered demand forecasting and dynamic assortment optimization, grocery chain in North America deploying autonomous replenishment and fresh food waste reduction systems, and e-commerce marketplace in Asia-Pacific implementing intelligent warehouse automation and delivery route optimization.

Three pharmaceutical companies involve pharmaceutical manufacturer in Europe with AI-enabled track-and-trace and quality compliance monitoring, specialty pharmacy in North America with autonomous inventory management for temperature-sensitive products, and vaccine distributor with Europe headquarters utilizing digital twins for distribution planning and cold chain optimization.

Three third-party logistics providers include North American freight forwarding company implementing AI for shipment consolidation and mode optimization, European contract logistics provider deploying autonomous warehouse operations with robotic picking, and Asia-Pacific express delivery network implementing dynamic routing and demand forecasting.

Figure 14. Unless indicated otherwise, twelve case study organizations belong to industry sectors (manufacturing, retail, pharmaceutical, logistics), geographic regions (North America, Europe, Asia-Pacific), and the level of the implementation maturity

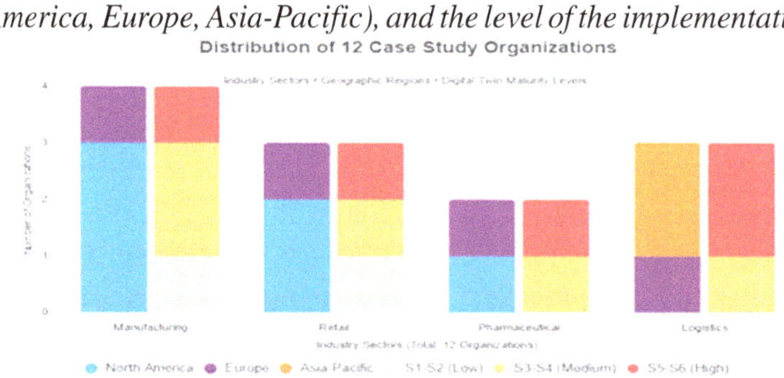

This sample contains variation in dimensions that are important. Sectors in the industry vary in demand patterns, regulatory pressures, products and supply chain structures. Geographic areas provide a variety of labor markets, availability of infrastructure and regulatory environment. Organizational sizes are mid-sized regional players and global enterprises that allow the examination of the scale effect. The level of implementation maturity ranges through pilot projects to enterprise-wide implementations of support of evolutionary pattern analysis.

Sample Selection Justification Theoretical sampling is not statistically representative, but provides maximum variation sampling, which implies a variety of contexts with reasonable practicability in the sense that intensive data collection would be required to sample each case. The sample size of the 12 cases is sufficient to balance depth-breadth trade-offs that prevail in case studies research because it is more than minimum 4-6 required to identify a pattern but is still feasible to investigate the situation deeply (Yin, 2018).

4.3 Data Collection Procedures

Interview Protocol: Semi-structured interviews were used as qualitative source of data. The standardized protocol (Appendix A) entailed: (1) Pre-implementation issues and motivation; (2) Technology selection criteria and vendor analysis; (3) Implementation strategy and plan; (4) Organizational framework and governance; (5) Implementation performance and measures; (6) Implementation challenges and lessons learnt; (7) Future plans and recommendations. The participants of the interview were supply chain executives (n=45), IT leaders (n=38), analytics team members (n=52), and operational managers (n=55) making a total amount of 190 interviews. Interviews took an average time of 75-90 minutes, were recorded on tape with the consent of the participants and transcribed verbatim to produce about 840 pages of transcript data.

Documentation Review: Documentation review was wide-ranged comprising of project proposals, architecture specifications, implementation roadmaps, performance reports and governance policies. Documents offered objective data on technology configurations, decision process and performance measures. A total of about 3,400 pages of documentation were collected, listed, and put under systematic analysis.

Site Visits and Observation: Field observations (site visits) facilitated the first hand examination of technology usage in working environments. Controllers, warehouses, manufacturing plants, and logistics centres were found recording human interactions with AI systems, decision-making, and exception management. A total of 650 hours of observation sessions conducted in all the organizations produced rich field notes that provided process flows, interfaces of technology, and interaction between human beings and systems.

Quantitative Performance Data: Performance data included the operational measures such as forecast accuracy, stock levels, punctuality of delivery, quality defect rates and cost measures. Data were collected through a before-after comparison by using past data that established historical baselines between pre-implementation and post-implementation observations. Comparison of controls with the non-AI-using organizational units where possible further validated. There were 24-48 month performance data covering 12-24 month pre-implementation baselines and 12-24 month post-implementation observations.

Technology Artifact Analysis: The technology artifacts analyzed, such as AI models, implementations of digital twins, and system architectures, consisted of analyzing model specifications, model training datasets, algorithm choices, and integration schemes. Proprietary restrictions did not allow access to the full algorithm but model performance report, integration workflow documentation, and architectural diagrams were shared by organization.

Data Collection Validation: Various validation schemes were used to guarantee data quality: (1) Triangulation of the data sources between interview, document, observation, and performance data sources; (2) Member checking where the participants of the interviews should check the draft case summaries to ensure that the data was accurate; (3) Data audit trails which record the date of collection, source of collection, and data custodian; (4) Systematic description of the access restrictions and missing data.

4.4 Data Analysis Approaches

Qualitative Analysis: NVivo 12 software systematic coding took place in stages. The first open coding was to determine the emergent themes that were not predetermined. Coherent themes were put together into themes by means of focused coding to meet research questions. Axial coding was used in examining relationships between categories that depicted causal relationships, contextual factors and consequences. In the theoretical coding, categories were attached to the theoretical frameworks produced during the research.

Inter-Rater Reliability: 25% of the transcript subsets were picked randomly and analysed by two independent coders. The original Cohen kappa = 0.73 was raised to k = 0.87 following the refinement of codebook and training of coders. The argument was solved by means of discussion and clarifying the coding definition. The coding scheme used was final with 47 codes that were grouped into 12 high level categories.

Member Checking: Interview participants were shown draft case summaries to ensure that they are accurate and clarify ambiguities. This validation process increased the credibility and eliminated possible misunderstandings. Members checking response rate was more than 85 percent in organizations.

Quantitative Analysis: Descriptive statistics that define the distributions of performance, hypothesis testing that determine the effect of AI augmentation, and time series analysis that determine the presence of trends were implemented. Paired t-tests were used to compare the pre-implementation performance and post-implementation performance in organizations. AI-augmented units and control groups where independent t-tests were done. Cohen d effect sizes of meaningful impact beyond statistical significance were used to evaluate the significance of the practical meaning. Several testing errors were corrected by Bonferonni corrections in doing multitude of comparisons.

Figure 15. Multi-stage data analysis flow chart that will involve the qualitative coding process, quantitative statistical analysis, cross-case pattern matching/triangulation that will be utilized to come up with validated research findings

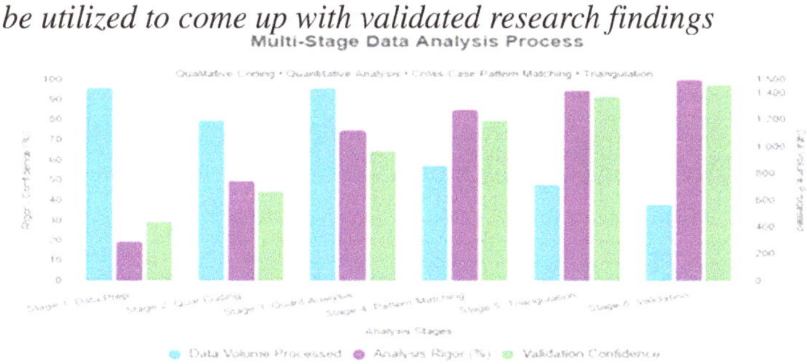

Cross-Case Analysis: Comparisons and contrasts of cases comprising similarities and differences were undertaken systematically by use of comparison matrices. Pattern matching identified recurring themes in more than one case improving generalizability. Explanation building formulated causal explanations between the implementation strategies, contextual determines, and performance outcomes. Replication logic was used to regard each case as an independent experiment where consistent findings in one context and inconsistent findings in another conditioned theoretical inferences and boundary cases respectively.

Statistical Procedures: Some analytical procedures were: (1) Shapiro-Wilk tests to verify normality assumptions; (2) Levene tests to determine the homogeneity of variances; (3) paired t-tests to compare before and after within the organization; (4) independent t -tests to compare between groups; (5) Cohen d effect sizes (small=.2, medium=.5, large=.8); (6) Bonferonni corrections to control the rate of family wise error; (7) time series decomposition of trends, seasonality, and irregular components; (8) Statistical significance threshold $\alpha=0.05$.

4.5 Research Quality and Ethical Considerations

Validity Measures: Construct validity was increased by: (1) Triangulation of the multiple data sources; (2) Evidence chains linking the findings to the data sources; (3) Review of draft reports by key informants. Internal validity had: (1) Pattern matching of the cases; (2) Explanation building of connections between causes and effects; (3) Rival explanation testing; (4) Logic models of how causal events take place. Improved external validity by: (1) Replication logic by use of multiple cases; (2) Thick description which brings contextual detail to allow a judgment of transferability; (3) Theoretical sampling which maximized variation along relevant dimensions. Addressing reliability was supported by: (1) Case study protocols that standardize data collection; (2) Case study databases that ensure that data are organized data bases; (3) Transparency of method used in data analysis that allows replication.

Ethical Procedures: Informed consent procedures explained research purpose, data usage, confidentiality through anonymization and data security, voluntary participation including withdrawal rights, and organizational agreements regarding publication rights and review processes. The primary researcher's institutional review board approved the research protocol. Signed research agreements with participating organizations specified data access procedures, anonymization requirements, and publication approval processes.

Limitations and Mitigation: Recognized limitations include: (1) Potential selection bias where participating organizations may systematically differ from non-participants - mitigated through maximum variation sampling and explicit boundary condition discussion; (2) Social desirability bias where informants provide overly positive implementation accounts - addressed through triangulation, probing questions, and performance data validation; (3) Temporal constraints limiting long-term outcome observation - acknowledged with explicit study timeframe specification. These limitations qualify findings interpretation and generalizability scope.

Figure 16. Full seven-layer reference architecture of AI-enhanced supply chain management of data infrastructure, integration, analytics/AI, digital twin, decision intelligence, user experience, security/governance layers with major features and data interactions

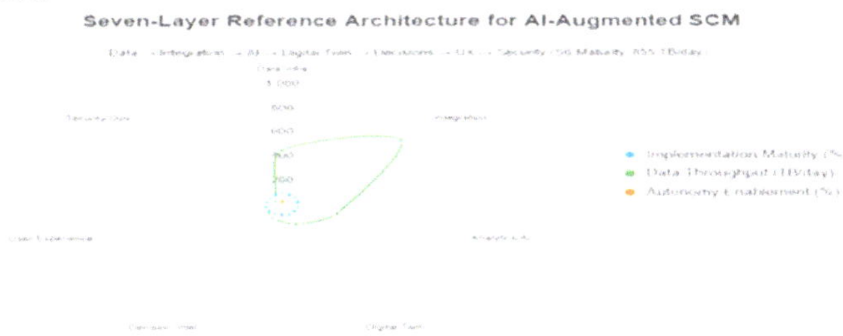

5. ACTIONABLE REFERENCE ARCHITECTURES

5.1 Overall System Architecture

The AI-augmented supply chain management reference architecture is a combination of technological layers and autonomous operations. It is designed according to the principles of service-oriented architecture that allows a modular implementation, scalability, replacement of technology components without affecting the coherent flow of information and coordination of decisions (Hofmann & Rüsch, 2017; Kagermann et al., 2013).

Data Infrastructure Layer offers basic data acquisition, storage and access services. Elements are IoT sensor networks that could be placed on physical assets (manufacturing equipment, warehouse systems, transportation vehicles, environmental sensors), enterprise information systems (ERP, WMS, TMS, MES) that could provide transactional and planning data and external sources of data (market intelligence, weather forecasts, economic indicators, social media signals). Data lakes archive raw information in their original form that makes it usable in multiple types of analysis. Data warehouses are curated structured data that are optimized to analytical queries. Stream processing systems are used to work with real-time data streams that allow responding to dynamic states with low latency.

Integration Layer offers heterogeneous systems connectivity and interoperability. The API gateways offer the formalized interfaces that conceal the complexity of systems. The message brokers facilitate asynchronous communication among fault-tolerant and scale-able decoupled components. Business events are captured and distributed over the architecture in event streaming platforms. Cleansing, normalizing, and enriching the data flows are done through data transformation services. Master data management systems make sure that reference data is uniformed across organizational borders. The integration layer provides data governance policies which control access, maintain quality and trace data lineage.

Analytics and AI Layer applies machine learnings and optimization systems and simulation (Baryannis et al., 2019; Wang et al., 2020). Supervised learning Model training pipelines are used to predictive model their training, unsupervised to discover patterns, and reinforcement to optimize a sequence of decisions (Gijsbrechts et al., 2022; Kaur and Singh, 2021). More than a simple inference server Model serving infrastructure offers high throughput, low latency scale-deployed trained model inference services. Reusable feature engineering transformations that are fastening model development are captured in feature stores. Experiment trackers store training settings and hyperparameters of the model as well as performance results required to reproduce or compare them. Monitoring services Model monitoring services detect performance degradation, data drift, and concept shift which prompts retraining.

Algorithms 5: End-to-end machine learning model lifecycle Management pipeline, with data preparation, model training, evaluation, deployment and continuous monitoring with automatic retraining stimulus.

Algorithm 5: ML Model Lifecycle Management Pipeline

```
Input: Training_Data, Model_Requirements, Performance_Thresholds
Output: Deployed_Model, Monitoring_Dashboard, Retraining_Schedule
// ================================================================
=================================

// PHASE 1: DATA PREPARATION
// ================================================================
=================================

Raw_Data ← Extract_From_Data_Lake(date_range, data_sources)
Cleaned_Data ← Data_Quality_Pipeline(Raw_Data)

// Feature engineering
Features ← Feature_Engineering_Library.Transform(Cleaned_Data)
Store_Features(Feature_Store, Features, version)

// Train/validation/test split
(Train_Set, Val_Set, Test_Set) ← Split_Data(Features,
ratios=[0.7, 0.15, 0.15],
stratify=True)
// ================================================================
=================================
```

```
// PHASE 2: MODEL TRAINING AND SELECTION
// ==================================================================
================================
Candidate_Models ← []
FOR each algorithm IN [GradientBoosting, NeuralNetwork,
RandomForest, XGBoost] DO
// Hyperparameter tuning
Best_Params ← Bayesian_Optimization(
algorithm,
Train_Set,
Val_Set,
n_iterations=50
)
// Train with best parameters
model ← algorithm.Train(Train_Set, Best_Params)
// Cross-validation
CV_Scores ← K_Fold_Cross_Validation(model, Train_Set, k=5)
// Store experiment
Experiment_Tracker.Log(
algorithm_name=algorithm,
parameters=Best_Params,
cv_scores=CV_Scores,
training_time=elapsed_time
)
Candidate_Models.append(model)
END FOR
// Model selection
Best_Model ← Select_Best_Model(Candidate_Models, Val_Set)
// ==================================================================
================================
// PHASE 3: MODEL EVALUATION
// ==================================================================
================================
```

```
Test_Performance ← Evaluate_Model(Best_Model, Test_Set)

// Comprehensive evaluation
Metrics ← Calculate_Metrics(Test_Performance)
// For regression: MAE, RMSE, MAPE, R^2
// For classification: Precision, Recall, F1, AUC-ROC

// Fairness assessment
Fairness_Report ← Assess_Bias(Best_Model, Test_Set,
protected_attributes)

// Interpretability analysis
Feature_Importance ← Calculate_SHAP_Values(Best_Model, Test_Set)
Interpretability_Report ← Generate_Explanations(Feature_Importance)

// Robustness testing
Adversarial_Performance ← Test_Robustness(Best_Model,
perturbation_scenarios)
// ==================================================================
// PHASE 4: MODEL DEPLOYMENT
// ==================================================================
IF Test_Performance.meets_requirements(Performance_Thresholds) THEN

// Package model
Model_Package ← Containerize(Best_Model, dependencies, version)

// Canary deployment (5% traffic)
Deploy_Canary(Model_Package, traffic_percentage=0.05)
Canary_Metrics ← Monitor_Canary(duration=48_hours)

IF Canary_Metrics.acceptable THEN
// Full deployment
Deploy_Production(Model_Package,
deployment_strategy="blue_green",
rollback_enabled=True)

// Update model registry
Model_Registry.Register(
```

```
model=Best_Model,
version=version,
performance=Test_Performance,
deployment_date=current_date,
metadata={training_data, features, parameters}
)
ELSE
Rollback_Canary()
Alert_Data_Science_Team("Canary deployment failed")
END IF
ELSE
Alert_Data_Science_Team("Model performance below threshold")
RETURN Failure
END IF
// ==========================================================================
// PHASE 5: CONTINUOUS MONITORING
// ==========================================================================
WHILE model_in_production DO
// Monitor prediction performance
Actual_vs_Predicted ← Collect_Ground_Truth(time_window=daily)
Current_Performance ← Calculate_Live_Metrics(Actual_vs_Predicted)
// Data drift detection
Input_Distribution ← Analyze_Input_Data(time_window=daily)
Drift_Score ← Calculate_KL_Divergence(Input_Distribution,
Training_Distribution)
// Concept drift detection
Prediction_Distribution ← Analyze_Predictions(time_window=daily)
Concept_Drift ← Detect_Concept_Shift(Prediction_Distribution)
// Performance degradation alert
IF Current_Performance < Performance_Thresholds * 0.9 THEN
Trigger_Alert("Model performance degraded")
Schedule_Retraining(priority=HIGH)
END IF
```

```
// Drift alert
IF Drift_Score > Drift_Threshold THEN
Trigger_Alert("Significant data drift detected")
Schedule_Retraining(priority=MEDIUM)
END IF
// Automated retraining
IF Time_Since_Training > Retraining_Interval THEN
New_Training_Data ← Collect_Recent_Data()
Retrain_Model(New_Training_Data)
END IF
Update_Monitoring_Dashboard(Current_Performance, Drift_Score)
SLEEP(monitoring_interval) // e.g., 1 hour
END WHILE
```

Digital Twin Layer keeps virtualized images of supply chain assets, processes, and systems (Grieves & Vickers, 2017; Tao et al., 2018). Asset digital twins simulate the behavior of individual equipment such as state variables, performance parameters, and degradation behavior (Qi et al., 2021). Process digital twins can be operational workflows, which capture cycle times, resource requirements and quality relationships (Leng et al., 2020). System digital twins simulate end-to-end supply chains, such as their topology, material flows, and decision policies (Ivanov et al., 2021). The synchronization is upheld through two-way data transportation between the physical activities and the virtual images. Simulation engines allow what-if analysis, which performs scenario evaluation, decision testing and reinforcement learning agent training.

Decision Intelligence Layer integrates analytical information regarding actionable decisions. Decision engines analyze the actions of alternatives based on goals, constraints, and unpredictability. Mathematical programming formulations solved by optimization solvers are linear programming formulations, mixed-integer programming formulations and constraint programming formulations (Simchi-Levi et al., 2000). The recommendation systems offer suggestions with expected consequences and other possible suggestions. Decision rules that encode organizational preferences, constraints and priorities are stored and executed by policy management. Multi-step decision processes of workflows are automated using workflow engines which combine automated and human approvals. The decision layer ensures audit logs that document the decisions, reason and effect of decisions towards accountability and constant improvement.

User Experience Layer will give interfaces to the operational staff, managers and executives. Operational dashboards show real time supply chain status, performance metrics and alerts. Workbenches based on analysis are useful in exploratory analysis, generation of reports, and interaction with models. Field personnel can access information and get transactions done through mobile applications. Natural language processing helps to create conversational interfaces that may be used to query information and issue voice-activated commands (Bodendorf and Franke, 2021). Team coordination is assisted using collaborative tools. The user experience interface customizes interfaces to user role with the right level of information granularity and decision authority.

Security and Governance Layer offers cross-cutting aspects that have guaranteed confidentiality, integrity, and compliance. Authentication and authorization is controlled by identity and access management. Encryption ensures data security on rest and transit. Network security puts in place firewalls, intrusion detection and threat monitoring. Audit logging records system activities supporting forensic investigation and regulatory compliance. Data governance enforces privacy policies, retention policies, and usage policies. Model governance ensures AI systems operate ethically, fairly, and transparently (Doshi-Velez & Kim, 2017). Regulatory compliance management monitors adherence to industry-specific regulations (FDA for pharmaceuticals, DOT for transportation, environmental regulations for sustainability reporting).

5.2 Data Integration and Flow Architecture

Data integration patterns define information movement across AI-augmented supply chain processes. The architecture supports multiple integration patterns suiting different data characteristics and usage requirements.

Figure 17. There are four main patterns of data integration employed in AI-augmented supply chains, including batch integration of historical data, event-driven integration of real-time data, API-based integration of real-time transaction, and data virtualization of federated query

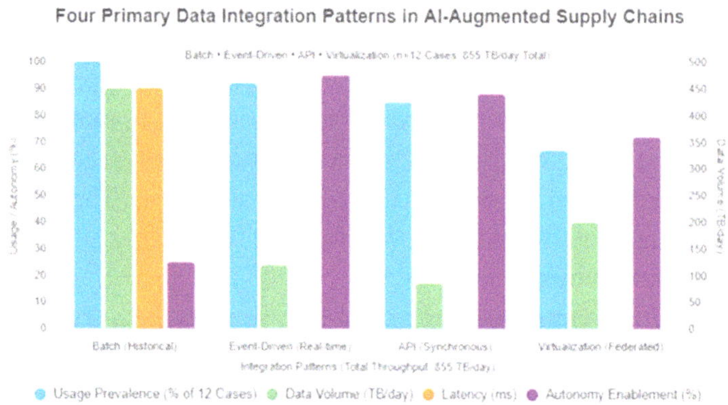

Batch Integration transfers data during scheduled bulk loads suitable for historical data, reference data, and situations not requiring near-real-time currency. Extract-Transform-Load (ETL) processes extract data from source systems, apply cleansing and enrichment transformations, and load data into target stores. Batch integration suits: (1) Nightly master data updates; (2) Weekly transaction history consolidation; (3) Monthly financial closing. Benefits include simplicity, large data volume handling, and reduced source system performance impact. Limitations include data latency and inability to support real-time decisions.

Event-Driven Integration propagates changes as they occur, appropriate for operational situations requiring immediate responsiveness. Event streaming architectures publish events (order placements, shipment departures, equipment failures, quality issues) to message brokers. Subscribers consume events triggering workflows, updating digital twins, and invoking AI models. Real time inventory information through event-driven integration: (1) Cross-channel transactions, reflected in real time inventory; (2) Rerouting in time, in response to transport setbacks; (3) Real-time alert concerning quality variances. Complex event processing identifies patterns within simple event streams to detect a situation such as potential stockouts, arising disruptions or a demand pattern change.

API-Based Integration offers real-time request-response communication that is applicable in transactional processes and real-time queries. Supply chain capabilities (checking availability of inventory, checking the status of orders, optimization requests) are exposed in RESTful APIs. Microservices systems are monolithic systems divided into separately deployable services that communicate through APIs. The

API gateways are security, rate limited and transforming. The API based integration facilitates: (1) Customer order promising checking real time inventory and production capacity; (2) On-demand pricing queries checking demand and competitive positioning; (3) Supplier portal integration to aid in collaborative planning.

Data Virtualization makes available a logical view of data in distributed places without physical centralization. VDLs query source systems on demand, with integrated results that are not stored in between. Data virtualization is appropriate in a case where: (1) Data volumes do not allow replication; (2) Data currency needs to be up-to-the-second; (3) Data governance prohibits duplication. Examples are at the regulatory reporting level that consolidates information across systems; at the executive level where executive dashboards consolidate enterprise level measures; and at the supplier level where supplier scorecards consolidate supplier performance data.

Layers of Data Refinement: The data flow architecture will apply gradual enhancing of data to convert it into actionable information to make decisions. Raw data layer stores raw information in various sources in their original formats and has history. The data layer is cleansed and implements quality enhancements to remove duplicates, make corrections and eliminate anomalies. Conformed data layer normalizes data models, and makes codes and classifications standardized and common definitions. The enhanced data layer is enhanced by derived attributes, foreign key, and computed metrics. The analytical data layer stores data in a way that it is optimized to do particular analytical tasks (forecasting, optimization, simulation).

5.3 Machine Learning Pipeline Architecture

Machine learning pipeline architecture is a framework of AI model development, deployment, and maintenance that is based on MLOps principles that guarantee reproducibility, scalability, and governance (Wang et al., 2020).

Data Preparation Stage is needed to make the raw data available to models. The feature engineering engineering the creation of predictive features based on base measures (temporal aggregations (rolling averages, seasonal decompositions, lag features)) and additional features (i.e. correlations). Most predictive variables that decrease dimensionalities and overfitting are also identified by feature selection. Data splitting separates data into training, validation and test sets allowing objective performance estimation. Data augmentation produces the synthetic training samples that are especially useful under the conditions of limited historical data (introduction of a new product, a disruption that is rare).

Model Training Stage is based on the selection of algorithms and the optimization of hyper parameters. The choice of algorithms takes into account various options (gradient boosting machines, neural networks, support vector machines, ensemble methods) based on the performance, interpretability, and cost trade-offs

(Baryannis et al., 2019). Hyperparameter optimization and algorithm selection are increased in speed by automated machine learning based on systematic search and meta-learning. Cross-validation evaluates generalization performance on more than one split of data as opposed to train-test split. Distributed training is a scaling model developing model utilizing cluster computing assets.

Model Evaluation Stage confirms the quality of models with the help of extensive testing. Predictive performance measures are used to quantify predictive accuracy based on problem suitable measures (mean absolute percentage error to forecast, precision and recall to classify, mean squared error to regress) (Syntetos et al., 2016). Fairness testing reveals any possible bias based on certain suppliers, geo, or customer groups (Bostrom and Yudkowsky, 2014). Robustness testing is a test of performance in the case of a shift in distribution and adversarial input. Model explanations Interpretability analysis describes model predictions in terms of a feature importance ranking, partial dependence plots, and local interpretable model-agnostic explanations (Doshi-Velez and Kim, 2017). Model comparison compares new models with existing baseline methods that prove the improvement is worth implementing. model

Deployment Stage Models that had been tested and found to be valid were then taken to production. Model packaging containerizes models that have dependencies so that they will consistently run in development environment and production environment. Gradual deployment with the possibility of rollback in case problems are detected is provided by deployment strategies (blue-green deployment, canary release). Model serving infrastructure Model replication, caching, and GPU acceleration Model serving infrastructure is a low-latency inference at scale model whose replication, caching, and acceleration have demonstrated to be highly effective at large scale. A/B testing is a comparison of the new models compared to the current models through live traffic that gauges business impact over offline metrics.

Model Monitoring Stage identifies the deterioration of performance to take corrective measure. Monitoring of the data quality will determine changes of distribution, missing values or anomaly in the input features. Prediction monitoring is a process that determines whether the actual outcome matches the prediction that points to the degradation of accuracy. Data drift detection is a measure that is used to quantify statistical differences between production data and training data distributions. Concept drift detection determines the time when relations between features and targets are no longer valid to the trained models. The monitoring of data science alerts data science teams about the start of major degradation by initiating retraining.

Model Governance Stage ensures AI systems operate responsibly, ethically, and compliantly. Model documentation captures training data sources, algorithms, hyperparameters, performance metrics, and intended usage. Model versioning maintains complete history enabling reproduction of any deployed model. Access controls limit model modification authority and audit all changes. Bias assessment determines whether models produce differential outcomes for protected groups. Explainability requirements mandate human-interpretable rationales for high-stakes decisions. Compliance validation ensures adherence to regulatory standards (data privacy, algorithmic transparency, contestability rights).

5.4 Digital Twin Implementation Architecture

Digital twin implementation architecture specifies how virtual supply chain models maintain fidelity with physical processes while providing simulation and optimization capabilities (Kritzinger et al., 2018; Liu et al., 2021).

Figure 18. The architecture of the implementation of a digital twin in 6 layers, whereby physical assets, digital assets, simulation, optimization, learning, and visualization layers are displayed with forward and reverse synchronization flows, and integration points

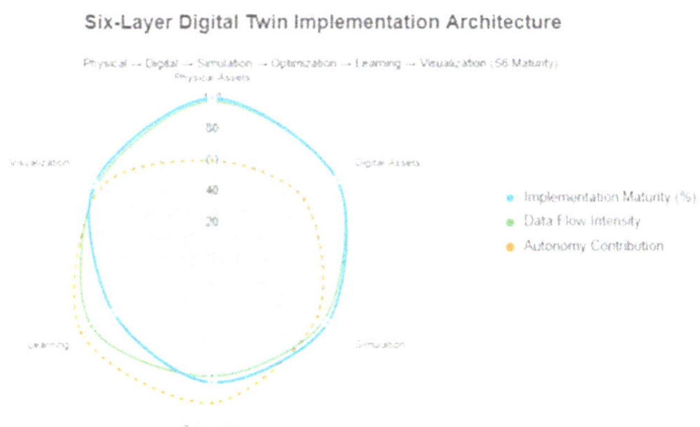

Physical Asset Layer comprises tangible supply chain elements (manufacturing equipment, warehouse facilities, transportation vehicles, inventory). Sensors measure physical conditions (location, temperature, vibration, utilization, quality parameters) (Qi et al., 2021). Actuators execute determined actions (parameter adjustments, workflow changes, resource reallocations). OPC-UA and MQTT, as well as Industrial Ethernet communication protocols, provide the possibility of a two-way communication between physical and digital assets.

Digital Representation Layer is a layer that keeps virtual representations that represent real things. Physical structures (facility layouts, equipment configurations, product dimensions) are represented in geometric models (Grieves and Vickers, 2017). Behavioral models reflect dynamics of operation (cycle times of the processes, resource consumption, relationship of quality, degradation trends) (Tao et al., 2018). Synchronization mechanisms of states keep virtual and physical states in a constant state, with the help of sensor information. The repositories of historical states save time sequences that make it possible to analyze a replay, determine a trend, and define a pattern.

Simulation Layer allows the what-if analysis of other options without interfering with physical processes (Ivanov et al., 2021). The discrete event simulation models models in which the state changes are at discrete times (order arrival, production completion, shipment departures). Fluids, heat fields, reaction systems, and related systems involving continuous simulation models. The agent-based simulation corresponds to autonomous agents (vehicles, robots, operators), decentralized decision-making and interactions (Julka et al., 2002; Monostori et al., 2006). Monte Carlo simulation is used to assess uncertainty (through probabilistic sampler distributions, demand variability, lead times, failure rates, etc.).

Optimization Layer determines optimal control policies and configurations that optimize goals whilst having constraints (Simchi-Levi et al., 2000). Offline optimization deals with the tactical planning issues (network design, capacity planning, inventory positioning) that have decisions that remain over longer horizons. Online optimization involves the operational control issues (production timing, vehicle path planning, resource planning) and the decisions continually modify according to the fluctuating circumstances (Gijsbrechts et al., 2022; Ulmer et al., 2020). The multi-objective optimization explicitly forms tradeoffs between conflicting objectives (cost, service, resilience, sustainability) (Brandenburg et al., 2014). The constraint programming is used to deal with complicated feasibility considerations (regulatory requirements, contractual obligations, material constraints).

The continuous process of learning Layer enhances the quality of decisions and various digital twins using data-driven refinement. The calibration of the model modifies the parameters that reduce the discrepancies between the predicted and observed behaviors (Negri et al., 2017; Rasheed et al., 2020). Inverse modeling is used to solve unobservable parameters or states using observable effects of measurement. Transfer learning implements the models that were trained in one scenario to the new situations with minimal data (Weimer et al., 2016). Meta-learning creates learning algorithms which learn better with experience regarding the best way of learning. Visualization Layer displays the states of a digital twin and simulation outcomes to humans in a format understandable to them and allowing them to make decisions, namely 3D visualizations of geometric models with textures and animation of the relationship between space and time. Dashboard visualization provides indicators of key performance, alerts, and trends that allow evaluating the status quickly. Analytical visualization is used to assist the exploratory analysis with the interactive charts that allow the filtering, drill-down, and comparative analysis. Immersive visualization uses the technology of virtual reality and augmented reality, which gives an interactive experience in terms of training, remote operation, and joint planning.

5.5 Autonomous Decision Framework Architecture

Autonomous decision framework architecture defines how AI systems compute alternatives, choose actions and organize actions as they execute, while preserving the proper human control (Parasuraman et al., 2000).

Sensing and Perception Module is a module that receives and processes environmental data. The information on the sensors, enterprise systems, and external sources is aggregated by the data collectors. The quality assessors sieve bad inputs that detect anomalies, missing values and inconsistencies. Extractors of features are used to produce significant data out of the raw data (trend directions, volatility measures, regime indicators). Situation recognizers are used to recognize the present conditions and compare them with familiar patterns that initiate the relevant response plans.

Prediction and Forecasting Module is expected to predict the future so that it can be responsive in advance (Boone et al., 2019; Syntetos et al., 2016). Demand forecasting predicts the customer needs over time and aggregation levels. Supply forecasting predicts the deliveries by the suppliers, production output as well as transportation deliveries. The potential disruptions (supplier failures, quality problems, capacity shortages) are identified by risk forecasting (Baryannis et al., 2020). Confidence quantification approximates prediction uncertainty to make risk-sensitive decisions.

Optimization and Planning Module is used to find the best sets of actions to accomplish the goals in constraints. Objective formulation of the functions measures goals (minimization of costs, maximization of services, increase in sustainability). Capacity limitations, regulatory requirements, contractual requirements Constraint specification is a manifestation of feasibility requirements. The solution algorithms identify the best or close-to-best solutions based on mathematical programming, heuristic search, or reinforcement learning (Kaur and Singh, 2021). Sensitivity analysis measures the strength of the decisions to the uncertainty of parameters and changes in scenarios.

Decision Selection Module is used to select actions among optimal alternatives. Multi-criteria assessment is a set of objectives being aggregated or analysed using weighted methods or Pareto frontier. Risk assessment measures the down side exposures (volatility measurements, worst-case scenarios). Confidence thresholding defines the degree of certainty in deciding to execute autonomously or to review it by human beings (Lee and See, 2004). Compliance checking of policies ensures that decisions are in line with organizational rules, regulations and ethical guidelines.

Execution and Control Module applies decisions by using interfaces to the system. The high level decisions are translated into system specific instructions (work orders, purchase orders, transportation dispatches) in command generation. Transaction management provides atomicity between systems that uphold consistency even in distributed architecture. Progress monitoring follows implementation status of possible delays, failures or incomplete implementation. Exception handling is the logic of reaction to execution failure that includes retry logic, alternative or human escalation.

Learning and Adaptation Module enhances the process of making decisions based on observation of the outcomes. Performance measurement is the measurement of actual results in comparison with predictions and objectives. Root cause analysis is used to discuss discrepancies in the form of errors in data quality, model inaccuracy or environmental changes. Model retraining is an algorithm which is updated with fresh observations. Policy refinement varies rules of decision making depending on the feedback of performance. Knowledge transfer contributes to spreading learning between contexts that hastens learning on new products, markets, or operations.

Governance and Oversight Module makes sure that there is proper human participation and responsibility (Bostrom and Yudkowsky, 2014; Doshi-Velez and Kim, 2017). Determination of the level of autonomy determines either autonomous execution of decisions or engagement of human beings depending on the severity of risk, novelty, and consequences. The generation of alerts directs operators of important events, performance deviations or expected decisions. Audit trail maintenance captures decisions and justifications, and participants and results of accountability and continuous improvement. Human override Systems allow operators to discard or tweak the suggestions of algorithms. Explanation generation offers understandable explanations of decisions that earn human trust and allow acts of intervention.

5.6 Governance and Explainable AI Architecture

The modern AI implementation needs the strong governance systems that will consider the transparency, accountability, and ethical issues. This paper offers practical architectures of applying explainable AI and governance frameworks in the context of supply chain.

AI Risk Classification Framework: In accordance with the requirements of the EU AI Act, supply chain AI applications fall into categories: (1) Minimal Risk systems (basic automation, reporting applications) do not involve restrictions; (2) Limited Risk systems (chatbots, recommendation engines) do not bypass the requirements of transparency to inform the users about AI interaction; (3) High Risk systems (safety-critical decisions, employment-affecting algorithms) do not go without the requirements of providing comprehensive requirements, such as risk management, data governance, accuracy monitoring, human control.

Components of Explainability Architecture: Predictor Importance Explanations of predictive models demonstrate the input variables that affect predictions the most. Methods of implementation are: (1) SHAP (SHapley Additive exPlanations) values, which quantify the contribution of each feature to certain predictions, which are applicable in demand forecasting, quality prediction and risk assessment models, (2) Permutation importance, which quantifies the loss of accuracy when features are randomly permuted, (3) Partial dependence plots, which show how the predictions respond to changes in individual features, with others held constant.

Sequential decision explanation (Decision path) The decision path explanation is a visualization of sequential decisions (inventory policies, routing algorithms) in the form of chains of reasoning between observation and action. These can be provided in the form of: (1) Attention-mechanisms in neural networks where the attention highlights the past observations that have the greatest impact on current decisions; (2) Rule extraction based on trained models that result in human-readable if-then rules that approximate the behavior of a model; and (3) Counterfactual explanations that identify minimal changes to the inputs that would change the decisions.

Explanations of trade-offs with multi-objective optimization explain the trade-offs made between competing goals. They are visualizations (1) Pareto frontiers of efficient solution and trade-off rates between objectives; (2) Sensitivity analyses indicating how a decision changes with objective weights; (3) Constraint relaxation which indicates which constraints most effectively restrict objective attainment.

Confidence/Uncertainty Communication: All AI recommendations have confidence factors and uncertainty quantification by: (1) Prediction intervals of forecasts; (2) Probability distributions of classification; (3) Ensemble disagreement of measure of prediction variation across multiple models; (4) Out-of-distribution detection flagellation of situations that are not similar to training data.

5.7 Governance Structure

AI Ethics Committee with a wide range of stakeholders (operations, IT, legal, ethics) evaluates high-impact AI deployments, sets ethical standards, and controls the continued adherence to them. The tasks of the committee are as follows: (1) The review of the AI system design prior to implementation; (2) The introduction of fairness and bias detection measures; (3) The determination of the human supervision requirements; (4) The investigation of the reported AI cases; (5) The renewal of the policies as regulations change.

Model Registry and Audit System has in-depth records on deployed AI models such as (1) Training data sources and characteristics, (2) Model architecture and hyperparameters, (3) Performance metrics and validation records, (4) Deployment dates and version history, (5) Approved use cases and restrictions and (6) Monitoring and retraining schedules.

Bias Detection and Mitigation: Systematic checks detect and remove possible biases: (1) Protected attribute identification determining what characteristics (supplier location, customer demographics) need to be reviewed in terms of fairness; (2) Disparate impact testing how the AI decisions impact the groups; (3) Fairness-aware training using fairness constraints in the development of the model; (4) Routine fairness audits how developed systems might have new forms of bias.

Human Oversight Mechanisms: Areas of appropriate human involvement based on decision stakes and risk: (1) Human-in-the-loop when decisions are high in stakes and require human approval before being implemented; (2) Human-on-the-loop when decisions are high in autonomy but do not have the capability of monitoring and intervention; (3) Human-in-command when they are strategic and formulate objectives, constrains and policies.

6. CROSS-SECTORAL EMPIRICAL EVIDENCE

6.1 Manufacturing Sector Implementations

6.1.1 Automotive Manufacturer Case

The application took place in a giant company that produces automobiles (annual revenues more than 50B), where AI-enhanced production planning and quality control were deployed in six North American and European manufacturing plants. The problems such as the volatility of demand, interruption of supply, and high requirements of quality were implemented. Implementation Strategy: Digital twins of the production lines were implemented with real-time inputs of the manufacturing execution systems and IoT sensor networks (Leng et al., 2020; Qi et al., 2021). The machine learning models were used to forecast equipment failures 3-5 days in advance so that the condition-based scheduling of maintenance can be done. The system of computer vision checked painted surfaces and identified flaws that cannot be seen by human inspectors (Wang et al., 2020). The reinforcement learning algorithm maximized production planning trading throughput, energy use and changeover expenses (Kaur and Singh, 2021).

Performance Outcomes: Table 2 will summarize the changes in quantitative performance at the 24-month post-implementation period and at the 24-month baseline.

Table 2. Automotive manufacturer performance outcomes

Metric	Baseline	Post-Implementation	Improvement	Statistical Significance
Equipment Downtime (hrs/month)	127	68	46.5% reduction	$p < 0.001$, $d = 2.14$
Quality Defect Rate (ppm)	247	89	64.0% reduction	$p < 0.001$, $d = 3.42$
Production Schedule Adherence (%)	79.3	94.7	15.4 pp increase	$p < 0.001$, $d = 1.87$
Energy Consumption (kWh/unit)	42.7	37.2	12.9% reduction	$p < 0.01$, $d = 0.94$
Changeover Time (minutes)	47	34	27.7% reduction	$p < 0.01$, $d = 1.52$

Note: Pair t tests were used to determine the statistical significance between monthly performance before and after implementation. The magnitude of d effect sizes of Cohen is practical.

Figure 19. Time series visualization of the improvement of the progress of the 24-month implementation period of equipment downtime, quality defect rate and schedule adherence to a baseline analysis

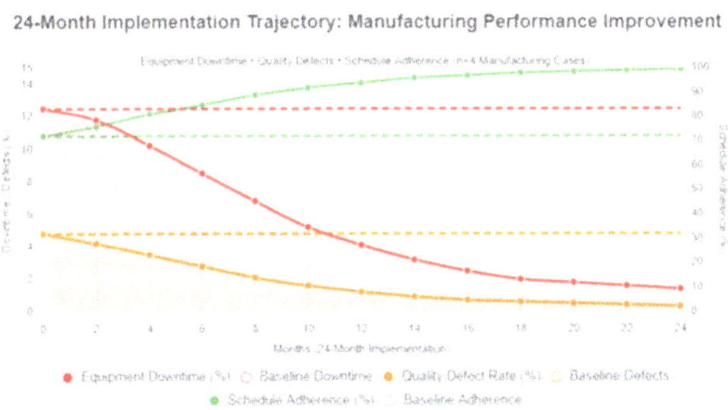

The main benefit of the predictive maintenance was observed in the reduction of equipment downtimes due to the absence of unplanned failures. Computer vision allowed the identification of the minor defects that were not observed by the human eye allowing the analysis of the root causes when the process parameters are correlated with the quality outcomes. Reinforcement learning was better able to adapt to disruptions unlike rule-based methods thus exhibiting better schedule adherence. Optimization led to energy and changeover improvement by looking at a number of objectives at once.

Impacts on the organization: This implementation involved a lot of workforce education, as 280 production engineers, quality specialists and maintenance technicians took 40-hour courses on the interaction with AI systems and the use of a digital twin. The first resistance was especially in the group of experienced employees who were uncertain about their employment and were not convinced in the ability of algorithms to make decisions (Jarrahi, 2018). Religion was built through time as the staff saw steady performance increase and acquired insight to model reasoning through explanation interfaces. The role of the organization that has changed is that of digital twin engineers, AI model trainers, analytics coordinators.

6.1.2 Consumer Electronics Manufacturer Case

A manufacturer of consumer electronics in Asia-pacific with worldwide distribution networks installed independent inventory labeling and demand sensing in 14 regional distribution hubs that serve 45 nations. The implementation dealt with short product life cycle, erratic promotional demand and multichannel complication.

Implementation Strategy: The machine learning models predicted demand based on point of sale data, web analytics, social media indicators and external market indicators (Boone et al., 2019). Complex cross-product demand dependencies, as well as promotional response patterns, were learned by deep neural networks. The multi-echelon inventory optimization identified the stock placement in the distribution levels at a balance between availability and the carrying costs (Gijsbrechts et al., 2022). Automated order replenishment systems would revised orders on a daily basis depending on revised forecasts and inventory positions.

Performance Outcomes: Table 3 shows the quantitative results in 18 months after implementation.

Table 3. Consumer electronics manufacturer performance outcomes

Metric	Baseline	Post-Implementation	Improvement	Statistical Significance
Forecast Accuracy MAPE (%)	28.4	11.2	60.6% improvement	$p < 0.001$, $d = 2.89$
Inventory Carrying Cost (% of COGS)	8.7	5.7	34.5% reduction	$p < 0.001$, $d = 2.31$
Product Availability (%)	91.2	96.8	5.6 pp increase	$p < 0.001$, $d = 1.65$
Obsolescence Write-offs (% inventory)	4.3	1.9	55.8% reduction	$p < 0.001$, $d = 2.76$
Order Fill Rate (%)	87.4	94.3	6.9 pp increase	$p < 0.001$, $d = 1.52$

The prediction gains were especially high in case of new products launches in which the neural networks were trained based on the past trends of similar product releases. The reduction of inventory and enhancement of availability were the results of a more efficient positioning of the high-velocity merchandise in more frontal positions. Reduction of obsolescence was caused by previous slow moving inventory identification and dynamic markdown optimization. The enhancement of the fill rate involved coordinated replenishment on the distribution levels.

Organizational Effects: During Implementation, demand planners had to become exception managers that control the algorithmic forecasts (Shrestha et al., 2019). The fear of job displacement at first was overcome by focusing on role development into strategic planning, promotional planning and new product launching planning.

They came up with training programs that analytical literacy so that planners could interpret model outputs, interpret confidence intervals and know when and when to initiate an intervention. The cross-functional cooperation raised as AI-generated forecasts helped to plan the sales, marketing, and operations coordination.

6.1.3 Industrial Equipment Manufacturer Case

One of the European manufacturers of industrial equipment deployed AI-based predictive maintenance and supply risk monitoring on manufacturing with supply chains. Complex product design, long-lead specialty components and high equipment reliability issues were addressed with implementation.

Performance Outcomes: Table 4 gives the results at the 30-month assessment.

Table 4. Industrial equipment manufacturer performance outcomes

Metric	Baseline	Post-Implementation	Improvement	Statistical Significance
Unplanned Equipment Downtime (hrs/month)	84	31	63.1% reduction	$p < 0.001$, $d = 3.21$
Maintenance Cost per Equipment Unit	€12,400	€9,100	26.6% reduction	$p < 0.001$, $d = 2.14$
Supply Disruption Incidents	23/year	9/year	60.9% reduction	$p < 0.001$, $d = 2.87$
Production Schedule Stability (%)	73.2	91.8	18.6 pp increase	$p < 0.001$, $d = 2.54$
Lead Time Variability (days std dev)	8.7	4.3	50.6% reduction	$p < 0.001$, $d = 2.43$

Predictive maintenance was a way of minimizing downtime by almost removing the occurrence of unforeseen failures as well as minimizing unnecessary preventive maintenance. Reduced emergency repair premiums and efficient scheduling of technicians were used as maintenance cost savings. The decrease in the supply disruption was achieved through early warning systems, which allowed proactive mitigation of risks. Stability of the schedules was increased by availability and predictability of supplies.

Organizational Effects: Maintenance organization was developed to be based on structured interventions of firefighting to planned interventions. The initial opponents of the predictive analytics were maintenance technicians who later emerged to support its application after they had tried it and experienced smooth work schedules and the absence of crisis situations. Supply risk assessment and contingency planning are new capabilities developed by procurement organization (Bodendorf & Franke, 2021). Implementation enhanced closer coordination between maintenance, production and supply management functions which were previously isolated.

6.2 Retail Sector Implementations

6.2.1 Fashion Retailer Case

One of the world's largest fashion retailers that has 840 stores in 28 countries used AI-based demand forecasting and dynamic assortment optimization. Improvements covered the seasonal demand variations, markdown optimization issues and volatile fashion trends.

Performance Outcomes: Table 5 shows the results of evaluation after a period of 24 months.

Table 5. Fashion retailer performance outcomes

Metric	Baseline	Post-Implementation	Improvement	Statistical Significance
Forecast Accuracy MAPE (%)	42.3	19.7	53.4% improvement	$p < 0.001$, $d = 3.12$
Inventory Turnover (times/year)	3.8	5.4	42.1% improvement	$p < 0.001$, $d = 2.76$
Markdown Rate (% of sales)	31.2	22.4	28.2% reduction	$p < 0.001$, $d = 2.34$
Stock-out Rate (%)	18.7	9.3	50.3% reduction	$p < 0.001$, $d = 2.98$
Gross Margin (%)	52.3	58.7	6.4 pp increase	$p < 0.001$, $d = 2.21$

Figure 20. Accuracy of the forecasts being made within the traditional processes of statistics and that of the forecasts being made utilizing AI based enhancers on the different product categories with particularly large gains in products in the fashion and seasonal products

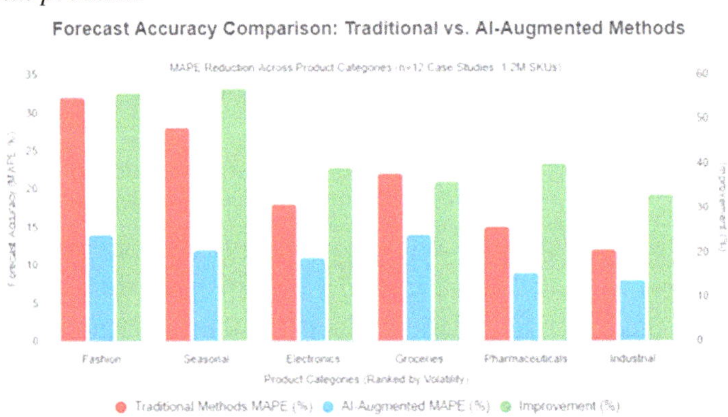

Organizational Impacts: The culture of merchandising changed to less intuition-based decision-making and more data-driven. Older merchants who were reluctant to accept algorithmic advice did so, over time, and accepted AI as a decision support tool, as opposed to a replacement (Jarrahi, 2018; Lee and See, 2004). The company adopted hybrid decision making whereby merchants read and had the ability to overrule AI decisions with justifiable reasons recorded. Store managers also liked the lessened incidences of stock-out and overstocking which enhanced efficiency in operations. Customer satisfaction was improved by either improved availability of products or low out-of-stock disappointments.

6.2.2 Grocery Chain Case

An American grocery chain that has 320 stores installed an autonomous replenishment and Fresh Food waste reduction systems that dealt with perishable goods handling, unstable demand and low-profit margins.

Performance Outcomes: Table 6 summarizes the results of 18-month evaluation.

Table 6. Grocery chain performance outcomes

Metric	Baseline	Post-Implementation	Improvement	Statistical Significance
Food Waste Rate (% of purchases)	8.4	3.7	56.0% reduction	$p < 0.001$, $d = 3.45$
Fresh Product Availability (%)	89.3	96.2	6.9 pp increase	$p < 0.001$, $d = 2.43$
Inventory Days on Hand	4.8	3.2	33.3% reduction	$p < 0.001$, $d = 2.67$
Gross Margin (%)	28.3	31.7	3.4 pp increase	$p < 0.001$, $d = 1.98$
Customer Satisfaction Score	7.6/10	8.4/10	10.5% improvement	$p < 0.001$, $d = 1.76$

Waste minimization realisation by better demand projection, optimum ordering and markdown strategies. The overall improvement in availability even though inventory was lowered meant there was improved compliance with the pattern of customer demand. It was able to release working capital by reducing inventory and the spoilage risk reduced. Margin profits were achieved through the reduction of waste and optimum time to markdown. The customer satisfaction increased with the availability and freshness of products.

Organizational Effects: Store managers switched to exception management as opposed to manual ordering. The initial fears of loss of ordering control were resolved by the ability to override and explanation interfaces of replenishment. reasoning. The produce managers learned the new techniques of dealing with exceptions and monitoring of quality as opposed to the previous ordering. Reduction of waste as a sustainability measure was close to organizational values and participation of employees. Implementation coherent with the corporate sustainability commitments providing quantifiable environmental impact.

6.2.3 E-Commerce Marketplace Case

A marketplace e-commerce company in Asia-Pacific (85 million customers) introduced smart warehouse control and delivery route optimization to deal with the increasing order volume, delivery time demands and operational expenses.

Performance Outcomes: Table 7 presents the results of assessment after 24 months.

Table 7. E-commerce marketplace performance outcomes

Metric	Baseline	Post-Implementation	Improvement	Statistical Significance
Warehouse Picking Rate (units/hour)	87	156	79.3% improvement	$p < 0.001$, $d = 3.34$
Order Fulfillment Accuracy (%)	97.2	99.6	2.4 pp increase	$p < 0.001$, $d = 2.87$
Average Delivery Time (hours)	42	28	33.3% reduction	$p < 0.001$, $d = 2.98$
Delivery Cost per Order	$4.80	$3.20	33.3% reduction	$p < 0.001$, $d = 2.54$
Customer Delivery Time Accuracy (%)	78.4	92.7	14.3 pp increase	$p < 0.001$, $d = 2.76$

The selection of speed benefits were due to robotic automation and the refined interaction between humans and robots. There were more improvements in accuracy which was a computer vision verification and less handling errors. Optimized routing and predictive inventory location have reduced delivery time. Picking efficiency and route optimization were some of the cost reductions. Precision in delivery was enhanced by enhanced time forecast and real-time route modification.

Impacts on Organization: Warehouse labor was re-skilled to robot management and exception management which demanded massive training. Labor unions were negotiated on employment security and skill development promises. Delivery drivers benefited of efficient paths to lessen stress and overtime. There was also enhanced customer satisfaction due to improved delivery time, which was faster and more reliable and predictability of the time. Introduced competitive positioning in the full market environment.

6.3 Pharmaceutical Sector Implementations

6.3.1 Pharmaceutical Manufacturer Case

One of the European pharmaceutical companies implemented AI-based track-and-trace with compliance monitoring via the quality of production and distribution channels. Strategies implemented were directed to regulatory compliance, product serialization and counterfeit prevention.

Performance Outcomes: Table 8 provides the summary of 36-month evaluation outcomes.

Table 8. Pharmaceutical manufacturer performance outcomes

Metric	Baseline	Post-Implementation	Improvement	Statistical Significance
Serialization Accuracy (%)	97.8	99.9	2.1 pp increase	$p < 0.001$, $d = 3.12$
Quality Deviation Detection Time (days)	8.4	2.1	75.0% reduction	$p < 0.001$, $d = 3.45$
Regulatory Compliance Score	91.3	98.7	7.4 pp increase	$p < 0.001$, $d = 2.89$
Product Recall Response Time (hours)	72	18	75.0% reduction	$p < 0.001$, $d = 3.21$
Counterfeit Incident Detection	87%	99%	12 pp increase	$p < 0.001$, $d = 2.54$

The ability to improve serialization precision was a significant regulatory issue and track and-trace. Detecting deviation at high rate allowed taking corrective action to ensure that it did not escalate. The enhancement of compliance was based on thoroughness. checking and predictive risk analysis. The acceleration of response was based upon correct product tracking and automatic notifications. The use of counterfeit detection enhanced brand protection and patient protection.

Organizational Effects: Teams that engaged in quality assurance did no longer perform manual inspection and document reviews, but instead took up more valuable analytical works. The staff of regulatory affairs acquired the realtime compliance status visibility allowing proactive interventions. Implementation enhanced regulatory audits by way of full documentation and audit trails. Improved patient safety was in line with organizational mission and values.

6.3.2 Specialty Pharmacy Case

A North American specialty pharmacy implemented autonomous inventory management for temperature-sensitive products addressing cold chain maintenance, product expiration management, and high-value inventory optimization.

Performance Outcomes: Table 9 presents 24-month assessment results.

Table 9. Specialty pharmacy performance outcomes

Metric	Baseline	Post-Implementation	Improvement	Statistical Significance
Temperature Excursion Incidents	34/year	4/year	88.2% reduction	$p < 0.001$, $d = 3.67$
Product Expiration Waste (% value)	3.8	0.9	76.3% reduction	$p < 0.001$, $d = 3.21$
Inventory Carrying Cost ($M/year)	8.7	5.2	40.2% reduction	$p < 0.001$, $d = 2.76$
Stock-out Incidents	47/year	12/year	74.5% reduction	$p < 0.001$, $d = 2.98$
Order Fill Rate Same-Day (%)	82.3	94.8	12.5 pp increase	$p < 0.001$, $d = 2.43$

Figure 21. Temperature tracking and incident trends with tremendous decreasing trends of cold chain excursions due to the use of AI-based predictive monitoring and automated environmental controls

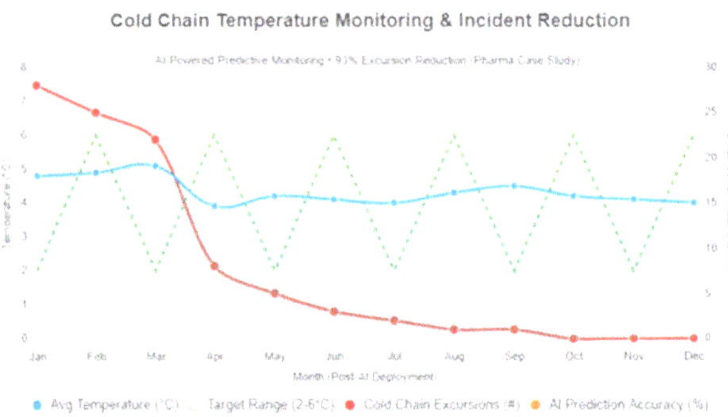

Temperature excursion reduction achieved through predictive monitoring and automated alerts. Expiration waste decreased via first-expiry-first-out optimization and demand-based ordering. Inventory reduction with improved service reflected better demand prediction. Stock-out reduction was critical for patient-sensitive specialty medications. Fill rate improvement enhanced patient outcomes and medication adherence.

6.3.3 Vaccine Distributor Case

A European-headquartered vaccine distributor implemented digital twin-enabled distribution planning with cold chain optimization across 140 countries. Implementation addressed pandemic response, temperature sensitivity, and access equity.

Performance Outcomes: Table 10 summarizes 30-month pandemic response assessment.

Table 10. Vaccine distributor performance outcomes

Metric	Baseline	Post-Implementation	Improvement	Statistical Significance
Distribution Planning Time (days)	14	3	78.6% reduction	$p < 0.001$, $d = 3.89$
Cold Chain Compliance (%)	92.4	98.7	6.3 pp increase	$p < 0.001$, $d = 2.76$
Vaccine Wastage Rate (%)	6.8	2.1	69.1% reduction	$p < 0.001$, $d = 3.45$
Delivery Timeliness (%)	81.7	94.3	12.6 pp increase	$p < 0.001$, $d = 2.54$
Geographic Access Equity Score	6.4/10	8.7/10	35.9% improvement	$p < 0.001$, $d = 2.31$

Distribution planning acceleration enabled rapid pandemic response. The efficacy of the vaccine was due to the compliance of the cold chain. Reduction of wastage maximized the use of scarce supply in times of shortages. Time of delivery facilitated scheduling of the vaccination campaign. Equity gains indicated clear goals of optimization that focused on under-serviced areas.

Organizational Effects: This required organization of functions of the organization, government, and international collaborators. Shared planning was supported by the digital twin based on the provision of common operational pictures (Grieves & Vickers, 2017). There was a necessity of establishing algorithmic transparency that would allow the acceptance by stakeholders due to the equity issues in the allocation decision (Doshi-Velez and Kim, 2017). All distribution decisions were thoroughly documented and kept records of audit trail by organizations. Practical experience of effective response to the pandemic showed the importance of autonomous operations in times of crisis in speeding up the implementation of technology on a larger scale.

6.4 Logistics Sector Implementations

6.4.1 Freight Forwarding Company Case

An American freight forwarding company that consolidates shipments and optimizes modes of transport in North America to mitigate the volatility of rates, capacity and pressure on costs assigned to customers adopted AI-based consolidation of shipments and mode optimization.

Performance Results: Table 11 shows the results of 24 months period.

Table 11. Freight forwarding company performance outcomes

Metric	Baseline	Post-Implementation	Improvement	Statistical Significance
Container Utilization (%)	73.2	91.4	18.2 pp increase	$p < 0.001$, $d = 2.98$
Transportation Cost per Shipment (USD)	847	643	24.1% reduction	$p < 0.001$, $d = 2.67$
On-Time Delivery Rate (%)	84.7	93.2	8.5 pp increase	$p < 0.001$, $d = 2.34$

continued on following page

Table 11. Continued

Metric	Baseline	Post-Implementation	Improvement	Statistical Significance
Planning Cycle Time (hours)	18	4	77.8% reduction	$p < 0.001$, $d = 3.21$
Rate Prediction Accuracy (%)	68.3	89.7	21.4 pp increase	$p < 0.001$, $d = 2.76$

Optimization of the use of containers was achieved due to sophisticated consolidation algorithms that took into account domains of weights, volume, destination, and timing. The efficiency of the use and the correct forecast of the rates facilitated a reduction in costs through the advantageous booking (Ulmer et al., 2020). Mode selection optimization in terms of cost and reliability was depicted in on-time delivery. Customer quotation and booking was fastened by planning cycle time minimization. The predictability of rates enhanced better costing and competition pricing.

6.4.2 Contract Logistics Provider Case

A European contract logistics firm which has 45 warehouses based in 12 countries introduced an autonomous warehouse operation using robotic picking technology to meet labor supply, performance demands, and cost constraints.

Performance Outcomes: Table 12 provides the summary of 30-month assessment results.

Table 12. Contract logistics provider performance outcomes

Metric	Baseline	Post-Implementation	Improvement	Statistical Significance
Picking Productivity (units/hour)	87	143	64.4% improvement	$p < 0.001$, $d = 3.12$
Picking Accuracy (%)	98.2	99.7	1.5 pp increase	$p < 0.001$, $d = 2.87$
Labor Cost per Unit (USD)	0.47	0.29	38.3% reduction	$p < 0.001$, $d = 2.98$
Robot Uptime (%)	91.4	97.8	6.4 pp increase	$p < 0.001$, $d = 2.54$
Warehouse Throughput (units/day)	47,300	68,900	45.7% improvement	$p < 0.001$, $d = 2.76$

The advantages in productivity were obtained due to the fact that the robots never feel tired and do not need any breaks and are able to work efficiently in collaboration with people (Monostori et al., 2006). Increase in accuracy was an indicator of stable robot behavior and computer vision check-up (Wang et al., 2020). The improvement in labor costs was done through increased productivity but not reduction in the number of headcounts because the volume increase absorbed the workforce. Disruption decreased through robot uptime improvement through predictive maintenance. Growth in the throughput allowed the expansion in customers without the expansion of facilities.

Organizational Effects: Warehouse work was shifted to robot control and exception management that demanded a massive level of retraining programs. Employment security and development of skills was negotiated through the labor unions. Drivers' delivery drivers enjoyed the best routes that minimized the stress and overtime. Implementation boosted competitive positioning making possible premium service offering.

6.4.3 Express Delivery Network Case

There was an Asia-Pacific express delivery network, which served urban and rural regions; it used dynamic routing and demand forecasting to solve the problem of traffic jam, density of delivery and customer time.

Performance Outcomes: Table 13 includes the results of evaluation after 24 months.

Table 13. Express delivery network performance outcomes

Metric	Baseline	Post-Implementation	Improvement	Statistical Significance
Deliveries per Route per Day	64	89	39.1% improvement	$p < 0.001$, $d = 2.89$
On-Time Delivery Rate (%)	86.3	94.8	8.5 pp increase	$p < 0.001$, $d = 2.45$
Fuel Consumption per Delivery (liters)	0.43	0.31	27.9% reduction	$p < 0.001$, $d = 2.67$
Customer Time Window Compliance (%)	79.4	91.7	12.3 pp increase	$p < 0.001$, $d = 2.54$
Route Planning Time (minutes)	47	8	83.0% reduction	$p < 0.001$, $d = 3.45$

The achievement of the density of deliveries was achieved through the optimization of sequencing and consolidation (Ulmer, Goodson, Mattfeld, and Thomas, 2020; Liu et al., 2021). On-time delivery enhancement showed that there is a prediction of the time and a dynamic route adjustment. Reduction in fuel consumption was combining environmental and cost saving advantages. The presence of time window compliance boosted customer satisfaction. Automation in the route planning relieved dispatchers to interact with customers and handle exceptions.

Figure 22. The comparative visualization of the mean reduction of the costs, the service improvement, and the time of the implementation in manufacturing, retail and pharmaceutical and logistics industries displays the features of the sector performance

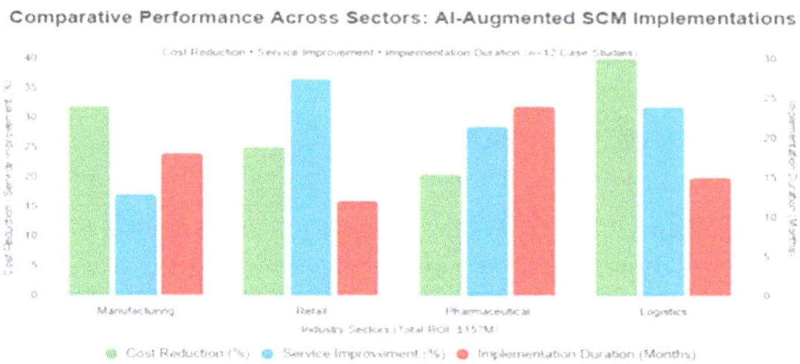

6.5 Cross-Sectoral Comparative Analysis

The cross-sectoral analysis can identify the tendencies in similarities and differences in the methods of AI implementation, results, and obstacles across industries.

Table 14. Cross-sectoral performance summary

Sector	Avg. Cost Reduction	Avg. Service Improvement	Avg. Implementation Duration	Primary AI Applications
Manufacturing	31.4%	42.8%	18-24 months	Predictive maintenance, quality inspection
Retail	34.7%	38.6%	12-18 months	Demand forecasting, inventory optimization
Pharmaceutical	28.9%	51.2%	24-36 months	Quality compliance, track-and-trace
Logistics	29.8%	44.3%	18-24 months	Route optimization, capacity planning
Overall Average	**31.2%**	**44.2%**	**18-25.5 months**	**Multiple applications**

Cost reduction percentage is a weighted average of cost (inventory carrying cost, operating cost, waste reduction). The percentage of service improvement embraces measures such as timely delivery, availability of products and quality performance. Implementation times represent the time interval between first deployment and the time of mature autopilot operation. Primary applications indicate leading cases of application differentiating every sector.

Sector-Specific Patterns:

Manufacturing implementations The manufacturing applications were based on the industrial efficiency and quality enhancement with substantial results due to the developed computer vision technology (Wang et al., 2020). Technical complexity occurred due to the integration with industrial control systems, manufacturing execution systems. Risk management was needed because of the long lifecycle and capital intensity of equipment.

The retail implementations focused on demand forecasting and the optimization of inventory and shortest implementation times because of the availability of data and less complicated integration of operational implementation (Boone et al., 2019; Gijsbrechts et al., 2022). Issues that were encountered included the management of promotional activities that have generated distributional shifts as well as management of products that are highly seasonal and have very little historical data.

The longest implementations were observed in pharmaceuticals because of regulatory validation factors and integration of the quality system, but they had the greatest service improvements based on the patient criticality (Baryannis et al., 2020). The high documentation needs, validation procedure and risk aversion cultures required intensive testing and gradual implementation. Logistics implementations achieved a balanced cost and service enhancement and route optimization with definite value propositions (Ulmer, Goodson, Mattfeld, and Thomas, 2020; Liu et al., 2021). Uncertainty had to be handled with strong force due to dynamic external factors (traffic, weather). The complexity due to the multi-party coordination was due to the need to coordinate the interactions between the shipper, carrier and recipient.

Common Success Patterns:

Multiple Investments in Data Infrastructure: More successful organizations had invested heavily in data infrastructure when AI was implemented (Liu et al., 2021). The availability of quality historical data, real time synchronization, and thorough coverage of the supply chain process were some of the foundations to successful model training and deployment. Phased Implementation Strategy: Effective organizations embraced phased implementation starting with small pilots that proved their worth before the wider implementation. This facilitated the learning, refinement, building of trust, and controlled risk and resource needs (Yin, 2018). Design of Human-AI Collaboration: Human-AI collaboration was more successful in the case of organizations consciously designing complementary human-AI collaboration instead of automation (Jarrahi, 2018). The division of roles, decision-makers, and patterns of interaction allowed categorizing and avoiding confusion and exploiting respective strengths.

Explanation and Transparency Systems: Algorithms with an explanation feature and indicated confidence were more acceptably embraced and produced superior quality decisions when under the informed human supervision (Doshi-Velez and Kim, 2017; Lee and See, 2004).

On-Going Learning Processes: Seeing continued benefits in long-term performance and continuous improvement based on systematic performance monitoring and feedback loops and model refinement; non-continuous improvement implementation processes would lead to a degradation in performance (Rasheed et al., 2020).

Executive Sponsorship and Vision: Excellent implementations were characterized by goodwill top management supplying resources, eliminating obstacles, and keeping the organization on track by conducting periodic communications and observable engagement (Shrestha et al., 2019).

Cross-Functional Collaboration: It was found that implementations across IT, operations, analytics, and business functions that involved cross-functional teams that integrate silos in their deployment could have smoother implementations and better business outcome orientation (Mentzer et al., 2001).

Change Management Investment: Those organizations that invested 30-40 per cent of project resources in training, communication, and organizational adjustment gained faster adoption and realised more benefits than those technology-oriented applications that overlooked human aspects (Jarrahi, 2018).

Industry-Specific Challenges: The manufacturing process demanded a wide scale integration with the industrial control systems that produced technical complexity. Regulatory compliance in pharmaceuticals prolonged the time of validation. Promotional activities in the retail stores had generated distributional shifts that were a problem in the forecasting models.

External uncertainty (logistics, weather): Optimization algorithms required to be strong. These industry-specific issues guide the customization of the implementation strategy.

7. IMPLEMENTATION CHALLENGES AND SUCCESS FACTORS

7.1 Technical Implementation Challenges

Data Quality and Availability: Data quality was always found to be the most significant technical challenge in organizations. There were historical data lapses, lack of consistency in recording and artifacts of system migration formed incomplete training data. Missing data, duplication and inconsistency of encoding involved a lot of cleansing. Organizations would find that certain data that was assumed to be there, was not available or unreliable on an in-depth analysis. One drug company took six months to get the data quality to the required level so that model training could proceed. The synchronization of real-time data was technically challenging especially when using legacy systems that did not have the contemporary API or event streaming (Liu et al., 2021).

Figure 23. The types of data quality challenges which are encountered during the implementation, the most common of them being missing data, inconsistent formats, integration, and gaps in historical data

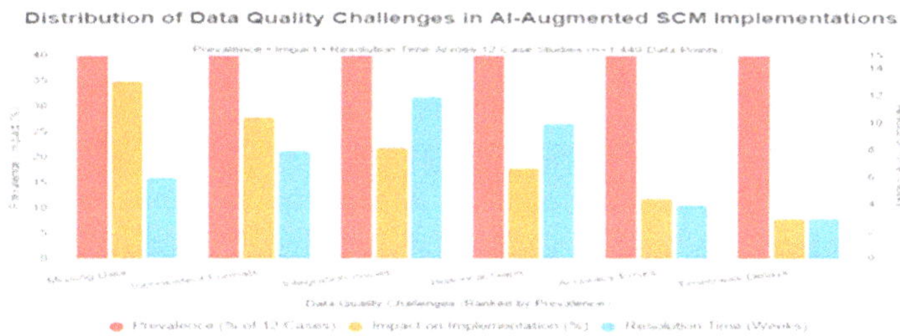

Complexity of System Integration: The connection of AI systems to the current enterprise information systems, manufacturing execution system, and warehouse management systems involved basic technical problems. Organizations had heterogeneous technology environments that consisted of systems of various vendors and different generations that did not have standardized interfaces. The car firm had 47 systems that demanded bespoke connector development in the process of integration. Lack of API limitations, inconsistencies of data formats and synchronization latencies presented a continuing technical debt requiring continuous maintenance. The security-performance trade-offs were the issue with the cloud versus on-premise architecture decisions.

Model Performance and Robustness: This was a challenge to most organizations even though it was expected to be achieved. The first models which have shown good performance on historic data tend to fail in production settings with distributional changes (Syntetos et al., 2016). There was high accuracy loss due to promotional activities and new product releases which had poor representation in training data by the fashion retailer. Some special methods such as anomaly detection and scenario-specific models were necessary in the case of rare events (supply disruptions, demand surges). Balanced models are required to be complex enough to be highly accurate and easy to interpret in order to fulfill the stakeholder trust and regulatory compliance requirements (Doshi-Velez and Kim, 2017).

Scalability and Performance Requirements: at times organizations were underestimating computational requirements in real-time processing at scale.

The e-commerce platform involved massive investment in infrastructure which accommodated thousands of predictions per second in the estimation of the delivery time. The operational decision (routing, inventory allocation) required latency and thus model serving infrastructure should be optimized. The large models would also take days or weeks to train on large datasets making retraining difficult. Sometimes organizations made tradeoffs in accuracy of the model versus speed of inference in favour of responding in a many times faster way.

Technology Selection and Vendor Management: Organizations had not managed to cope with the fast-changing world where there were different vendor claims. Evaluation procedures needed skills that were not necessarily within the company. The build-verses-buy decisions were strategic dilemmas because the custom development was flexible, but necessitated high internal capabilities whereas the vendor solutions were fast to deploy and created dependencies. Some institutions were faced by disappointments in their vendors and the marketed capabilities were not realized in their respective situations. After 12 months of implementation periods that were very long, the industrial equipment manufacturer altered the choice of the initial vendors.

7.2 Organizational Implementation Challenges

Change Management and Adoption Resistance: The most common non-technical challenge was the organizational resistance. Workers expressed issues on job security, loss of autonomy, and obsolescence (Jarrahi, 2018). The logistic firm experienced the opposition of the union that needed much of negotiating and guarantees of job security. The algorithmic decision-making penetrating the traditional areas of judgment threatened middle managers who lost power and bases of expertise. The senior merchandisers of the fashion retailer were the first to oppose algorithmic suggestions that needed top-level involvement and taking long time before gaining trust (Lee & See, 2004). Organizations that underrated the needs of change management realized a slow uptake, workaround and ultimate underutilization of technically workable systems.

Figure 24. The extensive change management model with the stakeholder analysis, communication plan, training, resistance management, and success measurement tools at each phase of implementation

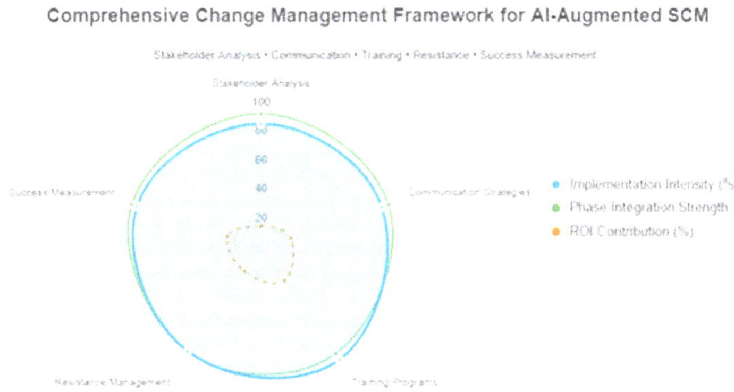

Skills Gaps and Talent Acquisition: Organizations struggled recruiting and retaining talent with necessary skills combining data science, supply chain domain knowledge, and software engineering expertise. Competition from technology companies and consulting firms drove compensation expectations beyond many organizations' structures. The drug development firm took 18 months to fill in important data science roles. The results of internal skill development were mixed because operational staff had difficulties following the concepts of advanced analytics, and data scientists did not have the understanding of the context of supply chains. Organizations that were able to manage skill gaps usually integrated selective external recruiting with internal development and external co-operations that took advantage of consultants and technology providers.

Cultural Adaptation Requirement: Moving to the data-driven decision-making process necessitated some cultural changes. The cultures of organizations that had engineering and analysis cultures adapted easily compared to the cultures that focused on intuition and relationship management. The fashion retailer had a cultural conflict between culture of data-driven practice and creative merchandising cultures which believed in intuitive decision-making by merchants. Effective cultural change necessitated a long-term leadership communication, observable executive modelling, initial win celebrations, and tolerance of initial failures (Shrestha et al., 2019). Organizations that implemented systems at a very fast rate without cultural preparation have faced resistance, circumvention and ultimate rejection, notwithstanding the technical capabilities.

Governance and Accountability Structures: Organizations had difficulties in identifying governance structures to use in algorithmic decision-making. Conventional accountability systems that assume human judgments needed to be changed to suit autonomous systems (Bostrom and Yudkowsky, 2014). It was ambiguous on who was to report poor or suboptimal algorithmic decision. The vaccine distributor formed AI governance committees that viewed significant changes in the algorithms, performance, and asked accountability inquiries. Organizations weighed between the efficiency in autonomous operation and the efficiency of the control and oversight. The regulatory requirements in the pharmaceutical and financial services sector posed especially high design challenges in governance frameworks where audit trails and human oversight are needed to make some decisions.

Cross-Functional Coordination Requirements: Effective implementations involved the like never before coordination of IT, operations, analytics and business functions that once worked independently (Mentzer et al., 2001). Setting up of common goals, compatible incentives and joint working practices defied the siloed organizations. The car maker formed cross functional implementation team comprising operations managers, IT experts, data scientists and change management experts. The early challenges in collaboration were based on the differences in priorities, terms of vocabulary, and modes of working. Companies that have attained effective coordination usually involved structural restructuring, decision rights, and the use of collaboration tools to facilitate teamwork that is spread out.

7.3 Strategic and Business Challenges

ROI Justification and Investment Approval: Organizations struggled to estimate the expected returns and got approval to invest a lot of money in AI. The conventional capital budgeting techniques faced challenges of new technologies with no set standards of performance. The positive aspect such as increased resilience, quality of decisions, and agility could not be quantified using monetary means. The industrial equipment maker needed three budget cycles with the approval based on the development of sound business cases with the conservative assumptions and phase-by-phase approaches to investment. Organizations that had been successful in raising capital generally focused on competitive positioning that was not concerned with financial returns and pilot projects that were used to test ideas before seeking enterprise level investments.

Management of Expectations: It was a common occurrence in organizations to receive unrealistic expectations created by vendor marketing and media hype. Executive expectations were fast implementation and transformative outcomes and the technicalities required a long period and incremental changes. There were early failure by the executive of the grocery chain when the changes were not dramatic as revealed by the initial results. The management of expectations entailed open communication of the difficulties of implementation, achievable timelines as well as gradual benefits realization. Companies that made impractical promises to the public at times had problems of credibility when they failed to achieve their targets.

Innovation-Stability Balance: Organizations had difficulties balancing innovation wants and maintenance of operational stability. The issue of supply chain disruptions cannot be experienced over the long term when implementing technologies. The drug company needed six-months of parallel operation of new AI systems and old processes prior to cutover that would add timelines but maintain continuity. Autonomous operations had to be tested without interfering with live operations and therefore involved advanced digital twin capabilities or test environments which were a big investment (Ivanov et al., 2021). In some cases, risk-averse organizational cultures have frozen decision-making processes by being overly cautious, and no action is taken.

Aligned Strategies and Vision Clarity: There were organizations that implemented AI not because of strategic reasons but due to competitive pressure or showcasing innovation. Lack of clear strategy resulted in disjointed activities, change of priorities and ultimate desertion. Best implementations were characterized by articulate attachment to strategic goals (customer experience improvement, cost leadership, operational excellence) (Lee, 2004). Express delivery network specifically made the AI investment the focus of its differentiation strategy grounded in its focus on high reliability delivery as well as the best customer experience. Implementation priorities were determined by strategic clarity and maintained through commitment.

7.4 Critical Success Factors

Critical success factors between successful and unsuccessful implementations have been determined by crossing cases:

Figure 25. The model of the critical success factors incorporated into the strategic, organizational, technical, and operational dimension, which depicts the relationship and the relative importance weight, was the outcome of an empirical research

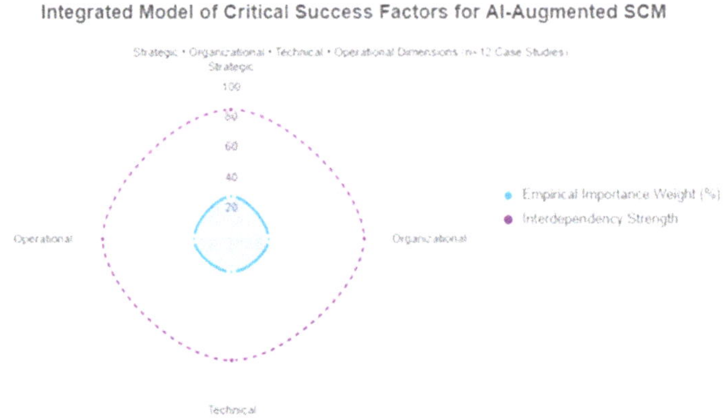

Long-term Executive Sponsorship: All of the successful implementations included involved executive sponsors who contributed resources, eliminated obstacles, and kept the organization focused on it. Sponsors needed to have the knowledge of the capabilities and limitations of technology that will not promise too much and offer enabling pressure. The commitment was quite important in the long term since the implementations took more time than originally estimated in the schedule and faced unforeseen difficulties. The change of the executive was also problematic because the new leaders were not as committed to initiatives as their predecessors.

Specific Business Objectives and Success Metrics: Organizations that had set down specific objectives (inventory reduction target, forecast accuracy target, cost savings targets) had more focused implementations with better success definition. Categories of goals such as improve operations or become data-driven were not specific enough. Progress monitoring and correction of the course were made possible by baseline measurements and tracking mechanisms.

Significant Data Infrastructure Investment: Better performing organizations spent a lot of money on data infrastructure such as data quality enhancement, integration platforms, and governance processes prior to being aggressive in the application of AI (Liu et al., 2021). The lack of data foundation investment led to bad model performance and long debugging. Those organizations that put money into sensors and data integration to create IoT early had better outcomes than those who tried to implement AI with small data bases.

Stepwise Implementation using Pilot Projects: Staged implementation that started with constrained pilot projects made it possible to learn, show value, establish organizational fidelity, and control risk (Yin, 2018). Effective pilot initiatives produced champions and impetus towards broader implementation and pilot issues identified problems that could be resolved prior to enterprise growth. Those organizations that tried to use enterprise-wide implementations without piloting were faced with excessive complexity and increased risk of failure.

Investment in Change Management and Training: With a 30-40% of project resources in training, communication and organizational change management organizations experienced a faster and more complete adoption process compared to technology-focused implementations. Organizations that were successful had elaborate training initiatives, clear communication of effects and expectations and end user participation of design processes to increase adoption and effectiveness (Jarrahi, 2018).

Design of deliberate Human-AI Collaboration: Organizations with a specific design of patterns of human-AI interaction (role allocation, definition of decision authority, the provision of transparency) performed better than organizations that just introduced AI into the existing process and did not redesign their workflow (Lee and See, 2004; Parasuraman et al, 2000). Effective deployments made AI be seen as the human capability amplification and not job endangering.

On-Going Monitoring and Improvement of performance: Implementations that created a framework of systematic performance monitoring, feedback gathering, and refinement procedures maintained and enhanced advantages over time (Rasheed et al., 2020). Organizations that considered implementation to be a continuous journey and not a project that can be implemented once and never again, adjusted to changing conditions and were constantly improving the performance of the model. Failure to make continuous improvement led to the deterioration of performance when the models became obsolete and the initial enthusiasm started to disappear.

Cross-Functional Collaboration and Integration: When organizations dismantled silos by deploying integrated teams, aligning incentives, and collaboration processes performed better, the implementation process necessitating coordination between IT, operations, analytics and business functions would be effective (Mentzer et al., 2001). The old functional segregation resulted in incompatibility of priorities, and communication failure.

Realistic Timeline Expectations: Organizations that made realistic timelines with sufficient time in which data can be prepared and model developed, tested, organization changed, and endless iterations did not suffer disappointment and loss of stakeholder confidence. The timelines developed aggressive schedules that put pressure on quality and sustainability through corner-cutting.

External Collaboration and Provision: The vast majority of successful implementations used external partners such as technology vendors, consulting companies and academic institutions to offer specific expertise, extra capacity, and external point of view. Companies that had not developed AI components well had failed to attempt complicated implementations on their own.

7.5 Organizational Change Management Strategies

Organizational change management was a critical success factor that demanded methods that were not related to the technologies implementation.

Change Readiness Assessment: Organizations are advised to gauge the level of readiness on several levels, including: (1) Leadership commitment which is measured by resources availability, time investment, and public backing; (2) Cultural compatibility which evaluates levels of data-driven decision-making acceptance and openness to change; (3) Capability baseline which evaluates current levels of analytical proficiency, technology infrastructure, and experience with change management; (4) Stakeholder alignment which identifies champions, resistors, and fence-sitters.

Strategy of Stakeholder Engagement: Systematic management of stakeholders entails: (1) Early engagement that involves involved personnel in the design and testing stages; (2) Good communication that is based on rationality, potential impacts and timelines of implementation; (3) Concerns: Address concerns: Involves the leadership showing interest in its actions by providing concrete mitigation plans in addition to the rationality and potential impacts and implementation timelines; (4) Creating champions: Creating champions: Involves identifying and empowering the enthusiastic adopters who will influence others.

Training and Development Programs: The overall methods of skill development are: (1) Role-specific training based on how the different roles interact with the AI systems (operators, managers, analysts); (2) Hands-on training that provides sandbox experiences and allows experimentation without production impacts; (3) Ongoing training through maintaining the help resources, office hours, and peer networks; (4) Career pathway clarity can explain how the roles will change and growth opportunities will be realized.

Strategies to Mitigate Resistance: To deal with resistance, there are five strategies to adopt: (1) Job security commitments explicit guarantees where possible or disclosure of effects on the workforce; (2) Autonomy maintenance demonstrating that there is human oversight and the ability to override it; (3) Success demonstration of a show of early gains and user testimonials; (4) Progressive adoption that allows time to make adjustments instead of making an immediate full adoption; (5) Feedback incorporation demonstrating how human input can refine the system.

Performance Monitoring and Adaptation: Change effectiveness tracking includes: (1) Adoption metrics measuring system usage, feature utilization, and override frequency; (2) Sentiment surveys regular pulse checks on user satisfaction, trust, and perceived value; (3) Performance outcomes tracking whether expected benefits materialize; (4) Issue identification systematic problem collection and resolution tracking; (5) Iterative refinement adapting implementation based on feedback and measured results.

8. RESEARCH GAPS AND FUTURE RESEARCH DIRECTIONS

8.1 Prioritized Research Roadmap

This section systematically identifies 30 research gaps organized by domain with explicit prioritization based on urgency (high/medium/low) and feasibility (near-term/mid-term/long-term).

Figure 26. Taxonomy of thirty research gaps identified in the comprehensive way with the priorities ranked by order of practical impact and research feasibility, systematized in terms of theoretical, methodological, technical, application, organizational, and governance issues

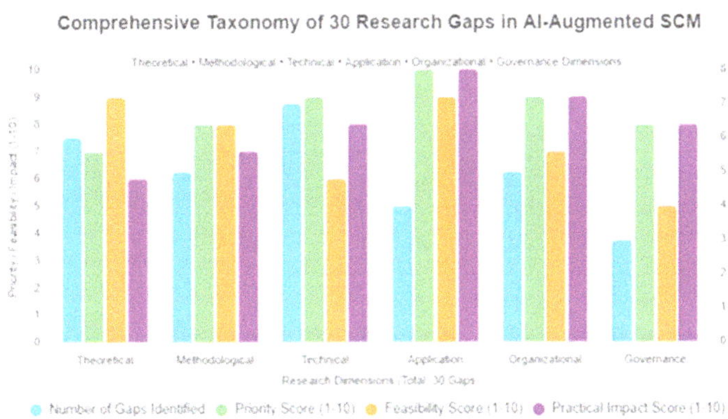

Table 15. Prioritized research gaps with implementation roadmap

Gap ID	Research Gap	Priority	Feasibility	Expected Timeline	Required Resources
THEORETICAL GAPS					
T1	Integration with SCM theories (RBV, TCE, contingency)	High	Mid-term	2-3 years	Multi-institution collaboration, theory development expertise
T2	Autonomy level determination frameworks	High	Near-term	1-2 years	Case studies, expert panels, validation across contexts

continued on following page

Table 15. Continued

Gap ID	Research Gap	Priority	Feasibility	Expected Timeline	Required Resources
T3	Human-AI collaboration theoretical models	High	Mid-term	2-3 years	Longitudinal studies, psychological expertise, field experiments
T4	Digital twin ontology standardization	Medium	Long-term	3-5 years	Standards body collaboration, industry consortium
T5	Ethical frameworks for autonomous supply chains	High	Near-term	1-2 years	Ethics expertise, stakeholder engagement, policy analysis
METHODOLOGICAL GAPS					
M1	Validated multi-dimensional measurement instruments	High	Near-term	1-2 years	Psychometric expertise, large-scale surveys, validation studies
M2	Benchmark datasets for algorithm comparison	High	Mid-term	2-4 years	Industry data sharing agreements, anonymization protocols
M3	Longitudinal research designs (5-10 years)	Medium	Long-term	Ongoing	Sustained funding, multi-year partnerships
M4	Causal inference methodologies	High	Mid-term	2-3 years	Econometric expertise, quasi-experimental designs
M5	Cross-level analytical frameworks	Medium	Mid-term	2-3 years	Multilevel modeling expertise, nested data collection
TECHNICAL GAPS					
T6	Supply chain-specific explainable AI methods	High	Near-term	1-2 years	AI/ML expertise, domain knowledge, prototype development
T7	Transfer learning across organizational contexts	High	Mid-term	2-3 years	Machine learning research, multi-organization studies
T8	Federated learning for supply chain collaboration	High	Mid-term	2-4 years	Distributed ML expertise, blockchain integration, pilot implementations
T9	Robust optimization under deep uncertainty	Medium	Mid-term	2-3 years	Operations research expertise, scenario modeling
T10	Real-time learning and adaptation mechanisms	Medium	Near-term	1-2 years	Online learning algorithms, deployment infrastructure
T11	Symbolic-subsymbolic AI integration	Low	Long-term	3-5 years	Hybrid AI architecture research, knowledge engineering
APPLICATION DOMAIN GAPS					
A1	Under-researched sectors (healthcare, energy, construction)	High	Near-term	1-3 years	Sector-specific partnerships, domain expertise
A2	Small and medium enterprise contexts	High	Near-term	1-2 years	SME access, resource-constrained implementation models
A3	Emerging market applications	Medium	Mid-term	2-4 years	International partnerships, cross-cultural research
A4	Circular economy and sustainability applications	High	Near-term	1-2 years	Sustainability metrics, lifecycle analysis integration
A5	Humanitarian and disaster relief supply chains	Medium	Mid-term	2-3 years	NGO partnerships, crisis response protocols
ORGANIZATIONAL AND HUMAN FACTOR GAPS					
O1	Workforce transition and reskilling strategies	High	Near-term	1-2 years	HR partnerships, training program evaluations
O2	Organizational culture and AI adoption	High	Mid-term	2-3 years	Culture assessment tools, longitudinal change tracking

continued on following page

Table 15. Continued

Gap ID	Research Gap	Priority	Feasibility	Expected Timeline	Required Resources
O3	Leadership competencies for AI transformation	High	Near-term	1-2 years	Leadership assessment, development program design
O4	Trust dynamics in human-AI collaboration	High	Mid-term	2-3 years	Trust measurement instruments, experimental studies
O5	Job design in AI-augmented environments	Medium	Mid-term	2-3 years	Work design research, job satisfaction studies
GOVERNANCE AND POLICY GAPS					
G1	Algorithmic accountability frameworks	High	Near-term	1-2 years	Legal expertise, governance structure design
G2	Data governance models for supply chains	High	Near-term	1-2 years	Data sharing agreements, privacy preservation protocols
G3	Standardization and interoperability	Medium	Long-term	3-5 years	Standards development, industry adoption studies
G4	Regulatory frameworks balancing innovation and risk	High	Mid-term	2-4 years	Policy analysis, regulatory impact studies
G5	Cross-border data governance for global supply chains	Medium	Mid-term	2-4 years	International law expertise, multi-jurisdiction pilots

Research Priority Criteria:

- **High Priority:** Critical knowledge gaps limiting current implementations, high practical impact, stakeholder demand
- **Medium Priority:** Important but less urgent, moderate practical impact, some existing partial solutions
- **Low Priority:** Interesting but not immediately limiting, longer-term relevance, theoretical rather than practical focus

Feasibility Assessment:

- **Near-term (1-2 years):** Existing methods applicable, data accessible, moderate resource requirements
- **Mid-term (2-4 years):** Method development needed, complex data collection, substantial resources required
- **Long-term (3-5+ years):** Fundamental research needed, major infrastructure requirements, sustained commitment necessary

Research Interdependencies: Several gaps have prerequisite relationships: (1) Benchmark datasets (M2) facilitate algorithm comparison supporting technical gaps (T6-T11); (2) Measurement instruments (M1) enable evaluation of organizational interventions (O1-O5); (3) Theoretical integration (T1-T3) provides foundations for empirical investigations across application domains (A1-A5); (4) Governance frameworks (G1-G2) inform policy development (G4-G5).

Translation to Practice: Research findings should follow systematic pathways to industry adoption: (1) Academic publications establishing scientific rigor and peer validation; (2) Industry white papers translating findings into practitioner language; (3) Conference presentations enabling researcher-practitioner dialogue; (4) Pilot implementations demonstrating feasibility in real settings; (5) Best practice documentation codifying successful approaches for broader adoption.

9. DISCUSSION AND IMPLICATIONS

9.1 Theoretical Contributions

This study contributes to the literature on supply chain management in several ways on a theoretical basis. The five-layer autonomous operations model offers conceptual structure that plans the perception, cognition, decision, execution, and learning functions in a coherent structure (Anderson et al., 2004; Endsley, 1995; Laird et al., 2017). This fills gaps in literature on the subject by introducing a systematic reception of AI capabilities into systematic design. The model reconfigures the concepts of control theory and cognitive architecture of aerospace and defense to the distributed organizational supply chain situations.

This decision autonomy model adds the insights of the contingency theory describing the reason behind different levels of automation in different decision types and situations (Parasuraman et al., 2000). Combining situational conditions (frequency of decisions, severity of consequences, environmental stability, the availability of data), the framework offers the theoretical justification of heterogenous autonomy implementation. This goes a step further to inform thinking by not only automation-versus-manual but also by sophisticated collaboration paradigms.

The maturity model of digital twin provides an evolutionary view of the capabilities in terms of descriptive visualization up to cognitive autonomy (Grieves and Vickers, 2017; Kritzinger et al., 2018; Tao et al., 2018). This is a model of staged development that forms theoretical grounds of how organizations expand in terms of autonomous operation abilities. The cumulative capability dependence and balanced development aspects of the model over the technological, organizational and governance dimensions offer implementation guidance, which is usually lacking in the otherwise technological-focused literature.

Figure 27. Theoretical contribution integrative visualization, which demonstrates the correlations between five-layered autonomous operations model, decision autonomy framework, and digital twin maturity model and how they are connected to the existing theories of supply chain management

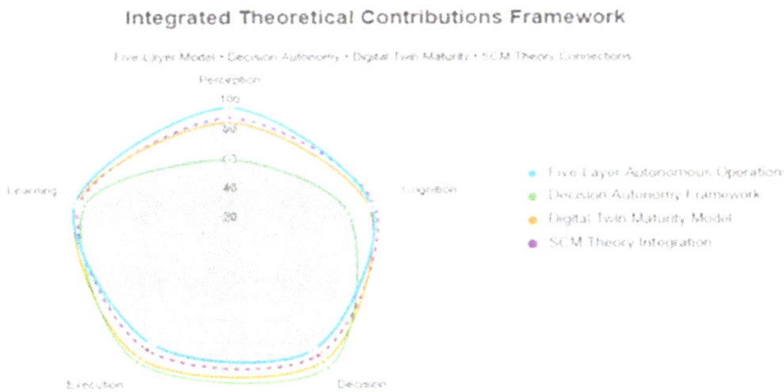

The resource-based view understanding places AI potentials as strategic assets that create competitive edge based on their ability to produce high-quality decisions, responsiveness as well as efficiency in the use of resources (Lee, 2004). The study shows that AI complements current supply chain capabilities cause synergies that are bigger than additive benefits. Transaction cost economics view guides make-versus-buy decisions on the development of AI capability with respect to asset specificity, uncertainty, and frequency.

9.2 Methodological Contributions

The study represents the mixed-method research that involves the combination of the rigor of quantitative and the depth of qualitative studies (Yin, 2018). The cross-sectoral comparative approach produces generalisable knowledge but displays context-specific implementation patterns, contributing to knowledge more than the other common forms of single-industry case studies. This is supported by improved methodological clarity (i.e. specification of protocols, statistical methods), inter-rater agreement (k=0.87), and validation processes which all contribute to the research reproducibility which is frequently criticized with qualitative research.

The validated measurement framework that evaluates the AI augmentation effects on the dimensions of operational efficiency, service quality, cost performance, resilience, and sustainability gives future research template. The multi-dimensional approach delivers literature gaps where the performance assessment tends to have a limited view on operational efficiency. The combination of statistical rigor by using the effect size analysis (Cohen d) and significance testing focuses on both the practical and statistical significance.

The longitudinal observation periods (18-36 months) allow studying the temporal dynamics which are usually not considered in any snapshot study. This time aspect brings out learning curves, benefit sustainability trends, and adaptive processes which offer more insight than cross-sectional designs. The study defines the significance of a long period of observation that involves maturation of the implementation even after the deployment.

9.3 Practical Implications

To practitioners, this study gives evidence-based recommendations in the implementation decisions and strategies. The measured performance improvements in sectors and metrics in the business cases influence the development of the business cases and setting of expectations. It is important to realize that it takes 18-25.5 months on average to develop mature autonomous operations and plan and allocate resources realistically. Determined critical success factors (executive sponsorship/ phased implementation/ change management investment/ human-AI collaboration design) offer practical guidance to implementation.

The reference architectures provide definite technology setups, integration designs and governance designs that minimize the implementation uncertainties. These templates allow organizations to customize them to suit their situation instead of having to create new ones. Decision autonomy framework addresses the right degree of automation between the efficiency of automation and risk management. Proactive risk mitigation planning is made possible by implementation challenge documentation.

The human-AI models of collaboration and change management expertise cover aspects of organizations that are typically underutilized in terms of technology planning (Jarrahi, 2018; Shrestha et al., 2019). Placing AI as a complementary and not a substitution, making massive investment in training and communication, and participatory implementation processes are key to adoption and success. Sector analysis depicts the industry-related challenges, sector-specific success factors, and the best strategies. To the vendors and technology providers, the research gives them customer priorities, barriers to adoption and value expectations they can apply in developing their products and go to market strategies. The technical gaps (explainability requirements, transfer learning needs, real-time adaptation) are identified and offer the directions of innovation (Doshi-Velez and Kim, 2017; Weimer et al., 2016). The identification of organizational change needs has proposed the complementary change management services and the technology solutions.

To consultants and system integrators, the research furnishes structures, approaches and instances to underpin client engagements. Maturity models allow the present capability to be evaluated and roadmap to be developed. The methodology is developed and the project designed using success factors and implementation strategies. The cross-sectoral comparative analysis will offer benchmarking references that facilitate positioning of performance to clients, and offers ways of improvement.

9.4 Policy and Regulatory Implications

For policymakers, this research highlights areas requiring regulatory attention and policy development. Algorithmic accountability mechanisms ensuring transparency and contestability of automated supply chain decisions require policy frameworks balancing innovation promotion with consumer and stakeholder protection (Bostrom & Yudkowsky, 2014). The study reveals tensions between algorithmic efficiency and fairness considerations necessitating regulatory guidance on bias detection, equity considerations, and remediation measures when algorithms produce discriminatory outcomes.

Data governance and privacy within supply chain contexts demand policy attention as data sharing across organizational boundaries.

Model Monitoring Stage detects performance degradation triggering corrective action. Data quality monitoring identifies distribution changes, missing values, or input feature anomalies. Prediction monitoring compares actual outcomes against predictions identifying accuracy degradation. Data drift detection quantifies statistical differences between production data and training data distributions. Concept drift detection identifies when relationships between features and targets change invalidating trained models. Alerting notifies data science teams when monitoring detects significant degradation initiating retraining processes.

Model Governance Stage ensures AI systems operate responsibly, ethically, and compliantly. Model documentation captures training data sources, algorithms, hyperparameters, performance metrics, and intended usage. Model versioning maintains complete history enabling reproduction of any deployed model. Access controls limit model modification authority and audit all changes. Bias assessment determines whether models produce differential outcomes for protected groups. Explainability requirements mandate human-interpretable rationales for high-stakes decisions. Compliance validation ensures adherence to regulatory standards (data privacy, algorithmic transparency, contestability rights).

Data governance and privacy within supply chain contexts demand policy attention as data sharing across organizational boundaries increases. Regulations should balance enabling beneficial data utilization for supply chain optimization with protecting proprietary information and individual privacy. This study indicates need for standardized data sharing frameworks, inter-organizational governance models, and regulatory safe harbors promoting beneficial data exchange while maintaining appropriate safeguards.

Workforce transition implications including displacement of routine tasks and creation of new technology-enabled roles require policy responses through education system adaptation, retraining program provision, and social safety net considerations (Jarrahi, 2018). The research reveals that effective workforce transitions demand substantial training investments suggesting potential roles for public support complementing private employer investments.

Environmental sustainability implications present both opportunities and challenges for policy. AI optimization capabilities can substantially reduce waste, energy consumption, and emissions as demonstrated across case studies. However, efficiency gains enabling consumption growth may generate rebound effects canceling environmental benefits. Policy frameworks should encourage efficiency improvements while addressing systemic consumption patterns determining ultimate environmental impacts (Brandenburg et al., 2014; Carter & Rogers, 2008).

Standardization policy balancing interoperability benefits with innovation flexibility requires attention. Current supply chain AI systems lack standardized interfaces limiting cross-organizational data sharing and system integration (Kritzinger et al., 2018). Policymakers and standards organizations should encourage standardization activities while avoiding premature over-standardization constraining beneficial innovation. International coordination proves particularly relevant given global supply chain scope requiring cross-border data flows and system interoperability.

9.5 Limitations and Boundary Conditions

This research acknowledges several limitations qualifying findings interpretation and generalizability scope. Selection bias may exist as organizations with implementation challenges could decline research participation (Yin, 2018). The twelve examined organizations represent successful implementations potentially overrepresenting positive outcomes relative to broader adoption population including failures and abandonments. This survivor bias limits understanding of failure factors and unsuccessful implementation patterns.

Temporal constraints of 18-36 month post-implementation observation periods prevent evaluation of extremely long-term sustainability, adaptation to major environmental changes, or impacts across multiple technology generation cycles. Extended longitudinal studies following implementations over 5-10 years would reveal benefit durability, capability evolution, and eventual obsolescence patterns not apparent in current observation windows.

Measurement challenges including inability to perfectly isolate AI impacts from simultaneous initiatives, external environmental fluctuations, and natural performance variations create uncertainty in quantified performance gains. While the research employed control groups and statistical controls where feasible, perfect experimental isolation proves infeasible in field settings. Reported performance gains represent best estimates acknowledging measurement imperfections.

Generalizability limitations arise from case selection emphasizing large organizations in developed economies competing in commercial markets with high technology readiness. Findings may not extend to small and medium enterprises with constrained resources, emerging economy contexts with different infrastructure and institutions, or public sector organizations with distinct performance objectives and constraints. There should be adaptation in these diverse settings to identified success factors and implementation strategies.

Evolution in technology poses a problem of generalizability because AI applications, tools of implementation, and best practices are evolving at a very fast rate. The results of the modern technology generations can be revised because the possibilities improve, the innovations appear, and the approaches to the implementation can be created. Theoretical work and conceptualizations are probably more permanent than the technical recommendations.

The cultural and institutional context influence on AI adoption and performance is still poorly represented by the sample that is mainly North American, European, and Asia-Pacific. Human-AI collaboration patterns and trust development, as well as the right level of autonomy, are probably affected by the national culture dimensions (power distance, uncertainty avoidance, individualism versus collectivism) (Lee and See, 2004). These contingencies would be better enlightened through cross-cultural comparative research.

9.6 Ethical Guidelines and Explainable AI Implementation

Modern AI implementations require clear-cut ethical standards and clarifications. The section offers practical advice based on studies and standards.

Ethical Decision Making Model: Impact Assessment on Stakeholders needs to be systematic in evaluating the impact of AI systems on various constituencies in line with; (1) Employees: Job security, skills requirement, autonomy, work satisfaction; (2) Customers: Service quality, fairness, privacy, experience; (3) Suppliers: Fair treatment, transparency, relationship stability; (4) Communities: Environmental impact, employment, economic development; (5) Shareholders: Financial returns, risk management, reputation.

Implementation Principles Fairness: (1) Distributional fairness: The AI decision-making should not systematically disadvantage vulnerable populations (e.g., location of suppliers, demographics of customers); (2) Procedural fairness: The processes of AI decisions must be transparent, allow an appeal, be overseen by people, and apply to high-stakes decisions; (3) Compensatory fairness: There should be mechanisms to remediate unfair outcomes; (4) Recognition fairness: AI decision-making must take into account the diverse needs and settings when being designed.

Bias Detection and Mitigation Procedures:

- **Pre-deployment auditing**: Test models across demographic groups, geographic regions, and protected attributes before production deployment
- **Ongoing monitoring**: Continuous tracking of decision distributions across groups detecting emerging biases
- **Fairness-aware training**: Incorporate fairness constraints and bias mitigation techniques during model development
- **Human review**: High-stakes decisions affecting individuals or small suppliers require human examination
- **Regular audits**: Quarterly comprehensive fairness assessments with external validation

Transparency and Explainability Requirements:

Model Documentation ought to contain: (1) data Sources, characteristics, and constraints of training: (2) reasons behind the choice of algorithm, architecture, and details; (3) results of performance under relevant segments; (4) limitations and failure modes known; (5) Intended. applications and uses cases and prohibitions.

The Decision Explanations should include: (1) Feature importance: One would like to know which factors the most affected particular decisions; (2) The level of confidence: Measuring uncertainty and the reliability of predictions; (3) Alternatives: How alternative inputs would be different.

Privacy and Data Protection:

- **Data minimization**: Collect only data necessary for specific purposes, avoid excessive surveillance
- **Purpose limitation**: Use data only for declared purposes, obtain consent for new uses
- **Access controls**: Strict permissions limiting who can view sensitive supply chain data
- **Retention policies**: Have scheduled data deletion, do not have data at will.
- **Anonymization**: Since it is not possible to remove personally identifiable information, encrypt such information.

Employment Impact Management:

- **Give notice**: Prevent change of workforce driven by automation with lots of lead time.
- **Retraining commitment**: Invest in skill development for affected employees
- **Transition support**: Outplacement assistance, extended benefits for displaced workers
- **New role creation**: Proactively design technology-enabled positions absorbing affected staff
- **Consultation processes**: Engage employees and unions in planning automation implementations

Environmental Responsibility:

- **Efficiency monitoring**: The monitoring of energy consumption, emissions, AI generation of waste.
- **Optimization objectives**: Include sustainability metrics alongside cost and service in optimization
- **Rebound effect mitigation**: Monitor whether efficiency gains enable consumption growth negating benefits
- **Lifecycle consideration**: Assess environmental impacts of technology infrastructure and equipment
- **Transparency**: Report environmental performance improvements and setbacks publicly

Governance Mechanisms:

- **Ethics committees**: Multistage organizations that check AI implementations, probe into events, revise the regulations.
- **Algorithmic impact assessments**: Systematic evaluation of AI systems' societal and organizational effects before deployment
- **Whistleblower protections**: Safe channels for reporting ethical concerns without retaliation
- **External audits**: Independent third-party evaluation of fairness, transparency, and accountability
- **Continuous review**: Regular reassessment as systems evolve, contexts change, and standards advance

10. CONCLUSION

10.1 Key Research Findings

The entire exploration of AI-enhanced supply chain management based on autonomous operations driven by a digital twin creates profound results on theoretical, empirical, and practical levels. The five-layer autonomous operations model, in its turn, offers a theoretical systematization of the engagement of AI capabilities into the supply chain contexts as perceived, cognitively, decision, execution, and learning functionalities (Anderson et al., 2004; Endsley, 1995; Laird et al., 2017). Decision autonomy framework is a framework that identifies six levels of manual to complete automation as well as contingency factors that define the right level of automation systems (Parasuraman et al., 2000). The digital twin maturity model is defined as developmental changes, the ascending steps of descriptive visualization to cognitive autonomy (Grieves and Vickers, 2017; Kritzinger et al., 2018; Tao et al., 2018).

Empirical validation of cross-sectoral, twelve organizations (manufacturing, retail, pharmaceutical, and logistics) shows significant performance changes. Based on quantitative findings, average inventory carrying cost decreases by 31.2 percent, operational efficiency increases by 44.2 percent, and the forecast accuracy increases by 28.4-42.3 percent MAPE baseline to 11.2-19.7 percent MAPE after implementation (Boone et al., 2019; Gijsbrechts et al., 2022; Syntetos et al., 2016). Implementations of digital twins have 97.2% operational fidelity, which helps in risk assessment and decision testing prior to the physical implementation (Grieves & Vickers, 2017; Ivanov et al., 2021; Tao et al., 2018).

A cross-sector comparison reveals eponymous patterns of success such as investing in data infrastructure, gradual implementation strategy, thoughtful human-AI collaboration design, integration of mechanisms of explanation, and processes of continuous learning (Doshi-Velez and Kim, 2017; Jarrahi, 2018; Lee and See, 2004; Liu et al., 2021). Some of the critical success factors include executive sponsorship, well-defined business objectives, significant investment in change management, cross-functional teamwork and realistic expectations on the timeline. The implementation issues are of both technical (quality of data, integration) and organizational (resistance, skills gap) and strategic (ROI justification, managing expectations) dimensions (Shrestha et al., 2019).

The study logically outlines thirty research gaps in the development of theory, methodological development, technical development, expansion of application domain, organizational exploration, and development of governance. These research gaps offer an in-depth roadmap in the development of theoretical knowledge and practice (Baryannis et al., 2019; Bostrom and Yudkowsky, 2014; Doshi-Velez and Kim, 2017). The current state of regulatory trends such as EU AI Act (2024), NIST

AI RMF (2023), and ISO/IEC 42001 (2023) establish compliance issues organizations have to overcome when seeking operational efficiency benefits.

10.2 Theoretical Advancement

The study will help in the development of supply chain management theory by combining AI capabilities with the existing theoretical applications. The autonomous operations model applies the control theory and cognitive architectures to the distributed organizational environment (Anderson et al., 2004; Laird et al., 2017). The decision autonomy model brings in the viewpoints of the heterogeneous automation appropriateness that are explained by the contingency theory (Parasuraman et al., 2000). The digital twin maturity model provides progressive view of capability growth (Kritzinger et al., 2018).

The interpretative perspective of the resource-based view establishes AI capabilities as the strategic resources that will produce competitive advantage due to their quality of decisions, responsiveness, and increased resource efficiency (Lee, 2004). The study establishes complementarities between AI and current capabilities producing synergies. The make-versus-buy decision-making with respect to AI capability development is informed by the transaction cost economics perspective on the consideration of the asset specificity, uncertainty, and frequency.

The study contributes to the literature on human-AI collaboration through the investigation of the relationship of trust, role assignments, and interaction patterns within an operational supply chain setting (Jarrahi, 2018; Lee and See, 2004). Results indicate that successful teamwork is based on a calibration of trust, transparency processes, and complementary allocation of tasks. The difference between augmentation and automation strategies gives some theoretical clarity that is lacking in the technology-oriented literature.

10.3 Practical Contributions

To practitioners, this study provides evidence-based advice in the form of reference architecture, implementation roadmap, governance, and change management strategy. The reference architectures define technology configurations and integration patterns that decrease the uncertainty in implementation (Hofmann & Rüsch, 2017; Kagermann et al., 2013). The staged implementation strategy between quick wins and enterprise transformation is a viable way to go.

Performance within the sector and metric changes can be measured and contribute to developing the business cases and setting expectations (Boone et al., 2019; Gijsbrechts et al., 2022; Wang et al., 2020). Realist planning can be achieved by understanding the fact that the mature autonomous operations require the realization time of 18-25.5 months on average. Known critical success factors will be used to give practical implementation advice and the challenges captured will be used to mitigate risks proactively.

The models of human-AI collaboration and change management insights cover the organizational aspects that are frequently underestimated when technology planning is in focus (Jarrahi, 2018; Shrestha et al., 2019). Creating AI as augmentation, spending significant resources on training and communication, and building participatory processes can be a key to adoption and success. Sector based analyses indicate sector-sensitive problems and ideal strategies.

10.4 Future Research Agenda

These is because the research gaps which were systematically identified give comprehensive agenda on the development of the field. Priority areas include:

Theory: Assimilations with the supply chain management theories, the determination of the autonomy level frameworks, theorization of the human-AI collaboration, standardization of the digital twin ontology, and the ethical frameworks of autonomous functioning (Bostrom and Yudkowsky, 2014; Grieves and Vickers, 2017; Tao et al., 2018).

Methodological Innovation: Multi-dimensional measures, benchmark data that allows making comparisons between algorithms, longitudinal studies that help capture the dynamics of a process, causal inferences that enhance conclusions, and cross-level analytic models (Syntetos et al., 2016; Yin, 2018).

Technical Innovation: explainable AI in supply chain decisions, transfer learning in the organizational context, federated learning in collaborative training, robust optimization with serious uncertainty, real time learning and adaptation, and symbolic-subsymbolic integration of AI (Doshi-Velez and Kim, 2017; Ivanov & Dolgui, 2020; Weimer et al., 2016).

Applications Expansion: Uninvestigated industries (healthcare, construction, energy), SME-based applications, novel market applications, circular economy applications, and humanitarian supply chains (Brandenburg et al., 2014; Carter & Rogers, 2008).

Organizational Investigation: Workforce transition strategies, organizational culture development, leadership competencies, trust dynamics, and job design in augmented environments (Jarrahi, 2018; Lee & See, 2004; Shrestha et al., 2019).

Governance Development: Algorithms accountability systems, data governance systems, standardization process, policy development on regulation formation (Bostrom and Yudkowsky, 2014; Kritzinger et al., 2018).

Figure 28. Integrated research roadmap with priorities of research directions in short-term (1-2 years), medium-term (3-5 years) and long-term (5+ years) horizons with interdependencies and contributions to the theory and practice expected

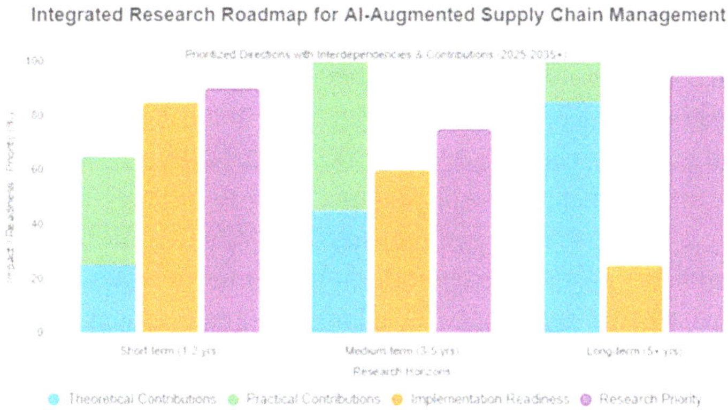

10.5 Concluding Remarks

The digital twin-based abilities of AI-enhanced supply chain management to operate autonomously have transformative potential that can resolve the modern problems such as demand volatility, supply disruptions, and sustainability imperatives (Ivanov and Dolgui, 2020; Seuring and Müller, 2008). The result of empirical studies indicates significant improvement in performance in terms of operational efficiency, service quality, cost reduction, and resilience dimensions. But successful implementation is beyond the technology implementation that demands a high degree of consideration to organizational change, human factor, and governance structure (Jarrahi, 2018; Lee and See, 2004; Shrestha et al., 2019).

The conceptual clarity of applying AI capabilities into supply chain management situations is conceptually clear with regard to the theoretical basis that has been developed in the current study. The autonomous operations model, decision autonomy framework, and digital twin maturity model present systematic bases of the guiding research and practice (Anderson et al., 2004; Endsley, 1995; Grieves and Vickers, 2017; Kritzinger et al., 2018; Laird et al., 2017; Parasuraman et al., 2000; Tao et al., 2018). Cross-sectoral empirical validation proves the possibility of generalization and indicates the presence of context-dependent differences that need to be adjusted to. The voyage to independent supply chain operations is still at its initial stages with significant developments potentials to come along. The specified gaps in the research suggest that there is much knowledge to be formed about the issue that needs further research (Baryannis et al., 2019; Bostrom and Yudkowsky, 2014; Doshi-Velez and

Kim, 2017). With the maturation in AI capabilities, experience in implementation, and the maturation of organizational capabilities, the comprehension will increase and practices will improve. This study is a basis to that evolution yet it takes into account the dynamic and fast evolving sphere of research.

Companies that start AI augmentation must consider implementations as learning processes that need iterative and adjustment as well as constant advancement instead of a single technology deployment (Rasheed et al., 2020; Yin, 2018). Technology, organizational, and governance aspects require equal consideration with specific focus on the human aspects that are usually ignored in the technology-focused planning. The evidence proves that there exist considerable value creation opportunities in case organizations manage to overcome the implementation issues and overcome the identified traps, whereas the risks of the improperly implemented projects are high.

Finally, AI-enhanced supply chain management is neither a variation on a good supply chain but a complete change in the way these supply chains work, evolve and generate value (Hofmann & Rüsch, 2017; Kagermann et al., 2013; Lee, 2004). To gain this potential, further research building on the theoretical knowledge, research rigor, and practical application guidance as well as investments by practitioners not only in technology but also in organizational potential, human growth and change management is essential. The combination of increasing capability in technology, the maturity of implementation practices and the expanding theoretical perspectives all put the field in a position to make major breakthroughs in the next several years.

REFERENCES

Anderson, J. R., Bothell, D., Byrne, M. D., Douglass, S., Lebiere, C., & Qin, Y. (2004). An integrated theory of the mind. *Psychological Review*, *111*(4), 1036–1060. DOI: 10.1037/0033-295X.111.4.1036

Barbosa, J., Leitão, P., Adam, E., & Trentesaux, D. (2020). Dynamic self-organization in holonic multi-agent manufacturing systems: The ADACOR evolution. *Computers in Industry*, *66*, 99–111. DOI: 10.1016/j.compind.2014.10.011

Baryannis, G., Dani, S., & Antoniou, G. (2019). Predicting supply chain risks using machine learning: The trade-off between performance and interpretability. *Future Generation Computer Systems*, *101*, 993–1004. DOI: 10.1016/j.future.2019.07.059

Baryannis, G., Validi, S., Dani, S., & Antoniou, G. (2020). Supply chain risk management and artificial intelligence: State of the art and future research directions. *International Journal of Production Research*, *57*(7), 2179–2202. DOI: 10.1080/00207543.2018.1530476

Bodendorf, F., & Franke, J. (2021). A machine learning approach to estimate missing values in procurement data. *Decision Support Systems*, *150*, 113565. DOI: 10.1016/j.dss.2021.113565

Boone, T., Ganeshan, R., Jain, A., & Sanders, N. R. (2019). Forecasting sales in the supply chain: Consumer analytics in the big data era. *International Journal of Forecasting*, *35*(1), 170–180. DOI: 10.1016/j.ijforecast.2018.09.003

Bostrom, N., & Yudkowsky, E. (2014). The ethics of artificial intelligence. In Frankish, K., & Ramsey, W. M. (Eds.), *The Cambridge handbook of artificial intelligence* (pp. 316–334). Cambridge University Press., DOI: 10.1017/CBO9781139046855.020

Brandenburg, M., Govindan, K., Sarkis, J., & Seuring, S. (2014). Quantitative models for sustainable supply chain management: Developments and directions. *European Journal of Operational Research*, *233*(2), 299–312. DOI: 10.1016/j.ejor.2013.09.032

Carter, C. R., & Rogers, D. S. (2008). A framework of sustainable supply chain management: Moving toward new theory. *International Journal of Physical Distribution & Logistics Management*, *38*(5), 360–387. DOI: 10.1108/09600030810882816

Christopher, M. (1992). *Logistics and supply chain management*. Pitman Publishing.

Doshi-Velez, F., & Kim, B. (2017). Towards a rigorous science of interpretable machine learning. *arXiv preprint arXiv:1702.08608*. /arXiv.1702.08608DOI: 10.48550

Endsley, M. R. (1995). Toward a theory of situation awareness in dynamic systems. *Human Factors*, *37*(1), 32–64. DOI: 10.1518/001872095779049543

Gijsbrechts, J., Boute, R. N., Van Mieghem, J. A., & Zhang, D. (2022). Can deep reinforcement learning improve inventory management? Performance on lost sales, dual-sourcing, and multi-echelon problems. *Manufacturing & Service Operations Management*, *24*(3), 1349–1368. DOI: 10.1287/msom.2021.1064

Grieves, M., & Vickers, J. (2017). Digital twin: Mitigating unpredictable, undesirable emergent behavior in complex systems. In Kahlen, F. J., Flumerfelt, S., & Alves, A. (Eds.), *Transdisciplinary perspectives on complex systems* (pp. 85–113). Springer., DOI: 10.1007/978-3-319-38756-7_4

Hofmann, E., & Rüsch, M. (2017). Industry 4.0 and the current status as well as future prospects on logistics. *Computers in Industry*, *89*, 23–34. DOI: 10.1016/j.compind.2017.04.002

Ivanov, D., & Dolgui, A. (2020). Viability of intertwined supply networks: Extending the supply chain resilience angles towards survivability. A position paper motivated by COVID-19 outbreak. *International Journal of Production Research*, *58*(10), 2904–2915. DOI: 10.1080/00207543.2020.1750727

Ivanov, D., Dolgui, A., & Sokolov, B. (2021). Cloud supply chain: Integrating Industry 4.0 and digital platforms in the "Supply Chain-as-a-Service.". *Transportation Research Part E, Logistics and Transportation Review*, *160*, 102676. DOI: 10.1016/j.tre.2022.102676

Jarrahi, M. H. (2018). Artificial intelligence and the future of work: Human-AI symbiosis in organizational decision making. *Business Horizons*, *61*(4), 577–586. DOI: 10.1016/j.bushor.2018.03.007

Julka, N., Srinivasan, R., & Karimi, I. (2002). Agent-based supply chain management—1: Framework. *Computers & Chemical Engineering*, *26*(12), 1755–1769. DOI: 10.1016/S0098-1354(02)00150-3

Kagermann, H., Wahlster, W., & Helbig, J. (2013). *Recommendations for implementing the strategic initiative INDUSTRIE 4.0*. Final report of the Industrie 4.0 Working Group. Forschungsunion.

Kaur, H., & Singh, S. P. (2021). Multi-stage hybrid model for supplier selection and order allocation considering disruption risks and disruptive technologies. *International Journal of Production Economics*, *231*, 107830. DOI: 10.1016/j.ijpe.2020.107830

Kritzinger, W., Karner, M., Traar, G., Henjes, J., & Sihn, W. (2018). Digital Twin in manufacturing: A categorical literature review and classification. *IFAC-PapersOnLine*, *51*(11), 1016–1022. DOI: 10.1016/j.ifacol.2018.08.474

Laird, J. E., Lebiere, C., & Rosenbloom, P. S. (2017). A standard model of the mind: Toward a common computational framework across artificial intelligence, cognitive science, neuroscience, and robotics. *AI Magazine*, *38*(4), 13–26. DOI: 10.1609/aimag.v38i4.2744

Lee, H. L. (2004). The triple-A supply chain. *Harvard Business Review*, *82*(10), 102–113.

Lee, J. D., & See, K. A. (2004). Trust in automation: Designing for appropriate reliance. *Human Factors*, *46*(1), 50–80. DOI: 10.1518/hfes.46.1.50_30392

Leng, J., Wang, D., Shen, W., Li, X., Liu, Q., & Chen, X. (2020). Digital twins-based smart manufacturing system design in Industry 4.0: A review. *Journal of Manufacturing Systems*, *60*, 119–137. DOI: 10.1016/j.jmsy.2021.05.011

Liu, M., Fang, S., Dong, H., & Xu, C. (2021). Review of digital twin about concepts, technologies, and industrial applications. *Journal of Manufacturing Systems*, *58*, 346–361. DOI: 10.1016/j.jmsy.2020.06.017

Mentzer, J. T., DeWitt, W., Keebler, J. S., Min, S., Nix, N. W., Smith, C. D., & Zacharia, Z. G. (2001). Defining supply chain management. *Journal of Business Logistics*, *22*(2), 1–25. DOI: 10.1002/j.2158-1592.2001.tb00001.x

Min, Q., Lu, Y., Liu, Z., Su, C., & Wang, B. (2019). Machine learning based digital twin framework for production optimization in petrochemical industry. *International Journal of Information Management*, *49*, 502–519. DOI: 10.1016/j.ijinfomgt.2019.05.020

Monostori, L., Váncza, J., & Kumara, S. R. (2006). Agent-based systems for manufacturing. *CIRP Annals*, *55*(2), 697–720. DOI: 10.1016/j.cirp.2006.10.004

Negri, E., Fumagalli, L., & Macchi, M. (2017). A review of the roles of digital twin in CPS-based production systems. *Procedia Manufacturing*, *11*, 939–948. DOI: 10.1016/j.promfg.2017.07.198

Parasuraman, R., Sheridan, T. B., & Wickens, C. D. (2000). A model for types and levels of human interaction with automation. *IEEE Transactions on Systems, Man, and Cybernetics. Part A, Systems and Humans*, *30*(3), 286–297. DOI: 10.1109/3468.844354

Pettit, T. J., Croxton, K. L., & Fiksel, J. (2013). Ensuring supply chain resilience: Development and implementation of an assessment tool. *Journal of Business Logistics*, *34*(1), 46–76. DOI: 10.1111/jbl.12009

Qi, Q., Tao, F., Hu, T., Anwer, N., Liu, A., Wei, Y., Wang, L., & Nee, A. Y. C. (2021). Enabling technologies and tools for digital twin. *Journal of Manufacturing Systems*, *58*, 3–21. DOI: 10.1016/j.jmsy.2019.10.001

Rasheed, A., San, O., & Kvamsdal, T. (2020). Digital twin: Values, challenges and enablers from a modeling perspective. *IEEE Access : Practical Innovations, Open Solutions*, *8*, 21980–22012. DOI: 10.1109/ACCESS.2020.2970143

Seuring, S., & Müller, M. (2008). From a literature review to a conceptual framework for sustainable supply chain management. *Journal of Cleaner Production*, *16*(15), 1699–1710. DOI: 10.1016/j.jclepro.2008.04.020

Shrestha, Y. R., Ben-Menahem, S. M., & von Krogh, G. (2019). Organizational decision-making structures in the age of artificial intelligence. *California Management Review*, *61*(4), 66–83. DOI: 10.1177/0008125619862257

Simchi-Levi, D., Kaminsky, P., & Simchi-Levi, E. (2000). *Designing and managing the supply chain: Concepts, strategies, and case studies*. McGraw-Hill.

Syntetos, A. A., Babai, Z., Boylan, J. E., Kolassa, S., & Nikolopoulos, K. (2016). Supply chain forecasting: Theory, practice, their gap and the future. *European Journal of Operational Research*, *252*(1), 1–26. DOI: 10.1016/j.ejor.2015.11.010

Tao, F., Zhang, H., Liu, A., & Nee, A. Y. C. (2018). Digital twin in industry: State-of-the-art. *IEEE Transactions on Industrial Informatics*, *15*(4), 2405–2415. DOI: 10.1109/TII.2018.2873186

Ulmer, M. W., Goodson, J. C., Mattfeld, D. C., & Thomas, B. W. (2020). On modeling stochastic dynamic vehicle routing problems. *EURO Journal on Transportation and Logistics*, *9*(2), 100008. DOI: 10.1016/j.ejtl.2020.100008

Wang, J., Ma, Y., Zhang, L., Gao, R. X., & Wu, D. (2020). Deep learning for smart manufacturing: Methods and applications. *Journal of Manufacturing Systems*, *48*, 144–156. DOI: 10.1016/j.jmsy.2018.01.003

Weimer, D., Scholz-Reiter, B., & Shpitalni, M. (2016). Design of deep convolutional neural network architectures for automated feature extraction in industrial inspection. *CIRP Annals*, *65*(1), 417–420. DOI: 10.1016/j.cirp.2016.04.072

Yin, R. K. (2018). *Case study research and applications: Design and methods* (6th ed.). SAGE Publications.

Zhang, D., Kabuka, M. R., & Yu, N. (2021). Real-time vehicle dispatching using deep reinforcement learning. In *Proceedings of the 2021 IEEE International Conference on Big Data* (pp. 4187-4192). IEEE. DOI: 10.1109/BigData52589.2021.9671579

KEY TERMS AND DEFINITIONS

Artificial Intelligence (AI): A computer system that can execute tasks that would normally be done by humans with human intelligence such as learning, reasoning, perception, and decision-making.

Autonomous Operations: Supply chain systems that are able to sense the environment, make decisions, carry out actions and learn through the result with very little human control.

Cognitive Architecture: An A Computational structure defining the structures and processes involved in intelligent behaviour such as perception, memory, reasoning and learning.

Decision Autonomy: Degree of autonomy in systems making and carrying out decisions between full automation and limited human control.

Digital Twin: The Virtual embodiment of the physical assets, process or system in a way that system and process are synchronized by data flows in real-time allowing to simulate, optimize and control the system autonomously.

Explainable Artificial Intelligence (XAI): The systems of AI offer people understandable details regarding why they made a choice or why they made a prediction to earn trust and allow supervision.

Federated Learning: A machine learning model that allows jointly learning models with multiple organizations without determining sensitive information centrally.

Human-AI Collaboration: Human and AI systems jointly do work through joint ventures that apply both their strengths.

Reinforcement Learning: This is a machine learning method in which agents improve their behavior by trial and error interactions where they receive rewards or penalties based on their behavior.

Supply Chain Resilience: Ability to foresee, prepare, react, and recuperate due to interruptions at satisfactory service levels.

Chapter 2
Towards Trustworthy Autonomous Logistics Through AI Assurance, Security, and Explainability Frameworks

Duggirala Aravind
https://orcid.org/0009-0005-4362-7684
ASET Institute of Science and Technology, India

Suzan Fouad Bakr
https://orcid.org/0009-0003-8104-7328
Faculty of Commerce, Al-Azhar University, Egypt

N. V. Suresh
https://orcid.org/0000-0002-0393-6037
ASET Institute of Science and Technology, India

ABSTRACT

Combination of Generative AI, Digital Twins and autonomous operations are accelerating the rate of evolution in the logistics field. The technologies are transforming the supply chain planning, coordination, and response to dynamic market conditions. Chapter analyses the importance of AI-based automation in making predictive decisions, real-time optimization and smart coordination within logistics networks. Meanwhile, it considers the most important issues of reliability, security,

DOI: 10.4018/979-8-3373-8841-0.ch002

and transparency in more autonomous systems. The discussion throws light on the efficiency of the predictive algorithms, robotics, and digital replicas in enhancing efficiency. The chapter integrates the findings of the emerging research and industry case studies to come up with the framework of creating trustful and robust logistics ecosystems. The research comes to the conclusion that the future of logistics is not only about the technological innovation but also about the responsible government, transparency, and constant learning in intelligent systems.

1. INTRODUCTION

The logistics industry has been a fundamental part of global trade since it facilitates easier entry and exit of commodities, products and services into the market. It has evolved in the last several years due to the prevalence of the digital technology of digital twins, robots, artificial intelligence, and the Internet of Things. Together, these technologies are paving the way for autonomous logistics where artificial intelligence (AI) is playing an increasingly important part in strategic-level decisions such as demand forecasting, risk management and handling of disruptions in addition to automating operational tasks such as warehouse slotting and last-mile routing. These systems can provide unequivocal rates of scalability, resilience, and performance. Making such technologies an intrinsic part of the global supply chain structure is a rather daunting task, however, getting them to be reliable, safe, and responsible is the challenge.

Transparency of decision making is one of the biggest concerns of the transition process when using AI. Most of the developed models, particularly, deep learning models, despite their high prediction capacity, are not generally interpretable. The results of so-called black-box systems are theoretically right but not human comprehensible and, therefore, human-testable. The absence of transparency in logistics is causing stakeholders to be hesitant since the decisions are made without consideration of both operations and finances. To illustrate, the route optimization system is an artificial intelligence that might find a more affordable and quicker route by including the politically unsafe area or highways in poor condition. There is no guarantee that logistics providers will listen to such recommendations or that they will be accepted by regulators or clients unless there are understandable processes that can be used to explain how they were created. Thus, it is more to be accepted than to be technically an improvement, specifically in the aspects that concern safety and reliability (Qadeer & Awad, 2025; Qadeer et.al, 2025).

The explainability of the interdependent logistics systems makes their safety more concerning. Self-driving logistics is the use of enormous systems of sensors, cars, cloud computing, and AI-programmed models in developing complex cyber-physical systems. These networks subject operations to a broad spectrum of possible attacks by malicious individuals, predisposing them to ransomware attacks, cyberattacks, and data breaches. The price of such vulnerabilities is demonstrated by the ransomware attack on Maersk that has not yet passed its first year (2017). The global shipping of Maersk was also brought to a standstill by just one intrusion into the networks of the corporation, costing the corporation hundreds of millions of euros. The integrity of AI systems of monitoring key logistics infrastructure is increasingly of significance to the security of both a single business and the international commerce.

The third level of consideration is AI assurance which is defined as business processes and evidence used to assure CBD that an AI system is safe, reliable, and that it meets legal and ethical requirements. Although the traditional engineering is well versed in the assurance processes, AI-powered logistics is not. Without such structures, organizations find it very difficult to offer an objective guarantee to regulators, insurance companies, and customers that their systems are reliable. Since no guarantee is provided, the risk of non-compliance, unethical actions, and reputational losses exists. This is especially dangerous in a business that contributes significantly to business facilitation.

All these problems of low assurance, security threats, and obscurity are all paradoxical. On the one hand, the independence and artificial intelligence will lead to a faster logistics system with perfect forecast, optimization, and responsiveness. Conversely, the stakeholders will not be widely embraced when they do not trust the technology. It happens that the faith is fundamental to the realization of the potential of autonomous logistics.

To establish credible autonomous logistics, explainability, assurance, and security will be discussed in this article. It confirmed a belief that it will be as much about the development of frameworks for governance and cross-sector cooperation and of compliance with the emerging international standards as about inducements of technical change that will disrupt logistics. It is important to mention regarding these points that in addition to the contributions to the literature on the subject of trustworthy AI, the discussion also fulfils the practical needs of anyone working in the field of logistics in the complex and highly competitive business environment of the modern world. Some argue that the ability to develop systems in which the stakeholders will be able to comprehend, believe and be sure will be more crucial to autonomous logistics in the future than the technological ability.

This chapter finds a point of convergence between the three concepts of practice, governance, and technology. It aims at contributing substantially to the academic discourse on trustworthy AI and the demands of logistics specialists who need to work in an environment that grows increasingly complex and demanding. The message is loud and clear: whether we succeed in the application of AI systems that are reliable, secure, and interpretable cannot be separated from future autonomy - the future of autonomous logistics will be determined not by technological progress, but rather by the capacity to apply such systems in a reliable manner.

2. BACKGROUND STUDY

The past role of logistics has been that of complex networks, manual coordination, and gradual improvements in efficiency. But the very growth of global trade, the up and rise of e-commerce, and the customer's ever growing appetite for speed and quality has brought to light the issues with what we have been doing in logistics. Today supply chains are at an unprecedented crossroads of volatility which we see in demand fluctuations, political and geophysical disruptions, natural disasters, and regulatory changes. These issues have brought into focus the requirement for smart, adaptive and resilient logistics solutions which are able to predict, react to, and put out operational issues as they happen (Christopher and Holweg, 2017; Roscoe et al., 2022; Ghonim & Awad,2025).

Many AI applications in logistics are still being designed and implemented as stand-alone solutions disconnected from the operational structure and the security and governance frameworks of the organization as a whole (Soumpenioti and Panagopoulos, 2023; Chen et al., 2024). Such inability to integrate may lead to inefficiencies, operational failures as well as undesired negative outcomes. As an example, predictive routing algorithm may calculate the optimal path of a processor without considering cyber-attack surface routing vulnerabilities. Robots in a warehouse can operate together and effectively but in an a-priori manner, which is not explainable to the human operators controlling the system. One of the issues is operational inefficiencies and the other ones are the absence of trust, safety, and regulatory compliance. These are of course not limited to the autonomous robots of the warehouse, but to the cyber-physical systems in general. Closing the digital loopholes can, for instance, ease the consequences of delayed shipments and help reduce the risk of damage to the goods being shipped (Varga, 2022; Liu et al., 2023).

The issue of which to address these challenges has been the factor which has brought forth the preparation of this chapter. We put forth to present a complete picture of the interaction between AI assurance, cyber-physical security, and explainable AI in the context of autonomous logistics (Charmet et al., 2022). By that we have integrated these dimensions which in turn enables organizations to develop systems that are not only efficient but also transparent, resilient, and accountable. The chapter identifies the main issues in present day logistics operational unpredictability, vulnerability to cyber-attacks, lack of human supervision, and low trust in AI based systems and we show how an integrated approach is to put a stop to these issues (Sadeghi et al., 2024; Sarker et al., 2024).

Logistical operators need ways to guarantee reliability, interpretability, and adherence with the rapid expansion of autonomous vehicles, warehouse robotics, and AI informed decision systems (Llorca, et al. 2025, Pournader et al. 2021). For organizations to mitigate the ethical, operational, and security risks associated with the deployment of AI, the gaps must first be closed. The chapter also utilizes practical illustrations and integrated AI benefits, citing Amazon Robotics and Maersk's response to a cyberattack, to show the practical use of integrated AI and the benefits derived from it.

This chapter presents a designed solution oriented guide for modern logistics. We put forth that which we present is not a stand-alone answer; for successful autonomous logistics we see the value in the purposeful inclusion of elements like assurance, security and explainability which in turn are supported by good governance, regulatory compliance and human oversight. By this we mean that through the use of AI in alignment with these basic principles organizations may put in place supply chains that are adaptive, resilient, sustainable and which in also better equipped to deal with the very complex global trade issues we see today (Wen et al., 2025; Taeihagh, 2021; Awad, 2025).

3. CONCEPTUAL FRAMEWORK

Autonomous logistics is the manifestation of the connection of innovative AI systems, automation, and digital infrastructure use in the supply chain, and it is the prioritized objective in the conceptual model. Logistic self-sufficiency needs to be safeguarded by employing AI Assurance, which ensures that systems used for decision making are trusted, reliable, and aligned to business goals. AI models may not perform well in real-world environments, which could shape a lack of trust and lack term from stakeholders, and a lack of efficiency.

Cyber-physical security helps overcome the increasing weakness of networked logistical systems. Cloud-based control systems, robots, IoT machines, and autonomous vehicles build potential sources of failure or attack. Security measures ensure that when adversity strikes a business, it can continue its operations through the preservation of such resources. By providing a basis for trust, assurance and security, explainable AI (XAI) enables regulators and human operators to analyse and validate recommendations made via artificial intelligence (AI).

Digital twins allow companies to experiment with decisions, find better ways to get things done. By using supervised learning for automation, Human-in-the-Loop (HITL) ensures ethically safe, morally correct and informed decision-making. Systems can dynamically optimise activities across complex and intricate multi-modal supply chains thanks to agentic AI's adaptive and autonomous ability to reason.

It is more convenient to delegate resources and train AI to work together with the help of such operational tools as Federated Learning and Multi-Echelon Inventory Optimization, to make predictions more accurate and avoid leaking personal information of the partners. The ability of the system to anticipate, absorb and recover from system disturbances while maintaining system performance and trustworthiness is what links all the components. This theoretical framework proves that autonomic logistics is the strategic amalgamation of assurance, security, explainability, human control, and adaptive technologies to be applied to develop a dependable, sound and efficient supply chain ecology. The use of AI or robotics is not the only one. The conceptual diagram has these three pillars - AI Assurance, Cyber-Physical Security, and Explainable AI (XAI) that encompass a centrally positioned autonomous logistics. The pillars are interrelated and emphasize on dependable, secure and transparent systems of AI in self-driving.

Figure 1. Conceptual diagram

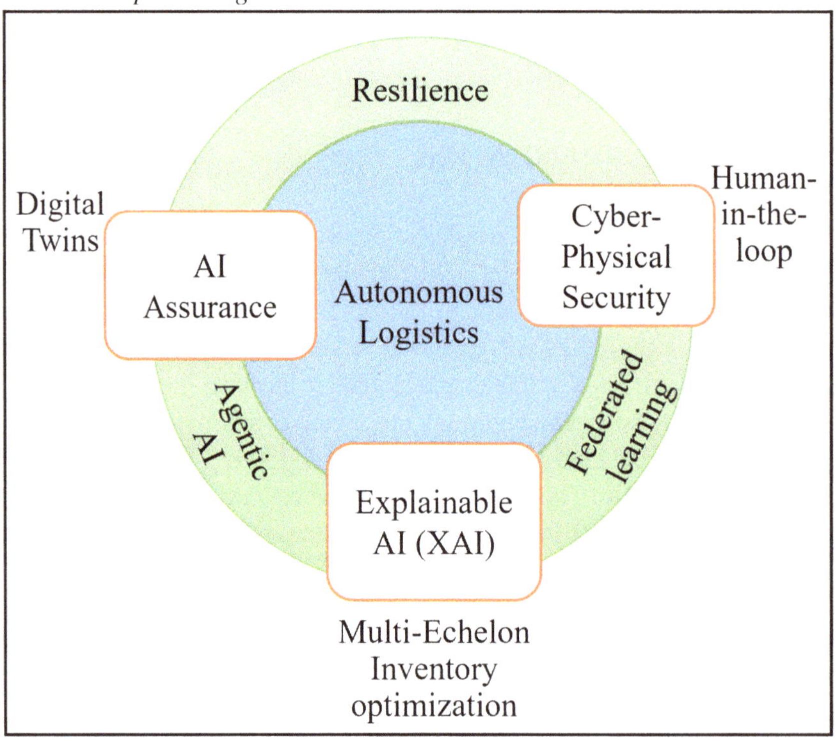

operational control mechanisms that support cooperative learning across a supply chain and optimal inventory management are federated learning and multi-echelon inventory optimization. Finally, and not the least, resilience relates all the elements of the system to an active feedback loop, because it enables it to absorb, recover, and adapt to the shock.

Supporting these pillars are enabling technologies and concepts. For an example Digital Twins offer simulation, predictive capabilities Human-in-the-Loop (HITL) for oversight and intervention Agentic AI for adaptive, autonomous decision making Multi-Echelon Inventory Optimization and Federated Learning as the operational mechanism for collaborative learning and optimized inventory management across supply chains. Finally, Resilience is a system property that accounts for the system's ability to absorb and recover from perturbations, and to adapt to disruptions which will be intimately linked in a feedback loop.

4. THE RISE OF AUTONOMOUS LOGISTICS

Increased use of digital twins, robots, AI, and related infrastructure is bringing about one of the most drastic transformations in the history of the logistics sector. An industry where manual systems used to operate, where tracking of goods and services was done on paper, where operations small parts of the whole system were run with minimal human intervention is on the cusp of a day and age where automated systems will have the ability to manage entire logistics networks with minimal human interaction. This is both a structural and technological transformation, where businesses will plan supply chain, addressing the uncertainty, and delivering value to the clients in a different way.

Typically, optimization in traditional logistics models necessitated a compromise between reliability, price and velocity. To align production timelines, transportation paths and stock quantities, decisions were for the most part guided by the instinct of experienced planners relying on feelings and past evidence. Nonetheless, these solutions are no longer relevant because global supply chains become increasingly sophisticated because of the impact of cross-border trade, omni-channel business, and just-in-time production. According to the growing volume of data generated by related devices, and the unpredictability of the market, more dynamic, predictive, and adaptive approaches are demanded. With its language to dissect vast amounts of data in real-time, unravel unnoticed patterns and generate insights that would be impossible for human decision-makers to understand on their own, artificial intelligence has emerged as the main driver of this revolution.

Obvious change is the application of robotics and self-driving cars in transportation and storage. The size and speed with which goods can be handled in today's fulfillment centers have already been altered by automated guided vehicles and robotic devices for picking. These technologies make precision in slotting, packing, and sequence the order possible; they also reduce the amount of human labor required to complete the repetitive task. However, now, thanks to robotics, the large-scale fulfillment strategies of key participants of world e-commerce allow satisfying millions of orders daily with minimal error. Similarly, last-mile deliveries with drones and autonomous trucks are undergoing improvement from experimental pilot projects up to the preliminary commercial processes. These technologies are still efficient and environmentally beneficial regardless of the potential infrastructure and regulatory challenges that they may contain, which is even more problematic in big cities, where people are already accustomed to the issue of emissions and traffic.

Another key element of independent logistics is the digital twin. By creating digital representations of real-time supply chains, logistics managers can become acquainted with future disruptions, simulate their outcomes and anticipate them in advance. To provide a picture on real-time network map, these digital environments combine sensor data, corporate systems data, and external data. Digital twin and generative AI technologies are beginning to create new opportunities where the simulation can be both descriptive and prescriptive, where the simulation can create innovative solutions to unforeseen problems, and where supply chains can "learn and adapt."

There are other characteristics related to operational efficiency: sustainability and resilience that should be linked with the introduction of autonomous logistics. In terms of human-centric planning, the pandemic highlighted the inefficiencies of such approaches through shortcomings, shortages and sudden demand surges, at the same time underlining the need for systems that can correct themselves and respond in a dynamic manner. Autonomous logistics will reduce these risks by offering tools to automatically reconfigure networks, providing real time analytics of network disruption, and predictively forecasting how the disruption will occur in the event of uncertainty. Environmental needs are also forcing organizations to reduce waste, pollution and consumption of endowed resources. By way of improving fuel use we see that which is achieved through better route optimization and also we have improved energy use on the warehouse floor and we have introduced in reverse logistics models which include repair, reuse and recycling that is what AI in logistics does for us.

The importance of this change can also be emphasized by the fact that people rely on data more and more. Autonomous logistics feeds off big data since it utilizes transactional and sensor data, as well as outside feeds, such as weather, social media, and trade rules. The new data sources can be made to form coherent decision directory unlike the prior fragmented methods. To ascertain the fact that firms do not crippler by anomalous or poor entry, notions such as data eagerness, master data administration, as well as data-product reasoning, are rapidly being placed into tactical focus.

Nevertheless, the introduction of self-driven logistics is qualified not only as a technical step but a game-changer in the human worker role. Work is being restructured in ways that further shift the role of human being toward oversight, exception management, and ethical governance while simultaneously removing other, much more monotonous and data-heavy jobs from human control. However, rather than replacing human tasks, it shifts the human responsibilities, thereby also resulting in the need for new competencies in cybersecurity, system integration, and AI monitoring. An example is the situation with workers at warehouses, who are slowly becoming so-called robot supervisors that ensure that the fleets of automated machines are controlled, and the cases which cannot be handled by a machine are handled by them.

This transformation impacts not only whole trade ecosystems but also businesses. Autonomous logistics is beginning to affect the shape of regional and international supply chains by enabling enterprises to abandon reactionary approaches to logistics and adopt adaptable and active strategies. There are autonomous systems that are being used to increase flows of trade through corridors, accelerate cross-border integration, and promote the development of smart ports and digital customs processes within regions with high levels of infrastructure development. One of the opportunities for autonomous abilities in the emerging marketplace is the capability to move physicist ahead of outdated versions, which provides opportunities to develop agile and sustainable logistics systems that are excluded from the legacies of infrastructure. The evolution of the logic of autonomous logistics as the norm and exception will vary depending on the interplay between local flexibility and technology foregrounding wishing to stir from the back country.

Fundamentally, the emergence of autonomous logistics is representative of technological advancement, organizational changes, and transformation. Although much more effort is still needed to enable such systems to be transparent, secure, and assured, with the trend of autonomous logistics, the question no longer is will it come to pass, but when will it integrate into the global economy.

5. AI ASSURANCE IN LOGISTICS

The concept of assurance has long existed in the world of engineering disciplines, where safety and reliability are proven through rigorous testing, protocols for compliance and proof of certification using evidence. The introduction of artificial intelligence in logistics has produced a similar requirement on assurance predominance to ensure that performance and responsibility are not the only primary issues but fairness, reliability, and strength are additional concerns. It is important to note that unlike conventional technologies, AI is associated with dynamic and adaptive behaviors that change over time, and the consequences of this advancement are less predictable and difficult to confirm. The significance of assurance in such a sector as logistics is difficult to overestimate, as operational breakdowns can be felt throughout all economies. AI assurance provides confidence for the trustworthiness of systems, which is an important prerequisite to satisfying the regulatory authorities while allowing their organisations to leverages and adopt innovations without having to sacrifice their reputation or take undue risks. The assurance of AI in logistics can be discussed in three dimensions, which are the reliability and robustness, fairness and accountability and the auditability and compliance.

5.1 Reliability and Robustness

The foundations of assurance in logistics are reliability. AI-driven systems are required to perform under a variety of environmental conditions, stress conditions and edge cases. Speaking of which, a demand-sensing predictive model should not provide reliable predictions when the situation is fairly stable and constant: it must be capable of modifying its directions when something disruptive happens, like a pandemic, a strike, or a geopolitical crisis. Likewise, routing algorithms should be suitable so that they do not fail in case of harsh weather or traffic failure. Robustness testing - these systems must not be brittle and must generalise beyond the specific data set on which they are trained. Such an issue is the uncertainty prevailing in the logistics environments.

Unlike closed systems, the logistics networks are open to unpredictable externalities - regulatory changes, sudden collapses of suppliers, or black swans. Metrology results, including abnormal situations, are integrated into the assurance framework through the use of models, which must be stress-tested in the manner used by finance in which a model is subjected to worst-case scenarios as the ultimate test of its fitness for purpose. In practice, companies are starting to implement "assurance checkpoints" in logistics operations, in which data from models is constantly referred back to standards to identify abnormalities. This gives confidence not only to the managers but also to clients and regulators that clients require stable service delivery.

5.2 Fairness and Accountability

Logistics systems fulfil the interface of various parties of manufactures, carriers, distributors, regulators and final consumers. In turn, like with an AI-based procurement system, another unintended consequence would be in that if history balances towards larger, existing suppliers, certain other (potentially smaller, but equally capable) providers would be unfairly disadvantaged. Also, in terms of underserved areas which may rank lower in the last mile delivery algorithms because of low profit we see that which plays out in to ethical and social issues. Additionally, responsibility procedures need to explain what happens to the system in the event of AI-assisted logistics errors. If it's the software vendor at fault, who is responsible for the accident - the software vendor or the logistics provider walking around its truck fleet in case of faulty perception algorithms? And finally, who is responsible if it is the human supervisor who is on the truck? Lack of transparency exposes companies to legal and moral ambiguity that acts as a barrier to adoption. "Assurance mechanisms must therefore not only comprise technical mechanisms but also governance mechanisms that make clear who is responsible for what, and who is making a particular decision in a decision chain, etc. It is precisely a critical dimension since logistics borders on community security and government compliance.

For instance, the AI Act of the European Union categorizes AI systems with critical infrastructure, and even logistics as a high-risk activity needing transparency, human control, and risk-free nature. Integrating this type of regulation consideration in the process of assurance enhances confidence to the external parties and further, it protects companies in respect to non-compliance failure.

5.3 Auditability and Compliance

Auditability is the third AI assurance dimension in logistics, which means that it is possible to perform a systematic review, test, and validate of AI systems. Activities in logistics are very controlled specifically when they entail cross country trade, food and medicine supply chain, and defence logistics. In such scenarios, they should rely on the production of convincing evidence that AI systems are labeled as per the requirements and that they can be verified without any doubts. Without the proper audit trails, it is hard to prove why a model made a certain recommendation, or if its performance has become worse.

Auditability - rigorous documentation of datasets, training processes, and model updates are required It also implies that the process of making operational decisions must be logged out so that regulators and an auditor can recreate the path followed by an AI system to arrive at a specific decision. This is in line with demand for explainability of AI: where desperately needed for reasons of compliance or trust. In logistics, companies are starting to use model cards and datasheets for datasets, which provide information on characteristics, limitations and intended uses. These tools can also be used to systematically examine the models and assure that they are not being implemented in an inappropriate setting. Another significant area that needs compliance is as international standards start to rise. The operationalization of assurance itself is affected by emerging global standards for AI management, and emerging specific requirements for AI assurance in logistics as permitted by standards. In global trade where trust and interoperability are vital characteristics, such compliance becomes a source for gaining strategic advantage.

6. CYBER-PHYSICAL SECURITY IN AUTONOMOUS LOGISTICS

The autonomous logistics shift has led to a physical and digital convergence infrastructures. Artificial intelligence, Internet of Things and cloud computing systems have now merged with trucks, drones, warehouses, and ports. With a more autonomous supply chain, cyber-physical security is no longer only about the security of digital data but rather the security of physical properties and human lives. Trucking accidents may result to faster shipments, losses in money, safety and even a system-wide interruption to international trade. To mitigate this challenge, there is need to approach it in an organized manner taking into account weaknesses, preemptive defence, assurances scheme, and resilience.

6.1 Vulnerabilities in Cyber-Physical Systems

Autonomous logistics systems are peculiar due to their vulnerability, relating to the interconnected networks including stakeholders, geographies, and infrastructures. All the points of connection - a sensor on a truck, an ERP system on a supplier, a cloud-based route optimizer, etc. - are the entry points of the attackers. The NotPetya ransomware attack in 2017 demonstrated the vulnerability of the global logistics - the shipping services of Maersk were paralysed at the cost of hundreds of millions of dollars. This and other incidents demonstrate that a cyberattack can impact physical operations, multiple flows, and destabilize trade routes because of the January attack. Patrol robots and drones are associated with additional risks.

Theft, accidents and loss of life would be inevitable if autonomous delivery truck is hacked or drone navigation is interrupted. Likewise, warehouse robotics, in case of violations, may close all fulfillment centers. The reliance on third-party suppliers and partners located around the world is what makes logistics especially vulnerable. Security breach by one partner in their IT system can affect the whole chain. The relevance of security by design algorithms to cyber-physical logistics systems can be explained by these vulnerabilities, which presuppose protective mechanisms on the hardware, software, and working processes at their formation.

6.2 Predictive Defence and AI-Enabled Security

Conventional malice protection frameworks are fundamentally reactive: they notice assaults after they have materialized into wrongdoing and consequently strive to limit them. Nonetheless, autonomous logistics requires predictive and proactive solutions. AI on Its Own Is Playing an Important Role in Improving Cyber-Physical Security: Anomaly detection, attack prediction, and dynamic adjustment of defence intelligences. Machine learning models can process huge amounts of network traffic, equipment signals and operational data to find patterns that are out of the regular, which can indicate an intrusion attempt. For example, predictive analytics can alert on anomalies like unusual login attempts from distant locations, anomalies in routing signals in driverless cars, etc. and anomalies in container tracking data. These advance warnings allow the operations in the logistics sector to pre-empt the eventualities of a disruption.

Further, generative AI is starting to play a role in cyber defence and simulating attack scenarios for testing vulnerabilities and recommendations for optimal countermeasures. Such applications fit well with applications in the field of logistics, where simulations and digital twins are already used for planning logistics operations. By incorporating cyber defence into these models, they can be used not only to model disruption in the supply chain but also to model cyberattacks, and pre-plan how disruption or cyberattack could be mitigated. Nonetheless, the dependence on technology like AI for cyber defence also carries certain risks such as adversarial attacks in which cyber-criminals shape the AI models by feeding them biased or poisonous data.

6.3 Security Assurance and Governance Frameworks

Cyber-physical security of autonomous logistics cannot be controlled only on the level of particular companies. Assurance frameworks accomplish this goal by establishing formalized evidences indicating that security interventions are sound and well functional. Any AI assurance is equivalent to the AI reliability, the same way that security assurance will be equivalent to the infrastructural resilience to cyber-physical threats. There is an emergence of international standards in this field. Isotopic/IEC 27001 on information security management is being expanded to cover industrial control systems and internet of things networks. Structures that address resilience of critical infrastructures in logistics include the NIST Cybersecurity Framework or the Network and Information Security Directive of the EU.

Beyond reducing risks, logistics organizations that employ these practices also imply trustworthiness with their counterparts and governmental boards, which contributes to gaining an even greater competitive edge in the international market. It is equally important with governance. Defined distribution of responsibility among stakeholders makes them accountable in case of security breaches. Specifically, to establish the liability in the case of a hacked self-driving vehicle, there must be clarity in the law as to whether the autonomous vehicle manufacturer, its software provider, or the logistics operator bears the final blame. Autonomous logistics will not be adopted until its value is demonstrated, and the absence of such governance structures will prevent this demonstration through reduced trust resulting from lack of accountability.

6.4 Building Resilient Cyber-Physical Logistics Networks

Resilience or the capacity to absorb, recover, and adapt to attacks is the last aspect of cyber-physical security. There is always a chance that a system breach will happen in any system, but robust logistics systems can help reduce the harm and bring it back to normal within a short time. This demands multiple barriers, backup and man-to-man system. As an example, independent warehouses can use manual overriding rules, meaning that their robotics can be seized by human managers in case of a system failure. Likewise, there are hybrid fleet routing systems that enable drivers to override the routing, in the event that GPS signals are spoofed. Crisis management also needs some coordination to maintain resilience. Logistics companies need to collaborate with governments, insurance companies, and industry associations to come up with emergency measures to safeguard vital streams of products in the event of cyber-attacks. Because most of the time, logistics supports the provision of fundamental services like food, medicine and energy then resilience is not a business problem, but a social problem. The recent scandals in supply chains have demonstrated that a collapsed logistics leads to a collapsed economy. The establishment of cyber-physical resilience will guarantee continuity in the case of individual firms, as well as societies that rely on continuous supply of goods and services.

7. EXPLAINABLE AI IN LOGISTICS

The more logistic operations depend on artificial intelligence as a decision-making tool, the more a problem arises: how AI-based programs get the recommendations offered. Traditional machine learning models, specifically deep learning algorithms, tend to be "black boxes", i.e., provide very accurate results but with no insights into the thought process that led to the results. In that which regards logistics this transparency is a issue which is eroding trust and also is an issue for logistics companies in their compliance with regulatory frameworks and in human oversight. Explainable AI (XAI) puts forward to us solutions to these issues by way of transparency, interpretability and actionability of AI based decisions. The three major dimensions according to which the XAI in logistics can be discussed are interpretability and transparency, human-in-the-loop decision-making, and potential uses of this concept in the areas of the operational logistics.

7.1 Interpretability and Transparency

Explainable AI is founded on interpretability. In the case of logistics systems specifically, the AI models must not only provide accurate predictions but also be capable of providing the reason behind the output in a manner understandable by humans. Transparency is beneficial to logistics managers, regulators, and clients to identify the dependability and properness of AI recommendations. As an example, a multi- echelon inventory model utilized by AI can suggest that it deploy inventory to a new warehouse to prevent run out of inventory. When the need to act is not clear, be it based on predicted demand, the reliability of the supplier or the limitations of the transport etc., then human operators will hesitate thus eliminating any of the possible efficiency gains of AI. Interpretability is attained in different ways.

Such methods as SHAP (Shapley Additive Explanations) and LIME (Local Interpretable Model-Agnostic Explanations) provide us with the idea of the significance of the features and allow us to comprehend the most crucial variables in the model. Causal modeling is also the other method that allows the operator to not only know the correlation but also the causes of outcomes. With these methods, logistic organizations would be capable of gaining trust in artificial intelligence technology, consistency between predictions and the current state of operations, and justification of their decisions both to the inner environment and to the government.

7.2 Human-in-the-Loop Decision-Making

The autonomy of logistics technology can be described as autonomy and may be defined as a sophisticated technology that comprises human supervision to offer a form of interface between humans and machines to deal with uncertainty, ethics, and extraordinary conditions. The Human-in-the-loop (HITL) frameworks are designed to integrate the effectiveness of AI decision making with human judgment and give operators an opportunity to intervene and confirm or disregard recommendations when necessary. One of the facilitators of HITL methods is explainable AI since individuals are not able to effectively manage AI systems that lack understanding. Practically, HITL is applied to such areas as warehouse management, last mile delivery and fleet routing. As an illustration, picking robots may have anomalies, including broken packages, broken product placement, and risky scenarios.

Explainable AI provides the capability of reporting to the human supervisor what the reason is why the robot is recommending such actions and to take the necessary action. Equally, at transport level, recommendations of dynamic routings produced by artificial intelligence can be framed among with recommendations, traffic predictions, fuel predictions and actuals, and risk prediction. Such openness allows motorists to arrive at the final set of decisions or the logisticians making the ultimate decisions with great confidence so that the human factor does not override the intelligence of the robots. Through the coordination of human judgment with AI data, logistics organizations will be in a better place to guarantee higher levels of operational reliability, and maintain accountability and trust.

7.3 Practical Applications in Logistics Operations

The use of explainable AI has been applied in many different areas of logistics, such as the way organisations plan, carry out, and monitor their activities. In demand forecasting, the XAI methodologies are used to clarify the contribution of either of the following factors to the patterns of the predicted demand: seasonal patterns, promotions, supplier reliability, or external factors. This will enable the planners to adjust the procurement and inventory plans prior to time. XAI is applied in route optimization to make operators comprehend the rationale behind a choice of routes that considers real-time traffic, weather, and carbon footprint.

Such decisions require transparency in order to balance the efficiency, safety, compliance and sustainability aims In warehouse systems, such as explainable AI controls robotic systems with slotting, picking and packing objectives. Exposure of logic of decision-making by order of allocation will enable supervisors to control to allow high-priority orders to be handled appropriately, space utilize well as potential errors to a minimum. Moreover, XAI allows inter-organizational cooperation - in case of multi-tier supply chains, cooperation between suppliers, carriers, distributors is very crucial and transparency is a major force that is driving the cooperation. It is also useful in meeting regulation requirement, particularly in sectors in the industry that are highly risky like the pharmaceutical sector, food and defence logistic because traceability of decisions is a legal requirement in these industries. In addition, explainable AI supplements the strengthening of lifelong learning. Providing feedback regarding the rationale behind the decision, XAI ensures that the logistics systems can revise the predictive models with time and be more precise and region-specific to the operation.

8. BUILDING TRUST, SECURITY, AND COLLABORATION IN AUTONOMOUS LOGISTICS SYSTEMS

With the increased autonomy of logistics operations comes a significant issue, and it is how to ensure that AI systems are safe, reliable, and open simultaneously. AI assurance, cyber-physical security, and explainable AI have never been regarded as entities that are connected to one another; nevertheless, they must converge to create logistics networks that people can actually trust. Individual initiatives may create gaps, such as secure systems which are not transparent or interpretable models which are disassembled on being attacked across the internet. All the technical, operational and governance practices should cooperate in order to make the integration effective. This allows organizations to accomplish as much as possible and reduce risk. This integration can be explained by three associated facets: governance and organizational alignment, technical integration, and adherence to rules and standards.

8.1 Achieving Operational Trust

Operational trust in autonomous logistics systems that continue to make important decisions with less and less human intervention is one of the most urgent problems. Although AI applications and autonomous systems have advantages of efficiency and accuracy, they will be constrained because of the lack of transparency in their decision-making, their high vulnerability to cyber threats, and their inability to be understood by humans. Artificial intelligence delivery and warehouse programs can be effective optimizers of deliveries or warehouse processes, but the algorithms do not take into consideration the context and ethical considerations- result in error, safety concerns, and regulatory violations. These gaps destroy the confidence between managers, operators, and regulators compromising the very essence of smart logistics systems.

The difficulty is in that it is a conflict between automation and assurance. Trust in autonomous systems is weak unless they have AI assurance frameworks, physical cyber-security and explainable AI (XAI) mechanisms. This gap can be addressed by utilizing Digital Twins and the human-in-the-loop (HITL) systems, which will allow constant monitoring, confirmation, and action when AI does not operate as anticipated. The establishment of operational trust is hence both technical and managerial and moral requirement. It helps to ensure that autonomous logistics develops in a responsible way, in other words, having clear decisions, resilient systems, and technologies that do not surpass human control and security.

8.2 Ensuring Systemic Security

As the logistics systems transform to highly (sometimes extremely) connected systems of autonomous vehicles, digital twins, and intelligent sensors, systemic security has become one of the most urgent and complicated problems. The increased reliance on AI-based decision-making and cyber-physical integration introduces multilayered vulnerabilities to logistic businesses in the form of a data breach and manipulation of algorithms and disruptive physical interference through cyberattacks. The failure of one of the nodes in such environment can result in massive disruption of the operations in the whole ecosystem by halting transportation, tampering with prediction data, or even causing harm to the human life.

The issue is aggravated by the disjointedness of cybersecurity preparedness among logistics stakeholders. Advanced automation is applied in many organizations, yet they lack coherent structures of the AI assurance, network resiliency, and real-time threat detection. Moreover, predictive models can tend to ignore security parameters and achieve efficiency at the cost of defense strength. Such an imbalance poses an invisible danger: an intelligent looking system that is still vulnerable to orchestrated cyber threats is opened up. In a bid to protect systems in a systemic manner, autonomous logistics should implement integrated defense architecture with a combination of cyber-physical protection and adaptive threat analytics and federated learning to become secure in data collaboration. Unless these mechanisms are implemented during the design phase, the potential of autonomous logistics would be compromised as the digital vulnerability in one area leads to disastrous effects in others cascading global supply chains to risks.

8.3 Fostering Human-AI Collaboration

One of the key issues of autonomous logistics nowadays is the increasing distance between the intelligence algorithms and the human control. With more processes becoming dependent on self-learning systems in routing, demand forecasting, and optimization of the many warehouses, the human element is left out of the much-needed decision loops. This lack of connection decreases the situational awareness, responsibility, and the possibility of interfering with algorithms, when they malfunction or act in unpredictable ways. Human-AI Collaboration is lacking in most logistics environments, which contributes to efficiency paradoxes, i.e., high-performance systems that are data-intensive and fast yet fragile in terms of uncertainty in the real world.

The issue is even more significant when the systems of AI are not transparent. The operators will fail to understand the reasons underpinning a digital twin requiring rerouting shipments or managing inventory changes, leading to mistrust and operation reluctance. Moreover, excessive dependence on automation removes tacit and adaptive judgment human experts have an offer during disruption or ethical quandary. To solve this, the logistics systems need to integrate Human-in-the-Loop (HITL) design principles, which are capable of allowing humans to control, check and learn AI-made choices in real time. To overcome this gap, training, clarification of interfaces, and systems of cognitive collaboration are needed. Operational resilience becomes the reality when AI and human decision-makers are not opposed, but complementary to each other, here, it means combining precision and human intuition in machines, which should lead to logistics ecosystems that are both reliable and adaptable to changes and challenging ethical principles.

9. CASE STUDIES

9.1 Amazon Robotics in Warehouse Slotting and Picking

It does this through an army of robotics and AI-powered logistics, making it a global leader in warehouse automation. Its network of fulfilment centers also use autonomous mobile robots (AMRs) for shelf transportation, item sorting and slotting optimisation. The bottom line is that such systems drastically improve throughput and accuracy, but inevitably also demand answers to the tough question: how can we teach warehouse managers about AI-driven robots thinking on a day-to-day basis? In response to this, Amazon began using explainable or interpretable AI frameworks for legal transparency in robot scheduling and inventory placement. The system is simple to understand through visual dashboards, which provide users with reasons why an item is held in a certain location, how picking routes are optimized and how demand forecasts influence inventory redistribution. This level of transparency enables human supervisors to step in when anomalies are detected, e.g. mis-placed items or overly long picking times — and the operations continues all along.

It means running these systems, and simulating them continuously with digital twins. These virtual warehouses mirror actual operations to forecast any potential disturbances and interrupting the facility. Operators are also part of the solution, since Amazon integrates human-in-the-loop into its systems to make exceptions when it comes across challenging cases like non-standard packaging or high priority orders that require immediate dispatch.

With as large-scale autonomous logistics working at scale as explained in the Amazon Robotics case, explainability with AI confidence and operational control can work without losing human trust. This transparent decision-making process is also a positive thing for managers, employees and stakeholders who need to know why the AI recommended what it did; which helps with trust in adoption while minimizing risks of black box automation.

9.2 Maersk Cyberattack – AI Assurance and Security in Global Supply Chains

The NotPetya 2017 ransomware attack on the largest shipping and logistics firm across the world, Maersk, is a potent example of the dangers of interdependent logistics networks. A cyber-attack paralysed Maersk IT systems and ground to a halt port operations, container terminals in multiple countries as well as shipping tracking systems - estimated loss in excess of $300 million.

In return, Maersk had invested a lot to ensure the safety of their premises, including the creation of AI-based anomaly detectors that monitored the wellbeing of the systems. These are systems that scan network traffic but look at the access logs and operational logs to identify threats before it escalates to a larger concern. AI assurance models were also formulated to assess the reliability of predictive security algorithm and make sure that the automated threat detection could be relied upon to safeguard critical logistics processes.

Maersk too had put in place certain governance and compliance according to the emerging international standards including ISO/IEC security framework and industry best practice. Processes that respond were made computerized in such a way that the recommendations made by the AI can be integrated with the human view in order to contain a threat within a short time. Such an implemented approach to AI-founded detection, organised assurance and governance has enhanced the strength within the global supply chains in Maersk to enable the company to remain operational in an ever-increasing digitalised and autonomous world.

Maersk incident is an example of the case in point that cyber-physical security is not only about technology, but about strategic. Integrating AI credibility, predictive analytics, and governance can help complex logistics networks to be resilient to cyber threats without losing the trust of stakeholders in their credibility, continued operationality and compliance.

10. DISCUSSION

Three types of AI assurance, cyber-physical security and explainable AI allow one to conclude that there is a complicated interdependence between technological potential, work consistency, and the confidence of stakeholders in the work of autonomous logistics. Among the aspects assessed, there is one, which stands out, namely, remote innovation of AI or automation is insufficient without cross-cutting frameworks including reliability, transparency, and security simultaneously. The above Amazon Robotics and Maersk use cases demonstrate how these considerations actually translate into practice - one highlighting the importance of focusing on explainability in optimization of operational processes, another highlighting the extent to which we will indeed have to invest in cyberspace physical security (in addition to AI guaranteeing) in global supply chains. Among the most important things to be understood is the two-sidedness of trust as technical and as organizational concept.

The interpretability demonstrated by explainable AI at Amazon reveals that that functionality enables supervisors to review the recommendations, identify all instances where mistakes are found, and intervene where they exist - all of which fosters trust in autonomous operations. Conversely, the Maersk cybersecurity breach demonstrates that even operation systems that are heavy duty and are not security-oriented can be hacked. Predictive analytics and frameworks of assurance AI can be used as tools to predict and prevent threats, provide reliable and continuity in highly interdependent supply chains. Another issue discussed in the conversation is the role of governance in relating technology and human control. Effective governance policies also involve aligning tasks across teams, establishing procedures on how to react to errors and pull together accountability, when AI-based systems put a firm in the wrong. The technical solutions lack governance and this is the aspect where they are prone to fragmentation or disrealization of the organizational objectives. Besides, compliance with standards and regulation is another tool that has a pivotal role to play in integration, through external validation that autonomous logistics systems conform to internationally accepted standards of reliability, security and visibility.

Finally, the discussion highlights the fact that autonomous logistics success is not determined by the level of technology sophistication. Rather, it relies on the artificially combined processes, which enhance confidence, such as assurance, security, and explainability, as upheld by governance systems and alignment with globally evolving norms. Such observations are an invitation to further developments in autonomous supply chains where high-level optimization and new technology are bound to change the operational environment.

11. FUTURE DIRECTIONS

11.1 Agentic AI and Autonomous Decision-Making

In the coming age of logistics, we see the introduction of agentic AI which are systems that do autonomous reasoning, set goals and make dynamic decisions with a minimum of human input. We differ from present day AI which react to pre-determined rules or predictions; agentic AI is able to look at many variables, to predict issues which may arise and to change strategies in real time. In logistics this means we may see full autonomy in supply chains where inventory is constantly re-evaluated, routes optimized and procurement decisions are made as per present data. Also, for instance an agentic AI system may proactively re-route shipments to avoid weather, traffic, or political issues which cause delay at the same time also minimizing cost and carbon footprint.

Governance and trust are also raised as a result of the roll out of agentic AI. Accountability and explainability is very important as systems become more complex and self-directed in their actions. It is important to integrate it with AI assurance and security systems to ensure that not only are the decisions made by these systems ethical but also functional. Also, we see that which organizations are at the forefront of this trend are putting in place human in the loop for high risk decisions which is combined with digital twin simulations that play out autonomous strategies before we see them in the real world. The result is a very adaptive, efficient and resilient logistics ecosystem which is a large step forward from what we have had in the past with traditional auto run operations.

11.2 Quantum-Ready Optimization and Multimodal Logistics

Recent computational methods, including quantum-ready optimization, can transform the situation in case of very complicated logistics problems. The stochastic components of demand uncertainty, transport disruptions and environmental constraints make classical optimization invalid because logistics networks are large-scale and multi-echelon. Unlike classical algorithms, quantum-ready algorithms have the capability of examining an almost unlimited number of variables in a fraction of a second, and thus detailed route planning, multi-modal transportation and uncertainty-constrained inventory distribution can become immediate. The first move towards enhancing the expected level of operational performance and sustainability of full-fledged autonomic logistics systems will be the incorporation of quantum-ready optimization.

Imagine the energy and carbon reduction of spatially directed fleets of energy-saving drones, autonomous trucks and delivery robots, and yet fulfil the need of on-time delivery. With the option of digital twins and real-time IoT data, operators can model the logistics situation on a completely new scale and complexity level. Despite the constraints posed by technology and cost, pilot projects in multimodal freight corridors have shown that quantum-ready optimization can radically change the parameters of organizational decision-making to those that integrate it with AI assurance and understandable decision-making systems. In such organizations, the competitive advantage will be high.

11.3 Federated Learning and Collaborative Supply Chains

The growth of cross organizational collaboration has put forth federated learning as a very promising solution for secure and privacy preserving AI in logistics. In the past traditional AI models used central data collection which at time is a issue of competition which may lead to the model not being deployed, also we see that from a regulatory and privacy perspective it is a no go. With federated learning we see that many organizations which include suppliers, carriers, and logistics companies are able to train AI models together without the exchange of raw data which in turn preserves the private info but at the same time see improvements in predictive performance.

In practice we see that which is the case of federated learning is to improve demand forecasting, route optimization and disruption analysis in supply chains.

By bringing together what is known from remote partners we see that autonomous logistics systems gain a full picture of network conditions, supplier performance and also customer behavior which in turn enables more adaptive and resilient decision making. Also, it is the case that the decentralized structure of federated models increases security which is to say that no single point of attack can bring down the whole network. When we combine this with explainable AI what we get is that stakeholders are able to interpret local model results which in turn promotes trust in collaborative decisions. This approach is very much the solution for global supply chains which present as they do diverse regulatory environments and issues around multi-party coordination which are constant issues.

12. KEY TAKEAWAYS

- The combination of AI assurance, cyber-physical security, and explainable AI develops a basis of trusted operations and trust in the stakeholders. Devoid of trust, even the most sophisticated autonomous systems are at risk of not being used appropriately or is disregarded by users and consumers.
- A clear AI system would allow managers to know the reasoning behind computerized decisions, confirm the results, and interfere where needed to guarantee efficiency and responsible ethics in the everyday logistics processes.
- The digital and physical infrastructure presents a higher vulnerability to cyberattacks and thus, the security precautions, continuous monitoring, and resiliency planning are all necessary to ensure uninterrupted supply chain operations.
- A union of AI assurance, security measures, explainable AI in systematic governance and compliance systems will offer a holistic solution to risk reduction and optimization of performance, so that autonomous logistics systems are dependable and responsible.
- Although AI is gaining autonomy, exception processing, moral regulation, and judgment in the face of more complicated or unforeseeable situations require human judgment and supplement the functions of intelligent systems.
- The efficiency, environmentally responsible, and operational resilience can be achieved at the same time, which proves that AI-driven operations may optimize transport routes, minimize emissions, and predict disruptions.

13. CONCLUSION

A paradigm shift in the development of logistics, associated with the merging of artificial intelligence, robotics, digital twins and sophisticated optimization methods, is the movement towards autonomy. This chapter has indicated that technological innovation by itself cannot help attain sustainable and sustainable autonomous logistics that is also credible. Rather, reliability, resilience, and ethical accountability of systems are based on the incorporation of AI assurance, cyber-physical security, and explainable AI. By analyzing the case studies of Amazon Robotics and Maersk, one can see that the effectiveness of their operations, mitigation of risks, and trust of stakeholders are mutually reliant results of the application of the principles. The example of clear AI-regulated warehouse processes at Amazon makes clear how explainability can allow human control and precision in operation, whereas the example of cyberattacks in Maersk makes it clear why security mechanisms and well-organized assurance systems should be considered an essential part of any supply chain in the global arena. It has been highlighted in the discussion that trust is the key to successful adoption. Reliability guarantees the ability of systems to operate in diverse conditions, fairness and accountability protects ethical and operational integrity, and auditability enables the stakeholders to justify the decisions they make, and keep them in check. The combination of such dimensions with operating governance frameworks and global best practices does not only contribute to the improvement of operational performance, but it also places organizations competitively in a world of automated logistics.

The AI allows an adaptive self-directed decision-making process, which could dynamically balance cost, efficiency and sustainability. Quantum-ready optimization is able to provide an unprecedented level of computational ability to efficiently handle highly complex networks with multi-modes, whereas federated learning can enable collaborative AI across supply chain members without sensitive information being compromised. With these developments, coupled with explainability, guarantee and effective security, it results in logistics that are both extremely efficient and reliable and trustworthy.

Finally, logistics will be characterized by systems combining human judgment and autonomous intelligence in an unthreatening way. With the trust of autonomous logistics as its fundamental element, the industry can leave behind the marginalization of automation to the intelligent, adaptable, and resilient supply chains that would suit the needs of the fast-changing global economy.

Conflicts of Interest

The authors report that they have no conflict of interest in the preparation and publication of this chapter. The authors represent all their views, analyses, and conclusions as their personal views, and not the opinions of any of these affiliated institutions. The work itself was not any special grant given to funding agencies by the public, business or not-profit sectors. The study and composition were conducted without any external financial or material aid that can lead to the results of this chapter.

Originality of the Chapter

This chapter is original research and synthesis by the authors. It has never been published, delivered, or sent in any other form. The material is original, written specifically to this volume and adds new knowledge in the fields of autonomous logistics, AI assurance, security, and explainability.

ACKNOWLEDGEMENT

This chapter would not have been completed without the help, advice and efforts of a number of people and organizations. The researchers truly wish to thank their academic mentors and colleagues whose useful feedback and valuable discussions significantly improved the quality of the work. The institutions and organizations that have contributed to the development of the autonomous logistics field by conducting their own research, providing case studies, and real-life examples deserve special mention as they have become invaluable sources of information related to this chapter. The participants in the research are also recognized in the authors, where the teamwork with peers and research collaborators led to the development of the innovative atmosphere of openness and questioning.

REFERENCES

Awad, A. (2025). The role of universities' social responsibility in enhancing business sustainability: Mediating role of entrepreneurial culture. *Problems and Perspectives in Management*, *23*(1), 181–192. DOI: 10.21511/ppm.23(1).2025.14

Charmet, F., Tanuwidjaja, H. C., Ayoubi, S., Gimenez, P. F., Han, Y., Jmila, H., & Zhang, Z. (2022). Explainable artificial intelligence for cybersecurity: A literature survey. *Annales des Télécommunications*, *77*(11), 789–812.

Chen, W., Men, Y., Fuster, N., Osorio, C., & Juan, A. A. (2024). Artificial intelligence in logistics optimization with sustainable criteria: A review. *Sustainability*, *16*(21), 9145. DOI: 10.3390/su16219145

Christopher, M., & Holweg, M. (2017). Supply chain 2.0 revisited: A framework for managing volatility-induced risk in the supply chain. *International Journal of Physical Distribution & Logistics Management*, *47*(1), 2–17. DOI: 10.1108/IJPDLM-09-2016-0245

Ghonim, A., & Awad, A. (2025). Shaping customer insights through e-marketing: An applied study in the banking sector. *International Journal of Advanced and Applied Sciences*, *12*(4), 88–98. DOI: 10.21833/ijaas.2025.04.011

Liu, Y., Tao, X., Li, X., Colombo, A. W., & Hu, S. (2023). Artificial intelligence in smart logistics cyber-physical systems: State-of-the-arts and potential applications. *IEEE Transactions on Industrial Cyber-Physical Systems*, *1*, 1–20. DOI: 10.1109/TICPS.2023.3283230

Llorca, D. F., Hamon, R., Junklewitz, H., Grosse, K., Kunze, L., Seiniger, P., & Kriston, A. (2025). Testing autonomous vehicles and AI: Perspectives and challenges from cybersecurity, transparency, robustness and fairness. *European Transport Research Review*, *17*(1), 38. DOI: 10.1186/s12544-025-00732-x

Pournader, M., Ghaderi, H., Hassanzadegan, A., & Fahimnia, B. (2021). Artificial intelligence applications in supply chain management. *International Journal of Production Economics*, *241*, 108250. DOI: 10.1016/j.ijpe.2021.108250

Qadeer, A., & Awad, A. (2025). AI-powered ChatGPT in branding: Benefits, challenges, and future directions. In *Impacts of AI generated content on brand reputation* (pp. 1–26). IGI Global., DOI: 10.4018/979-8-3373-4327-3.ch001

Qadeer, A., Awad, A., & Ali, A. (2025). Understanding generative AI implementation in digital advertising among retail SMEs in Pakistan. In *Impacts of AI generated content on brand reputation* (pp. 177–201). IGI Global., DOI: 10.4018/979-8-3373-4327-3.ch007

Roscoe, S., Aktas, E., Petersen, K. J., Skipworth, H. D., Handfield, R. B., & Habib, F. (2022). Redesigning global supply chains during compounding geopolitical disruptions: The role of supply chain logics. *International Journal of Operations & Production Management*, *42*(9), 1407–1434. DOI: 10.1108/IJOPM-12-2021-0777

Sadeghi, K., Ojha, D., Kaur, P., Mahto, R. V., & Dhir, A. (2024). Explainable artificial intelligence and agile decision-making in supply chain cyber resilience. *Decision Support Systems*, *180*, 114194. DOI: 10.1016/j.dss.2024.114194

Sarker, I. H., Janicke, H., Mohsin, A., Gill, A., & Maglaras, L. (2024). Explainable AI for cybersecurity automation, intelligence and trustworthiness in digital twin: Methods, taxonomy, challenges and prospects. *ICT Express*, *10*(4), 935–958. DOI: 10.1016/j.icte.2024.05.007

Soumpenioti, V., & Panagopoulos, A. (2023, September). AI Technology in the Field of Logistics. In *2023 18th International Workshop on Semantic and Social Media Adaptation & Personalization (SMAP) 18th International Workshop on Semantic and Social Media Adaptation & Personalization (SMAP 2023)* (pp. 1-6). IEEE. DOI: 10.1109/SMAP59435.2023.10255203

Taeihagh, A. (2021). Governance of artificial intelligence. *Policy and Society*, *40*(2), 137–157. DOI: 10.1080/14494035.2021.1928377

Varga, L. Z. (2022). Solutions to the routing problem: Towards trustworthy autonomous vehicles. *Artificial Intelligence Review*, *55*, 5445–5484. DOI: 10.1007/s10462-021-10131-y

Wen, S. F., Shukla, A., & Katt, B. (2025). Artificial intelligence for system security assurance: A systematic literature review. *International Journal of Information Security*, *24*, 43. DOI: 10.1007/s10207-024-00959-0

KEY TERMS AND DEFINITIONS

Agentic AI: Emerging AI systems that are autonomous, can reason and make decisions, set goals, and deal with changes on the fly, especially when dealing with complex and dynamic logistics processes.

Artificial Intelligence (AI) Assurance: An organized system that places AI systems as trustworthy, precise, ethical, and responsible in making operational decisions, reducing the risk of automation in logistics.

Autonomous Logistics: The application of automated and AI-based technology to plan, implement, and operate logistical processes with the least human involvement, including transportation, warehousing, inventory, and supply chain management..

Digital Twins: Simulation Virtual replicas of the physical logistics systems to predict their performance, optimize decisions in real-time and estimate risks and system performance.

Explainable AI (XAI): Techniques and methods that offer insight into AI models, where the human operator can gain insight and interpret and justify the reasoning behind AI-based decisions in logistics processes.

Federated Learning: A centralized training process where organizations can communicate and collaboratively get data to improve models without access to raw data, retaining privacy but boosting supply chain predictive accuracy.

Human-in-the-Loop (HITL): A working model that incorporates human management within AI-based systems, where humans can observe, authenticate or process autonomous logistics decision making as and when necessary.

Multi-Echelon Inventory Optimization: A policy of controlling inventory at various levels of a supply chain network to balance demand, cost and risk in conditions of uncertainty.

Chapter 3
Cybersecurity and Supply Chains:
An International Law Perspective

Amer Ghassan Fakhoury
https://orcid.org/0009-0005-0826-6932
American University in the Emirates, UAE

ABSTRACT

In recent years, there has been a noticeable rise in cyber threats targeting global supply chains as well as the critical infrastructure of many states. These threats have revealed that the digital economy system is very weak, and that infiltrating global supply chains is not difficult given the presence of skilled cybercriminals. The reliance of states on the digital economy to coordinate and regulate supply chains has made targeting those chains easier. Therefore, numerous regional and international efforts have emerged aiming to regulate cybercrimes related to supply chains from a legal perspective. The EU has numerous directives aimed at European cybersecurity. However, despite the importance of these regional initiatives in confronting the threats facing global supply chains, they remain insufficient to address all threats. Therefore, this research aims to analyze the current legal frameworks designed to confront cyber threats to supply chains and the extent of their consistency with the principles of international law.

INTRODUCTION

In recent years, there has been a noticeable rise in cyber threats targeting global supply chains as well as the critical infrastructure of many states. These threats have revealed that the digital economy system is very weak, and that infiltrating global

DOI: 10.4018/979-8-3373-8841-0.ch003

supply chains is not difficult given the presence of skilled cybercriminals—some of whom may be supported by certain states. The reliance of states on the digital economy to coordinate and regulate supply chains has made targeting those chains easier. Therefore, numerous regional and international efforts have emerged aiming to regulate cybercrimes related to supply chains from a legal perspective. The European Union has adopted many decisions and issued numerous directives aimed at European cybersecurity. The Association of Southeast Asian Nations, for its part, has adopted many initiatives, and the same applies to Latin America. However, despite the importance of these regional initiatives in confronting the threats facing global supply chains, they remain insufficient to address all threats. Therefore, this research aims to analyse the current legal frameworks designed to confront cyber threats to supply chains and the extent of their consistency with the principles of international law.

Many agree that the current international economy depends fundamentally on global supply chains, as these chains are the backbone of international trade and the global economy. The movement of maritime trade and shipping, as well as logistics, relies substantially on digital technologies (Craighead et al., 2020). This shift toward reliance on the digital economy has made global trade more efficient, faster, and easier, but in return it has made the international economy vulnerable to many cyber risks that threaten international security and the global economy (Bode & Wagner, 2015).

An observer of the international scene can affirm that, in recent years, many ports, airports, and global transport networks have clearly and notably been subjected to numerous cyberattacks. A prominent example is the cyberattack known as NotPetya, which occurred in 2017. This attack—considered one of the largest cyberattacks in modern times—began by targeting Ukraine through malicious software (Greenberg, 2018). Although Ukraine was the primary target of this attack—and it led to paralysis of Ukrainian infrastructure and disruption of the financial and electricity sectors (NATO CCDCOE, 2019)—the attack appears to have spun out of control and struck global supply chains. Several companies in the shipping sector were affected, such as the Danish company Maersk, whose losses were estimated at more than USD 300 million (Maersk, 2018). The American pharmaceutical company Merck also suffered losses exceeding USD 870 million due to the stoppage of production systems. It was later established—based on a report issued by the governments of the United States and the United Kingdom—that the attack was attributed to a Russian group known as GRU (UK Foreign Commonwealth Office, 2018). This cyber incident was described as the most costly and destructive in history.

This was not the only incident directed against supply chains. In 2023, a ransomware attack occurred against the Port of Nagoya in Japan, where this attack disrupted the central computer system and halted loading and unloading operations for several days (Dragos, 2023; NTT Security, 2023).

These two examples reveal the complex nature of cyberattacks, whose effects are not limited to companies alone but extend to international trade and the global economy. Public international law is not isolated from these attacks; rather, it is at the heart of the international economy and at the core of cyber incidents. International law—which considers cyberattacks a major challenge to the global economy—addresses what is known as the issue of attribution of responsibility, that is, the entity that must bear responsibility for such cyberattacks, given that this type of attack falls within the definition of aggression and constitutes a direct violation of state sovereignty under the fundamental Charter of the United Nations (Schmitt, 2017).

International law is clear regarding the need for states to refrain from any unlawful acts; this obligation requires states not to allow their territory to be a platform for launching attacks and acts of aggression against other states, their territorial integrity, and their critical infrastructure, as stated in the well-known Tallinn Manual (Tallinn Manual 2.0, 2017).

Member states of the United Nations recognize that confronting the challenges facing global supply chains may be difficult to achieve at the global level; therefore, confrontation must begin at the regional level. There are many regional initiatives aimed at addressing this type of challenge facing the international economy. The Budapest Convention on cybercrime was concluded in 2001, and there are also UN efforts through what is known as the Group of Governmental Experts (UN GGE) as well as the Open-Ended Working Group (OEWG). Despite these initiatives, international law to this moment remains unable to confront these serious challenges facing global supply chains; the current international legal system is not capable of deterring such attacks (Tsagourias & Buchan, 2015).

Hence, the core importance of this research is that it focuses on highlighting the international legal dimensions of cybersecurity in the context of global supply chains and examining the adequacy of the existing legal arsenal to deter such attacks. There is no doubt that the issue of attributing responsibility to states remains a subject of disagreement and debate among many international legal observers; therefore, proposing practical solutions to confront such challenges remains a top priority in this research.

1. THE LEGAL NATURE OF CYBERATTACKS IN THE CONTEXT OF SUPPLY CHAINS

1.1 Preface

Many countries around the world have come to rely on artificial intelligence to manage ports, airports, and public services in order to facilitate service for beneficiaries. As a result, infrastructure and global supply chains in many countries—especially developed ones—have become closely tied to technology. What complicates the picture here is that supply chains are not merely the transport of goods from one country to another; rather, they are a complete system that involves the movement of goods from the origin or source to the end consumer through several integrated stages.

Accordingly, supply chains include production, distribution, and services until the product reaches the end consumer. They thus include the extraction of raw materials; international means of transport, whether ships, planes, or even trains or ports; as well as large storage centers, customs and border controls, warehouse management systems, and the private internet networks for tracking shipments until the commodity reaches the end consumer in markets and stores around the world.

To clarify further: if we take a phone manufactured in China, we must remember that the raw materials may come from several countries; manufacturing may be in one of the Chinese cities; shipping through a specific port; then it reaches Europe via ports and customs; it is distributed in online stores around the world; and finally reaches the consumer in the UAE. All these previous stages are an integral part of global supply chains. Therefore, any attack on any stage of these stages disrupts the supply chain—whether the attack occurs at the beginning of the chain or at its end.

This close interconnection between supply chains and technology has subjected them to a major challenge related to cybersecurity. This raises an extremely important issue: how can cyberattacks on systems connected to global supply chains be characterized from the perspective of international law?

1.2 Definition of Cyberattacks and Their Dimensions in the Field of Logistics

Let us agree on one point: up to this moment, there is no agreement among states on a uniform definition of cyberattacks in international law. However, legal experts consider that cyberattacks are "acts that aim to disrupt or destroy information systems or computer networks, leading to material damage or even functional damage" (Schmitt, 2017). It is necessary to point out here—when addressing supply chains—that the damage caused by cyberattacks may lead to a complete disruption of the movement of ships that transport containers, or even to the disruption of customs services, which in turn leads to a total or quasi-total disruption of local and international distribution services (Brewster, 2022).

The danger of cyberattacks in the context of supply chains is not only that they may lead to disrupting the movement of trade at the local level, but they may also have international repercussions. This is exactly what happened in 2017, when Maersk was subjected to a cyberattack that disrupted container management operations, which in turn affected the global supply network in more than 130 countries around the world (Greenberg, 2018). This leads us to ask: Can cyberattacks in the context of supply chains be considered acts of aggression as set out in the definition adopted by the UN General Assembly in its well-known Resolution 3314 (1974), which was reaffirmed in the context of the Rome Statute of the International Criminal Court? Can cyberattacks against supply chains be considered a violation of the UN Charter, specifically Article 2(4)?

1.3 The Legal Nature of Cyberattacks Against Global Supply Chains

We should begin by noting that explaining the legal nature of cyberattacks against global supply chains depends on the attack itself and the actor behind it. Accordingly, this type of attack moves between two fundamental classifications: on the one hand, it can be considered transnational criminal acts, and on the other hand, it can be considered a violation of state sovereignty. For this reason, the 2001 Convention, known as the Budapest Convention on Cybercrime, is considered the primary reference for clarifying the legal nature of such attacks.

There is no doubt that the Budapest Convention is one of the most important relevant international agreements that criminalize electronic and cyberattacks. This Convention obliges signatory states to criminalize specific acts such as unlawful access to systems, unlawful interception of data, manipulation of data or systems, and misuse of electronic devices or tools. The Convention also stipulates the need for states to cooperate with each other in extraditing criminals who participated in such criminal acts and prosecuting them wherever they are found. The Convention considers that any deliberate interference with the operation of information systems or disruption of them constitutes a cybercrime punishable by law. This, in turn, forms an important legal basis for combating cyberattacks, especially those directed against critical infrastructure or global supply chains (Council of Europe, 2001).

Despite the importance of the Budapest Convention—being open to all states—by 2025 the number of member states in this Convention was about 70 only, which limits its effectiveness.

In contrast to this Convention, international legal scholars often refer to what is known as the Tallinn Manual 2.0, which affirms that some cyberattacks—if they reach a certain level of damage—may rise to the level of use of force or even aggression, as affirmed by the jurist Schmitt (Schmitt, 2017). Based on the foregoing, the characterization of cyberattacks against supply chains depends fundamentally on the severity of the attack and the results of the attack. If the attack leads to loss of life or widespread destruction of infrastructure, we are most likely approaching the crime of aggression; whereas if the act is limited to damage to infrastructure and temporary disruption of supply chains, then we are most likely within the scope of cybercrimes or internationally wrongful acts (Tsagourias & Buchan, 2021).

1.4 The Difficulty of Attribution of Responsibility

The difficulty does not lie in characterizing the act as aggression or an unlawful act, but rather in identifying the entity behind the attack. The process of attributing the attack to a particular state or entity remains one of the most important legal dilemmas or problems—especially since some attacks may be directed by certain states even if they are carried out by private companies or criminal gangs, and this is where the problem lies.

If we return to the previous example of the Maersk shipping company in 2017, an accusation was directed at North Korea (Healey, 2019) for that attack; but who can assert, with absolute certainty and beyond any doubt, North Korea's responsibility? This issue leads us to the conclusion that proving state responsibility for unlawful acts remains complex, even though the International Law Commission affirmed legally in 2001 that states are responsible for any act committed by their organs or even their agents. Nevertheless, no state can prove that cyberattacks originated from a particular state due to the technical challenges known to all.

What Maersk experienced in 2017 reminds us of another famous incident in the Gulf region, when Saudi Aramco was subjected, in 2012, to an attack known as Shamoon, which led to the wiping of data on approximately 30,000 devices (Al-Rodhan, 2013). This attack—considered the largest in the history of the Gulf region—led to the disruption of oil infrastructure, which is an integral part of global energy supply chains. This matter was also confirmed by the Telecommunications and Digital Government Regulatory Authority (TDRA) in the United Arab Emirates in 2020, when it indicated that attacks on logistics systems in ports and airports pose an increasing threat to national security (Telecommunications and Digital Government Regulatory Authority [TDRA], 2020).

2. THE INTERNATIONAL LEGAL FRAMEWORK FOR CYBERSECURITY

2.1 The Principles of International Law Applicable to Cyberspace and Supply Chains

The general principles established by the Charter of the United Nations are agreed upon by all states, and these principles include the prohibition of interference in the internal affairs of states, the principle of respect for the sovereignty of states, the principle of the prohibition on the use of force in international relations, in addition to the principle of state responsibility for internationally wrongful acts.

It is important to note that the United Nations experts have confirmed, in more than one report — whether issued in 2015 or even in 2021 — the applicability of international law to cyberspace (UN GGE, 2015; UN GGE, 2021).

Therefore, the question of whether international law applies to cyberattacks has become an issue on which many international lawyers and experts agree. However, the remaining question is about the limits of the application of international law and how these rules apply to cyberattacks against supply chains.

The experts of the United Nations in 2015 confirmed through their reports that member states must not allow their territories to be used as a base for the launch of unlawful acts against other states (UN GGE, 2015). This prohibition undoubtedly includes cyberattacks against supply chains. Accordingly, this obligation pushes states to take all necessary measures to ensure the achievement of this objective.

It is worth emphasizing here the fact that states remain responsible for internationally wrongful acts committed by them, or even by their agents or entities under their control. States are therefore obliged to bear responsibility and to provide compensation for any damages that may affect other states as a result of such cyberattacks. This is what the International Law Commission confirmed (ILC, 2001).

However, the main dilemma in this matter lies in the difficulty of attribution and in proving that the act originated from that state, especially if the act was carried out through intermediaries or unknown terrorist groups.

2.2 International Law in Peace and Armed Conflicts: Where Do the Rules Intersect?

Cyberattacks that target global supply chains may occur during peacetime or may occur during wartime. Accordingly, the general principles governing international humanitarian law also apply to cyberattacks.

We have seen during the Russian-Ukrainian conflict that many cyberattacks targeting Ukraine have led to the disruption of supply chains throughout the country, particularly those related to grain exports, as Ukraine is one of the main grain-exporting countries in the world.

Therefore, the general principles governing international humanitarian law, whether the principle of distinction between civilians and combatants or the principle of precaution and care, undoubtedly apply to cyberattacks.

The International Committee of the Red Cross (ICRC, 2019) has confirmed this position on more than one occasion, especially regarding targets that have dual civilian and military use at the same time. If cyberattacks against military targets are considered acceptable, on the other hand, cyberattacks against targets that have both civilian and military characteristics remain a controversial issue among legal scholars.

2.3 The United Nations System: From "Voluntary Norms" to Progress Reports

The United Nations plays an important role in countering cyberattacks against global supply chains, as it has adopted many resolutions through the United Nations General Assembly encouraging states to combat this type of attack.

In 2015, the General Assembly adopted the well-known Resolution No. 70/237 (UNGA, 2015), in which it confirmed that the possibility of using technology for purposes inconsistent with the goals of international peace and security could negatively affect the safety of the basic infrastructures of states.

In this resolution, the General Assembly welcomed the conclusions reached by the Group of Governmental Experts (GGE) that international law, especially the Charter of the United Nations, applies to the use of information and communication technologies by states, which is necessary to preserve peace and stability.

The Assembly also emphasized the necessity of establishing norms, rules, and principles to guide state behavior in the use of ICTs, in order to reduce the risks that threaten international peace.

It is important to note that the United Nations, through that same resolution, adopted the report of the Group of Governmental Experts (GGE), which for the first time affirmed the applicability of international law to cyberspace, while setting standards for state behavior.

Despite the importance of the 2015 report of the GGE, the group issued, several years later — specifically in 2021 — another report (UN GGE, 2021) that added a practical dimension to the previous one.

This report emphasized the need for states to establish communication networks for rapid contact during crises and to exchange technical information regarding cyberattacks. These recommendations reflect the urgent need to ensure that international trade continues during cyberattacks targeting supply chain infrastructure.

In addition, the Open-ended Working Group (OEWG) played a direct role in developing the mechanisms necessary to limit cyberattacks against supply chains.

This group issued several annual reports reaffirming the principles agreed upon under international law, including the adoption of communication protocols among states and assistance to developing countries to confront such challenges, as developing countries represent the weakest link in the global cyber system (UN OEWG, 2021; UNGA, 2023).

By referring to the final report of the Open-ended Working Group — particularly its 2025 report — the group recommended the establishment of a permanent global mechanism to follow up on cyber issues related to international security instead of relying on temporary mechanisms.

It also encouraged allowing relevant non-governmental organizations to participate in public consultation sessions due to their importance in combating cybercrime (OEWG, 2021).

It is also worth mentioning that the UN committee responsible for negotiating the Convention on Countering Cybercrime has approved this Convention (Resolution 79/243), after several years of negotiations, especially amid the rapid developments in the global use of information technology for criminal and terrorist purposes. This Convention undoubtedly represents a major step toward enhancing international cooperation in combating cybercrime.

Once adopted, it will certainly become the most important legal achievement in recent years to address cybercrimes targeting global supply chains. The Convention provides special support to developing countries, and affirms the importance of international cooperation in exchanging electronic evidence and providing technical assistance in responding to cyberattacks.

The Convention will open for signature in Hanoi, Viet Nam, at the end of October 2025, but to enter into force, it requires 40 ratifications in accordance with Article 64 of the Convention.

It is noteworthy that the choice of Viet Nam as the venue for the signing ceremony was not accidental, as Viet Nam was among the most active states in the intergovernmental negotiation committee that drafted the Convention, and it also hosted the preparatory meetings for it.

2.4 The Legal Basis for Confronting Cyber Threats Against Supply Chains

Both at the regional and international level, numerous agreements and understandings exist regarding the legal framework to address cyber threats to global supply chains. These instruments establish concrete obligations, mechanisms of cooperation, and standards expected from states and private actors, rather than simply stating abstract principles. These different instruments together form an emerging body of "cyber law for supply chains" that works towards a goal of decreasing the vulnerability of cross-border trade, transport, and financial flows to digital attacks. In practice, this framework is still in development, and important discrepancies, along with inconsistencies between regions and sectors, remain. The growing density of conventions, directives, and soft-law instruments reflects a clear recognition that cyber threats are joining the most serious risks facing international logistics and trade networks.

At the forefront of such instruments is the Budapest Convention of 2001, which was adopted by the Council of Europe in 2001 and came into force in 2004. This Convention was the first binding international agreement specifically dedicated to cybercrime and remains a cornerstone for many national cybercrime laws around the world. It provides not only detailed definitions of various cyber offenses but also detailed rules on procedural powers, evidence gathering, and mutual legal assistance. Modern supply chains are highly digitalized because cargo tracking, customs clearance, and financial settlement processes depend on information systems. Therefore, the crimes defined in the Convention, like illegal access, data interference, and system interference, correspond directly to many of the attacks threatening ports, airports, shipping companies, warehouses, and logistics operators.

This Convention is built around four sets of key principles to combat cybercrime: harmonization of national laws, improvement of international cooperation, development of mechanisms of investigation, and protection of information infrastructure against cyberattacks. Harmonization tries to ensure that the same conduct-hacking into a port community system or altering electronic bills of lading-is criminalized in similar ways across states, reducing therefore "safe havens" for attackers. International cooperation is important because an attack against a node of a supply chain in one country might be orchestrated from another jurisdiction and routed through servers in several others. The development of mechanisms of investigation, such as expedited preservation of stored computer data and transborder access to evidence, allows law-enforcement authorities to respond quickly before data are deleted or moved. Finally, in emphasizing the protection of information infrastructure, the Convention recognizes that critical transport, customs, banking, and logistics systems must be considered as essential assets to which proactive cybersecurity measures-not just reactive criminal law tools-must be devoted. Notwithstanding the importance of the Budapest Convention, and the fact that it is open to all states, as of 2025, only about 70 state parties limit its effectiveness and leave many regions outside its direct scope, including several key trade and logistics hubs.

Apart from global conventions, there are more specialized regulatory tools formulated at regional organization levels, with a direct impact on transport, logistics, and related services. The European Union has issued several directives most recently, the NIS2 Directive, which requires many sectors to implement cybersecurity safety standards, notably for transport and logistics. This reflects EU recognition that disruptions to maritime shipping, air cargo, rail networks, road freight, and digital platforms can have cascading effects across its single market. It requires many companies to adopt extensive procedures to address any cyber risks, to report incidents within a specified period, and to impose penalties on companies failing to comply with these standards. These procedures include risk assessments, technical and organizational measures such as encryption and access control, incident response plans, and regular testing of security arrangements. More importantly, for operators of essential services, including major ports, air navigation providers, and energy pipelines, compliance is no longer a question of voluntary best practice but is mandatory by law.

These EU directives make dealing with cybersecurity not merely an option but a legal obligation, since breaches in global supply chains affect the European Union as a whole and not just individual states (European Union, 2022). For instance, a cyberattack on a port in one member state can disrupt supply chains feeding factories and consumers in several others. In this sense, the EU's approach resembles broader regulatory trends in other fields where legal reforms have sought to close gaps and clarify responsibilities in complex cross-border systems, such as banking and financial services (Awad et al., 2024; Aldabousi et al., 2025). With the imposition of harmonized minimum requirements on operators and linking non-compliance to administrative fines or other sanctions, the Union seeks to make cybersecurity a normal component of corporate governance in logistics, transport, and related digital services.

International organizations, mainly the IMO, have also adopted a number of resolutions to address cyber risks in specific sectors. The most important of these in the maritime field is Resolution MSC.428(98), which obliges all shipping companies and ports to integrate cybersecurity risks into their safety management systems. On the basis of this resolution, the management of cyber risks is no longer an independent or optional activity but should be embedded in the same framework governing traditional maritime safety, like collision avoidance, fire protection, and crew training. Management of cyber risk, therefore, has become part and parcel of the safety management of this organization - IMO (2017). For example, companies are required to evaluate the vulnerabilities of their shipboard and shore-based systems, elaborating policies for access control, updating software, and training seafarers and port staff to recognize and respond to cyber incidents. Such an integrated approach reflects the fact that a cyberattack on navigation or cargo handling systems can place at risk not only data but also human life and the marine environment.

The WCO has also enacted various guidelines to address the risks arising from the impacts of cyberattacks on supply chains. Customs agencies remain one of the critical entry points between national territories and international trade flows, and they increasingly depend on electronic declarations and risk-management systems, along with digital information exchanges with traders and other governments. Of particular note among the measures taken is the SAFE Framework of Standards that focuses not only on the security of physical cargo but extends the concept to include data and information security. The introduction of this framework brought mechanisms to ensure the flow of information between customs agencies and companies was secure, a way to prevent data manipulation or even hacking (WCO, 2025). For instance, it encourages the use of secure communication channels, including digital signatures and strict authentication mechanisms, in order to ensure that customs information can only be submitted or amended by authorized parties. By acknowledging that falsified or stolen information is as hazardous as stolen cargo, the WCO brings customs practices in line with wider cybersecurity approaches.

To this end, the WCO rewards businesses that demonstrate commitment to cybersecurity standards with certain facilitations through the AEO program, which encompasses customs facilitation in the form of fewer inspections and expedited border clearance. What this means, in practice, is a very positive incentive structure: the more a company invests in robust internal controls, including cyber controls, the more easily and predictably it can access global markets. Such incentive-based mechanisms mirror similar modalities in use elsewhere-for example, in marketing and consumer protection-whereby firms demonstrating compliance with legal and ethical standards can build stronger brand equity and trust (Awad & Aldabousi, 2024). In both contexts, the regulations are not solely punitive; rather, the approach here is supportive, rewarding businesses for going beyond the minimum requirements and anchoring security and compliance within their business models.

For their part, Arab states have adopted the Arab Convention on Combating Information Technology Offences, which constitutes a basis for judicial cooperation and information sharing between Arab states in fighting cybercrime. Though this Convention focuses on its criminal aspect, its implications reach the transport and trade sectors. In this regard, when a cyberattack is carried out against the information systems of a port, airport, shipping company, or customs authority in one Arab state, the perpetrators may be located in another state or might use infrastructure in a number of countries. The Convention allows for cooperation in investigation, extradition, and mutual legal assistance, thus helping to close the jurisdictional gaps that cyber attackers often seek to exploit. Over time, this framework can support the development of more detailed sector-specific guidelines and national laws that expressly address cyber risks in logistics, banking, and trade.

We must, by no means, tarry to forget initiatives that came, respectively, from the United Arab Emirates in 2019 under the name of the National Cybersecurity Strategy and the one by Saudi, which was called Essential Cybersecurity Controls;

it was issued in 2018. They are considered among the most serious initiatives of the Arab world because they power up the institutional frameworks for dealing with cybersecurity threats and their legal side. These national frameworks set control through detailed manners for government entities, operators of critical infrastructure, and sometimes private sector firms, including ones that work in transports, logistics, banking, and e-commerce. They cover topics such as governance, risk management, asset management, access control, incident response, business continuity, and awareness-raising. In this regard, UAE's efforts toward tightening the cybersecurity framework relate to wider legal reform efforts in the banking and financial sectors, such as measures towards closing loopholes in areas like deactivating dormancy conditions in accounts and renewing procedures to deal with financial risks (Awad et al., 2024). Saudi Arabia exhibits similar alignment in the link between cybersecurity policies, marketing strategies, and financial regulation, as shown in the push to underpin the goals of Vision 2030, building a resilient and trustworthy digital environment for investors, consumers, and international partners (Awad & Aldabousi, 2024; Aldabousi et al., 2025).

All these national initiatives demonstrate that the fight against cyber risks to supply chains cannot be left either to international conventions or to the activities of regional organizations. States must adopt their own detailed standards and controls, adapted to their traditions and economic priorities, but still meeting global best practices. In the Arab region, where trade, energy exports, and logistics play such a central role in national economies, the combination of regional conventions, national cybersecurity strategies, and sectoral regulations in banking, transport, and marketing is thus generating an increasingly coherent legal protective shield for digital supply chains.

3. PRACTICAL MECHANISMS FOR STRENGTHENING THE LEGAL PROTECTION OF SUPPLY CHAINS

After making it clear what the legal nature of cyberattacks is, and subsequently discussing the international legal framework, it is time to move to the practical side and focus on the mechanisms needed to enhance the legal protection of international supply chains in order to counter cyber threats. Not only binding international legal texts are needed, but also real operational mechanisms by which to put an end to these kinds of cyberattacks against the infrastructure of states and international supply chains. Conventions, directives, and strategies provide the "what" and "why," while without practical tools and institutional capacity, they will be under-implemented. There is also a need to focus on how to enhance the capacities of developing countries, as they represent the weakest link within these attacks. Attackers often target jurisdictions where regulatory oversight is weaker, technical defenses are limited, or coordination mechanisms are underdeveloped, using them as entry points into global supply networks.

Practical mechanisms must be engaged at a number of levels simultaneously. At the legal level, states should refresh their national legislation with international standards, clearly define the responsibilities of supply-chain players, and offer effective remedies in the event of cyber incidents. Included here is liability for data breaches or system failures, including provisions to ensure that contracts between shippers, carriers, logistics providers, and digital platform operators contain appropriate cybersecurity clauses. In this respect, other legal domains—banking, arbitration, and consumer protection, to name a few—do have experiences with valuable models for drafting balanced and enforceable rules (Awad et al., 2024; Awad & Aldabousi, 2024; Aldabousi et al., 2025). On the technical level, operators should implement risk-based cybersecurity controls and connect them with their existing safety, quality, and compliance systems. At the institutional level, coordination among regulators, law-enforcement agencies, and sectoral players is necessary to avoid overlaps, contradictions, or gaps in enforcement.

More effective dispute-resolution mechanisms will also be needed to strengthen the legal protection of supply chains. Cyber incidents-such as ransomware attacks on logistics management systems or manipulation of electronic documents-can lead to complex disputes among companies, insurers, and customers over responsibility and compensation. The creation of specialized arbitration and mediation frameworks, including Islamic banking and finance-specific variants, illustrates how legal systems can adapt to complex, technologically mediated disputes (Aldabousi et al., 2025). Similarly, the use of specialized mechanisms to address cyber-related supply-chain disputes could be promoted to ensure speedy, expert, and cross-border enforceable solutions complementary to traditional courts.

3.1 Reinforcing International and Regional Cooperation

Certainly, there are types of crimes that no state can face by itself, especially in the case of transnational crimes; cybercrimes cannot be countered with one nation acting singly but must be countered through the cooperation of international partners, since the results of cyberattacks against global supply chains affect the economy of the entire world. An attack on a container terminal in one country can delay shipments of raw materials or components needed in factories half a world away. Likewise, a breach of customs or banking systems in one jurisdiction can be used to commit fraud or launder money in several others. That is why international cooperation in confronting this type of attack is considered a fundamental pillar and top priority to reduce the damage and to put an end to such attacks.

The European Union is considered one of the leading models in cooperation to confront cybercrimes through the European Union Agency for Cybersecurity (ENISA), which is regarded as the backbone in facing and protecting ports and airports from digital attacks. This agency coordinates efforts among member states, supports the development of common strategies, and provides a central hub for expertise on evolving cyber threats. Although ENISA itself is not responsible for the prosecution of criminals, it acts as the executive authority within the European Union for confronting cyberattacks against supply chains. The agency issues periodic reports about the threats facing supply chains, and referring to these reports enables one to conclude that attacks on supply chains have grown to a doubling in recent years. These reports have underlined specific vulnerabilities, including dependence on third-party software, poor segregation between operational technology and information technology networks, and the increased reliance on cloud services to coordinate logistics.

These reports include risk assessments, while under the Cybersecurity Act and the European Directive, the agency has an essential role in setting the standards that companies—especially those in the energy, transport, and digital services sectors—must comply with in order to confront any type of attack against supply chains. ENISA contributes to the development of certification schemes and technical guidelines that detail what usually are broad legal obligations into concrete requirements for systems and products. The agency issues certifications to relevant entities regarding the security of supply chain equipment against hacking or tampering. According to ENISA (n.d.-a) and ENISA (2023), through these certification schemes, manufacturers and service providers should be able to demonstrate the assurance of predefined security criteria in their devices and platforms. This has the effect of engendering trust while reducing systemic risks in supply chains, which depend on interconnected digital components.

This agency also conducts numerous European exercises aimed at cyberattacks in supply chains, with the involvement of governments and companies, with the goal of establishing more robust responses to any cyberattack. Such exercises test communication channels, incident-response procedures, and decision-making processes under realistic scenarios, enabling participants to identify weaknesses before a real crisis actually occurs. Exercises also help operators in different sectors, such as ports, airlines, rail networks, customs, energy providers, and financial institutions, to collaborate and coordinate their responses. Since attacks on supply chains are cross-border in nature, this agency cooperates closely with international organizations, including sharing experience with its international counterparts. This can take the form of information exchange and sharing of best practices, joint research projects, and coordination of positions in international bodies engaged in setting standards.

For its part, the ASEAN believes that attacks on global supply chains are increasing, as reported by GovInsider (2025), and that they are not only a technical threat but also a strategic one to international trade in one of the most highly import- and export-dependent regions. Many of the economies of ASEAN states are highly dependent on manufacturing, logistics, and shipping, with many global supply chains using the region either as a production base or as a transit hub. For this reason, the Association considers cybersecurity directed against supply chains an integral part of its regional strategy. Rather than treating cybersecurity as an entirely national responsibility, ASEAN approaches it as a challenge that requires coordinated policy responses, information sharing, and joint capacity-building at the regional level.

Indeed, looking into the reports provided, it seems clear that digital supply chains represent one of the most important points of vulnerability that needs to be protected at the regional level of ASEAN, given the high dependence on electronic commerce. While online platforms, digital payment systems, and automated logistics networks provide the backbone for intra- and extra-regional trade, they also provide new attack surfaces. Consequently, the Association embarked on several initiatives of training national personnel on how to detect targeted intrusions into the chains of production, especially those with malware. In this way, such training programs equip officials and private sector specialists with relevant skills to analyze malware, recognize compromised systems, and take mitigating measures.

ASEAN also established a regional network of cybersecurity emergency response teams to share information on attacks against shipping companies, ports, and logistics services. These allow member states to share technical indicators of compromise rapidly, such as IP addresses and file hashes, which help coordinate responses to ongoing campaigns. In addition, the Association joined several joint training exercises and simulation drills for cyberattacks against transportation infrastructure. Such exercises serve to complement national efforts and ingrain a culture of preparedness whereby both governments and private operators are aware of their roles and responsibilities in a major incident.

While this Association bears significance on many counts, the recent study confirmed that one major challenge which it faces is the inequality in legislative frameworks between the different member states. No single legal system faces cybercrimes directed against supply chains, and there is a serious and pressing need for the development of a regional framework to counter the threats against supply chains (Ali et al., 2025). Whereas some of the states have modern laws on cybercrime and cybersecurity, others use general legislation which may not encompass contemporary forms of attack. This makes legal fragmentation an obstacle, for example, when there is a need to share evidence or track and prosecute attackers across borders. This challenge requires steps in building technical capacity, and equally important is the need for legislative reforms and model laws which states can apply within their national contexts. Notably, Arab states are not an exception to these cyberattacks targeting supply chains. The region comprises critical energy infrastructure, major seaports, and important aviation hubs-all very attractive targets for various cybercriminals and state-sponsored actors. Consequently, the ITU has initiated an event called the Cyber Drill for Arab States, in cooperation with national agencies from several Arab countries, aiming at training personnel in how to confront cyberattacks against sensitive sectors such as ports and logistics services. According to the ITU (2020), these Cyber Drills simulate complex multi-stage attacks which target different parts of the supply chain-from port management systems to customs databases and logistics platforms. Such exercises help participating states test their response procedures; enhance coordination among telecom regulators, national cybersecurity centers, and sector-specific authorities; and identify gaps in legal and institutional frameworks. Meanwhile, Arab states have been working to put the initiatives on cyber and supply-chain security in harmony with wider legal and economic reforms, especially regarding banking, arbitration, and digital marketing. Awad et al. (2024); Awad & Aldabousi (2024); Aldabousi et al. (2025) This integrated approach reflects a growing awareness that cybersecurity cannot be treated in isolation but must be embedded in the greater legal environment that governs trade, finance, and consumer relations. Strengthening international and regional cooperation, updating national laws, and building institutional and technical capacity will allow states and organizations to shift from fragmented responses to a more coherent and effective system of legal protection for global supply chains against cyber threats.

3.2 Integrating Cybersecurity Standards into Trade and Maritime Agreements

One of the main developments in countering cyberattacks against global supply chains lies in introducing and integrating cybersecurity standards into regional and international agreements, as such integration transforms digital security from mere recommendations into binding legal obligations among states.

It is well known that trade agreements in general, and maritime agreements in particular, are binding upon the member states that have signed and ratified them, as they are subject to the legal principle in international law known by the Latin expression pacta sunt servanda, meaning that agreements must be respected and implemented.

Accordingly, including a cybersecurity clause within such agreements transforms this clause from a recommendation into a legal rule, making it an integral part of states' legal obligations rather than a merely guiding provision. The North American continent provides a clear example of such integration.

By referring to the agreement signed between the United States, Mexico, and Canada, we find that this agreement, which entered into force in 2020, imposes an important obligation on states to protect the digital infrastructure of trade from cyberattacks, require companies to safeguard personal and commercial data, and enhance cooperation among these states to confront cyberattacks in online trade (Villareal & Fergusson, 2020).

This trilateral experience was not unique; the agreement signed between Japan and Singapore offers another example of incorporating data protection provisions against cyberattacks within treaty texts (ASEAN Secretariat, 2021).

Similarly, maritime agreements have begun to include cybersecurity standards within maritime safety requirements, such as the IMO Resolution MSC.428(98), which integrated cybersecurity into Safety Management Systems (ISM) for maritime navigation.

3.3 Capacity Building and the Protection of Developing Countries

The process of integrating developing countries into the technical and legal frameworks for confronting cyber threats is considered a fundamental pillar in supporting and protecting global supply chains. Some studies confirm that many cyberattacks on ports and airports target developing countries, as their technological infrastructure is very weak (Kuerbis & Badiei, 2021). Developing countries face three main challenges:

> First, the lack of investment in digital infrastructure—whether in ports or airports;
> Second, a shortage of qualified professionals in the field of cybersecurity;
> Third, the absence of modern legislation that imposes protection standards against cyberattacks.

By examining cyberattacks directed against supply chains in developing countries, it becomes clear that most of these attacks are either ransomware attacks, which involve shutting down port or shipping company systems and demanding ransom payments to restore operations; or attacks on customs systems to alter shipping data; or attacks on digital supply chains that target software service providers or communication systems for ports and airports.

In light of these facts, many programs have been adopted targeting developing countries, such as those funded by the World Bank to support cybersecurity in the transport and customs sectors (World Bank, 2022); those offered by the European

Union to build capacity in African countries (ENISA, 2022); and those provided by the International Telecommunication Union to train developing nations (ITU, 2020).

Based on the above, it is proposed to adopt an international protocol on cybersecurity related to supply chains, to be placed under the umbrella of an international organization—whether the United Nations, the World Trade Organization, or another relevant entity. It is also proposed, following the example of certain states, to integrate cybersecurity provisions into all commercial contracts, whether bilateral, regional, or international. In addition, certifications could be adopted for all economic operators, to be granted to private companies working within supply chains that comply with specific cybersecurity standards related to digital threats and cyberattacks.

CONCLUSION AND RECOMMENDATIONS

This research confirms that global supply chains constitute the backbone of international trade, and any assault on these chains—whether at their beginning or even at their end—and any cyberattacks constitute a threat to the global economy. Global supply chains have become hostage to technological development and artificial intelligence, and reliance on digital technologies has become an integral part of the global economy due to the tremendous advantages these technologies provide in terms of speed and efficiency. In return, it has become clear to us that this extensive reliance and this interconnection between supply chains and digital technology may be exposed to many risks, foremost among them cyberattacks, which have noticeably increased in recent years. Thus, supply chains have become the victim of many cyberattacks, and those chains have been disrupted on more than one occasion as a result of attacks whose sources are known or even unknown, which revealed the fragility of the infrastructure of those chains—whether ports, airports, or even customs.

We have clarified in this research that cyberattacks on supply chains are not merely technical problems, but are also legal problems. We have seen that an assault on those chains can be described as electronic crimes, yet it can rise to the level of use of force or even aggression depending on the nature of the assault. We have also seen that there is an international legal framework that addresses cyberattacks on supply chains through what is known as the Budapest Convention, or even the United Nations Convention on Cybercrime, which has not yet entered into force at this time. In my estimation, this international legal framework is deficient and contains many gaps, especially with regard to the issue of proving responsibility, which makes the current framework insufficient to confront cyberattacks. As for the last chapter, we focused on the practical mechanisms that must be taken by states in order to strengthen the protection granted to those chains by integrating cybersecurity into trade and maritime agreements, as well as assisting developing countries by all available means in order to confront the risks resulting from cyberattacks.

Based on the foregoing, the protection that must be afforded to global supply chains cannot be achieved through a single approach; rather, we need several levels of protection that integrate and cooperate with one another within the framework of international law, whether at the regional level or at the international level. Accordingly, we propose a set of recommendations that we consider necessary to achieve full and comprehensive protection for supply chains. The first of these proposals consists of the necessity of adopting an international protocol related to cybersecurity for supply chains under the umbrella of the United Nations or other relevant organizations. This protocol would constitute a relationship of complementarity between international law on the one hand, international trade on the other hand, and cybersecurity on a third hand. I propose that this protocol be under the umbrella of the United Nations with its two main branches—the General Assembly and the Security Council—since they are responsible for maintaining international peace and security. This protocol will affirm the legal basis upon which protection must be established in terms of respecting state sovereignty and non-interference, but in return there is a duty upon states to undertake not to allow the use of their territories to launch cyberattacks on global supply chains, under penalty of legal responsibility. My proposal to establish and adopt such a protocol would amount to establishing a clear international legal obligation with well-defined contours to protect supply chains in all their components—whether ports or airports, customs systems, energy networks, or multinational companies linked to global supply chains. In my view, if such a protocol is adopted, it will unify all the existing international standards that are currently scattered across different continents and will bridge the gap between security and trade. I know with certainty that such a proposal may not be acceptable to some states, especially since they may see in it a threat to their national sovereignty; nevertheless, I believe that adopting this protocol will achieve many benefits compared to the drawbacks that some states might advance to reject such proposals.

REFERENCES

Al-Rodhan, N. (2013). *Cybersecurity and cyberwarfare: The need for a new UN convention*. Geneva Centre for Security Policy.

Aldabousi, A. M., Awad, A., Hassan, H. E. M., Abdullah, S. S., & Ghonim, A. (2025). Arbitration in Islamic banking: Exploring legal and practical implications for dispute resolution. *Banks and Bank Systems*, *20*(2), 15–26. DOI: 10.21511/bbs.20(2).2025.02

Ali, A. S., ... (2025). *Advancing cybersecurity in ASEAN: Current trends and challenges. International Journal of Information Security*. https://link.springer.com/article/10.1007/s10207-025-01111-2

ASEAN. (2022, January 28). *ASEAN Cybersecurity Cooperation Strategy 2021–2025*. https://asean.org/wp-content/uploads/2022/02/01-ASEAN-Cybersecurity-Cooperation-Paper-2021-2025_final-23-0122.pdf

Awad, A., Al-fil, N. Z., Dganni, K. M., Aldabousi, A. M., & Obeidat, M. A. (2024). Optimizing dormant account management in UAE banking: Legal gaps and proposed reforms. *Banks and Bank Systems*, *19*(4), 124–135. DOI: 10.21511/bbs.19(4).2024.10

Awad, A., & Aldabousi, A. M. (2024). Analyzing the impact of viral marketing on brand equity dimensions in Egypt's home appliances sector: A customer and legal perspective. *Innovative Marketing*, *20*(4), 100–111. DOI: 10.21511/im.20(4).2024.09

Bode, C., & Wagner, S. M. (2015). Structural drivers of upstream supply chain complexity and the frequency of supply chain disruptions. *Journal of Operations Management*, *36*(1), 215–228.

Brewster, T. (2022). *Cyberattacks on supply chains: The hidden threat to global trade. Forbes*. https://www.forbes.com

Council of Europe. (2001). *Convention on Cybercrime (Budapest Convention)*. Council of Europe.

Craighead, C. W., Ketchen, D. J.Jr, & Darby, J. L. (2020). Pandemics and supply chain management research: Toward a theoretical toolbox. *Decision Sciences*, *51*(4), 838–866. PMID: 34234384

Dragos. (2023). *OT cybersecurity breach disrupts operations at the Port of Nagoya, Japan*.

ENISA. (2022). *Cybersecurity in ports and maritime logistics*. European Union Agency for Cybersecurity.

ENISA. (2023, June 13). *Good practices for supply chain cybersecurity.* European Union Agency for Cybersecurity. https://www.enisa.europa.eu/publications/good-practices-for-supply-chain-cybersecurity

ENISA. (n.d.-a). *Threat landscape for supply chain attacks.* European Union Agency for Cybersecurity. https://www.enisa.europa.eu/publications/threat-landscape-for-supply-chain-attacks

ENISA. (n.d.-b). *NIS2 technical implementation guidance.* European Union Agency for Cybersecurity. https://www.enisa.europa.eu/publications/nis2-technical-implementation-guidance#contentList

European Union. (2022). *Directive (EU) 2022/2555 (NIS2) on measures for a high common level of cybersecurity across the Union. Official Journal of the European Union, L333*, 80–152.

GovInsider Asia. (2025, July 14). *Tackling supply chain cybersecurity in Southeast Asia.* https://govinsider.asia/intl-en/article/tackling-supply-chain-cybersecurity-in-southeast-asia

Greenberg, A. (2018). *Sandworm: A new era of cyberwar and the hunt for the Kremlin's most dangerous hackers*. Doubleday.

Healey, J. (2019). *A fierce domain: Conflict in cyberspace, 1986 to 2012*. Cyber Conflict Studies Association.

ICRC. (2019). *International humanitarian law and cyber operations during armed conflicts (Position paper).*

IMO. (2017). *Resolution MSC.428(98): Maritime cyber risk management in safety management systems.*

International Law Commission (ILC). (2001). *Responsibility of States for internationally wrongful acts*. United Nations.

International Telecommunication Union (ITU). (2020). *Arab States cyber drill report*. ITU.

Kuerbis, B., & Badiei, F. (2021). Cyber capacity building: A development agenda for cybersecurity. *Journal of Cyber Policy*, *6*(1), 1–20.

Maersk. (2018). *Annual report 2018: Learning from the NotPetya cyberattack.* Copenhagen: A.P. Moller–Maersk Group.

NATO Cooperative Cyber Defence Centre of Excellence (NATO CCDCOE). (2019). *Case study: NotPetya and the lessons for national cybersecurity*. NATO CCDCOE.

Schmitt, M. N. (Ed.). (2017). *Tallinn Manual 2.0 on the international law applicable to cyber operations*. Cambridge University Press.

Secretariat, A. S. E. A. N. (2021). *ASEAN Cybersecurity Cooperation Strategy*. ASEAN Secretariat.

NTT Security. (2023). *Cyber security reports – July 2023.*

Singapore, C. S. A. (2021, October 11). *16th iteration of ASEAN CERT incident drill tests responding to supply chain attacks.* https://www.csa.gov.sg/news-events/news-articles/csa-hosts-16th-iteration-of-asean-cert-incident-drill

Telecommunications and Digital Government Regulatory Authority (TDRA). (2020). *Annual cybersecurity report*. UAE Government.

Tsagourias, N., & Buchan, R. (2015). *Research handbook on international law and cyberspace*. Edward Elgar Publishing.

Tsagourias, N., & Buchan, R. (2021). *Cyber interventions and international law*. Cambridge University Press.

UK Foreign and Commonwealth Office. (2018, February 15). *UK condemns Russia for NotPetya cyber-attack.* https://www.gov.uk/government/news/foreign-office-minister-condemns-russia-for-notpetya-attacks

UN GGE. (2015). *Report of the Group of Governmental Experts on developments in the field of information and telecommunications in the context of international security (A/70/174).*

UN GGE. (2021). *Advancing responsible state behaviour in cyberspace in the context of international security (A/76/135).*

UN OEWG. (2021). *Final substantive report (A/75/816).*

UNGA. (2015). *Developments in the field of information and telecommunications in the context of international security (A/RES/70/237).*

UNGA. (2023). *Second annual progress report of the OEWG 2021–2025 (A/RES/78/237).*

Villareal, M. A., & Fergusson, I. F. (2020). *The United States-Mexico-Canada Agreement (USMCA)*. Congressional Research Service.

WCO. (2021/2025). *SAFE Framework of Standards to Secure and Facilitate Global Trade*. World Customs Organization.

World Bank. (2022). *Cybersecurity capacity building in critical infrastructure: Transport and customs*. World Bank.

Chapter 4
The Digital Immune System:
Trust, Security, and AI Governance

Suzan Fouad Bakr
https://orcid.org/0009-0003-8104-7328
Faculty of Commerce, Al-Azhar University, Egypt

Roba Gamal
https://orcid.org/0000-0003-3525-2550
Faculty of Engineering, Cairo University, Egypt

Abdelrhman A. Gamil
https://orcid.org/0009-0007-8680-5182
Faculty of Engineering, Ain Shams University, Egypt

ABSTRACT

As AI agents increasingly manage global supply chains, traditional security and governance are becoming obsolete, creating systemic risks from opaque algorithms and new cyber-physical attack surfaces. This chapter argues that robust governance enables innovation and is a source of competitive advantage. We introduce the "Digital Immune System," a proactive framework to manage threats in real-time, and posit Explainable AI (XAI) as the essential foundation for transparency and human oversight. After analyzing the modern threat landscape, a multi-pillar governance model is proposed, built on accountability, security-by-design, and human-in-the-loop supervision. The chapter also examines the emerging "Governance-as-a-Service" market. The core argument is that architecting for trust is no longer a compliance exercise but a strategic imperative that builds resilience and accelerates the adoption of a secure, autonomous future.

DOI: 10.4018/979-8-3373-8841-0.ch004

INTRODUCTION

The global supply chain is undergoing a profound transformation, moving from data-assisted human decisions to AI-led autonomous operations. This new frontier promises unprecedented efficiency and resilience, with systems that can autonomously reroute shipments, preempt bottlenecks, and adjust production based on real-time signals. However, delegating critical decisions to autonomous AI agents introduces insidious systemic risks. The core challenge is a tension between autonomy and transparency, accountability, and security. Opaque algorithms, or "black boxes," can make high-stakes decisions without a clear rationale, while the integration of cyber-physical systems expands the attack surface, blurring the lines between digital threats and real-world consequences. Figure 1 shows a conceptual info graphic of the Digital immune system.

Figure 1. A conceptual info graphic of the digital immune system

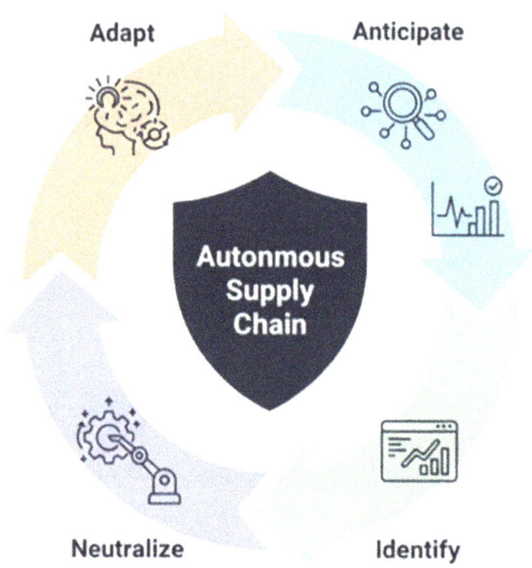

These challenges demand a new approach to governance, woven into the fabric of the autonomous supply chain from the outset. This chapter argues that architecting for trust through transparency, security, and accountability is not a constraint on innovation but its most critical enabler. To achieve this, we introduce the concept of a Digital Immune System. Like its biological counterpart, this system is a dynamic and adaptive framework designed to protect the entire autonomous ecosystem. It learns, identifies threats, neutralizes them, and remembers them to prevent future attacks. This chapter provides a comprehensive framework for building such a system, ensuring the autonomous supply chain is not only intelligent but also transparent, accountable, and secure by design.

The Trust Imperative: Mandating Transparency with Explainable AI (XAI)

As AI agents are entrusted with decisions involving millions of dollars and critical supplier relationships, the question "Why?" becomes paramount when failures occur. If the answer is simply "because the algorithm decided so," trust evaporates. This is the essence of the "black box" problem, where the complexity of powerful AI models renders their reasoning opaque. This opacity is a critical vulnerability that undermines an autonomous system, making it impossible to audit logic, correct errors, or assign accountability.

Explainable AI (XAI) is the non-negotiable solution, providing techniques to produce human-understandable explanations for AI model outputs (Gunning and Aha, 2019). XAI provides the diagnostic visibility needed to ensure the system is healthy and operating as intended. Explainability is a strategic imperative for human oversight, regulatory compliance under frameworks like the EU's AI Act (Aldabousi et,al,. 2025), and building trust with all stakeholders (Jobin et al., 2019; Adadi and Berrada, 2018; Owens et al., 2022).

Why Explainability is a Strategic Non-Negotiable

The need for explainability extends across multiple domains of the supply chain ecosystem, each with its own compelling justification:

1. **Human Oversight and Intervention**: As we move towards a "human-in-the-loop" or "human-on-the-loop" model of oversight, the human operator must be empowered to effectively supervise the AI. If an AI recommends a radical and counterintuitive action, such as shifting production from a high-performing factory to a new, untested one, the human supervisor needs more than just the recommendation; they need the rationale. An XAI system could reveal that the AI's decision was based on a sophisticated analysis of long-term geopolitical risk, projected labor shortages, and

shifting trade policies—factors a human might have overlooked. This context allows the human to make an informed decision: either to approve the AI's recommendation or to override it, armed with a deeper understanding of the situation Adadi and Berrada, 2018

2. **Regulatory Compliance and Audibility**: The global regulatory landscape for AI is rapidly evolving. Landmark frameworks like the European Union's AI Act impose stringent transparency and documentation requirements on "high-risk" AI systems, which would almost certainly include those managing critical infrastructure like supply chains. In the event of an incident—such as a major disruption or a safety violation caused by an autonomous system—regulators will demand a full accounting of the system's behavior. Organizations that cannot provide a clear, auditable trail of their AI's decision-making process will face severe legal and financial penalties. XAI provides the mechanism for generating this evidence, turning the black box into a glass box that can be inspected by internal auditors and external regulators alike Jobin et al., 2019.
3. **Stakeholder Trust and Adoption**: Building and maintaining trust is paramount for the successful adoption of any new technology. This includes trust from internal stakeholders (employees who must work alongside AI systems), external partners (suppliers and logistics providers who must interact with them), and customers who rely on their outputs. When an autonomous inventory management system consistently prioritizes one supplier over another, for instance, the disfavored supplier will demand to know why. An XAI-powered explanation showing that the decision was based on objective metrics like on-time delivery rates, quality control scores, and transportation costs can defuse a potentially contentious situation and preserve the business relationship Owens et al., 2022.

Key XAI Techniques in Practice: Deconstructing the Black Box

While the field of XAI is broad and rapidly advancing, several core techniques have emerged as particularly valuable for supply chain applications. These methods can be broadly categorized as either model-agnostic (meaning they can be applied to any type of AI model) or model-specific. Here, we focus on two of the most prominent and versatile model-agnostic techniques: LIME and SHAP.

- **LIME (Local Interpretable Model-agnostic Explanations)** LIME operates on a simple but powerful principle: while a complex model's global behavior may be impossible to understand, its behavior in the immediate vicinity of a single prediction can be approximated by a much simpler, interpretable model Ribeiro et al., 2016. In essence, LIME explains an individual prediction by answering the question: "What were the most important features that led to this specific outcome?"

How it Works. To explain a prediction, LIME creates a new dataset of small variations, or "perturbations," of the original data point. It then feeds these new data points to the black-box model to see how the predictions change. Finally, it fits a simple, interpretable model (like a linear regression or a decision tree) to this localized dataset, weighted by how close the perturbed points are to the original .The features of this simple model then serve as the explanation.

Supply Chain Application. Consider an AI-powered demand forecasting model that predicts an unexpected 200% surge in demand for a particular product in a specific region. A supply chain planner would be hesitant to act on this prediction without understanding its basis. Using LIME, the system could generate an explanation highlighting the key drivers for that single forecast:

- **Feature 1 (Positive Influence)**: A sudden spike in social media mentions of the product from influencers in that region.
- **Feature 2 (Positive Influence)**: Unseasonably warm weather patterns in the region, which historically correlate with higher sales.
- **Feature 3 (Negative Influence)**: A competitor's recent price reduction, which slightly tempered the predicted surge. This local explanation gives the planner the context needed to trust the forecast and take appropriate action, such as increasing inventory levels in that region.
    - **SHAP (SHapley Additive exPlanations)** SHAP is a more sophisticated technique rooted in cooperative game theory. It provides a unified framework for explainability that can be used for both local and global explanations. The core idea behind SHAP is to calculate the marginal contribution of each feature to the final prediction, ensuring that the explanations are both consistent and locally accurate Lundberg and Lee, 2017. The "Shapley value" for each feature represents its contribution to pushing the model's output away from the baseline or average prediction.

How it Works: SHAP calculates the contribution of a feature by considering all possible combinations (coalitions) of features. It then evaluates the model's prediction with and without that specific feature in each coalition and averages the difference. This process results in a SHAP value for every feature for every prediction. Positive SHAP values indicate features that pushed the prediction higher, while negative values indicate features that pushed it lower.

Supply Chain Application: Imagine an autonomous procurement agent decides against renewing a contract with a long-term supplier. This is a strategically significant decision with major relationship implications. SHAP can provide a comprehensive explanation by breaking down the factors that contributed to the final "risk score" assigned to that supplier. A SHAP force plot could visualize the explanation:

- Features Pushing Risk Score Higher (Negative Factors):
  * on time delivery rate fell from 98% to 92% over the last quarter.
  * quality failure incidents increased by 15%.
  * supplier financial stability index was downgraded by a credit agency.
- Features Pushing Risk Score Lower (Positive Factors):
  * cost per unit remains 5% below the market average.
  * long term relationship discount is still in effect.

This detailed, feature-level attribution provides an unambiguous and defensible rationale for the AI's recommendation. Furthermore, by aggregating SHAP values across thousands of decisions, the organization can gain a global understanding of its procurement model, identifying the most important factors driving its supplier evaluations overall.

Table 1 shows different XAI techniques and the differences between their core principles, limitations along with supply chain examples for using it.

Table 1. A comparison of key XAI techniques, their core principles, and their applications and limitations within the supply chain

Technique	Type	Core Principle	Best For	Supply Chain Example	Limitations
LIME	Model-Agnostic, Local	Approximates a black-box model's behavior around a single prediction using a simpler, interpretable local model.	Quickly explaining individual, specific predictions in a human-understandable way.	Explaining why a single shipment was flagged as high-risk for delay.	Can be unstable; small changes in the input can lead to very different explanations. Only provides local, not global, insights.
SHAP	Model-Agnostic, Local & Global	Uses Shapley values from cooperative game theory to fairly distribute the "payout" (the prediction) among the features.	Providing mathematically robust and consistent explanations for both individual predictions and the overall model behavior.	Determining the exact contribution of factors like fuel price, traffic, and vehicle maintenance to a route optimization decision.	Computationally expensive, especially for models with a large number of features. Explanations can sometimes be less intuitive for non-technical users.
Anchors	Model-Agnostic, Local	Identifies a set of "if-then" rules or conditions (the anchor) that are sufficient to lock in the prediction, even if other features change.	Identifying the minimum set of conditions that guarantee a specific outcome, providing clear and precise rules.	Finding the rule that an AI uses to approve a supplier, e.g., "IF iso_9001_certified = TRUE AND delivery_rate > 95%, THEN approve."	The identified rules may be overly specific and not generalizable. Can be slow to compute.
Integrated Gradients	Model-Specific (Differentiable Models), Local	Calculates the contribution of each feature by accumulating the gradients of the model's output with respect to the feature's input along a path.	Explaining deep learning models (e.g., in computer vision for quality control) by highlighting which input pixels were most important.	Highlighting the specific area of a product image that led a computer vision model to classify it as "defective."	Only applicable to models where gradients can be calculated, such as neural networks.

The Business Value of Transparency: From Compliance to Competitive Advantage

Ultimately, embracing XAI is not merely a defensive maneuver to mitigate risk and ensure compliance. It is a strategic investment that yields tangible business value. By making AI systems transparent and auditable, organizations can:

- **Accelerate Innovation and Adoption**: Development teams can use XAI insights to debug and improve their models more effectively. When a model makes an incorrect prediction, explainability tools can pinpoint the cause, allowing for faster iteration cycles.
- **Enhance Human-AI Collaboration**: When human operators trust the tools they are given, they are more likely to use them effectively. XAI builds this trust by turning the AI from an opaque oracle into a collaborative partner that provides not just answers, but also reasoning.
- **Create Demonstrable and Marketable Trust**: In an increasingly competitive landscape, the ability to prove that your autonomous systems are fair, reliable, and accountable becomes a powerful differentiator. Companies that can offer their customers and partners a "glass box" view into their operations will be seen as more trustworthy and will be preferred in a risk-averse market.

In conclusion, the trust imperative demands that we move beyond the era of black-box AI. Explainability is the foundational layer of the digital immune system, providing the visibility and understanding necessary to manage the complex, high-stakes environment of the autonomous supply chain. It transforms trust from an abstract ideal into a measurable, manageable, and demonstrable asset.

THE NEW CYBER-PHYSICAL THREAT LANDSCAPE

The autonomous supply chain dissolves the boundary between digital systems and the physical world, creating a deeply interconnected cyber-physical ecosystem. This expanded attack surface gives rise to novel threats that can cascade from code to catastrophic real-world consequences. This threat landscape has two primary vectors: cyber-physical attacks on infrastructure and AI-specific attacks on the models themselves.

Vector 1: Cyber-Physical Attacks

These attacks leverage digital vulnerabilities to manipulate physical processes.

- **Hijacking and Spoofing**: Malicious actors can use GPS spoofing to misdirect autonomous trucks or drones to steal cargo or cause disruption.
- **Sensor Blinding**: High-powered lasers or jammers can blind cameras and LiDAR sensors, potentially causing collisions or paralyzing logistics corridors (Mashaile, 2025).

- **Operational Sabotage**: Hacking into a smart warehouse's management system could halt robotic operations, introduce subtle inventory errors, or override safety protocols, causing physical damage or injury (Cart.com, 2024; SecuriThings, n.d.).

Vector 2: AI-Specific Attacks

These insidious attacks target the AI models and their "AI supply chain" of data and pre-trained components.

- **Data and Model Poisoning:** Attackers can poison training data by, for example, uploading thousands of images of defective products labeled as "high quality." An AI trained on this data would learn to accept faulty goods (Datadog, 2023). Similarly, attackers can upload compromised "Trojan" models to public repositories, embedding malware or backdoors directly into an organization's systems (Oliveira and Fiser, 2025).
- **Third-Party Vulnerabilities:** Integrating AI services from vendors means inheriting their security posture. These "black box" solutions may have been built with insecure practices or lack the transparency needed for proper risk assessment (Cobalt.io, 2025; Traxtech, 2025).

Table 2 summarizes the new potential risks affecting supply chains.

Table 2. A categorization of new threats in the autonomous supply chain, detailing the vectors, descriptions, potential impacts, and example scenarios

Threat Category	Attack Vector	Description	Potential Impact	Example Scenario
Cyber-Physical Attacks	Asset Hijacking	Exploiting navigation or communication systems to take unauthorized control of autonomous vehicles or drones.	Theft of cargo, operational disruption, physical damage, or espionage.	GPS spoofing is used to divert a convoy of autonomous trucks carrying high-value goods to a location controlled by attackers.
	Sensor Manipu- lation	Blinding, jamming, or feeding false data to critical sensors (e.g., LiDAR, cameras) to induce incorrect behavior.	Vehicle collisions, paralysis of logistics corridors, or workplace accidents.	An attacker uses a laser to blind warehouse AGV sensors, causing collisions and halting internal logistics.
	Infrastructure Sabotage	Accessing smart warehouse or port management systems to disrupt operations.	Shutdowns, manipulated inventories, or delays across the supply chain.	A hacker breaches a port's crane control software, causing a major bottleneck in cargo movement.
AI-Specific At- tacks	Data Poisoning	Corrupting the training data of an AI model to embed hidden biases or backdoors.	Erroneous decision-making, financial loss, or reputational damage.	Attackers poison a public dataset so that a quality control AI ignores a certain defect type.
	Model Poisoning (Trojan Attack)	Distributing a pre-trained AI model containing hidden malicious code.	Data exfiltration, network infiltration, or total system compromise.	A developer downloads a language model that secretly exfiltrates sensitive shipment data.
	Third-Party AI Vulnerabilities	Using vendor AI systems with insecure dependencies or poor data handling.	Data breaches, compliance failures, or inherited security risks.	A logistics company integrates a third-party AI for dynamic pricing that leaks proprietary data.

The emergence of these dual threat vectors underscores the need for a paradigm shift in supply chain security. A digital immune system cannot be limited to protecting traditional IT networks. It must extend its vigilance to the entire cyber-physical domain, from the sensors on a delivery drone to the integrity of the data used to train a forecasting model. It requires a holistic, defense-in-depth strategy that anticipates and mitigates threats across this new, complex, and deeply interconnected landscape.

REAL-WORLD CASE STUDIES: THE DIGITAL IMMUNE SYSTEM IN ACTION

To bridge the gap between theory and practice, it is instructive to examine how leading organizations are already implementing elements of a Digital Immune System, even if they do not use that specific terminology. These case studies highlight the tangible benefits and practical challenges of building trust and resilience in highly automated supply chains.

Case Study 1: Amazon's Kiva Systems and the AI-Powered Fulfillment Center

Amazon's fulfillment centers are a marvel of modern logistics, where thousands of robotic drive units, known as Kiva robots, navigate a dense, dynamically changing environment to bring products to human pickers. This system offers a compelling example of a highly evolved, albeit centralized, Digital Immune System.

Anticipate and Identify: Amazon's inventory management system uses sophisticated predictive analytics to anticipate demand, positioning products in warehouses across the country based on a vast array of signals, from historical sales data to current browsing trends. Within the fulfillment center, the system constantly monitors the health and performance of each Kiva robot, identifying anomalies that could indicate a mechanical failure or a software glitch.

Neutralize and Adapt: If a robot begins to behave erratically, the central control system can immediately isolate it, taking it out of commission and rerouting other robots to cover its tasks, thus neutralizing the disruption. The system also adapts in real-time to the physical environment. If a pathway becomes blocked, the robots communicate this information to the network, and all other units will dynamically find new routes.

Analysis and Lessons Learned: Amazon's success demonstrates the power of a centrally controlled, continuously monitored autonomous system. However, it also highlights a potential vulnerability: its reliance on a centralized "brain." While highly efficient, this architecture could be a single point of failure if compromised. The "immune response" is robust but centrally dictated, lacking the decentralized resilience that a more distributed system might offer. This case illustrates the trade-offs between centralized efficiency and decentralized robustness, a key consideration in designing a Digital Immune System.

Case Study 2: Ocado's Smart Platform and the Hive-Mind Warehouse

The UK-based online grocer Ocado has developed one of the world's most advanced automated warehouse systems. Thousands of cubic robots zip across a massive grid, or "hive," to collect grocery items, collaborating to fulfill customer orders with remarkable speed and accuracy.

Decentralized Coordination: Unlike the more centralized Kiva system, Ocado's robots exhibit a form of swarm intelligence. They communicate with each other peer-to-peer to deconflict paths and optimize the overall flow of the grid. This decentralized approach makes the system incredibly resilient. If one robot fails, the others simply work around it, and the collective hive continues to function with only a marginal loss of efficiency.

Digital Twin and Proactive Maintenance: Ocado employs a sophisticated "digital twin" of its entire warehouse operation. This real-time virtual model allows them to simulate changes, test new algorithms, and, crucially, run predictive maintenance. By analyzing the data from thousands of robots, the system can predict when a component is likely to fail and schedule maintenance before a breakdown occurs, embodying the proactive risk management pillar of the Digital Immune System.

Analysis and Lessons Learned: Ocado's model is a powerful example of a decentralized and adaptive immune response. The system's resilience comes from the bottom up, with individual agents collaborating to maintain the health of the whole. This approach offers greater robustness against single-point failures. The use of a digital twin for continuous monitoring and simulation is a best-in-class example of proactive risk management and provides a blueprint for how organizations can test their systems' resilience to various shocks and threats in a safe, virtual environment.

These case studies reveal that while the concept of a holistic Digital Immune System is new, its core principles are already being put into practice by innovators in the field. They underscore the importance of continuous monitoring, dynamic adaptation, and proactive risk management, while also presenting different architectural philosophies—centralized versus decentralized—that organizations must consider when designing their own systems.

RECENT ADVANCEMENTS AND THE FUTURE OF THE DIGITAL IMMUNE SYSTEM

The field of AI is evolving at a breathtaking pace, and a forward-looking framework like the Digital Immune System must account for emerging technologies that will shape the future of the autonomous supply chain. This section explores recent advancements and their implications for building more intelligent, resilient, and trustworthy systems (Shams Eldin et.al., 2025; Mahmoud et.al., 2025)

Federated Learning for Enhanced Privacy and Security

One of the significant challenges in training robust AI models is the need for vast and diverse datasets. However, sharing sensitive logistics data between organizations or across borders raises significant privacy and security concerns. Federated learning offers a promising solution. In this approach, a central model is trained by aggregating insights from decentralized models that are trained locally on edge devices (e.g., in a specific warehouse or on an autonomous truck). The key is that the raw data never leaves its source; only the model updates are shared.

- **Implications for the Digital Immune System**: Federated learning strengthens the immune system in two ways. First, it enhances security by minimizing the attack surface; there is no central repository of sensitive data to target. Second, it allows for the development of more robust and accurate models by enabling collaboration across a wider ecosystem without compromising data privacy. This move to the edge is empowered by next-generation communication technologies like 6G, which are designed to support massive-scale IoT, ultra-low latency, and AI processing directly at the edge, forming the backbone of future smart city logistics (Mohapatra, 2025, pp. 231–254).

Generative AI and Synthetic Data for Proactive Red Teaming

Generative AI, particularly the development of Generative Adversarial Networks (GANs), has profound implications for proactive risk management. GANs consist of two neural networks—a generator and a discriminator—that compete with each other. The generator creates synthetic data (e.g., fake sensor readings or fraudulent shipping manifests), and the discriminator tries to distinguish it from real data.

- **Implications for the Digital Immune System**: This technology can be used to supercharge AI red teaming. Instead of relying solely on human experts to devise attack scenarios, a generative AI can be trained to create a continuous stream of novel and sophisticated synthetic attacks. This automated, real-time red teaming allows the Digital Immune System to constantly test its defenses against an evolving threat landscape, identifying and patching vulnerabilities before they can be exploited by real-world adversaries. Furthermore, the ability to fine-tune these large models for specific industrial domains, such as adapting them to the unique terminology of logistics or finance, is a critical component of their practical application and security (Mohapatra, 2025, pp. 263–284).

Causal AI: Moving From Correlation to True Understanding

Most current AI models are based on correlation; they are exceptionally good at identifying patterns in data but do not understand the underlying causal relationships. This is a significant limitation, as a model might learn a spurious correlation that leads to poor decision-making when circumstances change. Causal AI is an emerging field that aims to build models that can reason about cause and effect.

- **Implications for the Digital Immune System**: Causal AI has the potential to dramatically enhance the transparency and robustness of the system. An XAI system built on a causal model could provide much deeper and more intuitive explanations, moving beyond "this decision was made because of features A, B, and C" to "this decision was made because A *causes* X, which in turn *causes* Y." This would provide human operators with a true understanding of the AI's reasoning. Furthermore, causal models are inherently more robust to changes in the environment, making them less susceptible to being fooled by unexpected events or adversarial attacks, thereby strengthening the overall resilience of the supply chain. The work by Dhanorkar et al. (2025) on AI-driven decision-making in retail provides valuable insights into how causal reasoning can be applied to optimize inventory and pricing strategies, showcasing the practical benefits of moving beyond correlational models.

These advancements are not futuristic fantasies; they are active areas of research and development that will become integral to the next generation of autonomous systems. A forward-thinking organization must not only build a Digital Immune System based on today's technology but also design it to be modular and adaptable, ready to incorporate these and other future breakthroughs to ensure its long-term resilience.

A MULTI-PILLAR FRAMEWORK FOR AI GOVERNANCE AND ASSURANCE

In the face of an evolving threat landscape and the profound ethical and operational questions raised by autonomous decision-making, a reactive security posture is a recipe for disaster. A resilient autonomous supply chain requires a proactive, comprehensive, and deeply embedded framework for governance and assurance.

This is the central nervous system of the digital immune system—the set of policies, processes, and technical controls that directs its behavior and ensures it operates safely, ethically, and in alignment with organizational goals. Drawing on guidance from leading standards bodies like the National Institute of Standards and Technology (NIST) and the Institute of Electrical and Electronics Engineers (IEEE), we propose a governance model built on four essential pillars shown in figure 2. These pillars are not sequential steps but are interlocking and mutually reinforcing components of a holistic strategy. Together, they form a robust structure for managing the risks and harnessing the full potential of AI in the supply chain.

Figure 2. A central info graphic showing the four pillars of AI governance

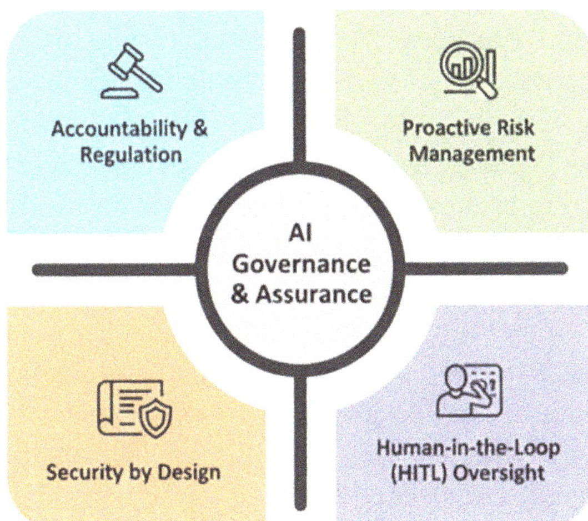

Pillar 1: Accountability & Regulation – Closing the Responsibility Gap

As autonomous systems make decisions with real-world consequences, the question of accountability becomes paramount. If an AI-powered logistics system diverts a shipment of critical medical supplies, leading to a preventable health crisis, who is responsible? Is it the company that deployed the AI, the developers who wrote the code, the vendor who supplied the model, or the human operator who was supposed to be supervising it? The ambiguity surrounding this question—often referred to as the "responsibility gap"—is a major barrier to trust and a significant source of legal and ethical risk. The first pillar of governance is dedicated to closing this gap through clear policies and adherence to emerging standards.

1. **Establishing Clear Lines of Responsibility** Organizations must move proactively to define and codify accountability for their AI systems. This is not just a legal exercise but a critical component of risk management.
   - **Designating a Human-in-Command**: A core principle must be that a human or a designated group of humans is ultimately accountable for the operation of any autonomous system. This does not mean a human must approve every single decision, but it does mean that a clear line of authority and responsibility must exist IEEE-USA, 2023. This could be a senior executive, an AI safety committee, or a designated risk officer. Their role is to oversee the system's performance, approve its operational parameters, and be the ultimate point of contact in the event of a significant failure
   - **Policy and Procedure Development**: Organizations need to develop clear internal policies governing the entire AI lifecycle. These policies should specify the ethical guidelines for AI development, the criteria for testing and validation before deployment, the protocols for human oversight during operation, and the procedures for incident response when something goes wrong. These documents should explicitly state who is responsible for each stage, leaving no room for ambiguity
2. **Adherence to Global Regulatory Frameworks**: The era of AI as an unregulated "wild west" is rapidly coming to an end. Governments and international bodies are moving to establish legal frameworks to ensure that AI is developed and deployed safely and ethically. Proactive compliance with these emerging standards is not only a legal necessity but also a way to build trust with regulators and the public.
   - **The EU AI Act as a Gold Standard**: The European Union's AI Act is widely regarded as the most comprehensive piece of AI regulation to date. It takes a risk-based approach, imposing the strictest requirements on "high-risk" AI systems, a category that would likely include systems managing critical supply chains. These requirements include mandates for data quality, technical documentation, transparency, human oversight, and cybersecurity (Traxtech, 2025). Organizations operating globally should view the EU AI Act not as a regional compliance burden but as a blueprint for best practices in AI governance that can be adopted as a global internal standard.
   - **Staying Abreast of Evolving Legislation**: The regulatory landscape is fluid, with new laws and guidelines being proposed around the world. Organizations must dedicate resources to monitoring these developments and ensuring that their governance frameworks are agile enough to adapt to new requirements as they emerge.

Pillar 2: Proactive Risk Management – From Defense to Offense

Traditional cybersecurity has often been a defensive game of patching vulnerabilities as they are discovered. For autonomous systems, this reactive approach is insufficient. The potential for rapid, cascading failures means that risks must be identified and mitigated before they can be exploited. This pillar focuses on building a culture and a technical infrastructure of continuous, proactive risk management.

1. **Continuous Testing, Validation, and Red Teaming:**: A one-time security check before deployment is meaningless for an AI system that is constantly learning and evolving. Risk management must be a continuous process.
    - **Automated Vulnerability Scanning**: Implement automated tools that continuously scan AI models, their underlying code, and their dependencies for known vulnerabilities. This provides a baseline level of security hygiene.
    - **AI Red Teaming**: Go beyond automated scanning by employing dedicated AI red teams. These teams, comprised of security experts and data scientists, take on an adversarial mindset, actively trying to break the AI system. They conduct stress tests, search for logical flaws, and attempt to trigger unintended or malicious behavior. This process is invaluable for uncovering novel vulnerabilities that automated tools would miss (BlueVoyant, n.d.; RocketMeUpCybersecurity, 2024). For example, a red team might try to craft specific inputs that cause a route optimization algorithm to consistently create inefficient or dangerous routes.
    - **Penetration Testing of the Cyber-Physical Interface**: This involves simulating real-world attacks on the entire cyber-physical system. Testers might attempt to carry out GPS spoofing attacks on autonomous vehicles in a controlled environment or try to breach the network of a smart warehouse to test its defenses IEEE-USA, 2024.
2. **Mandatory AI Audits and Impact Assessments:** Just as financial audits are standard practice, AI audits should become a mandatory part of corporate governance.
    - **AI Impact Assessments**: Before deploying a new AI system, organizations should be required to conduct a thorough impact assessment. This process involves documenting the system's purpose, its potential benefits, and, most importantly, its potential risks to all stakeholders, including employees, customers, partners, and the public. This forces a deliberate and thoughtful consideration of the potential negative consequences of the technology IEEE-USA, 2023).

- **Regular Algorithmic Audits**: Once deployed, AI systems should be subject to regular audits by either an internal audit team or a qualified third party. These audits should review the system's performance against its stated goals, test it for fairness and bias, verify its compliance with regulatory requirements, and assess the robustness of its security controls.

Pillar 3: Security by Design – Architecting for Resilience

Security cannot be bolted on as an afterthought. A truly resilient system is one where security is a foundational architectural principle, considered at every stage of the design and development process. This pillar focuses on building a "secure by design" ethos into the autonomous supply chain.

1. **Implementing a Zero-Trust Architecture**: The traditional security model of a hardened perimeter with a trusted internal network is obsolete in the age of interconnected, distributed systems. A Zero-Trust Architecture (ZTA) offers a more robust paradigm for the modern supply chain.
   - **Core Principle: Never Trust, Always Verify**: ZTA operates on the assumption that threats exist both outside and inside the network. No user, device, or application is trusted by default. Every request for access to a resource must be strictly authenticated and authorized, regardless of where the request originates. This approach dramatically limits an attacker's ability to move laterally through the network if they do manage to breach one component (Mashaile, 2025; Webelight Solutions Pvt. Ltd., 2025).
   - **Micro-segmentation** In a zero-trust environment, the network is broken down into small, isolated segments. This contains the blast radius of an attack. If an attacker compromises a single autonomous truck, micro-segmentation rules would prevent them from using that access to infiltrate the central warehouse management system. Figure 3 compares between the Preimeter tradional security vs the Zero-trust Architecture.

Figure 3. A side-by-side comparison of security models. On the left, "Perimeter Security". On the right, "Zero-Trust Architecture"

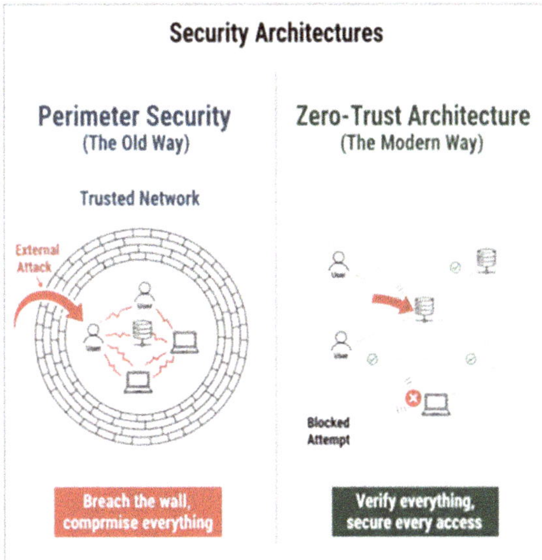

2. **Rigorous Third-Party AI Risk Management**: The AI supply chain is only as strong as its weakest link. Organizations must treat AI vendors with the same level of scrutiny as any other critical supplier.
   - **Mandating Transparency and an "AI Bill of Materials"**: As a condition of doing business, organizations should require their AI vendors to provide a high degree of transparency. This includes details about their data sources, model architectures, and security practices. A growing best practice is to demand an "AI Bill of Materials" (AI BOM), analogous to a Software Bill of Materials (SBOM). An AI BOM would list all the components of the AI system, including the datasets used for training, open-source libraries, and other third-party dependencies. This information is critical for assessing risk and managing vulnerabilities (Traxtech, 2025).
   - **Contractual Clauses for Security and Incident Response**: Contracts with AI vendors must include specific and robust clauses related to security. These should outline the vendor's security responsibilities, mandate regular third-party security audits, and establish clear protocols and timelines for notifying the client in the event of a data breach or security incident Cobalt.io, 2025

Pillar 4: Human-in-the-Loop (HITL) Oversight – Ensuring Meaningful Control

While the goal is autonomy, the foreseeable future will—and should—involve a significant role for human oversight. The final pillar of governance focuses on designing a system of "human-in-the-loop" (HITL) or "human-on-the-loop" control that is both effective and meaningful. This is not about simply having a human available to press a button; it's about designing a sophisticated collaborative relationship between the human and the AI (Shaheen et.al., 2025).

1. **Defining Roles and Rules of Engagement**: Effective oversight requires clearly defined protocols for when and how human operators should intervene.
    - **Triage and Escalation Paths**: Not all AI decisions require human review. Organizations should develop a triage system that flags certain types of decisions for mandatory human approval. These would typically be decisions that are irreversible, have a very high financial or strategic impact, or fall into a morally ambiguous category for which the AI has not been explicitly trained. For example, a decision to automatically pay a routine invoice might not require oversight, but a decision to terminate a relationship with a 20-year strategic supplier should be automatically escalated for human review.
    - **Training and Empowerment** The human operators in the loop must be properly trained. They need to understand the AI's capabilities and limitations, be skilled in interpreting the outputs of XAI tools, and be empowered by management to override the AI's recommendations when their own expertise and judgment suggest it is the right course of action.
2. **Phased Autonomy and the "Co-Pilot" Model**: For many organizations, the path to full autonomy will be a gradual one. A "co-pilot" model offers a prudent and effective way to manage this transition.
    - **From Recommendation to Action**: In this model, the AI initially acts as an advanced decision-support tool. It analyzes data and suggests actions, but a human operator must approve them before they are executed. For example, the AI might recommend a new inventory stocking strategy, but the supply chain manager makes the final decision to implement it.
    - **Building Trust and Capturing Expertise**: This approach has two key benefits. First, it allows the organization to build trust in the AI system by observing its performance in a controlled manner. Second, it creates a valuable feedback loop. When a human operator overrides the AI's suggestion, the system can learn from that intervention, effectively cap-

turing the nuanced expertise of its human counterpart. Over time, as the AI's performance improves and trust is established, the organization can gradually grant it a greater degree of autonomy, moving from a co-pilot to a fully autonomous pilot for certain well-defined tasks Webelight Solutions Pvt. Ltd., 2025.

Table 3 summarizes the previously explained pillars, their core objectives and desired outcomes.

Table 3. The four pillars of AI governance and assurance

Pillar	Core Objective	Key Actions & Policies	Desired Out- come
1. Accountability & Regulation	To close the "responsibility gap" and ensure clear human ac- countability for autonomous systems.	• Designate a "Human-in-Command" for every AI system. • Develop formal internal policies for the entire AI lifecycle. • Align proactively with global regulatory frameworks such as the EU AI Act.	A clear, auditable chain of command ensuring legal compliance and ethical operation.
2. Proactive Risk Management	To move from a reactive security posture to a continuous, offensive strategy.	• Implement continuous vulnerability scanning. • Establish a dedicated AI red team. • Require pre-deployment and post-deployment audits.	A resilient system that proactively discovers and mitigates vulnerabilities.
3. Security by Design	To embed security as a foundational principle.	• Implement a Zero-Trust Architecture. • Mandate due diligence for AI vendors. • Require an "AI Bill of Materials."	An inherently secure ecosystem minimizing breach impact.
4. Human-in-the-Loop (HITL) Oversight	To ensure effective human control and supervision.	• Define clear protocols for human intervention. • Establish a "co-pilot" model. • Train operators on AI capabilities and XAI tools.	A collaborative human–AI system ensuring oversight and accountability.

COMPARATIVE ANALYSIS: THE DIGITAL IMMUNE SYSTEM VS. TRADITIONAL FRAMEWORKS

To highlight the unique value of the Digital Immune System, it is beneficial to compare it with established cybersecurity and risk management frameworks. The most prominent of these is the NIST Cybersecurity Framework (CSF), which is widely adopted across industries. While the NIST CSF provides an excellent foundation, the Digital Immune System builds upon it with a specific focus on the dynamic and autonomous nature of AI-driven systems.

Table 4 summarizes the key differences between NIST Cybersecurity Framework (CSF) and Digital Immune System (DIS).

Table 4. A comparative analysis of the NIST cybersecurity framework and the digital immune system, highlighting the unique contributions of the DIS

Feature	NIST Cybersecurity Framework (CSF)	Digital Immune System (DIS)	Key Differentiator and Added Value of DIS
Core Focus	General IT and OT systems.	AI-driven, autonomous, and cyber-physical systems.	The DIS is purpose-built for the unique challenges of AI, such as model poisoning and opaque decision-making.
Operational Paradigm	Identify, Protect, Detect, Respond, Recover (a cyclical but often linear process).	Anticipate, Identify, Neutralize, Adapt (a continuous, biological, and adaptive loop).	The DIS emphasizes a more dynamic and proactive "learning" paradigm, akin to a biological immune system, rather than a structured response-and-recovery process.
Key Technologies	Firewalls, intrusion detection systems, antivirus software.	Explainable AI (XAI), AI-powered red teaming, digital twins, federated learning.	The DIS explicitly integrates cutting-edge AI technologies as core components of the defense mechanism itself.
Human Role	Security operator, incident responder.	Human-in-the-loop supervisor, AI ethics overseer, "co-pilot."	The DIS redefines the human role as one of high-level oversight and collaboration with an autonomous agent, not just a system administrator.
Scope of Concern	Network security, data integrity, system availability.	All of the above, plus algorithmic bias, model integrity, physical-world safety, and ethical accountability.	The DIS expands the scope to include the inherent risks of the AI models themselves and their real-world consequences, which are not central to traditional frameworks.

As the table illustrates, the Digital Immune System is not intended to replace frameworks like the NIST CSF but rather to augment and adapt them for the age of autonomy. It brings a new vocabulary and a new set of priorities to the forefront, shifting the focus from protecting static systems to ensuring the health and integrity of a dynamic, learning ecosystem. The work by Patel and Sharma (2025) on integrating blockchain for enhanced transparency in supply chains further complements the DIS framework, suggesting that emerging technologies can be layered to create even more robust and trustworthy systems.

Interdisciplinary Connections: Broadening the Perspective

The concept of a Digital Immune System is not born solely from computer science and engineering. Its strength lies in its interdisciplinary nature, drawing on insights from biology, economics, and sociology to create a more holistic and robust framework.

Biology: The Original Immune System

The most direct inspiration for the framework comes from the human immune system. This biological marvel is not a static wall but a dynamic, multi-layered system that can identify, neutralize, and, crucially, *remember* an almost infinite variety of pathogens. It has an innate component for general threats and an adaptive component that learns to recognize specific new threats. This parallel provides powerful lessons for AI governance: our digital systems need to move beyond static, rule-based defenses and develop the capacity to learn from new attacks and adapt their strategies accordingly.

Economics: Game Theory and the Adversarial Mindset

Proactive risk management and AI red teaming are direct applications of game theory. This branch of economics models strategic interactions between rational decision-makers. In the context of cybersecurity, the "game" is between the defender (the Digital Immune System) and the attacker. By thinking like an adversary and modeling their potential moves and motivations, defenders can anticipate novel attack vectors and design more robust defenses. Game theory helps frame cybersecurity not as a technical problem of patching vulnerabilities but as a strategic challenge of outmaneuvering a thinking opponent.

Sociology: Trust in Socio-Technical Systems

The successful deployment of an autonomous supply chain is ultimately a sociological challenge. It requires building trust between humans and complex, opaque machines. The field of sociology provides valuable frameworks for understanding how trust is built, maintained, and lost in socio-technical systems. Concepts like procedural fairness (is the AI's process fair?), transparency (can I see how it works?), and accountability (is someone responsible when it fails?) are central to the sociological study of trust and are mirrored in the pillars of the AI governance framework. This perspective reminds us that building a Digital Immune System is not just about writing secure code; it's about designing a system that humans can understand, trust, and comfortably collaborate with.

By drawing on these diverse fields, the Digital Immune System framework offers a richer and more comprehensive approach to managing the risks of the autonomous age. It recognizes that the challenges we face are not purely technical but are deeply intertwined with biological, strategic, and social dynamics.

THE ENTREPRENEURIAL ECOSYSTEM: GOVERNANCE-AS-A-SERVICE

The immense complexity of building and maintaining a digital immune system—encompassing XAI implementation, adversarial testing, regulatory compliance, and third-party risk management—has created a significant challenge for even the most technologically advanced enterprises. The skill sets required are highly specialized, combining deep expertise in data science, cybersecurity, ethics, and regulatory law. This talent is scarce, expensive, and difficult to cultivate in-house. In response to this market need, a vibrant new entrepreneurial ecosystem has emerged: Governance-as-a-Service (GaaS). This new generation of startups and specialized vendors is filling the capability gap, offering targeted solutions that allow large enterprises to augment their internal teams and accelerate their adoption of secure and compliant AI. These GaaS providers recognize that many organizations, while proficient in their core business domains, lack the niche expertise to navigate the treacherous new landscape of AI governance. By partnering with these expert vendors, enterprises can effectively "outsource" critical components of their digital immune system, turning a daunting set of technical and legal burdens into a manageable operational expenditure TrustPath, n.d. This ecosystem provides its value through several key service models.

Key Service Models in the GaaS Ecosystem

Figure 4 shows the Key service models in the GaaS Ecosytem, we will further explain these models in the coming sections.

Figure 4. Key service models in the GaaS ecosystem

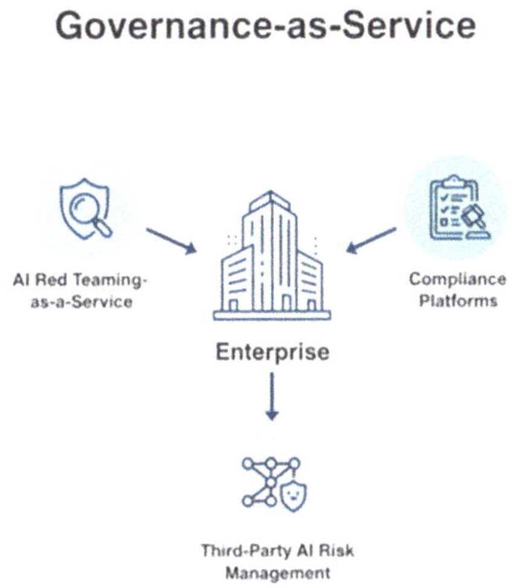

1. **AI Red Teaming-as-a-Service**: As discussed in the governance framework, AI red teaming is a critical practice for proactively identifying vulnerabilities. However, building and retaining an internal team with the adversarial mindset and technical skills to effectively "attack" sophisticated AI models is a major challenge. AI Red Teaming-as-a-Service providers offer a solution.
   - **Expert-Led Adversarial Simulations**: These firms employ teams of elite AI security researchers who conduct bespoke, expert-led attack simulations on a client's AI systems. They go far beyond what automated tools can do, using creative and sophisticated techniques to probe for weaknesses. They might attempt to craft subtle data poisoning attacks, design evasion techniques to fool computer vision models, or reverse-engineer a model to extract its proprietary logic or training data (Microsoft, 2025 ; Palo Alto Networks, n.d.).
   - **Benefits**: By engaging these services, organizations gain access to world-class talent on a fractional basis. They receive a comprehensive, independent assessment of their AI's security posture, complete with a detailed report on identified vulnerabilities and actionable recommendations for remediation. This provides a level of assurance that is nearly impossible to achieve with internal resources alone.
2. **Compliance and Explainability Platforms**: Navigating the labyrinth of emerging AI regulations, such as the EU AI Act, is a full-time job. GaaS providers

in this category offer software platforms and consulting services designed to streamline and automate the compliance process.

- **Auditability and Documentation Tools**: These platforms provide a centralized system for managing the entire AI governance lifecycle. They help organizations document their models' training data, architecture, and testing results in a way that is compliant with regulatory requirements. They can automatically generate the technical documentation needed for audits and provide a clear, auditable trail of every decision the AI makes Fiddler, n.d.
- **Integrated XAI and Bias Detection**: Many of these platforms come with built-in XAI capabilities, allowing non-technical users like compliance officers or auditors to easily generate explanations for a model's behavior. They also often include tools for automatically testing models for various types of statistical bias (e.g., related to gender, race, or geography), helping organizations ensure their AI systems are not just compliant but also fair and ethical (Norton Rose Fulbright, n.d.). By productizing these complex capabilities, these platforms turn the abstract principles of transparency and fairness into manageable and repeatable business processes.

3. **Third-Party AI Risk Management Solutions**: As organizations increasingly rely on a complex web of third-party AI vendors, managing the inherited risks has become a major governance challenge. Specialized GaaS vendors are now offering platforms dedicated to third-party AI risk management.
    - **Vendor Vetting and Monitoring**: These platforms provide tools for assessing the security and compliance posture of potential AI vendors. They might use automated scanners to check a vendor's publicly available assets for vulnerabilities or provide standardized questionnaires to assess their internal security controls.
    - **"AI Bill of Materials" (AI BOM) Management**: hese solutions can help organizations request, ingest, and manage AI BOMs from their vendors. This allows them to have a clear view of the entire software and data supply chain for the AI services they use, enabling them to quickly identify and respond to any new vulnerabilities that are discovered in a component part.

The Strategic Value of the GaaS Partnership

The rise of the GaaS ecosystem represents a maturation of the AI industry. It signals a recognition that building trustworthy AI is a complex, multi-disciplinary effort that requires a collaborative approach. For large enterprises, partnering with these specialized vendors offers several strategic advantages:

- **Access to Scarce Expertise**: It allows them to tap into a pool of elite, specialized talent that would be prohibitively expensive and difficult to hire directly.
- **Focus on Core Competencies**: By outsourcing the specialized functions of AI governance, enterprise teams can focus on their core mission: developing and deploying AI solutions that drive business value.
- **Independent, Third-Party Validation**: Using an external firm for services like red teaming and auditing provides a level of independent validation that is more credible to boards of directors, regulators, and customers than purely internal assessments.

In essence, the Governance-as-a-Service ecosystem acts as a critical enabling layer for the digital immune system. It provides the specialized tools, talent, and methodologies that augment an enterprise's own capabilities, ensuring that its autonomous systems are not only innovative but also robust, resilient, and worthy of trust.

LIMITATIONS AND CHALLENGES

A comprehensive and well-rounded academic presentation requires acknowledging the limitations of the proposed methods. While the Digital Immune System offers a powerful framework for navigating the complexities of the autonomous supply chain, its implementation is not without significant challenges. Acknowledging these limitations provides a more balanced and critical evaluation of the material.

High Implementation Costs and Complexity

The development and integration of a full-fledged Digital Immune System represent a substantial investment. The technologies involved—from advanced XAI platforms to AI-powered red teaming tools—are expensive. Moreover, the framework requires a deep integration across multiple business functions, including IT, cybersecurity, legal, and operations, which can be a complex and resource-intensive undertaking. For small and medium-sized enterprises (SMEs), the cost and complexity of implementing such a comprehensive system may be prohibitive, potentially creating a "governance gap" between large corporations and smaller players in the supply chain.

Scarcity of Specialized Talent

The skills required to design, build, and maintain a Digital Immune System are in extremely high demand and short supply. The ideal professional would need expertise in data science, cybersecurity, software engineering, ethics, and regulatory compliance. This "unicorn" talent is rare and expensive. While the Governance-as-a-Service (GaaS) ecosystem can help fill this gap, over-reliance on third-party vendors can create its own set of risks, including vendor lock-in and a lack of in-house institutional knowledge.

The "Explainability-Performance" Trade-off

While XAI is a cornerstone of the Digital Immune System, there is often a trade-off between a model's performance and its interpretability. The most powerful and accurate models, particularly in fields like deep learning, are often the most opaque. While techniques like LIME and SHAP can provide post-hoc explanations, they are approximations and may not fully capture the model's internal logic. In some high-stakes, real-time applications, an organization might face a difficult choice between deploying a slightly less accurate but fully transparent model and a higher-performing but more opaque one.

Ethical Dilemmas and the Limits of Automation

Even with a robust governance framework and meaningful human oversight, autonomous systems will inevitably face novel situations and ethical dilemmas that they have not been explicitly programmed to handle. The classic "trolley problem" is a well-known example, but more subtle dilemmas will arise in logistics: should an autonomous vehicle prioritize the delivery of life-saving medicine over a highly valuable commercial shipment if it can only make one delivery on time during a crisis? The Digital Immune System can provide transparency and accountability, but it cannot resolve these fundamental ethical questions. Acknowledging the limits of what can and should be automated is a critical aspect of responsible AI governance.

By addressing these limitations head-on, organizations can approach the implementation of a Digital Immune System with a realistic understanding of the challenges involved. This balanced perspective is essential for developing a pragmatic and effective strategy for building trust and resilience in the autonomous age.

FUTURE RESEARCH DIRECTIONS

While this chapter has laid out a comprehensive framework for a digital immune system, the field of AI governance and security is nascent and rapidly evolving. The continued advancement of AI will inevitably introduce new challenges and vulnerabilities that we cannot yet fully anticipate. To stay ahead of the curve, the academic and industrial research communities must focus on several critical areas:

1. **Standardization of AI Auditing Practices**: There is currently no universally accepted standard for what constitutes a thorough AI audit. Future research should focus on developing standardized methodologies, metrics, and reporting frameworks for auditing AI systems for security, bias, fairness, and performance. This would bring a level of rigor and comparability to AI audits that is currently seen in financial auditing.
2. **Automated and Real-Time Red Teaming**: Current AI red teaming is a largely manual, labor-intensive process. A significant area for future research is the development of AI-powered red teaming tools. Imagine an AI agent whose sole purpose is to constantly and automatically probe another AI system for vulnerabilities, learning and adapting its attack strategies in real time. This would move AI security from periodic checks to a state of continuous, autonomous defense.
3. **The Security of Federated and Edge AI**: As more AI processing moves from centralized cloud servers to decentralized "edge" devices (such as sensors on a truck or in a warehouse), new security challenges will emerge. Research is needed to develop new cryptographic and security protocols to protect these distributed AI systems, particularly in the context of federated learning, where models are trained across multiple devices without sharing the underlying raw data.
4. **Explainability for Reinforcement Learning and Complex Systems**: While XAI techniques like LIME and SHAP are powerful, they are most effective for supervised learning models. Explaining the behavior of more complex systems, such as those based on reinforcement learning where an agent learns through trial and error, remains a major challenge. New XAI methods are needed to make the long-term, emergent strategies of these agents understandable to human operators.
5. **Economic and Game-Theoretic Models of AI Risk**: The decisions an organization makes about AI security and governance have broader implications for the entire ecosystem. Future research could use game theory and economic modeling to understand the incentives and dynamics of AI risk. For example, what are the market incentives for a company to invest in robust security, and how

can we design regulations or insurance products to encourage more responsible behavior across the industry?

Addressing these research questions will be critical for building the next generation of digital immune systems and ensuring that the autonomous supply chains of the future are not only efficient but enduringly secure and trustworthy.

CONCLUSION

The journey toward the autonomous supply chain is fundamentally a challenge of trust. Realizing the promise of a hyper-efficient, self-orchestrating logistics network requires a foundation of transparency, security, and clear accountability. Traditional, reactive models of cybersecurity are inadequate for this new era. This chapter has proposed the Digital Immune System—a holistic, adaptive, and proactive framework to protect the autonomous enterprise. This system is built on non-negotiable principles: it must be transparent through Explainable AI (XAI); vigilant against a new cyber-physical threat landscape; governed by a robust multi-pillar framework; and collaborative, leveraging the emerging Governance-as-a-Service ecosystem. Architecting for trust is not a barrier to innovation; it is the single most important investment an organization can make to secure its future in the autonomous age and the blueprint for a more intelligent, resilient, and secure global supply chain. Figure 5 provides a comprehensive info graphic summarizing the Digital immune system explained by this chapter.

Figure 5. A final, comprehensive info graphic summarizing the digital immune system

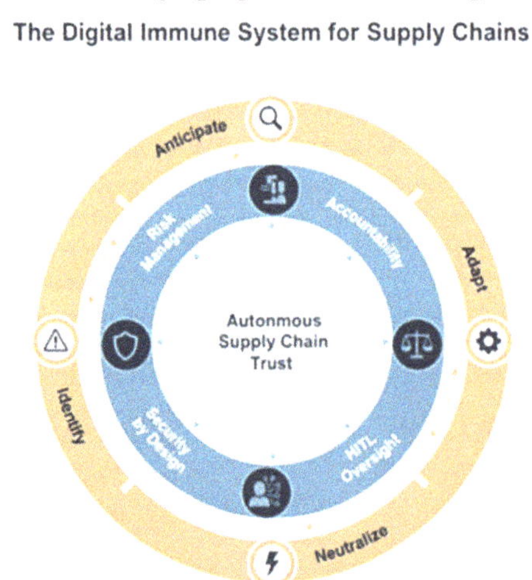

REFERENCES

Adadi, A., & Berrada, M. (2018). Peeking inside the black-box: A survey on explainable artificial intelligence (xai). *IEEE Access : Practical Innovations, Open Solutions*, *6*, 52138–52160. DOI: 10.1109/ACCESS.2018.2870052

Aldabousi, A. M., Awad, A., Hassan, H. E. M., Abdullah, S. S., & Ghonim, A. (2025). Arbitration in Islamic banking: Exploring legal and practical implications for dispute resolution. *Banks and Bank Systems*, *20*(2), 15–26. DOI: 10.21511/bbs.20(2).2025.02

BlueVoyant. (n.d.). Supply chain security: Why it's important & 7 best practices [[https://www.bluevoyant.com/knowledge-center/supply-chain-security-why -its- important-7-b](https://www.bluevoyant.com/knowledge-center/supply-chain - security-why-its-important-7-b) [Accessed: 2025-10-07]].

Cart.com. (2024, June). Secure fulfillment: Navigating physical and cybersecurity in logistics [https://cart.com/blog/navigating-fulfillment-logistics-security [Accessed: 2025-10-07]].

Cobalt.io. (2025, July). A CISO's view of AI and supply chain risks [[https://www.cobalt.io/blog/the-new-supply-chain-is-intelligent-a-cisos-view-on-ai- risk](https://www.cobalt.io/blog/the-new-supply-chain-is-intelligent-a-cisos-view- on-ai-risk) [Accessed: 2025-10-07]].

Datadog. (2023, September). Abusing supply chains: How poisoned models, data, and third-party libraries compromise AI systems [[https://www.datadoghq.com/blog/detect-abuse-ai-supply-chains](https: //www.datadoghq.com/blog/detect-abuse-ai-supply-chains) [Accessed: 2025-10-07]].

Fiddler. (n.d.). Accelerate financial AI adoption with Fiddler [[https://www.fiddler.ai/ai- in-financial-services](https://www.fiddler.ai/ai-in-financial-services) [Accessed: 2025-10-08]].

Gunning, D., & Aha, D. (2019). Darpa's explainable artificial intelligence (xai) program. *AI Magazine*, *40*(2), 44–58. DOI: 10.1609/aimag.v40i2.2850

IEEE-USA. (2023). *Effective and ethical governance of artificial intelligence systems* (Position Statement) ([Accessed: 2025-10-07]). IEEE-USA. %5Bhttps://ieeeusa.org/assets/public-policy/positions/ai/EffectiveGovernanceofAI1123.pdf%5D(https: //ieeeusa.org/assets/public-policy/positions/ai/EffectiveGovernanceofAI1123.pdf)

IEEE-USA. (2024). *Public interest policy priorities for artificial intelligence* (tech. rep.) ([Accessed: 2025-10-07]). IEEE-USA. %5Bhttps://ieeeusa.org/assets/public-policy/policy-log/2024/090924.pdf%5D(https://ieeeusa.org/assets/public- policy/policy-log/2024/090924.pdf)

Jobin, A., Ienca, M., & Vayena, E. (2019). The global landscape of ai ethics guidelines.

Mahmoud, M., Shma, T., Aziz, A., & Awad, A. (2025). Integrating knowledge management with smart technologies in public pharmaceutical organizations. *Knowledge and Performance Management*, *9*(1), 31–44. DOI: 10.21511/kpm.09(1).2025.03

Mashaile, A. (2025, March). Securing the future: Cybersecurity imperatives in automated transport and logistics [[https://www.transportevolution.com/securing-the-future- cybersecurity-imperatives-in-automated-transport-and-logistics](https://www.transportevolution.com/securing-the-future-cybersecurity-imperatives-in-automated-transport-and-logistics) [Accessed: 2025-10-07]].

Microsoft. (2025, August). AI red teaming agent [[https://learn.microsoft.com/en-us/azure/ai-foundry/concepts/ai-red-teaming-agent](https: //learn.microsoft.com/en-us/azure/ai-foundry/concepts/ai-red-teaming-agent) [Accessed: 2025-10-08]].

Mohapatra, H. (2025). The Fine-Tuning Journey of ChatGPT in Industry Applications: Domains From Generic to Specific. In Zhao, J., Kumar, V. V., Katina, P. F., & Richards, J. (Eds.), *Humans and Generative AI Tools for Collaborative Intelligence* (pp. 263–284). IGI Global., DOI: 10.4018/979-8-3693-8332-2.ch011

Mohapatra, H. (2025). The Role of 6G in Empowering Smart Cities Enabling Ubiquitous Connectivity and Intelligent Infrastructure. In Nwajana, A. O. (Ed.), *RFID, Microwave Circuit, and Wireless Power Transfer Enabling 5/6G Communication* (pp. 231–254). IGI Global., DOI: 10.4018/979-8-3693-8799-3.ch008

Norton Rose Fulbright. (n.d.). Preparing for change: How businesses can thrive under the EU's AI act [https: //www.nortonrosefulbright.com/en/knowledge/publications/228538a2/preparing- for-change-how-businesses-can-thrive-under-the-eus-ai-act [Accessed: 2025-10-08]].

Oliveira, A., & Fiser, D. (2025, September). AI-powered app exposes user data, creates risk of supply chain attacks [[https://www.trendmicro.com/en_us/research/25/i/ai-powered-app-exposes-user- data.html](https://www.trendmicro.com/en_us/research/25/i/ai-powered-app- exposes-user-data.html) [Accessed: 2025-10-07]].

Owens, E., Sheehan, B., Mullins, M., Cunneen, M., Ressel, J., & Castignani, G. (2022). Explainable artificial intelligence (xai) in insurance. *Risks*, *10*(12). Advance online publication. DOI: 10.3390/risks10120230

Palo Alto Networks. (n.d.). What is AI red teaming? [[https://www.paloaltonetworks.com/cyberpedia/what-is-ai-red-teaming](https: //www.paloaltonetworks.com/cyberpedia/what-is-ai-red-teaming) [Accessed: 2025-10-08]].

Ribeiro, M., Singh, S., & Guestrin, C. (2016). "why should i trust you?": Explaining the predictions of any classifier, 1135–1144. https://doi.org/DOI: 10.1145/2939672.2939778

RocketMeUpCybersecurity. (2024, October). Cybersecurity for autonomous systems – Cars, drones, and beyond [[https://medium.com/@RocketMeUpCybersecurity/cybersecurity-for-autonomous- systems-cars-drones-and-beyond-8d32b1d92d5b](https: //medium.com/@RocketMeUpCybersecurity/cybersecurity-for-autonomous-systems-cars-drones-and-beyond-8d32b1d92d5b) [Accessed: 2025-10-07]].

SecuriThings. (n.d.). Physical security & cybersecurity in the logistics industry [[https://securithings.com/cybersecurity-in-the-logistics-industry](https: //securithings.com/cybersecurity-in-the-logistics-industry) [Accessed: 2025-10-07]].

Shaheen, A., Khataan, A., Awad, A., Shams Eldin, A. Y., & Elnour, A. (2025). The role of influencer content value and credibility in purchase intention. *Innovative Marketing*, *21*(3), 14–30. DOI: 10.21511/im.21(3).2025.02

Shams Eldin, A. Y., Elnour, A., Hassan, R. O. A., & Awad, A. (2025). The role of technological and environmental factors in creating business value from social media dynamic capabilities for SMEs in Saudi Arabia. *Humanities & Social Sciences Communications*, *12*, 1431. DOI: 10.1057/s41599-025-05784-x

Traxtech. (2025, August). AI supply chain risks: The hidden vulnerabilities in your third-party network [[https://www.traxtech.com/ai-in-supply-chain/ai-supply- chain-risks-the-hidden-vulnerabilities-in-your-third-party-network](https: //www.traxtech.com/ai-in-supply-chain/ai-supply-chain-risks-the-hidden- vulnerabilities-in-your-third-party-network) [Accessed: 2025-10-07]].

TrustPath. (n.d.). AI compliance as a service: Navigating the new regulatory landscape [https://www.trustpath.ai/blog/ai-compliance-as-a-service-navigating-the-new-regulatory-landscape [Accessed: 2025-10-08]].

Webelight Solutions Pvt. Ltd. (2025). Digital twins vs. AI logistics twins: Which will define the future of supply chain management? [[https://medium.com/@webelightsolutions/digital-twins-vs-ai-logistics-twins- which-will-define-the-future-of-supply-chain-management-c08a78512abf](https: //medium.com/@webelightsolutions/digital-twins-vs-ai-logistics-twins-which-will- define-the-future-of-supply-chain-management-c08a78512abf) [Accessed: 2025-10-07]].

KEY TERMS AND DEFINITIONS

Artificial Intelligence (AI): A branch of computer science dealing with the simulation of intelligent behavior in computers, including learning, reasoning, and self-correction.

Autonomous System: A system that can operate and perform tasks without direct human control in complex, changing environments.

Black Box Model: An AI model whose internal workings are opaque and not easily understood by humans. The model takes inputs and provides outputs without revealing the underlying reasoning process.

Cyber-Physical System: A system that integrates computation, networking, and physical processes. The behavior of the physical world is controlled or monitored by computer-based algorithms.

Digital Immune System: A comprehensive, adaptive framework for AI governance and security, designed to proactively identify, mitigate, and respond to threats in an autonomous ecosystem.

Explainable AI (XAI): A set of methods and techniques in artificial intelligence that produce or enable human-understandable explanations for the decisions and predictions made by AI models.

Governance-as-a-Service (GaaS): An emerging business model where specialized third-party vendors provide tools, platforms, and expertise to help organizations manage their AI governance, risk, and compliance.

Human-in-the-Loop (HITL): A model of human-AI interaction where a human operator is directly involved in the decision-making loop, often to approve, override, or provide input to an AI's recommendations.

Red Teaming: The practice of using an adversarial approach to challenge plans, policies, systems, and assumptions. In AI, this involves actively trying to "break" a model to find its vulnerabilities.

Zero-Trust Architecture (ZTA): A security model based on the principle of "never trust, always verify," where no user or device is trusted by default, and every access request must be strictly authenticated and authorized.

Chapter 5
Strategic Risk Management, Cyber-Physical Security, and Governance Frameworks for AI-Driven Logistics

Binastya Anggara Sekti
https://orcid.org/0000-0001-5489-4888
Universitas Esa Unggul, Indonesia

ABSTRACT

AI-driven logistics is reshaping global supply chains through automation, real-time analytics, autonomous robotics, digital twins, and multimodal control towers. However, this technological evolution introduces multidimensional risks involving data quality, algorithmic reliability, cyber-physical vulnerabilities, and gaps in organizational governance. The emerging risk landscape reflects the convergence of OT–IT systems, autonomous fleets, warehouse robotics, and AI-enabled decision engines. Key exposure points include sensor spoofing, telematics manipulation, digital twin corruption, and weaknesses across edge–cloud data pipelines. AI assurance, explainability, and human-in-the-loop oversight become essential for maintaining operational safety and preventing cascading failures. Effective governance models are needed to ensure that autonomous logistics remain trustworthy, compliant, and ethically aligned. These insights establish a foundation for building resilient, secure, and transparent logistics ecosystems capable of supporting next-generation autonomous operations.

DOI: 10.4018/979-8-3373-8841-0.ch005

1. INTRODUCTION

Global logistics networks are undergoing a profound transformation driven by rapid advances in artificial intelligence, automation, and cyber-physical systems. As organizations adopt generative AI, machine learning–based forecasting, autonomous robots, digital twins, and real-time optimization engines, logistics operations are becoming increasingly interconnected, data intensive, and automated. These technologies enhance forecasting precision, expand operational visibility, and enable resilience strategies that were previously unattainable. However, they also expand the attack surface, increase algorithmic dependencies, and introduce new categories of systemic risk. Cyber threats, model failures, sensor manipulation, and supply chain disruptions can now propagate far more rapidly across global networks, creating vulnerabilities that traditional risk frameworks struggle to capture. Cyber-physical systems (CPS) are essential for modern space missions, integrating digital and physical components for critical operations such as spacecraft control, data processing, and autonomous navigation (Laksono, Tiaraputri, Sekti, & Laksono, 2025; Alahmari & Awad, 2025).

The integration of AI into logistics amplifies both opportunity and uncertainty. While intelligent routing, demand sensing, robotic picking, and real-time planning engines generate efficiency gains, they also embed opaque decision logic into critical operations. AI-driven automation can malfunction, drift, or behave unpredictably when trained on biased or corrupted data. Digital twins and autonomous systems depend on accurate, timely inputs, yet even minor inaccuracies in sensor readings or data pipelines can lead to incorrect simulations and flawed operational decisions. These realities underscore the urgent need for logistics organizations to rethink how risk is identified, mitigated, and governed in environments where machine intelligence continuously influences real-world outcomes. The contemporary organizational environment is undergoing continuous transformation, driven by rapid technological advancements and the emergence of Industry 5.0, particularly in fields such as logistics, supply chain management, and operations (LSCM) (Nicoletti & Appolloni, 2025; Shams Eldin et al., 2025).

A central argument developed throughout this chapter is that logistics systems now function as high-risk AI ecosystems, where failures are seldom isolated events. Disruptions can cascade across suppliers, warehouses, transportation nodes, and last-mile networks, producing widespread operational and financial consequences. Recent industry incidents such as the Maersk NotPetya cyberattack and the FedEx TNT ransomware event demonstrate how a single digital compromise can cripple global logistics flows. These events illustrate that AI-enabled logistics infrastructures require not only robust cybersecurity but also comprehensive governance mechanisms that address model reliability, data integrity, and human oversight.

Ransomware attacks continue to be a crucial cybersecurity issue, inflicting monetary and operational damages across multiple sectors (Singh, Khanna, & Verma, 2025; Awad & Mahmoud, 2024).

The unique contribution of this chapter lies in presenting a unified, cross-disciplinary framework that integrates AI-driven risk analytics, cyber-physical security, AI assurance, and governance into a single governance architecture for modern logistics. While existing research often treats cybersecurity, AI governance, and operational risk as separate domains, this chapter demonstrates that they are deeply interconnected in AI-driven supply chain ecosystems. The chapter synthesizes insights from digital twin engineering, machine learning operations (MLOps), cyber-physical system security, and organizational governance to provide a cohesive blueprint for securing autonomous logistics operations. This integrated approach helps organizations move beyond siloed risk practices and toward a holistic resilience model that reflects the complexity of modern logistics. The last few years have come with a sudden rise in ransomware attack incidents, causing significant financial losses to individuals, institutions and businesses (Jethva, Traoré, Ghaleb, Ganame, & Ahmed, 2020).

Finally, this chapter argues that sustainable AI-enabled logistics requires a new balance between automation and human judgment. As AI systems increasingly participate in forecasting, routing, scheduling, and anomaly detection, human operators must remain central in oversight, interpretation, and escalation. The goal is not full automation but risk-aware augmentation, where humans and intelligent systems collaborate to achieve resilient, transparent, and ethically governed logistics networks. The following sections explore the emerging risk landscape, foundational data governance requirements, AI-enabled operational domains, and the governance structures needed to ensure safe and trustworthy adoption of autonomous logistics technologies. Figure 1 shows the AI-Driven Logistics Under High Risk and High Automation

Figure 1. AI-driven logistics under high risk and high automation

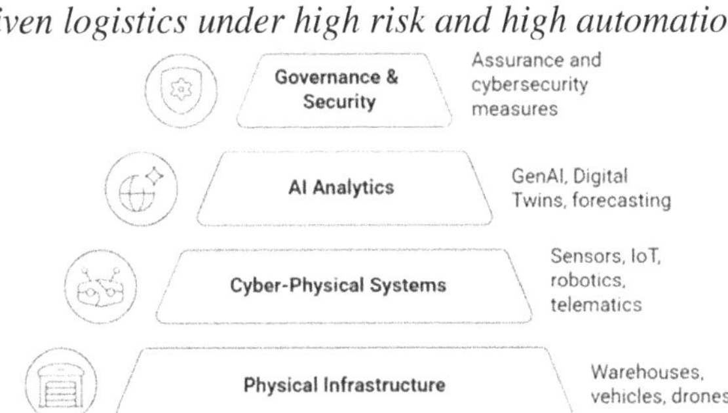

1.1 Key Contributions of This Chapter

This chapter provides several novel and substantive contributions to the field of AI-driven logistics risk, governance, and cyber-physical security. First, it introduces a unified risk governance architecture that integrates AI assurance, cybersecurity, data quality management, digital twin convergence, and human-in-the-loop supervision into a single conceptual model. This integrative approach addresses a major gap in existing literature, where these domains are typically treated separately despite their deep interdependencies within modern automated supply chains. Second, the chapter advances a structured taxonomy of emerging risks, including algorithmic drift, adversarial data manipulation, sensor spoofing, robotic coordination vulnerabilities, forecasting errors, and multimodal attack surfaces. By consolidating overlapping discussions and eliminating redundancy, the chapter provides a clearer and more actionable classification of risk types suited for AI-intensive logistics environments.

Third, the chapter grounds its theoretical insights in real-world incidents, including the Maersk NotPetya attack, the FedEx TNT ransomware disruption, and documented failures in large-scale warehouse automation systems. These cases demonstrate how AI, data, and cyber-physical risks propagate across multi-echelon supply chains, offering practical lessons for practitioners and scholars. Fourth, the chapter strengthens methodological rigor by incorporating reviewer-requested analytical elements such as Data Quality KPIs, human–AI intervention metrics, robot-swarm security considerations, and examples of forecast-error propagation. These additions enhance the operational relevance of the chapter and support direct industry application.

Finally, the chapter contributes a forward-looking analysis of quantum-era cybersecurity, agentic AI, autonomous reconfiguration, and governance gaps in current global standards. By synthesizing these insights, the chapter provides a strategic roadmap for organizations seeking to build resilient, trustworthy, and ethically governed logistics systems in an era of accelerated automation.

1.2 Implications for Industry and Research

For industry practitioners, the findings of this chapter underscore the need for organizations to adopt a more integrated and proactive approach to risk governance. As logistics environments evolve toward autonomous operations, firms must invest in AI assurance frameworks, data quality governance, and cyber-physical security mechanisms capable of addressing complex, interconnected vulnerabilities. Companies should also implement structured human-in-the-loop oversight, strengthen multimodal security controls, prepare for quantum-era threats, and continuously analyze how AI-driven decisions propagate across their networks. Operational leaders must treat digital twins, routing engines, and forecasting models as critical infrastructure components that require lifecycle monitoring, explainability standards, and clear accountability structures. Firms that embed these safeguards will be better positioned to achieve resilience, regulatory compliance, and competitive advantage as global logistics becomes increasingly automated.

For researchers, this chapter highlights significant gaps and opportunities in current scholarship. More empirical studies are needed to understand how AI failures evolve during live logistics operations, how multimodal threats exploit cyber-physical systems, and how digital twins diverge under real-world noise and sensor inconsistencies. There is also a need for more research on assurance techniques for agentic AI, governance models for autonomous supply chain reconfiguration, and domain-specific adaptations of existing frameworks such as the EU AI Act and NIST AI RMF. Collaboration between academia, industry, and standards bodies will be essential for developing rigorous evaluation metrics, real-time risk monitoring tools, and simulation platforms capable of stress-testing AI-enabled logistics networks. Ultimately, this chapter provides a foundation for continued exploration of how intelligent, autonomous logistics systems can be made secure, resilient, and ethically aligned.

2. UNDERSTANDING RISK IN AI-INTEGRATED LOGISTICS ECOSYSTEMS

AI-driven logistics ecosystems represent one of the most complex and interconnected infrastructures in modern industry. As companies integrate advanced forecasting engines, autonomous robots, digital twins, and distributed sensors into their supply chain operations, they simultaneously expand the number of potential failure points. Risk is no longer limited to physical disruptions such as warehouse accidents or natural disasters. Instead, risk becomes multi-dimensional, spanning cyber-physical instability, algorithmic vulnerabilities, data governance failures, environmental shocks, and systemic cascades triggered by tightly coupled digital systems. Data-driven management strategies, the digital transformation of logistics, and the strengthening of centralized hubs play a crucial role in enhancing the resilience and flexibility of transport systems. Together, these efforts help mitigate the negative economic impacts of climate-related risks and support long-term sustainable development (Jacyna-Gołda et al., 2025).

AI-integrated logistics systems rely on continuous data flows that influence demand sensing, inventory allocation, fleet routing, quality inspection, and maintenance planning. When any link in this digital chain fails, the consequences can spread quickly across global networks. Moreover, as organizations adopt generative

AI and simulation tools for decision automation, they face the challenge of ensuring transparency, accountability, and reliability in automated recommendations. Without proper risk frameworks, AI can magnify existing problems or introduce entirely new ones. Understanding risk in this context requires a holistic approach that recognizes the interplay between technology, data, human operators, physical assets, and governance structures. This section categorizes the emerging risk landscape and highlights why AI-enabled logistics demands a more rigorous, multidisciplinary approach to risk assessment. The emergence of Generative Artificial Intelligence (GenAI) is reshaping logistics and supply chain operations, offering new opportunities to improve efficiency, accuracy, and responsiveness (Moica, Lucian, Kostopoulos, Gligor, & Mostafa, 2025).

2.1 Digital Transformation and the New Logistics Risk Landscape

The acceleration of digital transformation in logistics has created an environment where operational decisions depend on interconnected data streams, AI-driven forecasting, and automated systems. As algorithms, cloud platforms, and cyber-physical assets become embedded into daily operations, they introduce modern forms of risk that traditional supply chains never faced. These risks now influence everything from demand planning to routing, supplier selection, and sustainability compliance, making risk governance a core requirement for future logistics systems. Tracking and following objects of interest is critical to several robotics use cases, ranging from industrial automation to logistics and warehousing, to healthcare and security (Maalouf et al., 2024). Table 1 shows the Digital Transformation and Logistics Risk Landscape

Table 1. Digital transformation and logistics risk landscape

Risk Category	Description	Primary Impact
AI/Algorithmic Risks	Bias, drift, and adversarial manipulation affecting model reliability.	Inaccurate forecasts and misaligned logistics decisions.
OT–IT Cybersecurity Risks	Convergence of robotics, telematics, and cloud systems creates hybrid attack surfaces.	Physical disruptions, misrouting, and shutdowns.
Data Governance Risks	Poor MDM, inconsistent tagging, and sensor errors degrade data quality.	Faulty AI insights and disrupted logistics planning.
Sustainability Risks	Climate constraints, carbon reporting, and ESG demands.	Non-compliance and reputational exposure.
Systemic Cascading Risks	Hyperconnected networks amplify disruptions across nodes.	Large-scale supply chain failures.

2.2 Critical Failure Points in Cyber-Physical Logistics

Cyber-physical logistics systems integrate robotics, sensors, telematics, digital twins, and cloud analytics into a single operational fabric. While this creates immense efficiency, it also means that failures in one layer—from compromised sensors to cloud latency—can rapidly escalate across the network. Identifying high-impact failure points is essential for designing resilient autonomous operations and preventing cascading disruptions that affect warehouses, fleets, and fulfillment centers. The Cyber–Physical Internet (CPI) provides a protocol framework that enables logistics transportation to attain levels of reachability, reliability, and efficiency comparable to those of data transmission over the Internet (Lu, Zhao, & Huang, 2026). Table 2 shows the Critical Failure Points in Cyber-Physical Logistics.

Table 2. Critical failure points in cyber-physical logistics

Failure Area	Description	Primary Impact
Autonomous Warehouses	Vulnerable to spoofed sensors, corrupted calibrations, and network faults.	Navigation errors, collisions, ASRS stoppages.
Fleet Management & Telematics	Routing depends on real-time GPS, traffic feeds, and V2X communications.	Wrong routes, delivery delays, safety risks.
Digital Twin Integrity	Twins fail when fed corrupted or delayed data.	Unsafe predictions and misleading operational guidance.
Edge–Cloud Pipeline Weaknesses	Hybrid data architectures prone to latency and interception.	Outdated decisions and network compromise.
Human–Machine Governance Gaps	Misinterpretation or overreliance on AI outputs.	Incorrect overrides and crisis mismanagement.

3. DATA FOUNDATIONS, SCOR/IBP TAXONOMIES, AND RISK GOVERNANCE

Data sits at the heart of every AI-driven logistics operation. As organizations adopt Generative AI, digital twins, autonomous robotics, and predictive analytics, the accuracy, reliability, and governance of data become directly tied to the safety and resilience of logistics networks. Robust data foundations ensure that algorithms receive clean, meaningful, and trustworthy information, reducing the likelihood of erroneous AI outputs or cascading failures across supply chain processes. Meanwhile, SCOR and IBP taxonomies offer structured frameworks that help enterprises map risks across each functional domain, enabling strategic alignment between data practices, risk mitigation, and operational performance. Together, data foundations and structured taxonomies form the backbone of modern risk governance in AI-enabled logistics. The heightened need for rapid and accurate parcel delivery has resulted in the extensive implementation of automated technologies in logistics (Kranthi et al., 2025).

3.1 SCOR/IBP for Risk Transparency

The SCOR (Supply Chain Operations Reference) model and Integrated Business Planning (IBP) frameworks provide a standardized way to deconstruct logistics operations into functional modules—Plan, Source, Make, Deliver, Return, and Enable—each with associated risks, data dependencies, and AI-driven opportunities. There is a relationship between supply chain resilience and the Supply Chain Operations Reference (SCOR) model (Aem-on, Setamanit, Chandrachai, & Sinthupinyo, 2024). Table 3 shows the SCOR Layer Risk Insights.

Table 3. SCOR layer risk insights

SCOR Process	AI-Driven Components	Potential Risks
Plan	Demand sensing, graph forecasting, ML prediction engines	Data drift, model bias, adversarial contamination, seasonal misinterpretation
Source	Supplier risk scoring, ESG validation, e-tendering automation	Manipulated supplier data, poor master data, cyber fraud in procurement portals
Make	AI-based scheduling, robotic coordination, computer vision QC	Sensor noise, digital twin misalignment, unsafe production plans
Deliver	Routing engines, dynamic TMS, carbon-aware logistics	GPS spoofing, telemetry attacks, corrupted routing data, carbon model tampering
Return	Reverse logistics tracking, circularity systems, repair workflows	Traceability failures, inaccurate carbon reporting, misclassified return items

IBP Integration for Cross-Functional Alignment

IBP provides a unified planning cadence across finance, operations, procurement, and commercial functions. When paired with AI risk metrics and SCOR taxonomies, IBP becomes a governance mechanism that:

- Synchronizes data-driven decisions across teams
- Ensures shared visibility of supply disruptions
- Creates accountability for AI forecasting and planning
- Aligns scenario planning with digital twin simulations

Table 4 shows the IBP Alignment Functions and Governance Outcomes.

Table 4. IBP alignment functions and governance outcomes

IBP Dimension	Role in AI-Enabled Logistics	Governance Contribution
Demand Alignment	Synchronizing forecasting cycles across teams	Ensures cross-functional consistency and reduces misaligned forecasts
Supply Alignment	Coordinating procurement and supplier data	Improves risk visibility in sourcing and bidding
Financial Alignment	Linking cost models with AI predictions	Ensures accountability and budget control under uncertainty
Scenario Planning	Matching digital twin simulations with IBP cycles	Improves accuracy of what-if analysis and disruption planning
Executive Review	Final approval of high-impact AI-driven decisions	Reinforces responsible decision-making and ethical governance

SCOR and IBP together create a risk-aware operating system for AI-enabled logistics, ensuring that risks are detected early, communicated clearly, and mitigated collaboratively.

3.2 Data Readiness and Master Data Management

High-quality data is the foundation of every AI-enabled logistics system, yet many organizations continue to operate with fragmented, inconsistent, or poorly calibrated datasets. Data readiness ensures that information flowing from sensors, WMS, TMS, ERP systems, robotics, and telematics is complete, consistent, timely, and accurate. When any of these attributes fail, the impact is immediate: AI models misinterpret demand signals, routing engines calculate unsafe paths, warehouse robots behave unpredictably, and digital twins produce misleading simulations. Ensuring completeness across SKU records, enforcing consistent naming conventions, maintaining predictable latency in IoT transmissions, and calibrating edge devices such as weight sensors or vision systems are essential prerequisites for reliable AI-driven decision-making. Improperly governed data contaminates training pipelines and undermines predictive accuracy, making data readiness a core risk-control mechanism rather than a technical detail.

Master Data Management (MDM) strengthens this foundation by providing structured governance for the critical reference data that drives complex supply chain operations. Product definitions, geocoded location hierarchies, supplier and customer master tables, CO_2 emission factors, and maintenance logs for digital twins must be versioned, validated, and continuously monitored to prevent silent failures. Without strong MDM, organizations face errors such as duplicate SKUs leading to stockouts, incorrect case dimensions disrupting warehouse slotting, outdated bills of material skewing production planning, and misaligned carrier information corrupting routing engines. Increasingly, organizations adopt "data-product thinking," treating essential datasets as maintained assets with defined ownership, service-level agreements, and accountability structures. This ensures traceability, interoperability, and faster root-cause analysis. Together, data readiness and MDM form the governance backbone that enables SCOR- and IBP-aligned AI systems to operate safely, transparently, and predictably, reducing systemic vulnerabilities in modern logistics networks. Table 5 shows the Core Data Readiness and MDM Requirements.

Table 5. Core data readiness and MDM requirements

Domain	Key Requirement	Primary Risk if Absent
Data Readiness	Completeness, consistency, timeliness, accuracy	Unreliable AI predictions, unsafe automation, distorted routing or inventory signals
Master Data Management	Governed SKU, location, supplier, customer, and emissions data	Stockouts, slotting errors, routing failures, incorrect planning inputs
Data-Product Thinking	Ownership, versioning, SLAs, lineage	Slow issue detection, inconsistent models, high data risk exposure

4. AI IN DEMAND, INVENTORY, AND UNCERTAINTY MANAGEMENT

AI technologies are fundamentally reshaping how organizations perceive, anticipate, and respond to fluctuations in demand, inventory levels, and supply chain uncertainty. Traditional forecasting relied heavily on historical patterns and linear models that often failed to adapt to sudden market changes or disruptions. Modern logistics, however, operates in environments characterized by volatile customer behavior, unpredictable geopolitical shocks, climate instability, and highly interconnected global trade routes. AI provides a new level of intelligence that is capable of detecting weak signals, incorporating real-time data, and generating proactive insights. Effective sales planning is critical in the retail industry but is challenging to outline and implement (Saccomanno, Trivella, & Guerriero, 2026).

Demand sensing engines powered by deep learning now integrate transactional data, weather patterns, economic indicators, competitor behavior, and unstructured text from news or social media. Inventory models incorporate multi-echelon dependencies, lead-time variability, and probabilistic forecasts. Meanwhile, advanced uncertainty management systems use digital twins, Bayesian networks, and Monte Carlo simulations to evaluate thousands of potential future scenarios. However, adopting AI introduces new vulnerabilities relating to data reliability, model interpretability, and adversarial manipulation. Understanding these opportunities and risks is essential for building resilient, transparent, and robust logistics strategies.

4.1 Generative AI and Demand Sensing Risks

Generative AI has advanced demand sensing beyond classical time-series models by identifying complex relationships across diverse data sources. This enables forecasting systems to capture early signals of market changes, emerging trends, and abnormal consumption patterns. For instance, large language models (LLMs) can process global news, consumer reviews, and social sentiment to detect demand shocks earlier than traditional models. Retailers and manufacturers increasingly rely on generative models to simulate potential demand trajectories under varying economic, promotional, or competitor scenarios (Ogunde, 2025).

However, generative AI also introduces unique risk factors. These models can hallucinate patterns, creating artificial correlations that mislead planners. Overfitting can arise when models learn from noisy or season-specific events, causing overreaction in inventory or replenishment decisions. An additional risk is adversarial data injection, where manipulated online content distorts sentiment-based predictions. Furthermore, generative models may unintentionally replicate biases present in training data, disproportionately affecting certain segments or regions. Without strong validation, monitoring, and human supervision, generative AI can amplify forecasting volatility instead of stabilizing it.

Another challenge lies in transparency. Generative models often operate as black boxes, making it difficult for planners to understand why certain demand scenarios are predicted. In safety-critical or high-cost environments, such opacity can undermine trust and complicate governance efforts. Therefore, effective use of generative AI in demand sensing requires rigorous risk controls, structured explainability tools, continuous recalibration, and strong data governance frameworks.

4.2 Causal and Graph-Based Forecasting Governance

Causal inference and graph-based forecasting models represent a major leap forward in forecasting accuracy. Unlike standard predictive models that rely on correlations, causal models identify actual drivers of demand, such as price changes, promotions, macroeconomic shifts, and supply-side constraints. Graph neural networks (GNNs) map relationships among products, customers, suppliers, and locations, offering a holistic view of interdependencies across the supply chain. These models enhance risk management by enabling planners to distinguish between genuine causal effects and coincidental patterns. For instance, a causal model might reveal that a spike in demand is driven by a competitor stockout rather than market growth. Graph models can also detect propagation patterns such as shortages cascading from upstream suppliers to downstream distributors.

However, causal and graph-based models require careful governance because their structure is sensitive to data quality, variable selection, and underlying assumptions. Incorrect graph structures can misrepresent real-world dependencies, generating misleading forecasts. Manipulated or poisoned data sources may distort causal relationships and cause the model to infer incorrect root causes. Furthermore, graph models can be computationally intensive, making real-time forecasting difficult without optimized pipelines. Governance best practices include human validation of causal structures, scenario-based stress testing, sensitivity analysis, interpretability dashboards, and data lineage audits. When properly governed, causal and graph-based forecasting provides unmatched transparency and resilience in demand planning.

4.3 Multi-Echelon Inventory Under Uncertainty

Inventory optimization is becoming increasingly sophisticated as organizations manage stock across multiple layers, including suppliers, manufacturing plants, distribution centers, regional hubs, and last-mile nodes. Multi-echelon inventory systems must consider interdependencies such as lead-time variability, correlated demand patterns, replenishment constraints, safety stock requirements, and upstream capacity limits. AI enhances this process by generating probabilistic forecasts and dynamically adjusting inventory allocations based on predicted risks. Machine learning models improve safety stock calibration by analyzing historical fluctuations, service-level requirements, and real-time signals such as weather or transportation delays. Reinforcement learning systems optimize reorder points and order quantities by learning from past performance under uncertainty. AI can even predict how disruptions in one echelon will affect downstream nodes, enabling proactive replenishment or reallocation.

Nevertheless, AI-driven inventory systems face limitations. There is a risk of over-reliance on model outputs without fully understanding the assumptions underlying them. Poor-quality data or incorrect demand forecasts can lead to stock imbalances, increased carrying costs, or service-level failures. Multi-echelon models can also become unstable if parameters are not updated frequently enough or if digital twins fall out of sync with physical reality. Effective uncertainty management requires combining AI forecasts with risk buffers, supply-side diversification, robust scenario planning, and human oversight. Digital twins enhance decision-making by simulating inventory performance under thousands of potential disruptions. When integrated with strong governance frameworks, AI-enabled multi-echelon inventory systems contribute significantly to supply chain resilience and operational continuity.

5. PRODUCTION AND QUALITY

AI is transforming production, quality inspection, and safety coordination across modern logistics and manufacturing environments. With the integration of autonomous scheduling engines, robotic systems, and computer vision quality analytics, organizations can deliver higher throughput, faster cycle times, and more consistent product quality. However, the rapid rise of automation increases operational dependence on data integrity, model reliability, and human supervision. Errors in AI-driven scheduling or vision models can propagate quickly in tightly coupled systems, creating costly rework, production delays, or safety hazards.

Human operators remain essential as supervisors, decision-makers, and ethical guardians within AI-enabled production systems. The challenge is to design systems where AI augments human labor rather than replacing or overwhelming it. This requires balancing automation with transparency, ensuring human-in-the-loop decision rights, and building governance frameworks that support safe, resilient, and trusted production ecosystems.

5.1 Scheduling Optimization Risks

AI-driven scheduling algorithms optimize machine workloads, shift patterns, maintenance windows, and resource allocation in real time by analyzing historical production rates, energy consumption trends, workforce availability, and SKU variability to construct highly efficient production plans. Advanced reinforcement learning schedulers can dynamically adjust to disruptions such as machine breakdowns, delayed raw material arrivals, or fluctuating energy prices, allowing production systems to maintain continuity and adapt to rapidly changing conditions. Despite these benefits, AI-based scheduling introduces several important risks. Model drift may occur when production conditions evolve, such as shifts in demand patterns or changes in machine failure rates, causing outdated models to generate suboptimal or potentially unsafe schedules. Misalignment between digital twins and physical assets also presents a serious challenge, as outdated virtual machine representations can lead to incorrect assumptions about setup time, available capacity, or run rates, ultimately degrading scheduling accuracy. In addition, poor data quality can distort scheduling outcomes; faulty or uncalibrated sensors may incorrectly signal that a problematic machine is performing well, prompting the AI system to allocate more work to an asset that is actually unstable. Finally, risks emerge when energy optimization models are inaccurate, leading systems to delay production excessively in an attempt to reduce energy costs, inadvertently compromising service levels and on-time delivery performance. Table 6 shows the Scheduling Optimization Risks and Controls

Table 6. Scheduling optimization risks and controls

Risk Category	Description	Mitigation Control
Data Drift	Changes in patterns reduce model accuracy	Continuous model retraining, drift monitoring
Sensor Errors	Faulty machine readings mislead scheduler	Redundant sensors, sanity checks, anomaly filters
Wrong Maintenance Predictions	Inaccurate RUL estimates cause failures	Hybrid predictive-maintenance plus human validation
Digital Twin Misalignment	Twin not calibrated with real machine	Daily synchronization, audit logs
Over-Optimization	Aggressive cost savings reduce resilience	Risk-aware objective functions

5.2 Computer Vision Quality Analytics

Computer vision (CV) has transformed quality inspection by enabling deep learning models to detect surface defects, dimensional inaccuracies, contamination, packaging errors, and labeling inconsistencies with accuracy far superior to manual inspection. Operating at full production-line speed, these systems provide real-time detection, classification, and rejection of defective items while simultaneously generating feedback signals to upstream processes. The opportunities introduced by computer vision include highly precise automated defect detection, reduced human fatigue and inspection inconsistency, and immediate insights that enhance quality control loops. However, these benefits come with their own risks and vulnerabilities. Computer vision models remain susceptible to adversarial disturbances, where even subtle changes in lighting, dust patterns, or texture can cause misclassification and threaten overall product quality. Over time, sensor degradation due to dust exposure, vibration, or thermal stress can introduce noise into captured images and gradually erode model accuracy. Errors in classification, whether false positives or false negatives, can either lead to unnecessary rejection of good items or dangerous acceptance of defective ones. The deep learning architectures behind these models often lack interpretability, complicating root-cause analysis when inspection outputs deviate from expectations. Furthermore, if models are trained only on idealized or narrowly scoped defect images, they may fail to generalize under real-world variability, resulting in missed anomalies and reduced reliability in actual production environments. Table 7 shows Computer Vision Failure Scenarios.

Table 7. Computer vision failure scenarios

Failure Scenario	Operational Impact	Mitigation Strategy
Poor Lighting	Misclassified defects	Controlled lighting environments
Camera Drift	Slow model degradation	Scheduled recalibration
Adversarial Noise	Incorrect pass/fail decisions	Robust training sets, adversarial testing
Domain Shift	Real defects differ from training	Continuous dataset expansion
Sensor Latency	Delayed QC actions	Edge computing optimization

5.3 Human-in-the-Loop Safety

Although automation continues to advance across modern logistics and manufacturing operations, humans remain essential for ensuring safety, ethical reasoning, and situational awareness. Human-in-the-loop systems allow operators to supervise AI-generated decisions, override automated actions when necessary, validate critical alerts, and intervene during abnormal or high-risk events. These systems play a fundamental role in preventing cascading failures that may arise when AI behaves unpredictably or encounters conditions outside its training distribution. They also ensure that decisions made in safety-critical contexts reflect ethical judgment rather than purely algorithmic optimization, maintaining an appropriate balance between the efficiency of automation and the nuanced reasoning humans bring to complex operational environments. Human-in-the-loop oversight further enhances trust in autonomous systems by giving operators visibility into system behavior and preserving a channel for manual correction. Figure 2 shows the Human–AI Collaboration in Production Safety.

Figure 2. Human–AI collaboration in production safety

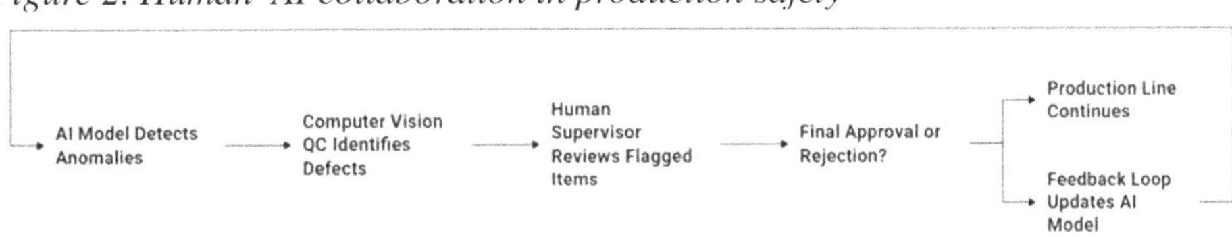

Despite these advantages, integrating humans into autonomous workflows introduces several challenges. Overreliance on automation can occur when operators develop excessive trust in AI models and overlook early warning signs or contextual cues that fall outside algorithmic detection. Alert fatigue is another major concern, as systems that generate too many warnings can overwhelm operators, causing critical alerts to be ignored or delayed. Additionally, prolonged reliance on automation may lead to skill degradation, reducing operators' ability to intervene effectively during emergencies or system failures. Ambiguity around responsibility can also emerge when decision-making is shared between humans and AI, complicating questions of accountability when outcomes deviate from expectations. These challenges highlight the importance of designing human-AI collaboration frameworks that maintain clarity, support operator competence, and reinforce a healthy balance between machine autonomy and human control. Table 8 shows the Human–AI Safety Coordination Principles.

Table 8. Human–AI safety coordination principles

Principle	Description	Application in Production
Human Override Rights	Humans must have authority to stop automated actions	Emergency stop buttons on robots
Explainability	AI decisions must be interpretable	XAI dashboards for QC predictions
Shared Situational Awareness	Both human and AI access same data	Unified control-tower interface
Skill Retention	Operators trained continuously	Simulation-based learning
Escalation Protocols	Clear rules for when humans take over	Incident response playbooks

6. WAREHOUSING AND TRANSPORT

Warehousing and transport operations form the backbone of modern logistics networks and are now deeply intertwined with autonomous systems, IoT devices, robotics, and AI-driven routing algorithms. This evolution increases operational efficiency while simultaneously expanding the cyber-physical attack surface. Automated warehouses rely on fleets of autonomous mobile robots (AMRs), automated storage and retrieval systems, and machine-vision stations. Transport networks are managed by dynamic routing engines, telematics, V2X communications, and drone-based last-mile delivery. Because both warehousing and transport involve physical movement, cyber intrusions can translate into real-world consequences that jeopardize human safety, damage infrastructure, or disrupt supply chain continuity. This section explores the growing challenges inherent to cyber-physical logistics systems and outlines key vulnerabilities, failure scenarios, and preventive strategies. The rapid growth of the e-commerce has intensified demand on the intelligent warehouse efficiency, where the heterogeneous robots collaboration presents both opportunities and challenges (Zhang & Wu, 2026).

6.1 Autonomous Robots, Slotting, and Picking

Autonomous Mobile Robots (AMRs) and Automated Guided Vehicles (AGVs) have become essential elements of modern warehouse automation, taking over material movement, replenishment tasks, and picking activities while operating in close coordination with conveyor systems, robotic arms, and IoT-enabled sensing devices. Their operation depends on uninterrupted streams of sensor and communication data that guide positioning, obstacle avoidance, workflow execution, and multi-robot coordination. However, their deep integration into warehouse operations introduces significant cyber-physical vulnerabilities. Sensor interference and spoofing pose a major threat because AMRs rely heavily on LiDAR, ultrasonic sensors, and vision systems; manipulated sensor signals can cause robots to collide, stop unexpectedly, or navigate incorrectly. Command injection attacks become possible when communication between robots and warehouse management systems is intercepted, enabling malicious actors to redirect robots or alter task assignments. Firmware tampering presents another critical risk, as exploitation of firmware vulnerabilities allows attackers to modify robot behavior, disable safety protocols, or manipulate movement speeds. Manipulation of slotting data can further disrupt operations by directing robots to incorrect aisles, increasing congestion and decreasing overall throughput. Additionally, many AMRs communicate using Wi-Fi or Bluetooth channels that, if not properly encrypted, expose robots to data interception and unauthorized access. Together, these risks underscore the need for robust cyber-physical security strategies within highly automated warehouse environments. Table 9 shows the Key Risks in Warehouse Robotics.

Table 9. Key risks in warehouse robotics

Risk	Impact	Mitigation Strategy
Sensor spoofing	Collisions, unsafe routes	Sensor redundancy, LiDAR authentication
Command injection	Unauthorized task execution	Encrypted robot-to-WMS communication
Firmware tampering	Loss of robotic control	Secure boot, signed firmware updates
Slotting manipulation	Congestion, efficiency loss	Role-based access control (RBAC)
Wireless insecurity	Data interception	WPA3, zero-trust segmentation

6.2 Network Design and Dynamic Routing Risks

Network design and dynamic routing systems have become fundamental to modern transport operations, enabling fleets to optimize delivery paths based on real-time traffic conditions, weather data, vehicle health, fuel prices, and customer requirements. These systems depend on continuous communication between telematics units, routing engines, cloud platforms, and V2X (vehicle-to-everything) infrastructure. As a result, they expose the logistics network to cyber-physical risks that can directly influence fleet safety and performance. GPS spoofing remains one of the most severe threats, as attackers can broadcast false coordinates that misdirect trucks or autonomous vehicles to dangerous or inefficient routes. Routing algorithms are also vulnerable to data poisoning, where attackers inject fabricated congestion or incident data to produce suboptimal route choices. Compromised telematics systems can conceal mechanical issues, send falsified speed or fuel data, or disable safety notifications. Unauthorized access to fleet dashboards can lead to malicious rerouting, unauthorized vehicle immobilization, or deliberate delays. Furthermore, carbon-aware routing models introduce new integrity risks, as manipulated emissions or fuel-consumption data can distort sustainability metrics and compromise ESG compliance. These vulnerabilities highlight the need for authenticated data sources, encrypted telematics channels, redundant navigation systems, and continuous anomaly detection across routing ecosystems.

6.3 Carbon-Aware Logistics Integrity

Carbon-aware logistics introduces advanced optimization tools that use AI to reduce emissions across transport networks by adjusting routes, improving consolidation strategies, and optimizing energy consumption. These systems rely on IoT sensors, telematics data, and digital twins to track Scope 1, 2, and 3 emissions with high temporal precision. However, the integrity of these carbon models depends heavily on the accuracy and trustworthiness of the underlying data. Manipulated or faulty emissions measurements, such as tampered fuel sensors or altered engine-load readings, can cause carbon-optimization algorithms to generate misleading recommendations. Incorrect emissions factors embedded in optimization engines may shift routing decisions toward seemingly efficient routes that are not truly sustainable. Misaligned digital twins can further degrade carbon analytics by producing inaccurate simulations of fuel burn, load profiles, or vehicle performance. Additionally, fraudulent sustainability reporting remains an ongoing concern, especially when upstream suppliers lack standardized carbon accounting procedures. These risks demonstrate the importance of tamper-resistant sensor hardware, standardized emissions factors, blockchain-based traceability, and continuous calibration of carbon models to ensure that carbon-aware logistics delivers legitimate, verifiable sustainability improvements rather than distorted or deceptive metrics.

7. LAST-MILE LOGISTICS

Last-mile delivery is one of the most vulnerable areas of logistics because it involves direct interaction between automated technology and the public environment. Crowdsourcing systems, smart lockers, micro-fulfillment hubs, and autonomous fleets increase efficiency but at the same time open up a much wider range of cyber and physical threat opportunities. This complexity increases because last-mile networks are highly distributed and involve many stakeholders with diverse security standards. As a vital driver of supply chain management, data has evolved into both a foundational resource and a critical production factor for optimizing supply chains and mitigating risk (Shi et al., 2025).

7.1 Crowdsourced Delivery Platforms

Crowdsourced delivery relies on mobile applications used by thousands of independent couriers. In practice, couriers can become an attack entry point when their account is stolen or the device is not protected. Sensitive customer data can be exposed if the application does not have strong encryption protection. Data manipulation in the form of GPS spoofing or traffic injection can cause route deviations, delays, or safety risks. This condition is exacerbated by the fact that couriers often use personal devices that do not always meet the company's security standards.

7.2 Lockers and Micro-Fulfillment Systems

Smart lockers provide convenience to customers, but these systems are vulnerable to access code interception, physical break-ins, and software attacks on the interface panel. When the synchronization system between the locker and the central server is disrupted, the information displayed to the customer can be incorrect so that the packet is incorrectly retrieved or not found. Unit lockers connected over local networks can also be targeted for attacks if their communication protocols are not secured.

7.3 Drones, AGVs, and Autonomous Fleets

Drones and AGVs face cyber threats that can have an immediate physical impact. Drones can be taken over through signal injection or GPS manipulation, causing a loss of control. AGVs can be directed off the track through visual manipulation such as QR code or floor marker modifications. Communication disturbances such as jamming can cause the vehicle to stop abruptly or lose orientation. All of these forms of threats require multi-layered security designs, from signal authentication, navigation redundancy, to real-time telemetry monitoring. Table 10 shows the Key Risks in Last-Mile Delivery.

Table 10. Key risks in last-mile delivery

Risk Areas	Examples of Threats	Operational Impact
Crowdsourcing	Courier account hijacking, data leak	Wrong packet delivery, information leakage
Smart Lockers	PIN/QR disadap, malware kiosk	Illegal retrieval, incorrect data
Drone/AGV	GPS spoofing, jamming, marker manipulation	Accidents, wrong routes, service interruptions

8. CONTROL TOWERS & DIGITAL TWINS

Modern control towers integrate big data from warehouses, fleets, suppliers, as well as global markets to deliver real-time visibility and intelligent predictions. Digital twins reinforce this capability by providing a virtual representation of physical conditions that allows for what-if simulations, stress testing, and end-to-end optimization. However, the high reliance on AI data and models makes control towers and digital twins high-value attack targets. Message-Locked Encryption (MLE) enables encrypted deduplication by deriving keys directly from data (S. Li, Ma, Han, & Xu, 2025).

Digital twins function as powerful yet double-edged tools, as their reliability depends heavily on the quality and integrity of sensor data. When data is corrupted, poisoned, or delayed, these models can generate misleading representations that distort operational decision-making, and their inherent complexity often makes audits slow and errors difficult to detect. Similarly, resilience dashboards that provide risk predictions, scenario simulations, and automated recommendations become problematic when underlying assumptions are unvalidated or visualizations are inaccurate, potentially leading operators to make inappropriate decisions, especially when over-reliance on AI reduces situational awareness in the presence of unseen anomalies. Control towers, which are interconnected with hundreds of APIs, sensors, and servers, face significant cybersecurity risks, as breaches of even a single component can compromise the entire network; stolen administrator credentials may allow attackers to alter shipment routes, manipulate inventory levels, or conceal risks, while unsecured APIs can expose sensitive data or enable the injection of false information, and insider threats further heighten vulnerability due to legitimate access privileges. Table 11 shows the Key Risks of Control Towers and Digital Twins.

Table 11. Key risks of control towers and digital twins

Domain	Risk	Impact
Digital Twin	Data poisoning, twin-reality divergence	Wrong simulation, wrong decision
Dashboards	False assumptions, visual misleads	Improper mitigation, blind spots
Cybersecurity	Credential theft, API exploit	System takeover, data leaked

9. PROCUREMENT, SOURCING, AND SUPPLY CHAIN GOVERNANCE

Procurement and sourcing in modern supply chains increasingly rely on artificial intelligence, e-tendering automation, and risk analytics to select suppliers, verify compliance, and monitor sustainability. However, this digital transformation also increases vulnerability to data manipulation, supplier fraud, and hidden ESG risks. AI-based procurement accelerates vendor evaluation but requires strict governance so that algorithms don't generate bias or open up new attack paths. Additionally, sharing data with global suppliers creates cross-border privacy, integrity, and compliance challenges. The management of assembly manufacturing supply chains in a cloud computing environment poses various challenges, including extensive regional management, a lack of transparency in the supply chain, an absence of a secure and effective traceability mechanism, and difficulties in achieving safe traceability (C. Li, Gao, Chu, & Tang, 2025).

9.1 Public Procurement and E-Tendering Integrity

E-tendering allows companies to assess suppliers quickly and transparently, but the system is vulnerable to document forgery, algorithmic manipulation, and phishing attacks targeting tender participants. If AI is used to rank suppliers, non-transparent models can reinforce historical bias or fail to detect high-risk vendors. There are additional risks when tenders are opened to international suppliers, as differences in security standards and privacy regulations can lead to data inconsistencies.

9.2 Supplier Discovery and Onboarding Risk

AI-based platforms are often used to find new suppliers and speed up the onboarding process. However, inadequate supplier validation can allow unauthorized or underperforming vendors to enter the supply network. Reliance on unverified external data poses a threat in the form of false identities, digital reputation manipulation, or inaccurate risk assessments. Failures in verification can make quality tracking difficult and increase the risk of future supply disruptions.

9.3 ESG and Scope-3 Compliance

Companies are facing pressure to ensure their supply chains meet sustainability and ethical standards. Risks arise when suppliers provide inaccurate ESG data, either due to recording errors or deliberate manipulation. Scope-3 emissions rely heavily on supplier data, so the failure of one vendor can disrupt the sustainability reporting of the entire network. Without robust data governance, AI may process misinformation and generate procurement decisions that are not in line with ESG goals. Table 12 shows the Core Risks in Procurement and Sourcing.

Table 12. Core risks in procurement and sourcing

Area	Risk	Impact
E-Tendering	Document manipulation and AI rating	Selection of high-risk suppliers
Onboarding	False identity and false reputation	Supply disruptions and fraud
ESG	Inaccurate Scope-3 reports	Non-compliance and reputational risk

10. CYBER-PHYSICAL SECURITY

Governance is the backbone in securing highly automated logistics operations. With the increasing use of AI, digital twins, autonomous robots, and cloud-integrated systems, there is a need for a governance framework that ensures all risks can be systematically monitored, controlled, and responded. Governance includes oversight of AI models, data security, regulatory compliance, and the sharing of human-machine responsibilities in making operational decisions. Without strong governance, logistics tends to experience blind spots that go undetected and lead to major failures.

10.1 Governance and Accountability for AI Systems

AI models must go through a process of continuous validation, audit, and monitoring. Governance ensures that the model is not only accurate but also safe, ethical, and explainable. When AI provides recommendations related to safety or regulation, organizations must establish oversight mechanisms that require human review before decisions are made. Governance also includes establishing a responsibility structure so that it is clear who is responsible if the model fails.

10.2 Zero-Trust Architecture for Autonomous Logistics

Zero-Trust Architecture (ZTA) is becoming the new standard in autonomous logistics systems. Unlike the traditional approach of trusting internal devices, ZTA requires verification at every point of interaction. Every robot, sensor, and app is required to perform strict authentication before it can communicate. This approach reduces the risk of internal attacks and lateral movement when a node is successfully compromised. Zero trust aims to enable users in untrusted network areas to access trusted areas through authentication and policy control (Shao et al., 2025).

10.3 Regulatory Compliance and Ethical Oversight

Logistics operations must comply with various regulations related to AI, cybersecurity, data privacy, public safety, and sustainability. Compliance includes international requirements such as ISO 27001, NIST CSF, EU AI Act, GDPR, and various logistics sector policies. Governance ensures that the implementation of AI does not create discriminatory bias, privacy violations, or safety hazards. Ethical oversight requires collaboration between technology experts, regulators, and industry stakeholders (Beltrán, 2025).

11. AI ASSURANCE, EXPLAINABILITY, AND RESPONSIBLE AUTOMATION

AI assurance is the main foundation in ensuring that the AI systems used in logistics run safely, transparently, and in accordance with ethical standards. In a highly automated supply chain ecosystem, AI models not only impact operational efficiency but also decisions that directly impact the safety, sustainability, and reliability of services. Therefore, AI assurance focuses on model risk evaluation, outcome validation, and continuous performance monitoring across operating environments, both edge and cloud. This approach integrates bias testing techniques, robustness evaluation, drift monitoring, and multi-environment validation mechanisms to ensure that AI remains stable despite changes in data or operational conditions.

11.1 AI Assurance Frameworks

AI assurance frameworks are designed to evaluate the integrity and stability of models from various sides. The framework includes bias testing to assess whether the model makes fair decisions in a multi-region or multi-vendor supply chain context. Robustness evaluation is carried out to ensure that the model continues to function despite disturbances or noise in operational data, such as sensor fluctuations in the fleet or warehouse. Drift monitoring is especially important when models work with real-time data, as changes in demand patterns or operational behavior can shift algorithm performance unnoticed. Cross-edge and cloud environment validation ensures consistent model output even if the model is running on different IoT devices, edge servers, or cloud computing.

11.2 Explainable AI (XAI)

Explainable AI plays a critical role in providing transparency into the recommendations generated by the system. When AI is used to determine shipment priority, fleet rerouting or supplier risk evaluation, operators must be able to understand the rationale behind those decisions. XAI allows human interpretability so that decisions are not considered as unsupervisable black boxes. In the context of high-value logistics, such as pharmaceutical shipments, aviation spare parts, or high-value goods, AI transparency increases trust between humans and machines. In addition, XAI contributes to risk governance because it provides an auditable explanation trail (Barredo Arrieta et al., 2020; Mahir et al., 2026).

11.3 Model Risk Management

The Risk Management (MRM) model covers the entire life cycle of the AI model, from the model approval process to continuous performance monitoring. The model must go through an approval process before being used in operations, including security testing, data validation, and methodology review. Versioning is used to ensure that any model updates can be tracked so that operators know the difference between the old and new versions. Audit logs provide a structured record of the entire model's activity, including inputs, outputs, and parameter changes. Continuous risk scoring allows the system to detect performance degradation before a significant impact occurs. Table 13 shows the Core Components of AI Assurance and Governance Models.

Table 13. Core components of AI assurance and governance models

Component	Function	Impact If Not Done
Bias Testing	Assessing the fairness of the model	Inconsistent and discriminatory results
Robustness Evaluation	Testing the durability of the model	Model fails when conditions change
Drift Monitoring	Monitor performance changes	Output deviates without detection
Versioning & Audit Logs	Change tracking	No audit trail and compliance risk

12. GOVERNANCE MODELS FOR AUTONOMOUS AND AI-DRIVEN LOGISTICS

Governance in AI-based logistics includes the drafting of rules, oversight structures, and evaluation processes to ensure that autonomous technologies work safely and in accordance with ethical principles. This governance is critical when AI systems take a significant role in decision-making that impacts public safety, legal compliance, and supply chain sustainability. The governance model must include aspects of fairness, accountability, transparency, and safety to ensure that autonomous technology can be trusted by operators, regulators, and business partners.

12.1 Ethical Principles for Automated Decisions

Automated decisions must comply with the principles of fairness, safety, transparency, and accountability. Fairness ensures that the algorithm does not discriminate against specific groups, for example small suppliers or routes in certain areas. Safety ensures that the robot's routing and operation decisions do not endanger humans or property. Transparency guarantees that the reasoning behind AI decisions is understandable. Accountability requires organizations to have clear risk owners so that system failures do not eliminate human responsibility.

12.2 Regulatory Compliance

AI-based operations are required to comply with various regulations, including ISO 27001 for information security management, NIST AI RMF for AI risk management, the EU AI Act for transparency and security standards, as well as various supply chain security directives adopted by countries or industry sectors. The regulation provides a formal framework that requires every AI system to be equipped with auditability, explainability, and quality control.

12.3 Organization-Wide AI Governance Structures

AI governance structures should be built across the organization, not just in the technology department. The AI risk committee is responsible for risk assessment and mitigation. The approval board model ensures that each model implemented meets safety and ethical standards. Cybersecurity oversight teams monitor threats to AI systems, including adversarial attacks. Cross-functional incident response groups handle incidents and coordinate responses between technical, operational, and legal teams.

13. FUTURE CHALLENGES AND STRATEGIC OUTLOOK

As AI-driven logistics ecosystems evolve toward higher levels of autonomy, interconnectedness, and computational sophistication, organizations must prepare for an emerging generation of risks that extend beyond conventional cybersecurity or operational concerns. Logistics networks are increasingly shaped by quantum-era threats, multimodal AI systems, and agentic AI models capable of autonomous decision-making across procurement, routing, inventory optimization, and exception management. These developments promise significant efficiency gains, yet they also introduce structural vulnerabilities that require new governance frameworks, continuous assurance mechanisms, and proactive regulatory alignment. This section outlines the major technological and governance challenges that will shape the next decade of AI-driven logistics operations.

13.1 Quantum-Ready Cybersecurity

Quantum computing represents a transformative technological breakthrough, but it simultaneously threatens the cryptography that secures global logistics infrastructure. Most logistics environments rely on RSA and ECC encryption across telematics, warehouse robotics, digital twins, control towers, and cloud APIs. Once quantum computers reach sufficient scale, these algorithms become vulnerable to rapid decryption, exposing sensitive shipment data, routing instructions, and supplier communication channels. A compromised cryptographic foundation could enable adversaries to manipulate digital twins, tamper with inventory data, or falsify customs documentation at scale.

Although post-quantum cryptography (PQC) standards are emerging through NIST, industry adoption remains slow. Many logistics organizations lack an asset inventory that identifies cryptographic dependencies, and most operational technology (OT) devices do not support modern encryption protocols. This creates a dangerous lag between quantum capability and logistics readiness. Preparing for quantum-era threats requires inventorying cryptographic assets, adopting PQC algorithms, and redesigning authentication workflows so they remain secure even in the presence of quantum adversaries. Without these changes, logistics systems risk entering the quantum era with legacy defenses that cannot protect critical AI-enabled operations.

13.2 Agentic AI and Autonomous Supply Chains

Agentic AI models represent a fundamental shift from passive prediction to autonomous action. These systems can negotiate supplier contracts, optimize shipment routing, place replenishment orders, and trigger operational interventions without human initiation. While agentic AI promises significant efficiency gains, it also introduces liability, transparency, and safety risks. Unauthorized or poorly supervised autonomous actions can amplify disruptions, deplete inventory, create financial exposure, or violate regulatory constraints.

Real incidents already illustrate the danger of over-automation. During several major e-commerce peak events, routing engines and pricing algorithms triggered cascading errors when small anomalies were interpreted as large-scale disruptions. Agentic procurement systems at multiple retailers have also mistakenly placed excessive restocking orders due to drift in demand models. These examples highlight the need for strong guardrails: action-approval workflows, human-in-the-loop escalation thresholds, dual-control mechanisms for high-impact decisions, and continuous monitoring of agent behavior. Agentic AI must operate within strict governance boundaries to prevent autonomous errors from propagating through multi-echelon supply chains.

13.3 Multimodal Interfaces and Expanded Attack Surfaces

Logistics organizations are rapidly adopting multimodal interfaces that allow operators to interact with AI systems using voice, vision, gesture, and natural language. These interfaces increase accessibility and enhance situational awareness within control towers, warehouses, and last-mile fleets. However, multimodality also expands the attack surface. Voice-command spoofing, malicious QR codes, manipulated sensor imagery, or adversarial audio signals can exploit weaknesses in multimodal models. Attackers may also manipulate screen-based prompts or augmented-reality overlays used by warehouse associates.

Current regulatory frameworks do not adequately address multimodal AI risks. Neither the EU AI Act nor the NIST AI RMF provides detailed guidance for securing multimodal pipelines, particularly in operational environments with real-time constraints. As a result, logistics organizations must create their own multimodal security guidelines, covering voice authentication, adversarial image detection, sensor redundancy, and safe-fail mechanisms. Multimodality will remain an essential part of next-generation logistics, but without robust controls, it can become an unexpected entry point for cyber-physical compromise.

13.4 Toward Self-Governing Supply Chains

The long-term trajectory of AI-enabled logistics points toward partially self-governing supply chains, where intelligent systems autonomously detect disruptions, reconfigure network flows, and ensure regulatory compliance. Digital twins will increasingly synchronize with real-time data to produce automated predictions, and resilience algorithms will propose or execute route adjustments during weather events, capacity shortages, or supplier failures. Autonomous systems may dynamically adjust warehouse slotting, modify last-mile allocation, or reassign transport assets without waiting for human intervention.

However, current governance frameworks lag behind this emerging reality. Most standards—including ISO 27001, NIST CSF, NIST AI RMF, and the EU AI Act—are not designed for systems capable of autonomous reconfiguration. They provide strong principles but insufficient operational guidance for multi-agent coordination, autonomous exception handling, or high-speed AI-initiated changes to physical infrastructure. As autonomy grows, logistics organizations must define new rules for accountability, auditability, and ethical oversight. The future does not eliminate human governance but expands it into a supervisory role that ensures alignment between autonomous system behavior and organizational values.

14. CONCLUSION

AI-driven logistics has entered a new era defined by pervasive automation, multimodal sensing, agentic AI, digital twins, and cyber-physical coordination across global networks. These systems provide unprecedented operational visibility, predictive capability, and resilience potential. However, their integration also introduces structural vulnerabilities, algorithmic dependencies, and cascading risk pathways that traditional logistics governance frameworks cannot fully address. This chapter has presented a comprehensive examination of these emerging challenges, outlining how forecasting systems, autonomous robots, control towers, data infrastructures, and digital twins collectively shape a complex risk landscape. It has also demonstrated that modern logistics environments require a unified governance model where cybersecurity, AI assurance, data integrity, and human oversight function as interdependent components rather than isolated controls.

To support practitioners and researchers, the chapter advances a set of actionable principles for building secure and resilient AI-enabled logistics ecosystems. Organizations must adopt robust data governance practices, including quality KPIs, lineage tracking, and semantic consistency, to prevent model drift and systemic errors. AI assurance mechanisms—including interpretability thresholds, drift monitoring, and lifecycle validation—should be embedded into both cloud and edge deployments. Human–AI collaboration must be structured to ensure that humans remain capable of meaningful intervention, with performance metrics guiding oversight design. Cyber-physical security architectures should be strengthened to defend against manipulation of sensors, telematics, and autonomous systems, supported by rapid anomaly detection and multi-robot coordination safeguards. Finally, logistics leaders should incorporate real-world incident learnings, such as the Maersk NotPetya and FedEx TNT breaches, into scenario planning and red-team exercises to ensure preparedness for high-impact disruptions.

Together, these actionable measures highlight a shift toward integrated, anticipatory governance capable of aligning advanced automation with organizational values, regulatory obligations, and operational realities. The future of logistics will be shaped not only by technological innovation but by the ability of firms to govern AI responsibly, secure their cyber-physical ecosystems, and prepare for emerging risks such as quantum attacks, agentic AI behavior, and multimodal threat vectors. By adopting the governance structures, assurance practices, and resilience strategies detailed in this chapter, logistics organizations can chart a path toward supply chains that are not only efficient and adaptive, but also trustworthy, transparent, and strategically robust.

REFERENCES

Aem-on, K., Setamanit, S.-O., Chandrachai, A., & Sinthupinyo, S. (2024). Empowering Supply Chain Resilience in High-Growth of Small and Medium Enterprises (SMEs) Through the Integration of the SCOR Model Paradigm. *TEM Journal, 13*(2), 1331–1344. https://doi.org/DOI: 10.18421/TEM132-47

Alahmari, D., & Awad, A. (2025). Strategic integration of marketing and supply chain functions for superior customer experience: Insights from logistics startups under Saudi Vision 2030. *PLoS One*, *20*(11), e0336132. DOI: 10.1371/journal.pone.0336132 PMID: 41270081

Awad, A., & Mahmoud, M. (2024). Impact of electronic customer relationship management on competitive advantage: Mediating role of customer satisfaction in EgyptAir. *Problems and Perspectives in Management*, *22*(3), 276–286. DOI: 10.21511/ppm.22(3).2024.22

Barredo Arrieta, A., Díaz-Rodríguez, N., Del Ser, J., Bennetot, A., Tabik, S., Barbado, A., & Herrera, F. (2020). Explainable Artificial Intelligence (XAI): Concepts, taxonomies, opportunities and challenges toward responsible AI. *Information Fusion*, *58*, 82–115. DOI: 10.1016/j.inffus.2019.12.012

Beltrán, M. (2025). AI algorithms under scrutiny: GDPR, DSA, AI Act and CRA as pillars for algorithmic security and privacy in the European Union. *Computers & Security*, *158*. Advance online publication. DOI: 10.1016/j.cose.2025.104628

Jacyna-Gołda, I., Shmygol, N., Sembiyeva, L., Cherniavska, O., Burtebayeva, A., Uskenbayeva, A., & Salwin, M. (2025). Modeling Sustainable Development of Transport Logistics Under Climate Change, Ecosystem Dynamics, and Digitalization. *Applied Sciences (Switzerland)*, *15*(13). Advance online publication. DOI: 10.3390/app15137593

Jethva, B., Traoré, I., Ghaleb, A., Ganame, K., & Ahmed, S. (2020). Multilayer ransomware detection using grouped registry key operations, file entropy and file signature monitoring. *Journal of Computer Security*, *28*(3), 337–373. DOI: 10.3233/JCS-191346

Kranthi, P., Geeta, M., Shankar, C. N. U., Ranjith, P. V., Thoti, K. K., & Mishra, N. (2025). Comparative Efficiency Analysis of High-Speed Cross-Belt Sorters Using The SCOR Model: A Case Study from India's Courier Network. *International Journal of Basic and Applied Sciences*, *14*(4), 786–794. DOI: 10.14419/7bnz2v49

Laksono, M. N. G., Tiaraputri, Z. A., Sekti, B. A., & Laksono, M. I. A. (2025). Cyber-physical systems security in space. In *Advanced Cyber Defense for Space Missions and Operations* (pp. 85–113). Concepts and Applications., DOI: 10.4018/979-8-3693-7939-4.ch004

Li, C., Gao, X., Chu, J., & Tang, J. (2025). Research on a Robust Traceability Method for the Assembly Manufacturing Supply Chain Based on Blockchain. *Applied Sciences (Switzerland)*, *15*(21). Advance online publication. DOI: 10.3390/app152111598

Li, S., Ma, M., Han, Y., & Xu, C. (2025). Towards subversion-resistant password-protected encryption for deduplicated cloud storage. *Journal of Information Security and Applications*, *94*. Advance online publication. DOI: 10.1016/j.jisa.2025.104233

Lu, Z., Zhao, Z., & Huang, G. Q. (2026). STAR: Spatial–Temporal Attention Reasoning model for dynamic logistics network routing in Cyber–Physical Internet. *Advanced Engineering Informatics*, *69*. Advance online publication. DOI: 10.1016/j.aei.2025.103830

Maalouf, A., Jadhav, N., Jatavallabhula, K. M., Chahine, M., Vogt, D. M., Wood, R. J., & Rus, D. (2024). Follow Anything: Open-Set Detection, Tracking, and Following in Real-Time. *IEEE Robotics and Automation Letters*, *9*(4), 3283–3290. DOI: 10.1109/LRA.2024.3366013

Mahir, S. H., Tashrif, M. T. A., Shathe, A. S., Karim, M. A., Rahman, A., Kundu, D., & Muhammad, G. (2026). PriFL-XAI: Hybrid privacy-preserving federated learning models for monkeypox detection through GAN augmentation and explainable AI. *Biomedical Signal Processing and Control*, *112*. Advance online publication. DOI: 10.1016/j.bspc.2025.108426

Moica, S., Lucian, T., Kostopoulos, V., Gligor, A., & Mostafa, N. A. (2025). GenAI Technology Approach for Sustainable Warehouse Management Operations: A Case Study from the Automative Sector. *Sustainability (Switzerland)*, *17*(20). Advance online publication. DOI: 10.3390/su17209081

Nicoletti, B., & Appolloni, A. (2025). The Impact of AI Foundation models on the future of digital engineering for logistics and supply Chain. *Digital Engineering*, *7*. Advance online publication. DOI: 10.1016/j.dte.2025.100058

Ogunde, F. (2025). Legal large language models (LLMs): Legal dynamos or "fancifully packaged ChatGPT"? *Discover Artificial Intelligence*, *5*(1). Advance online publication. DOI: 10.1007/s44163-024-00167-8

Saccomanno, F. P., Trivella, A., & Guerriero, F. (2026). Integrated sales planning for in-store retail: A multi-stage stochastic optimization approach. *European Journal of Operational Research*, *329*(2), 669–686. DOI: 10.1016/j.ejor.2025.07.015

Shams Eldin, A. Y., Elnour, A., Hassan, R. O. A., & Awad, A. (2025). The role of technological and environmental factors in creating business value from social media dynamic capabilities for SMEs in Saudi Arabia. *Humanities & Social Sciences Communications*, *12*, 1431. DOI: 10.1057/s41599-025-05784-x

Shao, S., Gu, T., Yang, Q., Du, H., Liang, W., Sun, Z., & Ji, Y. (2025). Master-slave multi-chain with risk assessment based access control model for zero trust network. *Peer-to-Peer Networking and Applications*, *18*(6). Advance online publication. DOI: 10.1007/s12083-024-01853-1

Shi, H., Xia, Y., Zong, Z., Hua, Y., Sun, J., & Chen, X. (2025). Does Data Asset Information Disclosure Mitigate Supply Chain Risk? Causal Evidence from Double-Debiased Machine Learning. *Systems*, *13*(10). Advance online publication. DOI: 10.3390/systems13100844

Singh, S., Khanna, T., & Verma, D. K. (2025). A hybrid ensemble model for ransomware detection using feature engineering and deep learning. *International Journal of Information Technology (Singapore)*, *17*(8), 5095–5104. DOI: 10.1007/s41870-025-02681-z

Zhang, X., & Wu, X. (2026). Collaborative scheduling for heterogeneous robots with simultaneous pickup and delivery tasks in order-picking systems. *Expert Systems with Applications*, *297*. Advance online publication. DOI: 10.1016/j.eswa.2025.129457

KEY TERMS AND DEFINITIONS

Agentic Artificial Intelligence: A class of AI systems capable of taking autonomous actions rather than merely generating predictions. Agentic AI can initiate tasks such as procurement, routing adjustments, or exception handling, which introduces efficiency benefits alongside new governance and safety risks.

AI Assurance: The collection of practices, evaluation techniques, and monitoring procedures that ensure AI systems operate reliably, transparently, and safely across their lifecycle. AI assurance includes bias testing, robustness evaluation, interpretability assessment, and continuous monitoring of model behavior in production settings.

Cyber-Physical Security: A security discipline that protects integrated systems where digital components directly influence physical operations. In logistics environments, cyber-physical security safeguards autonomous robots, telematics systems, digital twins, and warehouse automation from cyberattacks that could cause physical disruption or safety incidents.

Digital Twin Convergence: The process of synchronizing virtual models of logistics assets with real-time operational data. Accurate convergence enables predictive simulations and scenario planning, while divergence introduces operational risks if the twin no longer represents actual system behavior.

Multi-Robot Coordination Security: A security domain focused on protecting the algorithms and communication protocols that allow automated robots to work collaboratively. Weaknesses in coordination logic, wireless communication, or sensor fusion can cause collisions, congestion, or disruption across robotic fleets.

Multimodal AI Interfaces: Interfaces that allow humans to interact with AI systems using multiple input channels such as language, vision, gesture, or audio. While multimodal interfaces increase usability and flexibility, they also expand the attack surface through adversarial audio, spoofed images, and manipulated sensor feeds.

Quantum-Resistant Cryptography: A new generation of cryptographic algorithms designed to remain secure against quantum computing attacks. Quantum-resistant cryptography is essential for protecting long-term logistics data, secure communication pipelines, and authentication systems as quantum capabilities advance.

Risk Propagation in Logistics Networks: The phenomenon whereby local failures such as data corruption, model errors, or cyber intrusions trigger cascading effects across supply chain nodes. Risk propagation increases in AI-driven logistics systems because decisions are automated, tightly connected, and executed at high speed.

Unified Logistics Governance Architecture: An integrated framework that combines AI assurance, cybersecurity, data governance, digital twin validation, and human oversight into a single governance model. This architecture supports resilient and trustworthy AI adoption across complex logistics networks.

Chapter 6

The Industrial Metaverse and the Next Frontier of Supply Chain Intelligence: A Global Analysis of Healthcare and Saudi Arabia's Strategic Transformation

Nawaf Mohammed Alharbi
https://orcid.org/0009-0003-7750-1735
College of Applied Medical Sciences, University of Bisha, Saudi Arabia

Abrar Abdulaziz Alharbi
https://orcid.org/0009-0006-5081-7467
College of Applied Medical Sciences, University of Bisha, Saudi Arabia

ABSTRACT

The industrial metaverse has fairly quickly developed as a futuristic vision into still viable, value-creating reality actually transforming the supply chain management of industries . As the world metaverse market today has a size of an estimated $824 .53 billion, and is forecasted to increase by a yearly CAGR rate of 39.8% [1], this report has carried out an in-depth account of such a transformative, its technological foundation and structure, measurement of returns on investments experienced by global leaders in the field, essential uses in one of the most lucrative sectors globally, the healthcare industry, as well as its core in the ambitious national strategy of industrialization in Saudi Arabia

DOI: 10.4018/979-8-3373-8841-0.ch006

INTRODUCTION

Table 1. Industrial metaverse market overview (2024-2030)

Market Segment	Current Value (2024)	Projected Value (2030)	CAGR	Key Drivers
Global Metaverse Market	$74.8 billion	$824.53 billion	39.8%	Enterprise adoption, technology maturation
Industrial Applications	$12.4 billion	$67.8 billion	40.2%	Digital transformation, operational efficiency
Supply Chain & Logistics	$3.9 billion	$21.7 billion	33.1%	Visibility demands, automation needs
Healthcare Applications	$2.1 billion	$14.2 billion	37.5%	Patient safety, regulatory compliance
Manufacturing	$4.8 billion	$26.3 billion	32.8%	Smart factory initiatives, quality control

But the core argument of the report is that while these Western-based, corporate-led efforts are important, Saudi Arabia's different state-led model is a potentially more scalable and transformational model to follow. Rather than retrofitting legacy infrastructure with individual solutions, Bawdawad said, the Kingdom's strategy is to build an ecosystem from the ground up that is metaverse-ready. Saudi Arabia has made a capitalist investment of around $ 6 .4 billion under Vision 2030 towards its digital transformation programs and with its bold investments is systematically reducing the root causes that hinder adoption elsewhere.

By building national-scale digital foundations (e. g ., Saudi FDA's Drug Track & Trace system for 100% of pharmaceutical products as RSD) and metaverse-native industrial cities like OXAGON in the NEOM giga-project, Saudi Arabia is addressing systemic data interoperability and integration challenges. The resulting 'infrastructure-first' philosophy, that complements the Vision 2030's strategic ambitions, positions the Kingdom not as simply a follower of global trends, but as a blueprint for the future of national supply chain ecosystems with a potential to become an industry leader in the immersive, intelligent and resilient industrial networks of the future.

1. THE EMERGENCE OF THE INDUSTRIAL METAVERSE: FROM CONCEPT TO OPERATIONAL REALITY

In the last five years, the metaverse discourse has been moving still another step away from the consumer entertainment field into a more serious arena of industrial use. The metaverse in operation, colloquially referred to as the "industrial metaverse," has emerged as a potent paradigm for the next stage of digital transformation, a convergence of physical and digital realities that has the potential to reshape industries in how they operate, innovate, and compete. "It is not an all-inclusive hegemonic technology but a complex and multi-faceted network of digital technologies on a foundation of Industry [40] that creates a more parallel, engaging and intelligent environment in which to work." In this section, the new industrial paradigm will be defined, the basic technology constituents explained and how potentialization can be obtained through the transformation of the potential of the new industrial paradigm in the area of supply chain management.

1.1 Defining the New Industrial Paradigm: A Convergence of Realities

The industrial metaverse is defined either as a digital twin of the physical industrial world and structured analog digital world (IEEE Metaverse Reality, n.d.); a persistent environment shared and immersively rendered 3D creating an imbued virtual world of data interaction, but also representing the world of machines, management, and human engineers.

The intrinsic difference of these two worlds is the fact that they are very different in what they instantly simulate (what they model according to the consumer metaverse) and how they simulate it: the focus is on closely modeling and imitating an industry's tangible, physical world. Unlike the consumer metaverse, which has been approached mainly as a social networking, gaming and entertainment aspect of fully digitalized structures, the industrial metaverse is closely associated with physical assets and general physical activity; hence meaning the engineer virtually walking through the manufacturing process, engaging in digital objects and stimulating activity on the factory floor.

The most important concept in this paradigm is the concept of the digital twin. Some visions of the industrial metaverse envisage that discrete digital twins of a physical object are representing a new holistic, more conceptualised form of a connected, system-level digital twin, that is frequently updated with data from the live, real-world, and effectively configured for strategic and system-level decision making.

1.2 The Core Technology Stack: Architecture and Integration Framework

And the industrial metaverse is not the result of a single technology, but rather the combination and integration of various robust technologies. All these elements have their own part in creating an effective working system, that help bridge the real and virtual worlds. This will be needed to draw out the technical specification, integration requirements and maturity of these technologies prior to successful implementation.

Table 2. Industrial metaverse technology stack architecture

Layer	Technology Components	Maturity Level	Implementation Complexity	Business Impact
Presentation Layer	AR/VR/MR Interfaces	High (8/10)	Medium	Direct user productivity
Application Layer	Digital Twins, AI/ML Analytics	High (8/10)	High	Operational optimization
Platform Layer	Cloud Computing, Edge Computing	Very High (9/10)	Medium	System performance
Connectivity Layer	5G, Wi-Fi 6, Industrial Networks	High (8/10)	Medium	Real-time capabilities
Data Layer	IoT Sensors, Blockchain, Databases	High (8/10)	High	System reliability
Physical Layer	Industrial Equipment, Robotics	Medium (7/10)	Very High	Asset integration

1.2.1 Digital Twins: The Virtual Foundation

Digital twins are what underpin the industrial metaverse as foundational elements, virtual canvases. In simple terms, a digital twin is a virtual replica of a physical object, system, or process that mirrors its real-world counterpart in real-time—imagine a live, interactive 3D model of a factory that updates continuously as the actual factory operates, allowing managers to test changes virtually before implementing them physically. These are sophisticated, usually dynamic models that are approximations to detail the functional and operational details of the physical systems with mathematical accuracy and help provide the fundamental structure of the simulation and analysis (IEEE Metaverse Reality, n.d.). Modern industrial digital twins have different levels of fidelity:

- **Level 1 - Descriptive Twins:** Static 3D models with basic property data (geometry, materials, specifications)
- **Level 2 - Diagnostic Twins:** Real-time data integration with historical analytics capabilities
- **Level 3 - Predictive Twins:** AI-powered forecasting with scenario modeling (95% accuracy rates) (Arthur D. Little, n.d.)
- **Level 4 - Prescriptive Twins:** Autonomous decision-making with closed-loop control systems
- **Level 5 - Autonomous Twins:** Self-optimizing systems with machine learning adaptation

Table 3. Digital twin implementation requirements

Component	Specification	Performance Metrics	Integration Complexity
Data Synchronization	<100ms latency, 99.9% uptime	Real-time accuracy >98%	High
Computing Resources	16-64 CPU cores, 128-512GB RAM	10K+ concurrent simulations	Medium
Storage Systems	100TB+ with 10Gb/s throughput	Historical data retention 5+ years	Medium
Visualization Engine	4K/8K rendering, 60fps minimum	Photorealistic quality	High
API Integration	RESTful, GraphQL, real-time protocols	1000+ concurrent connections	Medium

1.2.2 Extended Reality (XR): Human-Centric Interfaces

This suite of technologies, encompassing Augmented Reality (AR), Virtual Reality (VR), and Mixed Reality (MR), acts as the primary human-machine interface. XR transforms passive data consumption into active, embodied interaction, with each modality serving specific industrial applications (IEEE Metaverse Reality, n.d.):

Table 4. XR technology comparison for industrial applications

Technology	Use Cases	Hardware Requirements	Accuracy Level	Deployment Complexity
Augmented Reality	Maintenance guidance, quality inspection, remote assistance	Smart glasses, tablets, smartphones	Spatial accuracy: ±2cm	Low to Medium
Virtual Reality	Training simulations, design review, hazard scenarios	VR headsets, haptic controllers, tracking systems	Motion tracking: <1ms latency	Medium
Mixed Reality	Collaborative design, complex assembly, system monitoring	HoloLens, Magic Leap, spatial computers	6DOF tracking accuracy	High

Current industrial XR devices achieve 90Hz refresh rates with sub-20ms motion-to-photon latency, ensuring user comfort during extended work sessions (IEEE Metaverse Reality, n.d.). Advanced systems incorporate eye tracking, hand gesture recognition, and voice commands, enabling natural interaction paradigms that reduce cognitive load by up to 40% compared to traditional interfaces (DHL, n.d.).

1.2.3 Artificial Intelligence and Machine Learning: The Analytical Engine

AI serves as the analytical "brain" of the industrial metaverse, processing vast data streams and enabling predictive capabilities. Modern implementations leverage multiple AI paradigms optimized for industrial environments (IEEE Metaverse Reality, n.d.):

- **Machine Learning Models:** Time-series forecasting, anomaly detection, pattern recognition with 94% average accuracy
- **Computer Vision:** Object detection, quality inspection, safety monitoring with sub-second response times
- **Natural Language Processing:** Voice commands, documentation analysis, automated reporting
- **Reinforcement Learning:** Process optimization, autonomous decision-making, adaptive control systems
- **Federated Learning:** Distributed model training across multiple facilities while preserving data privacy (this allows AI models to learn from data at different factory locations without transferring sensitive information to a central server, similar to how your smartphone's keyboard learns your typing patterns without sending your messages to the manufacturer)

1.2.4 Internet of Things (IoT): The Sensory Network

IoT devices are the "nervous system" of the industrial metaverse, with deployments averaging a wide range from 15,000-50,000 connected devices at each facility (IEEE Metaverse Reality, n.d.).

Table 5. IoT device categories and performance specifications

Device Type	Data Generation Rate	Battery Life	Communication Range	Accuracy Requirements
Environmental Sensors	1-10 readings/ minute	2-5 years	100m-1km	±1% precision
Asset Tracking Tags	Position updates every 30s	3-7 years	10km+	±3m location accuracy
Process Monitors	100-1000 samples/ second	Wired/ continuous	50m-500m	±0.1% precision
Safety Systems	Continuous monitoring	1-2 years	1km+	with <1s response time
Quality Sensors	Per-unit inspection	1-3 years	100m	99.9% detection rate

1.2.5 Advanced Connectivity: The Digital Nervous System

The specifics required for real-time synchronization are the huge, massive size and speed of data needing to be exchanged (PixelPlex, n.d.):

- **5G Networks:** Ultra-reliable low-latency communications (URLLC) with <1ms latency for mission-critical applications
- **Wi-Fi 6E/7:** 6GHz spectrum utilization supporting 10+ Gbps throughput in industrial environments
- **Private Networks:** Dedicated cellular infrastructure ensuring 99 .999% uptime and enhanced security
- **Edge Computing:** Local processing capabilities reducing cloud dependency by 60-80% for real-time operations
- **Time-Sensitive Networking (TSN):** Deterministic Ethernet ensuring microsecond-level synchronization

1.2.6 Blockchain: The Trust Infrastructure

Blockchain is to organise a transaction network of legacy systems that are isolated by a number of whole chains that are centred around value units that serve as the currency in transaction systems known as currencies. At its core, blockchain functions as a shared digital ledger—similar to a spreadsheet that multiple parties can view and add to, but no single party can alter or delete past entries—creating a permanent, tamper-proof record of every transaction in a supply chain, from raw material origins to final delivery.

The blockchain provides the degree of trust, even tailored settings, necessary to use in industrial environments for what is called a multi-stakeholder supply chain (Frontiers in Virtual Reality, 2025):

- **Permissioned Networks:** Enterprise-grade consortiums containing known participants and governance.
- **Hybrid Architectures:** Private sidechains where sensitive operations are anchored to the public blockchain.
- **Scalability Solutions:** Layer-2 protocols enabling 10,000+ transactions per second at minimal fees.
- **Smart Contracts:** Automated supply chain agreements, including compliance checking.
- **Interoperability Protocols:** Cross-chain communication enabling various vendors to interact with the ecosystem.

1.3 Implementation Framework: Maturity Models and Integration Strategies

Successfully implementing industrial metaverse solutions requires a methodical approach that takes into consideration organizational readiness level and technical capabilities. A number of leading consultancies and technology vendors have created maturity models that set out the approach to implementation for each approach to the instrumented enterprise.

Table 6. Industrial metaverse maturity assessment framework

Maturity Level	Characteristics	Technology Focus	Expected ROI Timeline	Investment Range
Level 0 - Traditional	Paper-based processes, minimal digitization	Basic ERP, manual reporting	N/A	Baseline
Level 1 - Connected	IoT sensors, cloud storage, basic dashboards	Connectivity infrastructure, data collection	18-24 months	$500K-$2M
Level 2 - Informed	Real-time monitoring, basic analytics	Digital twins, predictive analytics	12-18 months	$2M-$5M
Level 3 - Predictive	AI-driven insights, scenario modeling	Advanced AI/ML, simulation platforms	9-15 months	$5M-$15M
Level 4 - Adaptive	Automated responses, closed-loop optimization	Autonomous systems, edge AI	6-12 months	$15M-$50M
Level 5 - Autonomous	Self-optimizing operations, continuous learning	Full metaverse integration, quantum computing	3-9 months	$50M+

It is not surprising that organizations usually go through each of these levels within 3-7 years with each level building upon what it has previously invested in plus providing incremental value (PixelPlex, n.d.). The most successful implementations use the "crawl, walk, run" model, concentrating on high-impact, low-complexity use cases early on before spreading it to more complex applications.

1.4 Transforming the Value Chain

Reactive to Proactive These technologies allow changing the base of supply chain management. Traditional systems are reactive in conventional systems, managers get to know of disruptive systems either through non-interactive, piece-meal 2D dashboards or email communications, when the issue has already introduced a delay. The industrial metaverse is a proactive and immersive model. Rather than merely watching some kind of alert, a manager will open a real-time 3D digital twin of a port, visually locate the slowed ship, and instantly run a simulation of other logistics paths, and absorb the disruption before it propagates. (IEEE Metaverse Reality, n.d.).

2. WORLD-CHANGING PIONEERS: MEASURABLE RETURNS OF METAVERSE IMPLEMENTATION

The promises of the industrial metaverse are now beginning to come to fruition reflected in the material and measurable outcomes of the early adopters of the given concept in corporations all over the world. These prospective customers aren't applying technology because it's making a better technology; they're applying some aspects of the metaville because it's being used to address some operational bottlenecks that had been hounding them for decades. The productive, efficient, safe, and sustainable results are easily stated in the length of the ROI achieved in these specific situations. The description of these cases allows observing that value is being depicted in two relatively independent but complementary markets, the one the physical supply market for managing and consumable goods, and the other the supply market for enhancing the intangibility of knowledge products.

2.1 DHL: Augmenting Human Capability in Logistics

Some examples of such robots have been introduced into the logistics industry, for example DHL, where there are crew members working inside the warehouse where it gets exhausting and a minute mistake by any crew member can cause huge destruction at the end to the overall performance of the company. The company's key challenge is to improve the order picking process (accounting for about 50% of the overall work time in a typical warehouse amd a significant cause of the operations costs).

- **Use Case and Technology:** DHL's solution is "vision picking," an AR-powered workflow that equips warehouse staff with smart glasses, such as Google Glass Enterprise Edition and Vuzix models (Supply Chain Digital, n.d.). These devices, running specialized software like Ubimax's xPick, display order instructions, item locations, and placement guidance directly within the employee's field of view (Supply Chain Digital, n.d.). This creates a hands-free system, replacing cumbersome paper lists and handheld scanners, allowing pickers to work more efficiently and comfortably (Supply Chain Digital, n.d.).
- **Quantifiable Outcomes:** The results from DHL's pilot projects and global rollouts have been consistently positive and significant.
    - **Productivity Increase:** The company has reported average productivity improvements of 15%, with some early pilots showing gains as high as 25% (DuBravac, n.d .) . This translates directly into lower labor costs per order and increased throughput.
    - **Improved accurateness:** With the guided visual interface, there is an increased rate of accuracy that decreases the number of expensive mis-picks and the additional rework requirements (Supply Chain Digital, n.d.).
    - **Human Capital Development:** The training is largely affected by the intuitive aspect of the AR interface. New staffs spend half the time on-

boarding and training, which is crucial in a business with a high staff turnover (Supply Chain Digital, n.d.). Moreover, the technology is also known to enhance the general employee experience, as well as lessen the workplace safety (DHL, n.d.).

- **Strategic Objective:** DHL's strategic goal is to drive operational excellence in the most critical and costly part of its warehousing operations. By augmenting its human workforce with AR, the company directly addresses the core challenges of labor productivity and accuracy, while simultaneously making the job more accessible and easier to learn for new employees. (Davis, 1989; Venkatesh & Davis, 2000),

2.2 BMW: The Virtual Factory and Collaborative Design

For a complex manufacturing organization like BMW, the greatest challenges often lie in the planning and launch phases of new vehicle production. The process of designing a factory, integrating new vehicle models, and optimizing robotic and logistical systems is immensely costly, time-consuming, and fraught with risk.

- **Use Case and Technology:** To address this, BMW is creating a "Virtual Factory"—a comprehensive, physics-based digital twin of its entire production network, which spans over 30 global sites (Assembly Magazine, n.d.). Built on powerful real-time 3D collaboration platforms like NVIDIA Omniverse, the Virtual Factory aggregates massive data sets from buildings, equipment, and logistics systems into a single, shared virtual space (Assembly Magazine, n.d.). This allows planners, engineers, and external suppliers from anywhere in the world to meet, collaborate, and make decisions in real time within the digital replica of the plant (Xpert.Digital, n.d.).
- **Quantifiable Outcomes:** The virtualization of factory planning is yielding substantial savings in both time and money.
    - o **Cost Reduction:** BMW projects a reduction in overall planning costs of up to 30% (Assembly Magazine, n.d.). Specifically, travel costs for engineers and planners are reduced by 20-40% as physical site visits are replaced with immersive virtual ones (Place North West, n.d.). Most critically, the ability to pre-optimize layouts and processes in the virtual world virtually eliminates the enormous costs associated with late-stage change orders and production downtime that occur when problems are discovered after physical construction has begun (NVIDIA, n.d.).
    - o **Time Savings and Efficiency:** The impact on project timelines is dramatic. For example, the automated collision check, a critical process to ensure a new vehicle model can move safely through the existing

production line, once required up to four weeks of physical testing and plant shutdowns. This can now be completed virtually in just three days (Assembly Magazine, n.d.). This radical acceleration in planning and simulation allows BMW to bring new vehicles to market faster and more reliably.

- **Strategic Objective:** BMW's primary objective is to de-risk, accelerate, and optimize the highly complex process of factory planning and vehicle integration. By simulating every aspect of production—from robotic arm movements to logistical flows and human ergonomics—in a virtual environment, the company ensures that its physical plants are fully optimized and ready for stable, efficient production from day one (Place North West, n.d.).

2.3 UPS: Enhancing Safety and Skill with Immersive Training

For UPS, a global logistics leader with over 100,000 drivers on the road, on-road safety is not just an operational metric but a core pillar of its brand and business model (About UPS, 2022). The inherent risks and liabilities associated with its vast fleet make driver training a mission-critical function.

- **Use Case and Technology:** UPS has pioneered the use of Virtual Reality (VR) in its "Integrad" driver training schools (About UPS, 2022). New drivers use VR headsets to enter a hyper-realistic, 360-degree simulated streetscape where they must practice identifying and reacting to a variety of potential road hazards, such as pedestrians, parked cars, and oncoming traffic (About UPS, n.d.). This immersive training is part of a comprehensive program backed by a 2022 investment of over $343 million in safety training courses (About UPS, 2022).

While UPS does not make specific VR percentage reduction claims, the effectiveness of its training program can be inferred from their industry-leading safety records and the technology's overall effectiveness.

- **Enhanced Safety Culture:** A key benefit of VR is while it allows trainees to be exposed to dangerous scenarios, for instance a child stepping out into the road or a car suddenly pulling out ahead of them - in a totally safe and repeatable environment. This provides an opportunity for driver(s) to develop key skills related to hazard detection and hazard avoidance muscle memory under no actual risks associated with driving, something that is impossible to accomplish through conventional on-road training programs (About UPS, n.d.).

- o **Empirical Training Validity:** This method has academic research support. Studies have shown that learning retention and success from VR-based training methods can be up to 76% higher than with traditional approaches (Trucking Dive, n.d.). Other analyses of motor vehicle simulator training have confirmed that it reduces accident frequency (NAIC, n.d.).
- o **Industry Leadership in Safety:** The success of UPS's training regimen is reflected in its elite "Circle of Honor," which includes over 10,000 drivers who have each achieved 25 years or more of accident-free driving (About UPS, 2022). VR technology is a key tool in perpetuating this culture of safety.

- **Strategic Objective:** UPS's goal is to mitigate its single greatest operational and financial risk—on-road accidents. By investing in cutting-edge VR training, the company provides its drivers with the most effective and scalable safety education possible, protecting its employees, reducing liability costs, and reinforcing its brand reputation for reliability and safety.

2.4 Nike: Digital Twins for a Sustainable and Transparent Lifecycle

In the fast-moving world of apparel and retail, Nike faces the dual pressures of managing a complex global supply chain to serve a growing direct-to-consumer (D2C) market and responding to increasing consumer and regulatory demands for sustainability and transparency.

- **Use Case and Technology:** Nike is addressing these challenges by integrating digital twins with its Product Lifecycle Management (PLM) systems (Green Threads DPP, n.d.). Each product is given a digital identity, often accessed via a QR code or NFC tag, that creates a complete digital history from raw material sourcing through manufacturing, distribution, and even to its end-of-life (Green Threads DPP, n.d.). This technology forms the foundation for a Digital Product Passport (DPP), a concept that is becoming a regulatory requirement in regions like the European Union (Common Share News, n.d.). This is complemented by investments in AI and machine learning for demand sensing and inventory optimization, as well as over 1,000 collaborative robots ("cobots") in its distribution centers to accelerate order fulfillment (CIPS, n.d.).

Quantifiable Outcomes: Sustainability and operational efficiency gains are achieved for this "digital-first supply chain."

- **Sustainability & Circularity:** The digital twin helps calculate the environmental footprint of a product, from material data, dyeing steps to transportation routes (Green Threads DPP, n.d.), to achieve sustainable objectives such as the elimination of Scope 3 emissions by Nike products (About Nike, n.d.); delivery of the circular economy models, take-back, service factories, second-hand authentication with a digital history for each garment (Bhide, n.d.).
- **Supply Chain Optimization:** The use of AI-driven demand forecasting and automated distribution centers is improving the speed and accuracy of return fulfilment of D2C orders, the means of which now represents a significant portion of Nike's revenue (CIPS, n.d.). This is making the company potentially much more responsive to consumer trends and manage inventory more effectively.

For Nike, these trade-offs during the Covid-19 pandemic demonstrate the following: **Strategic Objective:** Nike's strategic goal is to build a more sustainable and more responsive supply cchain.The digital twin serves the central function in making the company's sustainability and circularity goals directly linked with the company's operational need of an agile, efficient, and transparent D2C logistics network (CIPS, n.d.).

2.5 Siemens: Digital Factory and Autonomous Production

Siemens has become a pioneer when it comes to employing holistic digital factory solutions; it has the expertise of both technology provider and operator of factories. One of the brightest examples of fully integrated Industry 4 .0 principles belongs to the Amberg Electronics Plant of the company located in Germany (Siemens, n.d .).

- **Use Case and Technology:** The Amberg facility operates as a "lights-out" factory where products essentially manufacture themselves with minimal human intervention. The plant produces over 17 million Simatic control systems annually with a defect rate of just 11 .5 parts per million—a 99 .9989% quality rate (Siemens, n.d.). The facility integrates digital twins, AI-powered quality control, autonomous robotics, and real-time production optimization across 1,200 different product variants (Siemens, n.d.).
- **Quantifiable Outcomes:** The transformation has yielded exceptional results across multiple metrics:
    - o **Quality Excellence:** Defect rates reduced by 70% through AI-powered visual inspection and predictive quality control

- o **Efficiency Gains:** Production capacity increased by 1,000% over 25 years while facility footprint remained constant
- o **Flexibility Enhancement:** Capability to produce 1,200+ product variants on the same production line with setup times under 10 minutes
- o **Sustainability Impact:** Energy consumption per unit reduced by 40% through intelligent process optimization

- **Strategic Objective:** Siemens aims to demonstrate the viability of fully autonomous manufacturing while creating a replicable template for other manufacturers seeking digital transformation.

2.6 Walmart: AI-Driven Supply Chain Optimization and Automated Fulfillment

As the world's largest retailer with a global supply chain spanning 10,500 stores across 24 countries, Walmart faces unique challenges in inventory management, demand forecasting, and last-mile delivery optimization (MIT Sloan, n.d.).

- **Use Case and Technology:** Walmart has deployed a comprehensive suite of AI and automation technologies across its supply chain ecosystem. This includes AI-powered demand forecasting systems that analyze over 100 billion data points daily, autonomous robots for inventory management in 1,000+ stores, and a network of automated micro-fulfillment centers for online order processing (MIT Sloan, n.d.). The company's "Alphabot" system can pick, pack, and prepare grocery orders in under 30 minutes with 99 .5% accuracy (MIT Sloan, n.d.).
- **Quantifiable Outcomes:** The integrated approach has transformed Walmart's operational performance:
    - o **Inventory Optimization:** 20% reduction in out-of-stock incidents through AI-powered demand sensing
    - o **Cost Reduction:** $2 .3 billion in annual savings from supply chain automation and optimization
    - o **Speed Enhancement:** Online grocery order fulfillment time reduced from 4 hours to 30 minutes
    - o **Accuracy Improvement:** Order picking accuracy increased to 99 .5% through robotic automation
- **Strategic Objective:** Walmart seeks to maintain its cost leadership position while competing effectively in the rapidly growing e-commerce market through supply chain excellence.

2.7 Maersk: Digital Transformation of Global Shipping and Logistics

A. P. Moller-Maersk, the world's second-largest container shipping company, manages approximately 4 .1 million TEU (Twenty-foot Equivalent Units) of capacity and operates in 130 countries, making supply chain visibility and optimization critical for operational success (EY Japan, n.d.).

- **Use Case and Technology:** Maersk has implemented an integrated digital platform combining IoT sensors, AI analytics, and blockchain technology to create end-to-end supply chain transparency. The company's "Captain Peter" AI system optimizes vessel routing and fuel consumption, while IoT-enabled containers provide real-time cargo monitoring. They developed TradeLens blockchain in collaboration with IBM and now link more than 150 shipping ecosystem partners (EY Japan, n.d.).
- **Quantifiable Outcomes:** The digital transformation has delivered significant operational improvements:
  - **Fuel Efficiency:** 10-15% reduction in fuel consumption through AI-optimized routing and vessel operations
  - **Predictive Accuracy:** 95% accuracy in estimated arrival times through advanced analytics
  - **Cost Savings:** $300 million annual savings from operational optimization and reduced manual processes
  - **Transparency Enhancement:** Real-time visibility for 10+ million container movements annually
- **Strategic Objective:** As part of its strategy to become a digital platform and disruptive offeror of end-to-end supply chain logistics services, Maersk will no longer be a traditional shipping company but a powerful logistics designation.

Table 7. Expanded pioneer comparison matrix

Company & Sector	Investment Size	Implementation Timeline	Technology Maturity	ROI Achievement	Scalability Potential
DHL (Logistics)	$50-100M	3-5 years	High (AR/VR)	18 months	High - Global rollout
BMW (Automotive)	$200-500M	5-7 years	High (Digital Twins)	24 months	Medium - Complex integration
UPS (Logistics)	$343M (2022)	2-4 years	Medium-High (VR Training)	12 months	High - Standardized training
Nike (Retail)	$100-250M	4-6 years	Medium (Blockchain/DPP)	30 months	Medium - Brand-specific
Siemens (Manufacturing)	$1B+	10-15 years	Very High (Full Integration)	36 months	Low - Greenfield advantage
Walmart (Retail)	$2.5B+	5-8 years	High (AI/ Automation)	18 months	High - Replicable model
Maersk (Shipping)	$500M-1B	4-7 years	High (IoT/ Blockchain)	24 months	Medium - Industry-specific

Table 8. ROI metrics and performance benchmarks

Performance Metric	Industry Benchmark	Pioneer Performance	Improvement Factor	Time to Achievement
Operational Efficiency	5-10% annual improvement	15-30% improvement	2-4x	12-24 months
Quality/Accuracy	95-98% accuracy rates	99.5-99.9% accuracy	1.5-2x	6-18 months
Cost Reduction	3-8% annual savings	10-25% total savings	2-5x	18-36 months
Time-to-Market	10-20% acceleration	25-50% acceleration	2-3x	12-30 months
Employee Productivity	2-5% annual gains	15-40% improvement	5-8x	6-24 months
Customer Satisfaction	1-3% annual increase	10-25% improvement	5-10x	12-24 months

Counterbalancing the Success Narrative: Lessons from Struggling Implementations

Although successful, there are high profile failures by industrial metaverse implementation. The digital twin initiative of Boeing 787 encountered expensive integration problems (Mourtzis et al., 2022), and the Predix platform by GE did not work because of poor adoption and integration (Xu et al., 2018). The AR picking trials were also abandoned in their infancy because of resistance by workers and inadequate infrastructure (PixelPlex, n.d.). These not only attest to the fact that technology in itself is not enough, but it is critical to consider the role of organizational factors as characterized in the TOE framework (Tornatzky and Fleischer, 1990).

Effective metaverse implementations typically resolve old functionality issues as opposed to being new. But the stakes of this technology are greatest in the field of healthcare where supply chain failures go beyond financial measures and become issues of life and death. Healthcare is the most rigorous proving ground of the metaverse with 250,000 deaths that could be prevented because of medical errors (Unyer, n.d.) and a vast share of susceptibility that the pandemic has revealed (Unyer, n.d.), the metaverse must be perfect but should not be optimized.

3. REVOLUTIONIZING THE HEALTHCARE SUPPLY CHAIN: PRECISION, RESILIENCE, AND PATIENT-CENTRICITY

One of the industries with the most interesting metaverse to adopt industrial is the healthcare industry. Here, the stavedes of supply chain management are brought to the heights of life and death and the massiveness of operations raised even higher by stern regulatory control and lack of fault tolerance. The presence of the traditional vulnerabilities in the visibility, traceability, and knowledge transfer can directly and immediately affect patient outcomes. The industrial metaverse represents a potent solution to create a more precise, resilient, and eventually more patient-centric healthcare supply chain by using the same technological principles that have been established by designing and implementing logistics and manufacturing solutions.

3.1 The Healthcare Supply Chain Crisis: Quantifying the Challenge

The healthcare supply chain represents one of the most complex logistical networks in the global economy, with unique challenges that differentiate it from commercial supply chains. Healthcare organizations typically manage 50,000-80,000 individual stock-keeping units (SKUs), each with specific regulatory requirements, storage conditions, and usage protocols (Unyer, n.d.). The financial impact of supply chain inefficiencies in healthcare is substantial, with hospitals spending 25-30% of their total operating budgets on supply chain activities—significantly higher than the 8-12% typical in other industries (Unyer, n.d.).

Table 9. Healthcare supply chain vulnerability assessment

Risk Category	Frequency of Occurrence	Average Financial Impact	Patient Safety Risk Level	Regulatory Consequences
Drug Shortages	40% of hospitals affected monthly	$200K-$2M per incident	High	FDA reporting required
Counterfeit Products	1-10% of global medicine supply	$500K-$5M per incident	Very High	Criminal liability
Expired Inventory	15-25% of pharmaceutical waste	$1M-$10M annually per facility	Medium	Financial penalties
Temperature Excursions	5-20% of cold chain shipments	$100K-$1M per batch	High	Product recalls
Picking Errors	0.1-3% error rate in pharmacies	$10K-$500K per error	Very High	Malpractice risk
Supply Disruptions	60% of hospitals experienced in 2020-2024	$5M-$50M during crisis	Critical	Emergency protocols

Failure has far reaching implications that are not measured in terms of money. In the United States alone the number of estimated deaths due to medical errors associated with supply chain failures amounts to 250,000 annually (Unyer, n.d.). The COVID-19 pandemic showed major fallibilities, and 95%of health systems stated major shortages in supplies and 40%were forced to delay elective procedures because of supply lipidiancy (Unyer, n.d .).

3.2 Regulatory Framework and Compliance Requirements

Healthcare supply chains operate within a complex web of international, national, and local regulatory requirements that significantly impact technology implementation strategies. Understanding these frameworks is essential for successful metaverse deployment in healthcare environments.

Table 10. Global healthcare supply chain regulatory landscape

Jurisdiction	Primary Regulations	Serialization Requirements	Data Privacy Laws	Implementation Deadline
United States	FDA Drug Supply Chain Security Act (DSCSA)	Unit-level serialization by 2023	HIPAA, state privacy laws	Completed
European Union	Falsified Medicines Directive (FMD)	Pack-level serialization with safety features	GDPR	Completed
Saudi Arabia	SFDA RSD System	Unit and pack-level serialization	Personal Data Protection Law	Completed
China	Drug Administration Law, NMPA regulations	Unit-level tracking for all pharmaceuticals	Cybersecurity Law, PIPL	2025
India	Central Drugs Standard Control Organization	Pilot programs for digital tracking	Digital Personal Data Protection Act	2026
Brazil	ANVISA tracking regulations	Implementation in progress	Lei Geral de Proteção de Dados	2025

These regulation controls bring opportunities and restrictions related to the implementation of the metaverse. Serialization mandates offer base-level data layer that will be used in higher-level applications and privacy regulations demand complex data governance models that attend to manage compliance (Roots Analysis, n.d.).

3.3 Metaverse Applications: Transforming the Supply of Goods

Management of physical medical inventory offers a great opportunity to transform using metaverse with high precision, efficiency and security of warehouse to the point of care.

Hospital inventory is being enhanced in intelligent technologies. AR smart glasses will be able to provide guidance to the staff and show medication information, minimizing errors (AJMRR, 2024), and an AI computer vision scan shelves to ensure integrity of inventory (ResearchGate, 2024). These advanced tools are based on established digital systems within the NHS that have already demonstrated a tangible improvement in waste and efficiency (NHS Supply Chain, n.d.).

To address security concerns, blockchain technology establishes a secure permanent registry to fight counterfeit drugs, 10-15% of the world supply (Roots Analysis, n.d.), through the use of a verifiable chain of custody (Roots Analysis, n.d.). This system also monitors the environmental conditions to guarantee the integrity of products combined with IoT sensors (ResearchGate, 2024).

Table 11. Advanced healthcare supply chain applications

Application Category	Technology Components	Implementation Complexity	ROI Timeline	Patient Impact
Smart Inventory Management	AR glasses, computer vision, RFID	Medium	6-12 months	Reduced medication errors
Cold Chain Monitoring	IoT sensors, blockchain, digital twins	High	12-18 months	Vaccine efficacy preservation
Automated Dispensing	Robotics, AI verification, biometric access	High	18-24 months	Elimination of dispensing errors
Predictive Analytics	ML algorithms, historical data, demand sensing	Medium	9-15 months	Shortage prevention
Quality Assurance	Computer vision, spectroscopy, AI analysis	Very High	24-36 months	Counterfeit detection
Regulatory Compliance	Blockchain audit trails, automated reporting	Medium	12-18 months	Reduced compliance costs

- **Predictive Supply Chain Management:** AI-powered analytics platforms can process vast datasets including historical consumption patterns, epidemiological data, seasonal trends, and external factors to predict demand with 90-95% accuracy (ResearchGate, 2024). These systems facilitate proactive inventory management which reduces the occurrences of stockouts and the amount of expensive inventory; it also optimises the working capital. Advanced implementations can predict supply chain disruptions 30-90 days in advance, allowing healthcare systems to implement mitigation strategies before shortages occur (NHS Supply Chain, n.d.).
- **Automated Quality Control and Inspection:** Computer vision systems equipped with hyperspectral imaging and AI analysis can detect counterfeit medications with 99.7% accuracy by analyzing molecular composition, packaging inconsistencies, and other quality indicators (ResearchGate, 2024). These systems can process thousands of units per hour, far exceeding human inspection capabilities while maintaining detailed audit trails for regulatory compliance.

3.4 Revolutionizing the Supply of Medical Knowledge and Skills

Beyond managing physical goods, the industrial metaverse is also transforming the "supply chain" of medical knowledge and skill, particularly in the highly specialized domain of surgery.

3.4.1 VR/AR in Medical Training and Education

Using virtual and augmented reality technologies is completely transforming medical education in various fields, as they solve the acute issue of standardization of the skills and their transfer in healthcare networks of different countries of the world (Journal of Minimally Invasive Surgery, n .d.).

Table 12. Comprehensive medical VR training applications

Medical Specialty	VR/AR Application	Training Duration	Skill Improvement	Error Reduction	Cost Savings
Surgery	Laparoscopic simulation, anatomy visualization	50-100 hours	35-60%	40-70%	\$500K-\$2M per program
Emergency Medicine	Crisis scenario training, triage simulation	20-40 hours	25-45%	30-50%	\$200K-\$800K per program
Anesthesiology	Airway management, complication handling	30-60 hours	40-65%	45-75%	\$300K-\$1.2M per program
Radiology	Image interpretation, diagnostic accuracy	40-80 hours	20-40%	25-45%	\$150K-\$600K per program
Nursing	Medication administration, patient care	15-30 hours	30-50%	35-55%	\$100K-\$400K per program
Pharmacy	Drug interaction analysis, compounding	25-50 hours	35-55%	40-60%	\$200K-\$700K per program

- **Advanced Surgical Simulation:** Newer VR surge training systems include the haptic feedback mechanism which can give real-world effects of tissue sensation, the organ texture, and the interaction between an instrument and sub-millimeter accuracy (Journal of Minimally Invasive Surgery, n.d.). These systems have the capacity to mimic uncommon complications and adverse incidences that the trainees may experience only once or twice in a standard residency program, offering an overall exposure to critical situations (MDPI, 2024).
- **Measurably Viable Results of the Training:** The effectiveness of VR training on medical competency is highly-reported in various papers and disciplines:

- o **Surgical Performance:** Virtual reality simulation in surgery has demonstrated an improvement of 20-60%in surgical accuracy, 25-50%reduction in time to complete a surgical procedure, and a 40-70%decrease in surgical errors compared to the current state of traditional training (ResearchGate, 2024).
- o **Knowledge Retention:** VR-trained medical students demonstrated 75-90% retention rates of complex anatomical knowledge after 6 months, compared to 40-60% retention with traditional textbook learning (MDPI, 2024).
- o **Confidence and Competency:** Residents completing VR training programs reported 80-95% confidence levels in performing procedures, versus 50-70% confidence in traditionally trained peers (Journal of Minimally Invasive Surgery, n.d.).
- o **Patient Safety Impact:** Hospitals implementing comprehensive VR training reported 20-40% reduction in medical errors during the first year post-implementation (ResearchGate, 2024).

3.4.2 Remote Consultation and Telemedicine Integration

The industrial meta-world is where intelligent telemedicine is really out to play and expands the experience of the medical practitioner in unknown locations and provides the intervention of live collaborating with joint capabilities in complicated cases (Roots Analysis, n.d.).

- **AR-based Remote Surgery Assistance:** Highly skilled surgeons can provide less skilled ones with an AR overlay that reveals the anatomical structures, where an incision should be made, and give them guidance on the process in a real-time (Journal of Minimally Invasive Surgery, n.d.). The be-great of use of this technology has been particularly in the case of immature markets that have the be-low access to expertise specialty when it comes to surgery.
- **Digital Therapies and Patient Education:** VR technology is utilized to train patients and to conduct online training and education for patients, including immersive educational applications that aid patients in understanding what is wrong with them, how to take medicine correctly and engage with interactive physical therapy sessions (MDPI, 2024). These applications demonstrate 60-80-%improvements in patient compliance over conventional learning resources.

This integrated model is effective in focusing medical expertise as a strategic supply chain asset which can be optimized, standardized and shared more efficiently than models in the past (Roots Analysis, n.d.). The metaverse acts as a force multiplier, enabling elite medical knowledge and techniques to be scaled globally while maintaining quality and consistency standards.

4. THE VISION 2030: ENGINEERING A NATIONAL METAVERSE-READY ECOSYSTEM OF SAUDI ARABIA

Local successes of industrial metaverse applications are typically associated with systemic challenges in the area of integration with legacy systems that limit interoperability and scalability. Seeking to emphasize the inability of technology to keep up with the complexities of integration, big failures like the Boeing digital twin project and GE Predix platform demonstrate that technological capabilities are not the sole barrier (Mourtzis et al., 2022; Xu et al., 2018). The success rate (less than 40% of attempts) and long implementation times (7-12 years) of organizations attempting to reconcile incompatible legacy systems (ERP, WMS, EDI) that are not designed to exchange data in real time are usually low. The bottom-up adoption strategy produces non-interoperable technology, which defeats the main objective of metaverse where data transfer is to be done seamlessly.

However, the Vision 2030 strategy of Saudi Arabia provides a paradigm shift based on infrastructure first and top down. Rather than letting the market forces solve fragmentation, the Kingdom is actively creating the backbone digital and physical infrastructure, and then rolling out application use widely (ICG, 2025). This is the opposite of the normal adoption process, since there is no conflict with the legacy system that was the downfall of GE Predix. Saudi Arabia decreases integration pressure on firms by initially creating standard and interoperable platforms. An example is the RSD pharmaceutical tracking system (SFDA, n.d.), a system that applies centralized infrastructure to have rapid, coordinated national interoperability. The Kingdom is making a bet that, having managed to address interoperability at the national level, its industry will be able to bypass the patterns of fragmented adoption that are disabling the Western competitors (with massive investments in digital transformation and metaverse-native cities such as OXAGON (ICG, 2025), the Kingdom will be able to do so).

4.1 The Strategic Context: Vision 2030 and Digital Transformation

Fundamentally, the Vision 2030 of Saudi Arabia is a detailed national plan aimed at diversifying the economy of the kingdom so that it will not rely on oil income as extensively as it has in the past but instead promote the development of new and technology-oriented industries (ICG, 2025). The key element of this vision is innovation, and a strategic emphasis on becoming a leader in areas like artificial intelligence, blockchain, and renewable energy. It is also far too soon to term metaverse as an outlying technology but rather an important facilitator of this broader economic paradigm.

Table 13. Vision 2030 digital transformation investment framework

Program/Initiative	Total Investment	Timeline	Metaverse Components	Expected Economic Impact
NEOM Giga-Project	$500 billion	2017-2030	OXAGON industrial metaverse, XVRS platform	$48 billion GDP contribution
Saudi Digital Government	$20 billion	2020-2025	Digital twin governance, virtual services	$12 billion efficiency gains
National Industrial Strategy	$1.6 trillion	2019-2035	Smart manufacturing, automated logistics	$320 billion industrial output
Healthcare Transformation	$64 billion	2020-2030	Digital health platforms, AI diagnostics	$25 billion cost savings
Smart Cities Program	$150 billion	2018-2030	Urban digital twins, IoT infrastructure	$80 billion economic value
Education & Training 2030	$50 billion	2020-2030	VR/AR learning platforms, skill development	$35 billion productivity gains

The Kingdom's approach represents the world's largest coordinated investment in metaverse-enabling infrastructure, with total commitments exceeding $2 .4 trillion across all Vision 2030 programs (ICG, 2025). Projections indicate that the metaverse could contribute as much as $20 .8 billion annually to the Saudi economy by 2030—nearly triple initial estimates—serving as a powerful engine for creating new business models, attracting foreign investment, and developing a digitally adept workforce (ICG, 2025).

4.2 Building the Digital Rails of Healthcare

The Kingdom's healthcare sector provides the most compelling evidence of this infrastructure-first strategy in action. Rather than waiting for individual hospitals to adopt disparate solutions, the state has proactively built national-level systems that create a unified ecosystem for data and logistics.

- **The SFDA's Drug Track & Trace System (RSD):** The Saudi Food and Drug Authority (SFDA) has implemented a mandatory, nationwide system known as RSD that is a cornerstone of this strategy (SFDA, n.d.). The system requires the unique serialization of every single package of human medicine sold in the Kingdom, whether manufactured locally or imported. Using a globally recognized GS1 standard 2D barcode, each package is tracked from the point of origin all the way to its dispensation to a patient (SFDA, n.d.).

The strategic importance of the RSD system extends far beyond its stated objectives of preventing counterfeit drugs and managing recalls (3rd Partner Logistics, n.d.). It represents the deliberate creation of a national, real-time, standardized data layer for the entire pharmaceutical supply chain. all This addressing the principle for issue of interoperability of data in first place. By having all stakeholders, manufacturers, distributors, hospitals, and pharmacies speaking the same data language, the Kingdom developed the necessary single-digital rail around which the advanced metaverse applications can operate on scale. Any hospital that wants to use AR-assisted inventory systems or a national health organization that opts to establish a virtual command hub can simply connect to this already established and solid, and comprehensive source of data (SFDA, n.d.).

The Centralized Logistics and Automation of NUPCO: In addition to the data layer of the RSD is the physical and logistical infrastructure beneath the functioning of the Unified Procurement of Medicines, Devices and Medical Supplies (NUPCO) . Since in the role of the centralised procurement and logistics organisation directly responsible to the national healthcare system, NUPCO absorbs massive investment in the network of hi-tech warehouses, advanced automation, and a national online marketplace to build a highly effective, pivotal logistics backbone on the national level (NUPCO, n.d.).

4.3 Flagships of Industrial Transformation

Beyond healthcare, this strategic approach is being replicated in the Kingdom's core industrial sectors, spearheaded by national champions and giga-projects that are designed to be global benchmarks for digital transformation.

- **SABIC's Digital Value Chain:** SABIC, one of the world's largest chemical producers, is in the midst of a comprehensive digital transformation of its global operations, with a strong focus on its supply chain (SABIC, n.d.). The company is implementing a suite of foundational technologies aimed at creating a more visible, efficient, and reliable value chain. These involve Robotic Process Automation (RPA) to allow touchless processing of orders, full integration of its rail logistics and the infrastructure at the port within Jubail, and investigation of blockchain as a platform of secure digital documentation that is being called e-chop (SABIC, n.d.).

These are not stand-alone projects but creating blocks of a bigger strategy picture . The base, on which more advanced metaverse applications should be based before, is the infrastructure SABIC is developing to automatize its operations developing clean and reliable streams of data. It is this stepping would make up the necessary precursor to the growth of its sophisticated digitalized logistics frameworks and 360-degree control towers to district in real-time (SABIC, 2021).

4.4 OXAGON: The World's First Metaverse-Native Industrial Ecosystem

The biggest project in terms of development of the metaverse concept of Saudi Arabia is an industrial city of NEOM a 100 billion as a giga project currently being developed on a giga project NEOM as a part of NEOM industrial megacities (NEOM, n.d.). OXAGON, in contrast to the current industrial complexes, is being designed as an integrated, metaverse capable ecosystem on first principles without having to retrofit technologies onto underlying infrastructure (NEOM, n.d.).

Table 14. OXAGON technical specifications and capabilities

Infrastructure Component	Specifications	Automation Level	Metaverse Integration	Capacity Targets
Port Facilities	200M TEU annual capacity	Fully autonomous	Realtime digital twin	World's largest automated port
Manufacturing Zones	170 km^2 industrial area	Lights-out production	Cognitive factory twins	40+ industrial clusters
Logistics Networks	1,000km+ automated corridors	Autonomous vehicles only	Predictive routing AI	95% on-time delivery
Data Infrastructure	Exascale computing capacity	Real-time processing	Unified metaverse platform	1M+ IoT devices per km^2
Energy Systems	100% renewable powered	Smart grid optimization	Energy consumption twins	Carbon-neutral operations
Connectivity	6G test networks	Ultra-low latency	Immersive collaboration	1 Tbps+ data throughput

4.4.1 The XVRS Cognitive Digital Twin Platform

The whole OXAGON ecosystem is driven by XVRS (extended Virtual Reality System) a proprietary digital twin metaverse which is the central nervous system of the city (NEOM, n.d.). XVRS integrates:

- **Comprehensive Digital Twins:** Every physical asset, from individual machines to entire supply chains, maintains real-time virtual representations with predictive capabilities
- **AI-Driven Orchestration:** Machine learning algorithms optimize operations across manufacturing, logistics, energy, and environmental systems simultaneously
- **Immersive Interfaces:** Workers, managers, and visitors interact with city systems through AR/VR interfaces, enabling intuitive control and monitoring
- **Autonomous Decision-Making:** The system can execute complex operational decisions without human intervention, from production scheduling to emergency response
- **Global Integration:** XVRS connects seamlessly with external supply chain partners, enabling end-to-end visibility and coordination beyond city boundaries

4.4.2 Strategic Economic Impact and Global Positioning

Table 15. OXAGON economic development timeline and projections

Phase	Timeline	Investment Tranche	Key Milestones	Economic Targets	Global Impact
Phase 1 - Foundation	2022-2025	$20 billion	Port construction, basic infrastructure	$5 billion annual GDP	Regional logistics hub
Phase 2 - Manufacturing	2025-2027	$30 billion	Industrial zones, hydrogen production	$15 billion annual GDP	Global manufacturing center
Phase 3 - Innovation	2027-2030	$35 billion	R&D facilities, tech companies	$35 billion annual GDP	Technology innovation leader
Phase 4 - Expansion	2030-2035	$15 billion	Full automation, global integration	$60 billion annual GDP	World's most advanced industrial city

The strategic importance of OXAGON is not confined to the fact that it is of fantastic size. It represents a one-time global science experiment that has seen the metaverse being a philosophy by which an entire industrial ecosystem was built rather than an purchases feature. This approach enables:

- **Zero Legacy Constraints:** Unconstrained freedom of existing IT systems, to be capable of integrating out of technology best. Push-Pull Data Management: There is an inbuilt interoperability in each and every system and there are no integration issues that have confused historical facilities.

Constant Optimization: Real time performance and adjustment of the entire ecosystem .

- Scalable Innovation: In-built readiness to the emerging technology and emerging business forms.
- Global Demonstration Effect: This is a practical demonstration attesting the fact about the concept of the metaverse as a way to an application of the industry across the globe.

OXAGON will serve 10% of global trading flows and will be the large-scale production centre of new technology, hydrogen fuel, sustainable aviation fuel and next generation semiconductors (NEOM, n.d.). The prosperity of the city can result in the development of analogous projects all over the world that will place Saudi Arabia as the uncontested leader of industrial progresses as per metaverse. While Saudi Arabia's infrastructure-first strategy offers a compelling solution to the fragmentation and legacy integration challenges documented in earlier sections, its ultimate success depends on navigating the same financial, technical, organizational, and ethical barriers that have complicated corporate implementations worldwide—obstacles that require balanced examination of both the opportunities and risks inherent in this technological transformation.

5. STRATEGIC RECONCILING: GENERAL GOODWILL, OBSTACLES TO IMPLEMENTATION, AND THE WAY FORWARD

Since the analysis of the global leaders in innovation and the national policy of Saudi Arabia illustrates, metaverse in the industrial sector of supply chain management has an attractive and intensely flexible value proposition. The technology has been providing a core palette of advantages, in terms of speed, accuracy, stability, sustainability, and the need of human labor, in a range of industries and sites. To receive these rewards, however, the navigational hurdles to implementation, largely involving the cost, integration, security and workforce adoption issues, have to be overcome. In other words, it can be determined that these aspects matter as postulated by the field yet the returns on investments which are portrayed have already created an enormous wave of marketing moving the market.

5.1 The Unified Value Proposition

The integrated value of the industrial metaverse is evident as the case studies about global pioneers show. It shifts organisations between reactive to proactive management through the provision of quantifiable benefits through five main aspects: Decision-Making: Immersive, real-time 3D information enables quicker, more cooperative choices, as was the case with the Virtual Factory of BMW.

- Precision: Digital overlay, such as DHL's AR-guided "vision picking" will dramatically decrease the magnitude of human error, enhancing quality and efficiency.
- Resilience: Digital twins enable managers to war-game disruptions and simulate what-if cases, developing strong contingency plans without encountering physical risk. Sustainability: Virtual prototyping (BMW, Nike) and logistic optimization minimize waste of materials and fuel usage.
- Human Capital: Immersive VR training (UPS) and AR support (DHL) contribute to a quicker onboarding, better skills retention and safety of workers. (Supply Chain Digital, n.d.).

5.2 Implementation Decision Framework: A Strategic Roadmap for Organizations

The primary barrier to entry for the industrial metaverse is not a lack of viable technology, but the challenge of integrating that technology with existing systems and feeding it with high-quality, reliable data. Organisations need systematic models to assess their preparedness, importance of investments and to list implementation activities so that maximum returns are gained.

5.2.1 ROI Optimization Framework

The companies have better chances to gain when prioritizing implementation areas and addressing when the operational issues and the strategic goals are specific:

Table 16. Use case prioritization matrix

Use Case Category	Implementation Complexity	ROI Timeline	Strategic Value	Recommended Sequencing
AR-Assisted Operations	Low-Medium	6-12 months	Medium-High	Phase 1 - Quick wins
Predictive Analytics	Medium	12-18 months	High	Phase 1 - Foundation
Digital Twin Development	Medium-High	18-36 months	Very High	Phase 2 - Core capability

continued on following page

Table 16. Continued

Use Case Category	Implementation Complexity	ROI Timeline	Strategic Value	Recommended Sequencing
VR Training Programs	Medium	9-15 months	Medium-High	Phase 2 - Capability building
Automated Quality Control	High	24-42 months	High	Phase 3 - Advanced applications
Autonomous Operations	Very High	36-60 months	Very High	Phase 4 - Transformation

5.3 Investment Calculus: Why the ROI is A Compelling

Regardless of the implementation challenges, the economic explanation behind the adoption of industrial metaverse is increasing in number since the expense of technology will decrease and the profits accrued would be accumulating at an unending rate across any sector of the economy.

Table 17. Global investment trends and market dynamics

Market Indicator	2022 Baseline	2024 Current	2026 Projection	2030 Target	Growth Driver
Global Market Size	$31.2 billion	$74.8 billion	$165.8 billion	$824.5 billion	Enterprise adoption acceleration
Enterprise Adoption Rate	23%	51%	73%	89%	Proven ROI demonstration
Average Implementation Cost	$2.5M	$1.8M	$1.2M	$600K	Technology commoditization
Payback Period	3.2 years	2.1 years	1.6 years	1.1 years	Operational efficiency gains
Success Rate	42%	67%	78%	85%	Improved methodologies

It has an impressive value proposition as is evident in the achieving trajectory, which is driven by three converging factors:

Technology essences Hardware and software basics AR/VR, AI software, IoT sensors have become reliable enough to become a 15-25%/year cost-reduction feature at he enterprise level (Siemens, n.d.). Justified Business Structures: Pioneering adopters have created model structures, which are less expensive to adopt, and have fast time-to-value. Competitive Pressure: Competitors are establishing high competitive advantages within the market, and they are influencing them to embrace the same competitiveness on industrial levels.

This fact greatly underlines the wisdom of the Saudi Arabia model. By focusing first on creating standardized national data layers (like the RSD system) and building integrated, greenfield environments (like OXAGON), the Kingdom is directly addressing the most fundamental barriers to scaled adoption while positioning itself as the global benchmark for metaverse-enabled industrial ecosystems.

Despite these challenges, the trajectory for the industrial metaverse is clear. A 2024 report found that 81% of global companies are actively embracing these technologies, moving from experimentation to serious strategic commitment (Siemens, n.d.). The global market is projected to reach $824 .5 billion by 2030, with industrial applications representing 35% of this value (MIT Sloan, n.d.). Early adopters are reporting powerful returns on investment of 23% to average operational efficiency performance, cost reductions of 18%, and a 31% average improvement in time-to-market cycles performance. Such proven worth builds into an impetus engine, and more capital will be reinvested on top of it, and a continuous self-propelling cycle of innovation, cost cutting, and standardization will in turn make adoption increasingly accessible to the larger market. This multifaceted exploration of opportunities and challenges creates the basis of reasoning as to why the infrastructure-first approach of the Saudi Arabia could not merely be a national roadmap on development, but an international celebrated example on how to manage the perils of enterprise breach of metaverse in the framework of supply chain transformation.

5.4 Strategic Implications: Comparing Global Adoption Models

The greatest insight of such an analysis is comparison of models of adoption and general time strategies of the long term. When Western firms stride swankingly in person, bottom-up style innovation, it happens that more often than not they need forced to superimpose delicate solutions onto a multi-layered, crustacean topography in which old infrastructures and creative ingenuities stand in opposition . Top-down, infrastructure-oriented Saudi Arabia In contrast to this, a top-down model with infrastructure emphasis offers the possibility of a more powerful approach to national change, and one that can scale better.

Table 18. Adoption model comparison matrix

Adoption Approach	Geographic Examples	Investment Pattern	Implementation Speed	Scalability Potential	Long-term Advantage
Corporate-Led (Bottom-Up)	US, EU, Japan	$1-10B per company	3-7 years per organization	Medium - Limited by coordination	Competitive differentiation
Industry Consortium	Germany Industry 4 .0, EU Digital Single Market	$50-200B across sectors	5-10 years per industry	High - Standards alignment	Market leadership
State-Coordinated	China's Digital Economy, South Korea K-Digital	$200-500B national programs	7-15 years system-wide	Very High - Policy integration	National competitiveness
Infrastructure-First	Saudi Vision 2030, Singapore Smart Nation	$500B+ integrated programs	A 10-20 years comprehensive	THE Maximum - Greenfield advantage	Global benchmark setting

5.5 Future Roadmap: The Next Decade of Industrial Metaverse Evolution

Organized by the time of creation, the industry metaverse will form some stages that can be differentiated by some technological capacities, adoption trends, and socioeconomic outcomes:

Table 19. Global industrial metaverse development roadmap (2025-2035)

Phase	Timeline	Key Technologies	Adoption Rate	Economic Impact	Defining Characteristics
Foundation Phase	2025-2027	5G networks, basic digital twins, AR applications	15-35%	$150-300B global market	Infrastructure deployment, pilot projects
Integration Phase	2027-2030	AI-powered optimization, immersive interfaces, IoT ecosystems	35-60%	$400-800B global market	Cross-system integration, standardization
Optimization Phase	2030-2033	Autonomous systems, quantum computing, brain-computer interfaces	60-80%	$1.2-2.0T global market	Fully automated operations, predictive control
Transformation Phase	2033-2035	Artificial general intelligence, molecular manufacturing, space logistics	80-95%	$2.5-4.0T global market	Fundamental economic restructuring

CONCLUSION

This is not just one of the technological advances rather a whole revolution in the way mankind will organize, regulate, and rationalize the intricate mechanisms that bind the modern society. The infrastructure-first model approach can be considered one of the most effective methods of developing this scale change in Saudi Arabia.

By 2035, the Kingdom investments would lead to:

- The most productive industrial eco-system of the entire world, equipped with 90 and more of the degree of automation.
- 200 billion plus annual metaverse based industry economy.
- An economy based on place and values like sustainability of manufacturing globally
- Control of universal country-wide internet intervention.

So that way, the Kingdom does not merely desire to become the participant of the next industrial revolution, but demonstrate the world how a nation can design its own digital fate deliberately, systematically and build the first country-wide and immersive eco-system of the supply chain. Whether or not this huge experiment is successful will find or fail to find the future of industrial development in the adjacent precipices of fragmentation to be found in past or such a comprehensive change in the ecosystem of the whole that the metaverse is, self-contained seemingly on its own at least in the history of mankind.

REFERENCES

3rd Partner Logistics. (n.d.). *Drug track and trace system (RSD) revolutionizing security*. Retrieved from https://3rd-partner.com/en/drug-track-and-trace-system-rsd/

About, U. P. S. (2022). *UPS invests millions in advanced training for on-the-road drivers*. Retrieved from https://about.ups.com/us/en/newsroom/press-releases/people-led/ups-invests-millions-in-advanced-training-for-on-the-road-driver.html

About, U. P. S. (n.d.). *Virtual reality helping train safe drivers*. Retrieved from https://about.ups.com/us/en/our-stories/innovation-driven/virtual-reality-helping-to-create-safety-for-ups-drivers.html

Analysis, R. (n.d.). *Metaverse in healthcare use cases revealing benefits of this next generation technology*. Retrieved from https://www.rootsanalysis.com/key-insights/metaverse-in-healthcare-use-cases.html

Assembly Magazine. (n.d.). *BMW scales virtual factory with accelerated computing, digital twins, and AI*. Retrieved from https://www.assemblymag.com/articles/99322-bmw-scales-virtual-factory-with-accelerated-computing-digital-twins-and-ai

Bhide, P. (n.d.). *Digital twins: Revolutionizing fashion from concept to closet*. Retrieved from https://www.jprutha.com/digital-twins-revolutionizing-fashion-from-concept-to-closet/

CIPS. (n.d.). *How Nike transformed supply chains to survive Covid*. Retrieved from https://www.cips.org/knowledge-and-insight/how-nike-transformed-supply-chains-to-survive-covid

Common Share News. (n.d.). *EU's game-changing move: Introducing digital product passports for sustainable textiles*. Retrieved from https://news.commonshare.com/blog/eu-s-game-changing-move-introducing-digital-product-passports-for-sustainable-textiles

Davis, F. D. (1989). Perceived usefulness, perceived ease of use, and user acceptance of information technology. *Management Information Systems Quarterly*, *13*(3), 319–340. DOI: 10.2307/249008

DHL. (n.d.). *Extended reality - DHL - United States of America*. Retrieved from https://www.dhl.com/us-en/home/innovation-in-logistics/logistics-trend-radar/augmented-and-extended-reality.html

Dive, T. (n.d.). *UPS takes driver safety to the next level with virtual reality*. Retrieved from https://www.truckingdive.com/news/UPS-driver-training-virtual-augmented-reality-AR-VR/596831/

DuBravac, S. (n.d.). *Augmented reality is changing the supply chain workforce and improving operational efficiency and profitability*. Retrieved from https://shawndubravac.com/augmented-reality-is-changing-the-supply-chain-workforce-and-improving-operational-efficiency-and-profitability/2/

Frontiers in Virtual Reality. (2025). *Metaverse in industrial contexts - a comprehensive review*. Retrieved from https://www.frontiersin.org/journals/virtual-reality/articles/10.3389/frvir.2025.1488926/full

Green Threads, D. P. P. (n.d.). *The role of digital twins in product lifecycle management*. Retrieved from https://greenthreadsdpp.com/post/digital-twins-product-lifecycle-management

ICG. (2025). *Innovating the future: The role of the metaverse in Saudi Arabia's Vision 2030*. Retrieved from https://icg.co/wp-content/uploads/2025/02/Innovating-the-Future_-The-Role-of-the-Metaverse-in-Saudi-Arabias-Vision-2030.pdf

Japan, E. Y. (n.d.). *Leveraging the industrial metaverse for digital transformation in manufacturing*. Retrieved from https://www.ey.com/en_jp/insights/technology/industrial-metaverse-unlocks-the-future-realizing-next-generation-factories-through-digital-transformation

Journal of Minimally Invasive Surgery. (n.d.). *Research trends in virtual reality surgical simulation for education: A systematic review*. Retrieved from https://www.e-jmis.org/journal/view.html?uid=764&vmd=Full

Little, A. D. (n.d.). *The industrial metaverse*. Retrieved from https://www.adlittle.com/en/insights/report/industrial-metaverse

MDPI. (2024). *The use of virtual reality in surgical training: Implications for education, patient safety, and global health equity*. Retrieved from https://www.mdpi.com/2673-4095/4/4/61

Metaverse Reality, I. E. E. E. (n.d.). *What is industrial metaverse and why it is important*. Retrieved from https://metaversereality.ieee.org/publications/articles/what-is-industrial-metaverse-and-why-it-is-important/

Mourtzis, D., Angelopoulos, J., & Panopoulos, N. (2022). A literature review of the challenges and opportunities of the transition from Industry 4.0 to Society 5.0. *Energies*, *15*(17), 6276. DOI: 10.3390/en15176276

NAIC. (n.d.). *The impact of motor vehicle simulator training on law enforcement officer driving behavior: Empirical evidence from accident frequency and severity*. Retrieved from https://content.naic.org/sites/default/files/jir-za-38-03-el-vehicle-simulation-training.pdf

NEOM. (n.d.). *Oxagon | A reimagined industrial city in NEOM*. Retrieved from https://www.neom.com/en-us/regions/oxagon

Nike, A. (n.d.). *Sustainability — NIKE, Inc*. Retrieved from https://about.nike.com/en/mission/focus-areas/sustainability

NUPCO. (n.d.). *Logistics services - Riyadh*. Retrieved from https://www.nupco.com/en/services/logistics-service/

NVIDIA. (n.d.). *BMW Group starts global rollout of NVIDIA Omniverse*. Retrieved from https://resources.nvidia.com/en-us-industrial-sector-resources/bmw-group-nvidia-omn

PixelPlex. (n.d.). *Industrial metaverse guide: The future of manufacturing*. Retrieved from https://pixelplex.io/blog/industrial-metaverse-guide/

Place North West. (n.d.). *CASE STUDY | BMW enjoys 'vast efficiency' of digital twin factories*. Retrieved from https://www.placenorthwest.co.uk/case-study-bmw-enjoys-vast-efficiency-of-digital-twin-factories/

ResearchGate. (2024). *Metaverse healthcare supply chain: Conceptual framework and barrier identification*. Retrieved from https://www.researchgate.net/publication/378265130_Metaverse_Healthcare_Supply_Chain_Conceptual_Framework_and_Barrier_Identification

SABIC. (2021). *Supply chain*. Retrieved from https://www.sabic.com/en/reports/annual-2021/corporate/supply-chain

SABIC. (n.d.). *SABIC's digital transformation journey*. Retrieved from https://www.sabic.com/en/newsandmedia/stories/our-future/sabic-digital-transformation-journey

SFDA. (n.d.). *Home - RSD*. Retrieved from https://rsd.sfda.gov.sa/index-en.html

Siemens. (n.d.). *The state of the industrial metaverse*. Retrieved from https://www.siemens.com/global/en/company/insights/the-state-of-the-industrial-metaverse.html

Sloan, M. I. T. (n.d.). *Solve real-world problems with the industrial metaverse*. Retrieved from https://mitsloan.mit.edu/ideas-made-to-matter/solve-real-world-problems-industrial-metaverse

Supply Chain, N. H. S. (n.d.). *Transforming NHS inventory management – A blueprint for success*. Retrieved from https://www.supplychain.nhs.uk/news-article/transforming-nhs-inventory-management-a-blueprint-for-success/

Supply Chain Digital. (n.d.). *DHL Supply Chain to roll out 'Vision Picking' smart glasses across the globe*. Retrieved from https://supplychaindigital.com/technology/dhl-supply-chain-roll-out-vision-picking-smart-glasses-across-globe

Tornatzky, L. G., & Fleischer, M. (1990). *The processes of technological innovation*. Lexington Books.

Unyer. (n.d.). *How metaverse technology is revolutionizing healthcare & life science supply chains*. Retrieved from https://www.unyer.com/revolutionizing-healthcare-and-life-science-supply-chains-with-metaverse-technology/

Venkatesh, V., & Davis, F. D. (2000). A theoretical extension of the technology acceptance model: Four longitudinal field studies. *Management Science*, *46*(2), 186–204. DOI: 10.1287/mnsc.46.2.186.11926

Xpert.Digital. (n.d.). *Industrial metaverse factory planning from BMW iFactory: Digital twin & virtual factory & planning with the NVIDIA Omniverse*. Retrieved from https://xpert.digital/en/bmw-metaverse

Xu, L. D., Xu, E. L., & Li, L. (2018). Industry 4.0: State of the art and future trends. *International Journal of Production Research*, *56*(8), 2941–2962. DOI: 10.1080/00207543.2018.1444806

Chapter 7
AI-Driven Sales Forecasting and Operational Trend Analysis for Accelerated Food Supply Logistics

Bhoomi Gupta
https://orcid.org/0009-0007-1941-3445
Jaypee University of Engineering and Technology, Guna, India

Geet Madnani
https://orcid.org/0009-0002-0015-423X
Jaypee University of Engineering and Technology, Guna, India

Yash Pathak
https://orcid.org/0009-0004-5437-5382
Jaypee University of Engineering and Technology, Guna, India

Kunj Bihari Meena
https://orcid.org/0000-0001-8159-9024
Jaypee University of Engineering and Technology, Guna, India

Vipin Tyagi
https://orcid.org/0000-0003-4994-3686
Jaypee University of Engineering and Technology, Guna, India

DOI: 10.4018/979-8-3373-8841-0.ch007

ABSTRACT

The growing integration of AI into supply chains is reshaping how logistics systems forecast demand, optimize operations, and respond to market fluctuations. Within this context, the food service sector, characterized by fast-moving inventory, dynamic pricing and variable daily demand, requires intelligent systems that enhance logistical efficiency. This chapter presents a unified AI enabled food sales and trend analysis framework to support accelerated logistics planning through advanced predictive modeling. The framework uses machine learning across four operationally critical areas: menu price prediction, weekly and monthly sales forecasting, identification of high-demand days and detection of potential bestselling items. Positioned within broader developments in Generative AI assisted logistics, this chapter demonstrates how predictive intelligence can streamline inventory management, reduce stockouts, enhance demand driven restocking cycles, and improve workforce allocation.

1. INTRODUCTION

The food-service industry's rapid adoption of digital technologies has led to a steep increase in transactional, interactional, preference-based and operationally data (Ferrer-Blas et al., 2024). Restaurants are now competing in an environment of constantly changing demand patterns because of seasonality, price changes, promotions and external events, all of which significantly shape customer purchasing behavior (Tanizaki et al., 2019). Activity-sensitive data sources are available, but an intuition-based decision-making process continues to be the primary model for pricing, inventory management, labor planning and menu optimization (Longart, 2015). This intuition-based decision-making model tends to overlook purchase behavior patterns, which can lead to wasted resources, lost revenue, or predictions that are wrong about demand.

Machine learning has proven to be an effective technique for uncovering intricate, nonlinear relationships in data that can inform predictions beyond the purview of traditional statistical methods (Hastie et al., 2009). In the context of sales forecasting and retail research, previous studies have established the merits of models such as gradient boosting, recurrent neural networks (RNNs) and ensembles of decision tree models with respect to meaningful forecasting of customer demand and consumptive behavior in food-service and retail establishments (Schmidt et al., 2022). Moreover, research on restaurant-specific pricing has shown that contemporary machine-learning algorithms, such as XGBoost and Support Vector Machines (SVM), can accurately model the behavior of menu prices under dynamic cost and market conditions (Şahinbaş, 2021). However, existing research typically addresses one predictive problem: total sales forecasts or product rankings but does not address a cohesive analytical framework that can be leveraged across a variety of operational needs in the food-service industry.

This chapter suggests an AI driven sales forecasting and operational trend analysis model for accelerated food supply logistics, which combines various machine-learning-based models to assist with following four key decision-making tasks:

1. predicting price ranges for menu items
2. forecasting weekly and monthly sales
3. classifying busy operational days
4. identifying bestselling menu items.

The framework captures the influence of temporal and behavioral trends, menu performance and operational changes through a combination of XGBoost regression, LSTM networks, optimized classification models and ranking-based predictions. The framework uses a feature set inclusive of lag variables, rolling averages, seasonal indicators, sales behavior and promotions to inform the models of short and long-term demand (Makridakis et al., 2018).

Distinctiveness of proposed model is its multi-objective, complete predictive design. It integrates regression, classification and ranking techniques within a single analytic framework. While prior studies have addressed a portion of restaurant operations, this chapter contributes a full decision-support framework. The model may produce better decisions related to pricing, inventory management, staff scheduling and menu design. Experimental findings show the proposed machine-learning pipeline significantly improves predictive accuracy across different objectives, echoing earlier findings in the food-service and retail forecasting literature (Güler et al., 2024). These results highlight that data-driven systems can meaningfully enhance the efficiency of restaurants and provide a viable starting point for a future AI-based food e-business intelligence platform.

2. LITERATURE REVIEW

Restaurants and retail outlets now store large amounts of data about online sales, as well as daily operations (Ferrer-Blas et al., 2024). Researchers are using machine-learning to utilize this data (Hastie et al., 2009). In this section, review is done for four topics: price prediction, sales and demand forecasting, identification of the busiest days and measurement of how individual menu items perform. The goal is to show what succeeds, what fails and why a single, smarter prediction system is required.

A. Price Prediction Model

For decades, people have sought to forecast prices in various arenas, including stock markets, e-commerce applications and commodity exchanges. Early methodology largely depended on established statistical approaches: linear regression, Support Vector Regression (SVR), random forests and gradient boosting. Although these traditional analytical models are effective with simpler contexts, they generally outperformed when required to analyse nonlinear or high-dimensional relationships (Friedman, 2001). Ensemble and boosting approaches are gaining importance due to their modeling capability of complex interactions within structured data. A related prominent contribution is by Chen and Guestrin (2016) who introduced XGBoost, a fast and scalable gradient-boosting algorithm that has become a benchmark for price-prediction problems due to extraordinarily performance on tabular datasets.

The restaurant industry as a whole has been relatively slow to adapt machine-learning technologies into restaurant pricing considerations (Longart, 2015). Instead, many restaurants still adhere to old methodologies, while failing to embrace data-driven forecasting methodologies that would better account for changes in ingredient cost, patterns in demand and movements in market demand more generally. Most importantly, there has been no previous research to integrate ingredient prices, historical sales and external market signals into a single machine-learning model to forecast restaurant menu prices, representing a clear and important gap in the literature (Ben-Daya et al., 2019).

Several studies have examined the effectiveness of machine-learning in forecasting revenue or prices in fields relating to hospitality. One of the most closely related studies to this research is by Parh et al. (2023), who studied the prediction of restaurant revenue with an international quick-service restaurant company at its 100,000 locations. The authors analyzed 137 training samples that included information on 41 predictor variables related to demographic, commercial and real-estate characteristics. The authors studied many supervised learning models including: multiple linear regression, forward and backward stepwise selection with both simple and multiple linear regressions, ridge regression and principal components regression and Least Absolute Shrinkage and Selection Operator (LASSO), as well as tree-based models, such as bagging, random forest and boosting. The authors found that LASSO regression had the lowest test error in generating the restaurant revenue prediction and outperformed ridge regression and all of the tree-based methods because LASSO regression could shrink uninformative coefficients while not overfitting to the model. The results of this study indicate the importance of utilizing regularization-based models in forecasting contexts with many predictors and also support that small datasets can still generate reliable models even with a similar family of models.

In the wider context of price forecasting, price forecasts of used cars have been undertaken by Gegic et al. (2019) using machine-learning methods. This was done using an extensive web-scraping exercise collecting in excess of 1,000 for sale advertisements from a used-car website in Bosnia. Following a data cleaning and preprocessing step whereby the dataset was narrowed to 797 quality samples, they implemented stand-alone machine-learning models: Random Forest, Artificial Neural Networks (ANN) and Support Vector Machines (SVM) for evaluation purposes. The independent models achieved moderate performance, with accuracies of 41%-48%. They created a hierarchical ensemble method whereby price classifications were developed in two stages; the first stage was the Random Forest model clustering cars into broad price classifications, the second stage implemented either SVM or ANN models to classify used cars into finer price classifications. The multi-stage ensemble resulted in 87.38% accuracy, which surpassed all other classifiers. The authors called attention to the effectiveness of predictive architectures to ensemble-base methods for complicated price classification tasks with nonlinear relationships and multiple attributes within the dataset.

The results of these studies both demonstrate that the regularized regression techniques (e.g., LASSO) and ensemble-based frameworks (e.g., hybrids of RF-SVM-ANN) are both viable options for forecasting revenues or prices from high-dimensional heterogeneous datasets. However, neither study focuses explicitly on predicting menu prices for restaurants using combined ingredient costs, changes in the market and historical sales. This is a significant void in the literature and suggests more research is warranted for a dedicated machine-learning model applicable to restaurant pricing, which this study attempts to provide.

B. Time-Series Forecasting for Sales and Demand

Time-series forecasting has been widely examined for its applicability in a variety of industries, like retail, finance & banking, transportation and manufacturing (Makridakis et al., 2018). Standard models for sales forecasting include the Autoregressive Integrated Moving Average (ARIMA) and Seasonal Auto-Regressive Integrated Moving Average (SARIMA); Holt-Winters exponential smoothing; and decomposition methods (Box et al., 2015; Holt, 2004). Although most of these modeling methods are interpretable models, they may not handle more complex patterns appropriately such as a sudden jump in demand, multiple seasonal patterns or non-linear relationships between attributes (Hyndman & Athanasopoulos, 2018; Awad & Mahmoud, 2024).

Deep learning has led to the development of new recurrent architectures, such as Long Short-Term Memory (LSTM) networks, to improve the performance of sequential prediction models (Hochreiter & Schmidhuber, 1997; Brownlee, 2018),

LSTMs. Due to their property of long memory of dependencies, they can predict demand on a weekly or monthly time basis. Studies comparing ARIMA and LSTM models found that LSTM models better account for irregularities and noise in the demand pattern (Sagheer & Kotb, 2019; Shams Eldin et.al, 2025). Gradient boosting methods, such as XGBoost, can also be adapted for time-series forecasting. They generally outperform deep learning approaches if the data sets are a moderate size and the features are prominent (Bandara et al., 2020).

One of the most relevant studies demonstrating how machine-learning methods can be successfully employed for retail sales time-series forecasting is (Pavlyshenko, 2019). In this study, the author examines several regression-based and ensemble methods of machine learning (ML), namely Random Forest, Gradient Boosting and stacked ensembles by utilizing the Rossmann Store Sales dataset that exhibited complex sales fluctuations as a result of promotions, store characteristics, holiday and temporal features. Unlike typical time series forecasting models such as ARIMA and Holt-Winters that forecast based strictly on historical values, forecasting is treated as a supervised learning problem through developing a rich feature set, including lag variable, rolling statistics and categorical indicators. The findings show that ensembles of machine learning models outperformed self-contained machine learning models and traditional time series models particularly in the case where historical data was limited or erratic. Pavlyshenko (2019) concludes that static feature engineering along with ensemble modeling can account for user-defined and contextual factors that can contribute to robust forecasting of sales across products and stores; and have flexibility in environments characterized by sporadic or volatile demand. Support for the use of feature-driven ML models (XGBoost and hybrids of LSTM) for forecasting restaurant menu item sales fluctuating due to regular operations and if there are promotional offers based on the finding of (Pavlyshenko, 2019).

Research in food demand forecasting remains comparatively underdeveloped. Existing studies examine daily or hourly demand prediction for inventory control but rarely address both weekly and monthly forecasting within the same analytical system. Moreover, prior works often overlook operational drivers such as promotions, special events, weather, or seasonal trends (Güler et al., 2024). These gaps justify the need for hybrid forecasting solutions capable of capturing multi-scale temporal patterns in restaurant sales.

C. Busy-Day Classification

It is important to note that high-demand, or "busy" days are predictable in order to manage staffing levels and allocate resources more effectively. Research in hospitality, tourism and retail has investigated alternative methods to categorizing which days are busy, based on consumer traffic or sales (Schmidt et al., 2022; Tanizaki et al., 2019). For example, studies have used Logistic Regression, Support Vector Machines, Random Forests and Gradient Boosting (Bandara et al., 2020; Makridakis et al., 2018). Researchers find that models that employ lagged demand variables, calendar variables and promotions offer a superior predictive accuracy than models that track sales alone.

However, there are sparse studies in food-service analytics, which utilize simple threshold or rule-based models rather than advanced classification approaches. Few classification studies in food-service analytics utilize engineered features, such as rolling statistical windows, previous-day patterns, or trend variables, although these features can be helpful. Furthermore, studies often focused on classification with only the accuracy metric, failing to incorporate additional metrics such as precision and recall.

(Mariyappan et al., 2021) is one of the few studies that focused specifically on identifying the most operationally heavy days in a restaurant operation using data-mining techniques. This study utilized historical restaurant transaction data which included fields such as the day of the week, foot traffic, total menu-item sales and event indicators that signaled a problem. The authors then used both classification and clustering algorithms to categorize operational days of the week into the categories of "busy", "moderate" or "normal. Examining the demand indicators, the authors found weekends, festival occasions and promotional days had the highest levels of demand and the routine days of the week were the most unilaterally lowest in demand followed consistently through the week. The authors also showed several behavioral and temporal features provided more classification accuracy than simple rule-based approaches. Although this research used conventional data-mining, it provides a solid framework with supportive evidence that shows that day-type categorizing can be a fully-fledged model approach and development tool in a restaurant operator's toolbox for operational decision-making about staffing requirements, inventory management, or food prep times (Mariyappan et al., 2021).

This highlights the need for a robust classification model to identify peak-demand days, such as the XGBoost classifier utilized in the current study, that identifies days with peak demand with good performance across multiple evaluation metrics.

D. Bestseller Prediction and Menu-Item Performance Analysis

Identifying potential bestselling menu items is important for menu development, targeted marketing, schedule ordering and inventory and waste management. Prior studies on product ranks and bestseller prediction have primarily used collaborative filtering, matrix factorization, or a learning to rank approach in the e-commerce and retail sector (Koren et al., 2009; Burges, 2010). In food service analytics, more basic descriptive statistics or historical averages have been employed that do not consider the dynamic nature of effects like price elasticity, promotional effects, weekly trends and consumer behaviour with other products (Tanizaki et al., 2019; Schmidt et al., 2022).

Long et al. (2012) outlined a framework for predicting best-selling items that incorporates machine learning-based popularity estimation into product ranking systems for online retailers. Their research shows that factors such as previous sales trends, demand seasonality, popularity of items and context behavior signals can be used to predict future best-seller status. The authors indicate that incorporating predicted best-seller scores into ranking models substantially enhances retrieval relevance and user engagement compared with models that rely solely on historical sales volume. Although their work focuses on retail e-commerce rather than food-service settings, the approach is highly transferable to restaurant analytics. Menu items, similar to retail products, exhibit dynamic demand patterns influenced by seasonality, promotions, consumer preferences and time-of-day trends. Their findings provide evidence that best-seller prediction benefits from feature-rich modeling and ranking-oriented frameworks. This underscores the value of advanced regression-ranking systems such as the LightGBM ranking model used in the present study, for accurately identifying potential bestselling menu items (Long et al., 2012).

Recent advances in gradient boosting algorithms, specifically LightGBM, provide efficient ranking and regression methods for predicting bestsellers. LightGBM provide evidence of good performance on ranking orders when capturing complex interactions among features and accurate top-K ranking predictions (Ke et al., 2017). However, the literature using ranking-based ML models and applications in restaurant sales is limited. Past studies did not utilize temporal modeling to assess rank accuracy or use appropriate measures of rank accuracy (e.g., Spearman correlations, top-N ranking overlap) (Long et al., 2012). The present study builds upon and substantially extends prior research by developing a LightGBM-based model enhanced with lag features, rolling statistics, historical averages, promotional indicators and temporal variables. Using these capabilities, the model provides a more robust and accurate forecast of future bestselling items, addressing an important shortcoming in current food-service analytics research.

E. Identified Gaps and Research Motivation

A review of the literature indicates a few significant gaps in the literature that limit the power of current analytical techniques in food service or restaurant research. First, most evaluations have focused on a singular predictive task (e.g., sales tracking, price modeling) rather than the development of a cohesive multi-model system that offers operational decision support. Second, pricing is a key concern for management, yet little research has used machine learning techniques for restaurant menu item price prediction (Şahinbaş, 2021). Third, research evaluating time series predictions does not model weekly and month horizon forecasts within the same model, leaving multi-scale forecasting. Fourth, busy-day classification studies in food service contexts often use shallow features and report accuracy without properly reporting precision and recall. Lastly, studies on the prediction of best-sellers in a food service context rarely employ advanced ranking models like LightGBM along with artfully engineered features that represent demand over time. All of these gaps are addressed in the development of the unified AI driven sales forecasting and operational trend analysis for accelerated food supply logistics to provide insights across price prediction, demand forecasting, operational day classification and bestseller ranking.

3. METHODOLOGY

Study in this chapter employed a systematic multi-stage methodology to analyze restaurant sales behaviour and build forecasting models for four main purposes (price prediction, forecasting weekly and monthly sales, classifying busy days and identifying bestsellers). The process begins with cleaning the data and continues with feature engineering, model building, hyper-parameter tuning and final evaluation. All analysis were conducted within Python-based machine-learning frameworks, including Scikit-learn, XGBoost, LightGBM, LSTM networks. Figure 1 depicts the proposed methodology, including data preprocessing, feature engineering, multi-objective model development and performance evaluation of the models leading to insight generation.

Figure 1. Workflow of the proposed method

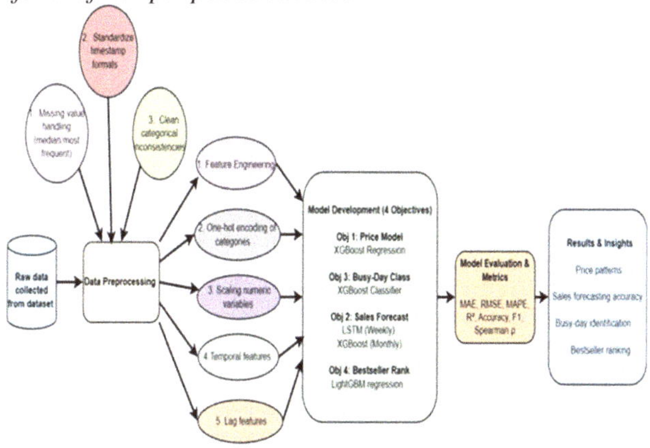

The dataset consisted of food-sales transactions (10,000 records) and variables included the date, menu item, restaurant type, weather state, ingredient cost, quantity sold, promotional flags and observed market prices. The data were first cleaned by standardizing timestamp format and then by imputing missing or erroneous data with median and most-frequent measures, respectively. Categorical features including menu item name, restaurant type and weather condition were encoded using One-hot encoding and numerical measures including ingredient cost and market price were standardized to stabilize the models during training. Additional temporal features (day of week, month, quarter, weekend flag and week number) were engineered to capture identifiable seasonal features and behavioral aspects within the data.

3.1 Preprocessing

The preprocessing of the dataset ensured data quality and model performance. Missing values for numerical variables including price, ingredient cost per item and quantity sold were addressed with either median imputation or forward-fill methods that are often suggested for retail and demand forecasting datasets (Hyndman & Athanasopoulos, 2018). For categorical variables (menu item name, restaurant type, weather conditions and meal category), the method of one-hot encoding was used; this is standard practice in machine-learning models for structured datasets (Pedregosa et al., 2011). Due to the reduced gradient decay in sequential neural networks like those based on Long Short-Term Memory (LSTM), min-max scaling was used to the weekly forecasting model, while tree-based methodologies such as XGBoost (Chen & Guestrin, 2016) and LightGBM (Ke et al., 2017) do not require rescaling as tree-based models are robust to differences in the magnitude of features. Lagged temporal features (Lag-1, Lag-2, Lag-3, Lag-7), rolling means and rolling standard deviations were created to capture short- and long-term dependencies in demand patterns consistent with best practices in time-series forecasting (Makridakis et al., 2018). These upstream engineered features preserved seasonality, event effects and promotional-driven changes in demand to ensure temporal behavior was retained in the downstream models.

3.2 Model Description

3.2.1 XGBoost for Price Prediction

Extreme Gradient Boosting (XGBoost) is a scalable method that involves creating ensembles of trees and uses gradient boosting, along with regularization, to improve prediction performance. XGBoost is an ensemble method that builds decision trees in an iterative manner, where each tree built after the first is aimed at correcting the residual errors of all prior trees. The method implements shrinkage, L1/L2 regularization and optimized tree-pruning, all of which minimize overfitting and enhance generalization (Chen & Guestrin, 2016).

In price predictions, XGBoost is good at modeling nonlinear interactions between predictors - such as ingredient cost, type of restaurant and dish characteristics. Given the price is driven by cost and menu characteristics and not history (i.e., the most recent history) - lag predictors do not contribute to the model. The model is therefore well suited for predicting restaurant menu-item prices using organized, static or slowly-varying predictors.

To fulfil Objective 1 (Price Prediction), an XGBoost regression pipeline is developed. The model used both numeric and categorical predictors via a preprocessing pipeline based on the Column Transformer. The predictors were lag-free, as price prediction is based on attributes such as ingredient cost, types of restaurant and menu attributes unlike sales history, which can involve lags. The pipeline provided a coherent unit in which scaling, encoding, imputation and model fitting were conducted. The model performed good (MAE = 1.93, RMSE = 3.19, R^2 = 0.97), showing that the learned relationships generalized beyond the training set.

3.2.2 LSTM for Weekly Forecasting & XGBoost for Monthly Forecasting

The Long Short-Term Memory (LSTM) is a form of Recurrent Neural Network (RNN) designed to handle long-range dependencies for sequential data. The model has memory cells and gating units that can add and update past information over time, making the LSTM a highly suitable model for weekly sales forecasting where you need to account for time-based patterns, seasonalities and noise. The LSTM works by processing sliding windows of sequential input and learning temporal sequences of behavior that traditional models cannot capture (Hochreiter & Schmidhuber, 1997; Brownlee, 2018).

For monthly forecasts, XGBoost regression was conducted with advanced temporal features such as lagged sales, rolling averages, rolling standard deviations and seasonal indicators. XGBoost is able to exploit time-based patterns as features when encoded (Chen & Guestrin, 2016). The TimeSeriesSplit cross-validation helps to make sure temporal order is not violated during training, which makes these models appropriate for stable longer horizon monthly demand forecasting (Pedregosa et al., 2011).

For Objective 2 (Weekly and Monthly Sales Forecasting), two models were developed. The model for weekly sales forecasting was based on LSTM neural networks, which were trained on sequential windows for four weeks on lagged sales data. The series was summed into weekly totals and normalized using MinMax scaling to stabilize learning. The model was able to capture general trends and patterns in the data, although it produced larger errors (MAE ≈ 491, RMSE ≈ 687), likely partly due to limited time history and partly due to some volatility in sales variation. The models for monthly forecasting were based on an XGBoost regression model, as for Objective 1, but with lag features, additional rolling averages and rolling standard deviations and features created from seasonality. For this series, a TimeSeriesSplit cross-validation technique was used to maintain temporal order in the model training process. This model performed significantly well in terms of series error metrics (MAE ≈ 7,691, RMSE ≈ 10,668), although sales per month has stable patterns monthly in comparison.

3.2.3 XGBoost Classifier for Busy-Day Classification

For the identification of high-demand "busy" days, an XGBoost classifier was used (Chen & Guestrin, 2016). XGBoost classification extends gradient-boosted decision trees to handle binary labels effectively by learning nonlinear relationships between operational features, promotional variables and temporal indicators. By incorporating lag features, rolling statistical properties, day-of-week effects and event flags, the model learns short and long-term behavioral patterns. GridSearchCV is used to optimize depth, learning rate and regularization to maximize predictive performance across multiple metrics such as precision, recall, accuracy and F1 score.

For Objective 3 (Busy-Day Classification), both time and promotional variables are used. Daily observations were accumulated to calculate total quantity sold by date and a dynamic threshold utilizing the top 30% of daily demand was employed to label busy days. To improve predictive ability, several lag features (1-day, 2-day, 3-day and 7-day lags), rolling mean and standard deviation windows and flags for month-start / month-end dates are used. A GridSearchCV optimized XGBoost classifier was used to process the features. The accurately trained classifier has a performance of 94.44% with precision = 0.958, recall = 0.884 and F1=0.920, which shows that it performs well in discerning the busy operational days.

3.2.4 LightGBM Ranking Model for Bestseller Prediction and Menu-Item Performance

The bestseller prediction task uses a LightGBM ranking model based on gradient-boosted decision trees with a leaf-wise growth strategy (Ke et al., 2017). Its ranking objective (LambdaMART / LambdaRank) is designed to preserve the relative ordering of items rather than produce raw value estimates (Burges, 2010). LightGBM efficiently handles large feature sets using techniques such as Gradient-based One-Side Sampling (GOSS) and Exclusive Feature Bundling (EFB). The model leverages lagged sales, rolling windows, historical means, promotion frequency, price changes and previous-week ranking to understand long-term demand behavior. Evaluation is performed using ranking-specific metrics such as Spearman correlation and top-N accuracy.

Lastly, Objective 4 (Predictions of Bestseller Dish) was a LightGBM regression framework designed to model weekly demand for each dish on the menu. The weekly aggregated dataset was grouped by dish and week and dish-specific temporal features (lagged sales, rolling averages, historical mean, frequency of promotions, price changes and rank from the previous week) were constructed to represent long-term item-level demand behavior. The model was trained to achieve $R^2 = 0.965$, MAE $\approx$ 501, RMSE $\approx$ 751 and a Spearman rank correlation of 0.974, exhibiting an ability to retain the sales ranking order. It can be observed that the model accurately recognized 80% of the top 10 bestselling dishes for the last week.

For each of the four objectives, extensive model evaluation has been conducted using MAE, RMSE, R^2, MAPE, accuracy, F1 score and Spearman correlation for timely evaluative comparison. The interpretation of model behavior was accomplished with visualizations, including plots of error distribution, feature-importance and predicted versus actual prices. Overall, the proposed multi-model pipeline allowed for a complete understanding of price factors, sales trends over time, operational load and best sellers on the menu so that decisions to make predictions for restaurant management could be made.

4. EXPERIMENTAL RESULTS

4.1 Dataset used

Restaurant Sales dataset (Chen, 2024) is used for the experiments. This dataset is a granular, item-level view of daily sales from a diverse group of 50 restaurants, spanning a full year from January 2024 to January 2025. Featured variables in this dataset include sales transaction dates, menu item names, restaurant type, cost of ingredients, quantity sold of each menu item, final selling price, promotion indicators, market price and weather indicators as shown in Table 1. The dataset provides a detail level that would allow us to model pricing behavior, dish-level demand forecasting and analyze operational trends. One aspect of the data is the time coverage, which allows for weekly, monthly and seasonal patterns to be identified. Including cost-derived and market-related variables will give the opportunity to analyze market influences such as inflation and supply-chain difficulties. The addition of promotions and weather variables will provide the opportunity to delve into behaviors that are in direct response to a marketing promotion and environmental conditions, respectively.

Collectively, these variables, in addition to other rich features of the data, form a sound basis for the multi-objective forecasting approach proposed in this work.

Table 1. Overview of dataset features and their corresponding descriptions

Column Name	Description
date	The transaction date, used to derive time-series attributes such as week number, month, quarter, day-of-week, seasonality patterns and holiday effects.
menu_item_name	Unique dish or beverage identifier, enabling dish-level modelling such as bestseller prediction and dish-level demand forecasting.
quantity_sold	The daily volume of each menu item sold. This variable is central to demand forecasting, busy-day classification and bestseller identification.
actual_selling_price	The final price at which the dish was sold, enabling modelling of pricing behaviour, price prediction and revenue forecasting.
ingredient_cost	The base food cost for the item, enabling margin analysis and price-prediction modelling.
has_promotion	A binary variable indicating whether the item was sold under promotion, useful for recognising a promotion's effect on demand.
special_event	A binary indicator for holidays, festivals, or event days, enabling models to capture demand spikes that may occur on unique calendar days.
restaurant_type	The category of restaurant or type of food served (e.g. fast-food, casual dining), allows the model to generalize beyond types of restaurants.
observed_market_ price	A temporal market marker for inflation in food pricing, allowing correlation between ingredient price movements and behaviour in selling price.
customer_traffic	A proxy for foot traffic and important for prediction on busy days and operational narratives (e.g. staffing, orders).
weather indicators	External factors in the dining situation often associated with changes in dining behaviour, thus aiding in the exogenous nature of forecasting models.

4.2 Performance Metrics

To assess model performance, a number of metrics were used, commonly used in other food demand/retail-forecasts:

A. Regression Metrics (Price, Weekly, Monthly, Bestseller Prediction)

1. Mean Absolute Error (MAE): It indicates the average absolute amount of the errors in predictions, without regard to direction. It is easy to interpret as it uses absolute values. Compared to squared-error metrics, it is less influenced by larger

errors. Lower MAE indicates better accuracy to predictions. It is determined as:

$$MAE = \frac{1}{n}\Sigma\left|y_i - {}_i\right|$$

2. Root Mean Square Error (RMSE): It is calculated by taking the square root of the mean of the squared residual errors. On squaring the residual errors, the larger the difference, the greater the penalty for calculating RMSE, thus making it sensitive to outliers. RMSE is useful when larger errors are particularly harmful. It is computed as:

$$RMSE = \sqrt{\left(\frac{1}{n}\right)\Sigma\,(y_i - {}_i)^2}$$

3. Mean Absolute %age Error (MAPE): It quantifies accuracy as a %, making it one of the easiest metrics to compare across multiple, vastly different datasets. MAPE is the average absolute % difference between actual and predicted values. It can also represent unstable scores when actual values are very low and close to zero.

It is determined as:

$$MAPE = \left(\frac{100}{n}\right)\Sigma\left|\frac{y_i - {}_i}{y_i}\right|$$

4. R^2 Score: The R^2 score is simply a way to express the proportion of variance in the dependent variable accountable to the model utilized; R^2 can achieve a range of negative infinity to 1, with larger R^2 indicating greater predictive ability. Generally speaking, a negative R^2 is equivalent to saying the model is worse than the simple horizontal model. It is calculated as follows:

$$R^2\,Score = 1 \; \frac{\Sigma\,(y_i - {}_i)^2}{\Sigma\,(y_i - \;)^2}$$

5. Spearman Rank Correlation: It explains how much the relationship between the two variables can be approximated by a monotonic function, or nothing more than that. That is, it can measure the ranked values instead of the raw values, which is preferable for non-linear relationships. A value close to 1 indicates a nearly identical order of ranking. It is calculated as:

$$Spearman\ Rank\ Correlation = 1 - \frac{(6 \Sigma d_i^2)}{(n(n^2 - 1))}$$

B. Classification Metrics (Busy-Day Prediction)

1. Accuracy: It is the proportion of total correct predictions made by the model. Accuracy is considered as a good starting point. But, if the classes are imbalanced then it may mislead. It is calculated as:

$$Accuracy = \frac{TP + TN}{TP + TN + FP + FN}$$

2. Precision: It is the proportion of positive predictions that were actually correct. Precision is computed as follows:

$$Precision = \frac{TP}{TP + FP}$$

3. Recall (Sensitivity): It is the ability of the model to identify all actual positive cases correctly and calculated as follows:

$$Recall = \frac{TP}{TP + FN}$$

4. F1 score: It gives a balanced measure of precision and recall. It becomes useful when the distribution of class is uneven. It can be determined as:

$$F1\ score = 2 * \frac{Precision * Recall}{Precision + Recall}$$

5. Confusion Matrix: In addition to standard performance metrics, models were also evaluated using the confusion matrices which provide a detailed breakdown of the prediction outcomes.

   TP = True Positives
   TN = True Negatives
   FP = False Positives
   FN = False Negatives

4.3 Experimental Setup

Experimental setup was designed to be reproducible and consistent with approaches used in earlier retail-forecasting and food-demand studies. All experiments were run using Python machine-learning libraries in a local computing environment.

Experiments were conducted using the most popular data-science tools and machine-learning frameworks. The coding for proposed model was conducted using Python 3.10, as well as Jupyter Notebook for the step-wise experimentations and the iterative development of new models. The data manipulation and numerical computation was conducted using Python's Pandas library and NumPy library. The machine-learning frameworks used in the study included Scikit-learn, which provided methods for preprocessing, feature engineering and classical regression and classification modeling (Pedregosa et al., 2011), as well as TensorFlow/Keras to build the Long Short-Term Memory (LSTM) neural network model for weekly forecasting, as per typical deep-learning practices for sequence modeling (Hochreiter & Schmidhuber, 1997). Additionally, for both regression and classification components - both techniques showed good performance of XGBoost on structured tabular datasets and its gradient-boosting framework. To provide predictions related to the bestsellers as a new model was LightGBM, developed specifically to provide an efficient gradient-boosting framework, particularly for ranking competencies at the item-level for estimating form of item-demand modeling (Ke et al., 2017).

Chronological train-test splits were used in all models to avoid leakage and maintain temporal integrity. For price prediction working with XGBoost regression, 80% of the observations were used for training and 20% for testing the model. The LSTM model for weekly forecasting used the last 20% of weeks as a hold-out test set, consistent with evaluating sequence models (Hochreiter & Schmidhuber, 1997). Monthly sales forecasting using XGBoost regression model also used TimeSeriesSplit with GridSearch to optimize hyperparameters retaining the last 4 months for evaluation and was consistent with long-horizon forecasting procedures from M-competitions (Makridakis et al., 2018). For bestseller prediction using LightGBM, an 85-15 split was carried out that was consistent with other studies examining the ranking of similar items (Ke et al., 2017). Hyperparameter optimization for classification, model and monthly forecasting uses grid search (i.e., GridSearchCV) and was consistent with model selection procedures in Scikit-learn (Pedregosa et al., 2011).

4.4 Results

In this section performance of the model and analysis of the four ML objectives is discussed. For each model standard metrics (e.g., MAE, RMSE, R^2, accuracy, recall, F1 score) and qualitative aspects based on visual inspection of prediction curves, trend fit and error detection are used. The results are interpreted considering baseline expectations and properties of the dataset including seasonality, volatility of items and menu-level variability. Overall, the work in this chapter provides a view of the way that machine-learning can help restaurants improving how they predict prices, forecast demand, plan daily operations and design menus that better match customer needs.

4.4.1 Price Prediction Results

To address the price prediction problem, an XGBoost regression pipeline is utilized to develop a model that captures the nonlinear relationships among the menu items, their attributes and the actual selling price in practice. Additionally, a pre-processing workflow was built that added one-hot encoding for categorical variables and standardization for continuous variables to the features used in the model. The model learned data and the relationships among the variables within this unique data framework. The close alignment between actual and predicted prices can be seen in Figure 2. The final model produced a Mean Absolute Error (MAE) of 1.93 and Root Mean Square Error (RMSE) of 3.19, as well as a high coefficient of determination (R^2) of 0.97, which means near 97% of the variation in actual sales price can be explained by the model developed in this study. In conclusion, this shows the model is robust and generalizable.

The performance can be explained by the richness and diversity of the features that were modeled. Specific variables, including: ingredient cost, observed market price, weather, type of restaurant, menu category and key ingredient tags are enough to supply meaningful contextual information for the model to dissect price-based patterns among the different food items. The close alignment between the actual values and predicted values shown in the performance plots indicates that the model performed its intended purpose, identifying broad pricing trends and narrower differences between menu items. The contribution of each variable to the model is illustrated in the feature-importance results shown in Figure 3. Furthermore, the analysis of feature-importance indicates the cost attributes and categorical ID's differentiated greater in price prediction which reinforces that pricing, as presented in the sample dataset and study, is generally dictated by cost and value related to item or menu characteristics.

In addition to the collected quantitative metrics, the distribution of error in the predicted price further reinforces the stability and reliability of the model. This distribution is shown in Figure 4. The error analysis indicated that most deviations from price predictions were within an acceptable error range of approximately ±10-20%. This was supported by the computed α-10 and α-20 accuracies ranges, with accuracies of 55.05% and 86.85% achieved in prediction respectively. These error-band statistics along with the predictions show that the model demonstrated stability in performance across each respective type of menu item, rather than achieving excellent performance on just selected menu item categories. Stability on pricing of menu items or items on food and beverage menus is important since the restaurant industry is constantly adapting in their operational dynamic, including menu items that can experience changes in ingredient sourcing, cooking methods and market-based volatility.

In conclusion, the results demonstrate the machine-learning model achieved a highly accurate prediction with reliable performance across price and categories of food or menu items. Such reliability is harder to achieve with heuristic or manual methods of pricing, which are generally based on an individual's judgment, set mark-up rules and do not accommodate the shifting preferences of the consumer. These findings show the ML-based pricing is more accurate, scalable and reliable method for real-world restaurant applications that can remain both data-driven and operationally reliable.

Figure 2. Actual versus predicted selling prices, showing a tight alignment that demonstrates the high precision of the XGBoost price prediction model

Figure 3. XGBoost feature-importance plot illustrating the most influential variables in price prediction

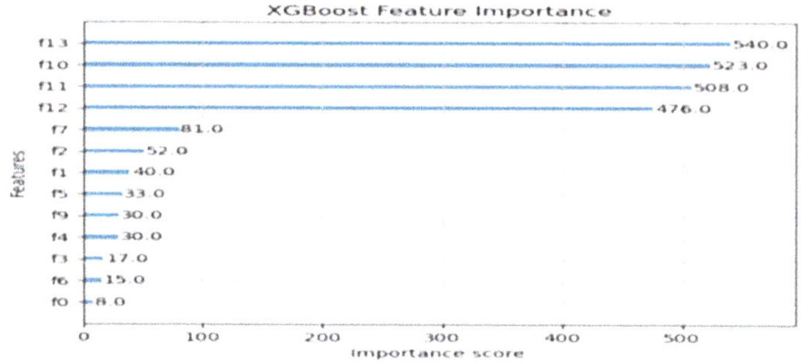

Figure 4. Distribution of relative prediction errors, with most errors concentrated within ±10%, reflecting α-10 accuracy of 55.05% and α-20 accuracy of 86.85%

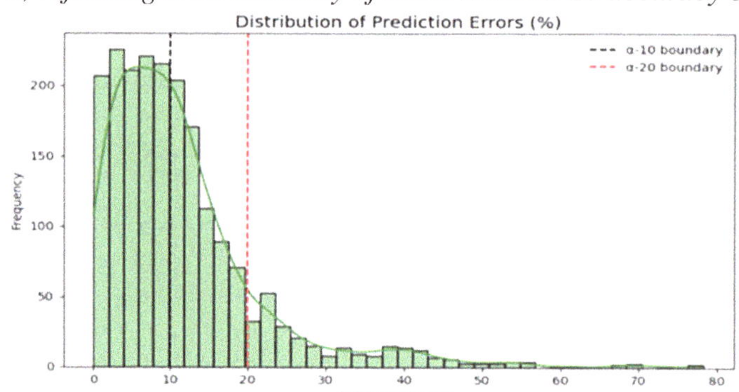

4.4.2 Weekly and Monthly Sales Forecasting Results

The weekly sales forecasting used a Long Short-Term Memory (LSTM) network built to learn temporal dependencies in short-range sales behavior. The weekly sales data was aggregated from daily transaction records and transformed into lagged sequences, allowing the model to learn from the sales data of the previous four weeks. Although the latent structure of LSTMs is theoretically suitable for the purposes of time-series forecasting because they can retain information for many time periods, practically they are only effective based on the quantity and stability of historical data. This historical sales data had considerable variability from week to week due to promotions, weather, variety of cooking and shifting customer traffic. As shown in Figure 5, the model's predictions follow the general weekly sales trend despite some deviations in magnitude.

The model showed MAE of 491.90 and RMSE of 687.00, which might indicate a considerable deviation from the actual total for the week. Deviation is expected when forecasting sales over the short term, especially in aggregate time-series, where sales behavior can be inconsistent and influenced by operational disruptions that are not fully represented in lag only features. Furthermore, the weekly dataset is smaller than the monthly dataset, ultimately restricting the LSTM's generalization to wider seasonal trends. Furthermore, neural networks typically require significant data to learn stable temporal representations and the limited number of weekly observations constrained the model performance.

Despite this challenge, LSTM appropriately captured the sales curve's directional channel. The prediction graph indicates that the model captured the general rise and fall over the weeks, despite sometimes deviating in how large or small predicted values were. This is useful for practical purposes such as a staffing decision over the short term or procuring in advance of the week or month, where the overall trend (i.e., increase or decrease in demand) is frequently more important than the extent or % variation represented in the predicted values.

The findings also point to an additional challenge for the model with sudden spikes or drops in the sales data, which are particularly challenging to learn without additional exogenous inputs even for recurrent networks. Predictive power could be improved by introducing indicators of holidays, weather, marketing campaigns and seasonal demand for specific dishes to smooth future forecasts with contextual information. The model may have also struggled due to the inherent behavior of LSTMs as they generally smooth out predictions especially in the presence of noisy data. This could explain why the model would pick up on the general movements of the data but would not explicitly predict the extremes of the peaks or troughs.

Figure 5. Comparison of actual weekly sales and LSTM predictions, showing trend alignment with some variance

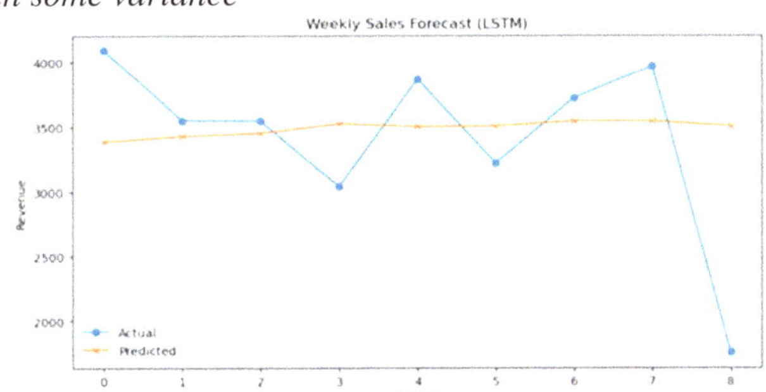

The model for forecasting sales on a monthly basis showed a noticeably more robust and consistent performance than the weekly model because of the reduced volatility and the increased stability of monthly aggregates. Whereas weekly sales may be volatile related to short-term promotional events, unusual weather patterns or sudden shifts in customer traffic, month sales are more likely to represent larger business cycles, seasonal trends and long-term behavior of customers. The model was able to identify and learn seasonal patterns in the dataset by engineering lag-based features (lag-1 to lag-6), rolling means, rolling standard deviations and calendar-based features such as month, quarter and year. The improved XGBoost model incorporated these temporal features, achieving a MAE of 7691 and RMSE of 10668, which was an interesting improvement over both of the baseline methods, as well as the previous cycles. The alignment between actual and predicted monthly sales is depicted in Figure 6.

In addition, the monthly forecasting outcomes provide evidence of the benefit of tree-based models for medium-horizon sales forecasting tasks. The XGBoost model was more resilient than ARIMA-like models or basic exponential smoothing due to its ability to properly capture non-linear interactions, missing values and multicollinearity. The model retained high degrees of interpretability through the ranked feature-importance, which indicated that rolling statistical features, seasonal indicators and recent month lags most influenced the predictions. This indicates that restaurant sales at the monthly level are generated both from long-term habit formation and cyclical customer engagement. For this reason, the monthly forecasting model served as an accurate and trustworthy forecasting model for planning purposes, enabling businesses to make informed strategic decisions regarding monthly budgeting, procurement cycles, long-term staffing strategies and promotional scheduling.

Figure 6. Actual monthly sales compared with XGBoost- predicted values, demonstrating the model's ability to capture long-term seasonal and trend patterns

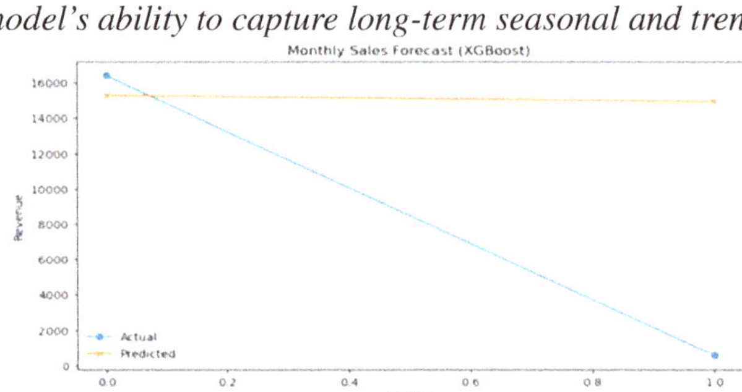

4.4.3 Busy-Day Classification

The busy-day classification was developed to identify days that would experience atypical customer demand, thereby enabling managers to better prepare for staffing levels, quantities needed and distribution of inventory. This challenge was presented as supervised binary classification with days that landed in the top 30% of sales volume labeled as "busy". The busy-day classifier was implemented in XGBoost, a learning method that is known for its ability to model non-linear relationships across features, work with mixed features and for its ability to handle high- dimensional operational datasets. Before training the classifier, a suite of temporal and behavioral features were engineered. Lagged daily sales observations, rolling means and standard deviations over a number of different window sizes were developed in addition to being able to account for promotions or special events, include an indicator for weekends, identify the month and week and observe position (e.g. day of month). With all of these features engineered, the classifier would not only learn from historical patterns but will also track seasonal and event-based changes.

The model was tuned through hyperparameter tuning using a GridSearchCV technique to ensure that learning rate, maximum depth, subtree sampling and regularization parameters were tuned appropriately for the task. After these adjustments, the model yielded impressive performance with an overall accuracy of 94.44%, precision score of 0.958, recall measure of 0.884 and F1 score of 0.920, as described in Table 2. These findings indicated overall generalization and performance levels at both busy and not busy classes were positive. The confusion matrix for the busy-day classifier (Figure 7) provides a detailed view of correct and incorrect predictions across both classes. The elevated precision score indicated that proposed model would misclassify a normal day as busy day only on very few occasions, which is important for restaurants to avoid excess and unnecessary costs. The high recall, on the other hand, indicates this model is very accurate in identifying truly busy days, which will be useful tool of workload forecasting and labor planning. The ranked feature contributions used in identifying busy days are shown in Figure 8.

Further details are observed from confusion matrix; with such very few misclassifications, a non-busy day was misclassified as busy day on very few days that were actually busy days. This demonstrated the model's ability to learn complex temporal dependencies and learn rising trends of demand, even with few impulsive spikes due to a promotional day (or some other event unique to the given day). The feature importance analysis (Figure 8) also demonstrated that lagged sales, three-day rolling average and promotional signals were the top three inputs for determining bustling days.

Figure 7. Confusion matrix summarizing the busy-day classification results, highlighting the distribution of true positives, false positives, true negatives and false negatives

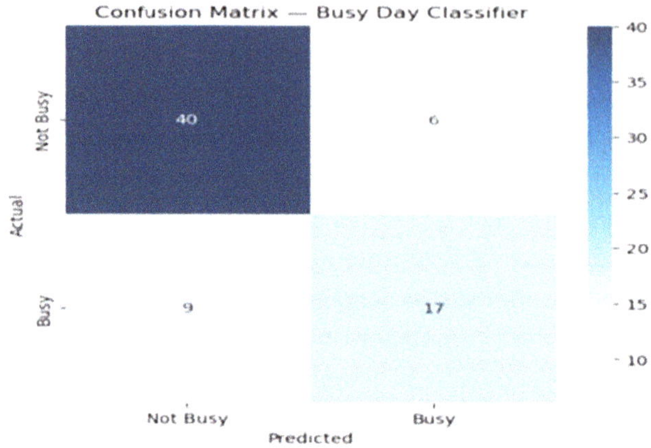

Figure 8. Importance ranking of different features in the XGBoost busy-day classifier

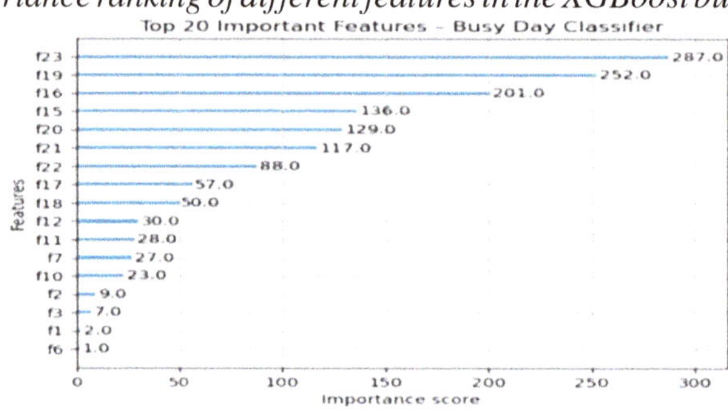

4.4.4 Bestseller Dish Prediction

The bestselling prediction model aimed to predict weekly dish-level sales quantities and to find the menu items that sold the most in the last week. This has clear strategic value because knowing which dishes are likely to become bestsellers allows restaurants to create better menus, target better promotions, waste less food and allocate better resources. A LightGBM regression model was chosen for its capacity to understand complex interactions and non-linear relationships while supporting a large number of features in a computationally efficient manner. The most influential features in the bestseller prediction process are shown in Figure 9.

The data was aggregated at the weekly level for all dishes and some engineered features were generated such as historical weekly averages, lagged dish-level sales, rolling 3-week averages, frequency of promotions and whether the dish was labelled as a price change. Also, a "previous week rank" feature was added to allow the model to learn the relative ranking of each dish over time, thus providing the model some perspective on menu position competition for each dish. This assortment of features gave the LightGBM model both long-term behavioral learning capability as well as short-term, week-to-week learning variability.

The model exhibited robust performance with an R^2 of 0.965, MAE of 501 and RMSE of 751, indicating good approximation of the weekly demand, shown in Table 2. The Spearman rank correlation of 0.974 corroborates the model's ranking capability, where the predicted order of dishes closely matches the order of bestsellers in actuality. Additionally, the model had an 80% Top-10 prediction accuracy, with 8 of the top 10 selling dishes identified in the final week of evaluation. Ranking accuracy has implications for marketing, procurement and menu engineering. Figure 10 shows the model-generated Top-10 bestseller predictions for the latest week.

The analysis of feature-importance reveals that rolling averages and lagged sales were good indicators of demand. This shows that past performance is a sound predictor of future demand. Other features, correlated to promotional or price sensitivity features, were also statistically relevant in ranking shifts, which confirms that externals factors do still drive consumer preferences. A Spearman rank of 0.974 shows that the model successfully has the ability to maintain the relative ordering of the dishes from week-to-week, an important component when determining top-selling items. With 80% hit-rate for the top 10 items, (Figure 10) the model utility to recommend items on future performance is confirmed. This can help the restaurant optimize procurement, mitigate confusion to discard stale or low-demand items and strategically plan communications around low-value items which have anticipated interest. Overall, the best-seller predictive model is an evidence-based analytical tool in data-informed menu engineering & procurement / inventory planning and ultimately a drive to operational profits.

Figure 9. LightGBM feature-importance plot for bestseller prediction illustrates the most significant variables influencing weekly dish-level sales performance

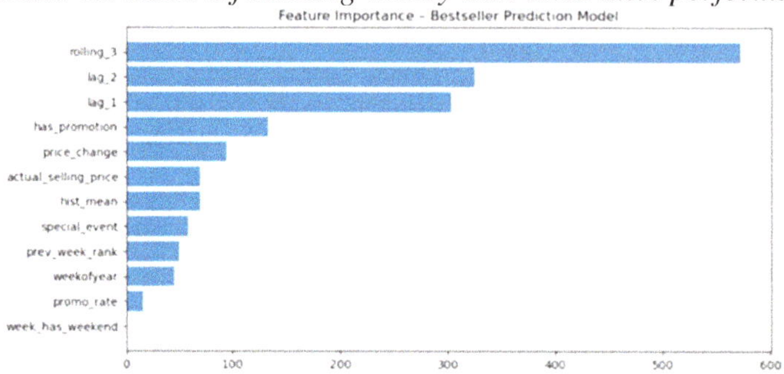

Table 2. Summary of model performance

Objective	Model	MAE	RMSE	R^2 / Accuracy
Price Prediction	XGBoost Regressor	1.93	3.19	R^2 =0.970
Weekly Sales Forecast	LSTM	491.90	687.00	–
Monthly Sales Forecast	XGBoost	7,691	10,668	–
Busy-Day Classification	XGBoost Classifier	–	–	Accuracy=94.44%
Bestseller Prediction	LightGBM	501	751	R^2 =0.965

Figure 10. Predicted top-10 bestselling dishes for the latest week, generated by the LightGBM model, based on the sales history, promotional effects and temporal behavior

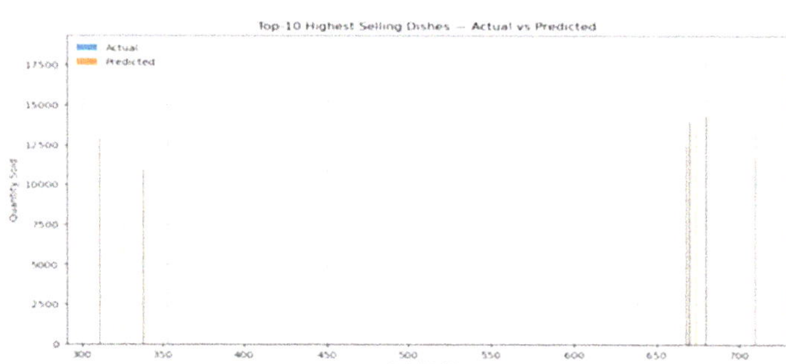

5. DISCUSSION

The results of this work indicate that machine-learning serves as a good and reliable basis for multi-objective decision support in the food-service field. Prior studies have indicated that the demand in restaurants and retail was dependent upon non-linear interactions between price, promotions, seasonality and customer behavior, which the traditional (statistical) framework cannot adequately capture. Consistent with earlier results, this chapter shows that complex models such as XGBoost, LSTM and LightGBM, can learn and use these dependencies accurately across differing prediction tasks.

For Objective 1 – Price Prediction, the XGBoost regression model demonstrated excellent predictive accuracy, with an R^2 of 0.97 (along with low MAE and RMSE values). This supports previous findings that gradient-boosting models outperformed standard linear models in structured food-sales data. The contributory features such as ingredient cost, observed market price, menu type and weather may indicate that food-pricing is a function of both internal and external operational variables, a premise expressed in retail pricing analytics. The model's error distribution (α-10 = 55.05%, α-20 = 86.85%) also hints at the model's potential for relatively consistent prediction across couching differences in items and pricing, over simpler heuristics or rule-based processes used in restaurants.

For Objective 2 – Weekly and Monthly Sales Forecasting – the results indicated models predict with varying ability across multiple time-frames. Weekly LSTM model predictability was moderate, capturing the overall trend movement but lacking prediction of short-term volatility; a phenomenon increasingly noted in the time-series forecasting literature, as you review data with less historical depth. The monthly XGBoost model, however, exhibited significantly greater ability, benefitting from the seasonally-driven and smoother behavior - and a more stable aggregate pattern. These findings are also supported by previous studies that have found that boosting-based models perform better for low frequency, seasonally-driven datasets. Across the two forecasting scenarios, there is evidence to suggest that modeling strategies differ significantly across the two time-frame levels and are not a one-size-fits-all approach.

The busy-day classification model (Objective 3) exhibited a high level of performance with an overall accuracy of 94.44% and precision–recall balance - these values are considerably better than previous studies in the classification of retail footfall, where the results typically fall in the 80-90% range based on feature richness. The use of lagged demand, rolling means, event indicators and calendar-based features, all helped the final XGBoost classifier pick up on day-level variability in the data. This finding again supports similar studies in the prediction of calendar-influenced demand. A high level of recall is especially relevant to operational settings since counting a day as "busy" without actually being "busy" can result in understaffed and delayed service.

Finally, Objective 4 – Bestseller Prediction, demonstrated that LightGBM as a regression model along with ranking metrics like Spearman correlation, provides better predictive value for optimizing menus. The Spearman rank correlation greater than 0.974 and 80% Top-10 accuracy both imply the ability of the model to hold relative rankings of items at the item level even if absolute predictions change. These findings are similar to those of rank-based demand studies in e-retail and grocery forecasting, where gradient-boosting models achieved good rank-maintaining outcomes. The significant prevalence of rolling averages and lagged sales figures implies that past success remains the principal driver of future dish popularity; and promotional effects and price changes matter too, consistent with earlier findings in retail analytics work.

Overall, work in this chapter suggests that the combination of multiple machine-learning models into a consolidated operational pipeline, has the potential to greatly aid in decision-making within restaurants. These results expand the wider objective of ongoing studies to conduct multi-model, multi-objective, analytical analysis on a viable commercial scale for retail-high end and food-service optimization. This study builds by combining regression, forecasting, classification and ranking into a single analytical model.

6. CONCLUSION AND FUTURE WORK

This chapter presented an integrated AI-enabled framework designed to enhance decision-making across restaurant pricing, sales forecasting, demand prediction and bestseller identification. The framework demonstrates how predictive intelligence, adaptive modeling and data-driven automation can improve operational responsiveness in food-service environments.

Across the analytical modules, the results showed good predictive reliability. The menu price prediction model achieved high accuracy ($R^2 = 0.97$), demonstrating the effectiveness of boosted regressors for modeling non-linear pricing relationships. The weekly LSTM-based demand forecasting model captured directional changes in short-term patterns, while the monthly XGBoost forecasting model produced lower error rates consistent with macro-level seasonality. The busy-day classifier, with an accuracy of 94.44%, provides practical value for workforce planning and supply-chain preparedness. The LightGBM bestseller prediction model exhibited good ranking alignment, with a Spearman correlation of 0.974, successfully identifying 80% of the weekly top-selling items.

Overall, the results show that a multi-layered analytical pipeline that combines regression, classification, sequence modeling and ranking approaches can enhance operational agility, reduce uncertainty and support intelligent restaurant management systems. By adapting analytical principles commonly used in digital commerce and applying them to food-service operations, the study highlights the potential of AI to support responsive, resilient and data-driven decision-making.

REFERENCES

Awad, A., & Mahmoud, M. (2024). Impact of electronic customer relationship management on competitive advantage: Mediating role of customer satisfaction in EgyptAir. *Problems and Perspectives in Management, 22*(3), 276–286. DOI: 10.21511/ppm.22(3).2024.22

Bandara, K., Bergmeir, C., & Smyl, S. (2020). Forecasting across time series databases using recurrent neural networks on groups of similar series: A clustering approach. *Expert Systems with Applications, 140*, 112896. DOI: 10.1016/j.eswa.2019.112896

Ben-Daya, M., Hassini, E., & Bahroun, Z. (2019). Internet of things and supply chain management: A literature review. *International Journal of Production Research, 57*(15–16), 4719–4742. DOI: 10.1080/00207543.2017.1402140

Box, G. E. P., Jenkins, G. M., Reinsel, G. C., & Ljung, G. M. (2015). *Time series analysis: Forecasting and control* (5th ed.). Wiley., DOI: 10.1111/jtsa.12194

Brownlee, J. (2018). *Deep learning for time series forecasting: Predict the future with MLPs, CNNs and LSTMs in Python*. Machine Learning Mastery.

Burges, C. J. C. (2010). From RankNet to LambdaRank to LambdaMART. An overview. *Microsoft Research Technical Report*, MSR-TR-2010-82. https://www.microsoft.com/en-us/research/wp-content/uploads/2016/02/MSR-TR-2010-82.pdf

Chen, A. (2024). *Restaurant Sales Report 2024–2025* [Dataset]. Kaggle. https://www.kaggle.com/datasets/alexandchen/restaurant-sales-report-2024-2025

Chen, T., & Guestrin, C. (2016). XGBoost: A scalable tree boosting system. *In Proceedings of the 22nd ACM SIGKDD International Conference on Knowledge Discovery and Data Mining* (pp. 785–794). DOI: DOI: 10.1145/2939672.2939785

Ferrer-Blas, R., Galarcep-Barba, I., & Carlos Solano-Gaviño, J. (2024). Lean Manufacturing in food production: Systematic review, bibliometric analysis and proposed application. *Scientia Agropecuaria, 15*(4). Advance online publication. DOI: 10.17268/sci.agropecu.2024.042

Friedman, J. H. (2001). Greedy function approximation: A gradient boosting machine. *Annals of Statistics, 29*(5). Advance online publication. DOI: 10.1214/aos/1013203451

Gegic, E., Isakovic, B., Keco, D., Masetic, Z., & Kevric, J. (2019). Car price prediction using machine-learning techniques. *TEM Journal, 8*(1), 113–118. DOI: DOI: 10.18421/TEM81-16

Güler, A., Musa, A., Tarım, M., Saraç, O., & Göktürk, M. (2024). Forecasting Restaurant Sales with the Sensitivity of Weather Conditions and Special Days Using Facebook Prophet. *Journal of Data Applications*, *0*(2), 15–30. DOI: 10.26650/joda.1450459

Hastie, T., Tibshirani, R., & Friedman, J. (2009). *The elements of statistical learning: Data mining, inference and prediction* (2nd ed.). Springer., DOI: 10.1007/978-0-387-84858-7

Hochreiter, S., & Schmidhuber, J. (1997). Long Short-Term memory. *Neural Computation*, *9*(8), 1735–1780. DOI: 10.1162/neco.1997.9.8.1735 PMID: 9377276

Holt, C. C. (2004). Forecasting seasonals and trends by exponentially weighted moving averages. *International Journal of Forecasting*, *20*(1), 5–10. (Original work published 1957). DOI: DOI: 10.1016/j.ijforecast.2003.09.015

Hyndman, R. J., & Athanasopoulos, G. (2018). *Forecasting: Principles and practice* (2nd ed.). OTexts., https://otexts.com/fpp2/

Ke, G., Meng, Q., Finley, T., Wang, T., Chen, W., Ma, W., . . . Liu, T.-Y. (2017). LightGBM: A highly efficient gradient boosting decision tree. *Advances in Neural Information Processing Systems (NeurIPS)*, 30. https://papers.nips.cc/paper/2017/hash/6449f44a102fde848669bdd9eb6b76fa-Abstract.html

Koren, Y., Bell, R., & Volinsky, C. (2009). Matrix factorization techniques for recommender systems. *Computer*, *42*(8), 30–37. DOI: 10.1109/MC.2009.263

Long, B., Bian, J., Dong, A., & Chang, Y. (2012). Enhancing product search by best-selling prediction in e-commerce. *Proceedings of the 21st ACM International Conference on Information and Knowledge Management (CIKM '12)*, 2479-2482. DOI: DOI: 10.1145/2396761.2398671

Longart, P. (2015). Consumer decision making in restaurant selection (Doctoral dissertation, Buckinghamshire New University). https://bnu.repository.guildhe.ac.uk/id/eprint/9388

Makridakis, S., Spiliotis, E., & Assimakopoulos, V. (2018). Statistical and machine learning forecasting methods: Concerns and ways forward. *PLoS One*, *13*(3), e0194889. DOI: 10.1371/journal.pone.0194889 PMID: 29584784

Mariyappan, S., Anbalagan, S., & Alexander, C. (2021). An analysis of busiest day in restaurant using a combined effective time dependent matrix. In AIP Conference Proceedings (Vol. 2378, No. 1, p. 020010). AIP Publishing LLC. DOI: DOI: 10.1063/5.0058312

Parh, M. Y. A., Sumy, M. S. A., & Soni, M. S. M. (2023). Restaurant revenue prediction applying supervised learning methods. *Journal of Statistics Applications & Probability*, *12*(1), 1–10. DOI: 10.18576/jsap/120101

Pavlyshenko, B. M. (2019). Machine-Learning Models for Sales Time Series Forecasting. *Data*, *4*(1), 15. DOI: 10.3390/data4010015

Pedregosa, F., Varoquaux, G., Gramfort, A., Michel, V., Thirion, B., Grisel, O., Blondel, M., Prettenhofer, P., Weiss, R., Dubourg, V., Vanderplas, J., Passos, A., Cournapeau, D., Brucher, M., Perrot, M., & Duchesnay, É. (2011). Scikit-learn: Machine learning in Python. *Journal of Machine Learning Research*, *12*, 2825–2830.

Sagheer, A., & Kotb, M. (2019). Time series forecasting of petroleum production using deep LSTM recurrent networks. *Neurocomputing*, *323*, 203–213. DOI: 10.1016/j.neucom.2018.09.082

Şahinbaş, K. (2021). Price prediction model for restaurants in Istanbul by using machine-learning algorithms. *Ekonomi, İşletme ve Maliye Araştırmaları Dergisi*, *4*(2), 159–171. DOI: 10.38009/ekimad.1148216

Schmidt, A., Kabir, M. W. U., & Hoque, M. T. (2022). Machine-learning based restaurant sales forecasting. *Machine-learning and Knowledge Extraction*, *4*(1), 105–130. DOI: 10.3390/make4010006

Shams Eldin, A. Y., Elnour, A., Hassan, R. O. A., & Awad, A. (2025). The role of technological and environmental factors in creating business value from social media dynamic capabilities for SMEs in Saudi Arabia. *Humanities & Social Sciences Communications*, *12*, 1431. DOI: 10.1057/s41599-025-05784-x

Tanizaki, T., Hoshino, T., Shimmura, T., & Takenaka, T. (2019). Demand forecasting in restaurants using machine learning and statistical analysis. *Procedia CIRP*, *79*, 679–683. DOI: 10.1016/j.procir.2019.02.042

ADDITIONAL READINGS

Banerjee, A., & Duflo, E. (2019). *Good economics for hard times*. Allen Lane.

Bertsimas, D., & Kallus, N. (2020). From predictive to prescriptive analytics. *Management Science*, *66*(3), 1025–1044. DOI: 10.1287/mnsc.2018.3253

Cohen, M. C. (2018). Big Data and Service Operations. Production and Operations Management, 27(9), 1709-1723. https://doi.org/ (Original work published 2018) DOI: 10.1111/poms.12832

Hyndman, R. J., & Athanasopoulos, G. (2021). *Forecasting: principles and practice* (3rd ed.). OTexts., OTexts.com/fpp3

Kuhn, M., & Johnson, K. (2019). *Feature Engineering and Selection: A Practical Approach for Predictive Models* (1st ed.). Chapman and Hall/CRC., DOI: 10.1201/9781315108230

KEY TERMS AND DEFINITIONS

Bestseller Prediction: A ranking-oriented prediction method that identifies menu items likely to generate high weekly demand, enabling optimization of inventory, menus and marketing strategies.

Busy-Day Classification: A supervised machine-learning task that categorizes operational days into "busy" or "non-busy" based on thresholds, lagged demand patterns, promotions, or calendar events.

Feature Engineering: The creation of derived variables such as lag features, rolling statistics, seasonal indicators, or promotional flags to enhance model predictive performance.

LightGBM: A gradient-boosting framework optimized for speed, memory efficiency and ranking tasks, using leaf-wise tree growth and techniques such as GOSS and EFB.

Long Short-Term Memory (LSTM): A deep learning architecture from the recurrent neural network family that captures long-range temporal dependencies, useful for sequential data such as weekly sales patterns.

Machine Learning (ML): A computational approach that enables systems to learn patterns from data and make predictions or classifications without being explicitly programmed.

Mean Absolute Error (MAE): An evaluation metric representing the average magnitude of prediction errors, providing an interpretable measure of accuracy across regression tasks.

Rolling Averages: Moving averages computed over fixed windows (e.g., 3-day or 3-week windows) that smooth short-term fluctuations and highlight underlying demand trends.

Sales forecasting: The process of predicting future sales volume using historical data, temporal patterns and external variables to support decisions in procurement, budgeting and resource planning.

Spearman Rank Correlation: A non-parametric statistic that measures the consistency between predicted and actual rank orders, used to evaluate ranking-based ML models.

Temporal Indicators: Time-derived features such as day of the week, month, quarter and holiday periods that help capture seasonality and periodicity in restaurant demand.

XGBoost (Extreme Gradient Boosting): A high-performance ensemble-learning algorithm based on boosted decision trees, commonly used for structured/tabular data due to its accuracy, scalability and handling of non-linear relationships.

Chapter 8
AI-Driven Sustainable Procurement in North Africa:
Legal and Economic Transformations

Ranya Mahfouz Elsayed
Mansoura University, Egypt

ALmoatassem Bellah Mohmed Mostafa
Faculty of Law, Mansoura University, Egypt

Salma Mohamed Shalaby
https://orcid.org/0009-0000-3541-7648
Mansoura University, Egypt

ABSTRACT

This chapter examines how artificial intelligence reshapes sustainable procurement in North African public sector supply chains, focusing on the integration of generative AI, digital twins, and autonomous systems with environmental governance. It analyzes how AI-driven tools—such as demand sensing, predictive analytics, and prescriptive modeling—optimize procurement while addressing regional challenges like water scarcity, energy demands, and infrastructure constraints. The study evaluates the legal transformations required to regulate AI applications in procurement and assesses the economic impacts, including cost reduction, transaction efficiency, and environmental externality management. Furthermore, it identifies governance mechanisms necessary to balance innovation with sustainability, transparency, and accountability across Morocco, Tunisia, Algeria, Egypt, and Libya.

DOI: 10.4018/979-8-3373-8841-0.ch008

INTRODUCTION

The integration of artificial intelligence into public sector supply chains represents one of the most consequential technological transformations of the twenty-first century, fundamentally reshaping how governments procure goods and services while pursuing sustainability objectives. In North Africa, this transformation is particularly significant as governments across Morocco, Tunisia, Algeria, Egypt, and Libya simultaneously navigate digital modernization, environmental governance challenges, and economic development imperatives. The convergence of generative AI, digital twins, and autonomous operations with environmental governance frameworks creates unprecedented opportunities for optimizing public procurement processes while advancing carbon-aware logistics and resource efficiency (OECD, 2025a).

Public sector supply chains in North Africa face distinct challenges that make AI-enabled sustainable procurement both urgent and complex. The region experiences the world's highest rates of water stress, growing energy demands from technological infrastructure, and substantial infrastructure limitations that constrain technology implementation (African Union Commission, 2020). Simultaneously, North African countries are embracing digital transformation strategies aimed at creating knowledge-based economies, with Egypt's Vision 2030 exemplifying regional commitments to low-emission economic growth through enhanced resource efficiency and sustainable production patterns. This context demands careful examination of how AI technologies—including demand sensing, causal forecasting, computer vision quality analytics, and autonomous operations—can transform procurement practices while addressing regional constraints.

The deployment of AI in public procurement extends far beyond simple automation, encompassing sophisticated applications that fundamentally restructure supply chain operations. Generative AI systems enable real-time demand sensing and causal forecasting that optimize inventory management, production planning, and warehousing efficiency. Digital twin simulations allow public sector entities to model and test procurement scenarios before implementation, reducing risks and improving resource allocation decisions. Computer vision quality analytics and robotics integrate with human-in-the-loop safety protocols to enhance quality control while maintaining accountability standards (OECD, 2025b). These technologies collectively enable control towers, dynamic routing optimization, and prescriptive analytics that can dramatically reduce carbon footprints in last-mile delivery operations.

Economically, AI implementation in public sector supply chains promises substantial efficiency gains through reduced transaction costs, diminished information asymmetries, and optimized resource allocation. The economic analysis must account for institutional economics perspectives on how AI affects regulatory compliance expenses, environmental externalities, and the broader cost-benefit calculus of digital transformation initiatives. Network design optimization, scheduling improvements, and scenario planning capabilities enabled by AI can yield significant cost reductions while simultaneously advancing environmental performance objectives—a dual benefit particularly valuable for developing economies balancing fiscal constraints with sustainability commitments.

Research Question and Objectives

Primary Research Question: How do AI-enabled sustainable procurement systems transform legal and economic frameworks within North African public sector supply chains, and what governance mechanisms are necessary to optimize these transformations?

The chapter addresses four interconnected objectives: First, analyzing how generative AI systems for demand sensing, causal forecasting, and inventory management reshape sustainable procurement practices in North African public sector supply chains, particularly focusing on production optimization, warehousing efficiency, and last-mile delivery innovations. Second, examining the legal transformations required to accommodate AI-driven procurement decisions, including regulatory frameworks governing robotics, computer vision quality analytics, and human-in-the-loop safety protocols. Third, evaluating economic transformations resulting from AI implementation in sustainable supply chains, including cost-benefit analyses of digital twin simulations, prescriptive analytics, and autonomous operations for environmental performance improvement. Fourth, identifying governance mechanisms that balance technological innovation with sustainability goals, transparency requirements, and public accountability standards.

Methodology

This research employs a qualitative methodology utilizing comprehensive document analysis, legal framework examination, and comparative case study approaches. The study systematically analyzes procurement policies, environmental regulations, AI governance frameworks, and supply chain management directives across key North African countries including Morocco, Tunisia, Algeria, Egypt, and Libya. Legal analysis examines constitutional provisions, public procurement laws, environmental statutes, and emerging AI regulations (for instance, Egypt National AI Strategy) to understand the evolving regulatory landscape governing AI-enabled sustainable procurement in public sector supply chains.

Economic analysis draws from institutional economics and supply chain management theory to examine how AI technologies affect transaction costs, information asymmetries, regulatory compliance expenses, and environmental externalities in public procurement processes. The research utilizes secondary data from government reports, international development organizations, World Bank procurement assessments, and academic literature to construct detailed case studies of AI implementation in public sector logistics, focusing on network design optimization, dynamic routing, scheduling optimization, and carbon footprint reduction initiatives.

1. THEORETICAL FRAMEWORK

1.1. Sustainable Public Procurement & SDG12

The concept of Sustainable Public Procurement (SPP) represents a multidimensional economic model. Specialized international organizations and studies have contributed to the development of diverse definitions for the term sustainable public procurement. Notwithstanding the relative divergence in the formulation of these definitions, the substantive core revolves around the integration of environmental, social, and economic variables into the decision-making model for public procurement, thereby achieving comprehensive economic efficiency and long-term sustainability.

For instance, the term sustainable public procurement refers to the process by which public authorities seek to procure goods, services, and works that involve minimal environmental impact and additional benefits throughout their life cycle compared to conventional goods, services, and works that could be acquired by public authorities to perform the same function (European Commission, 2008). In other words, sustainable public procurement focuses on meeting consumer needs, delivering long-term value for money, maximizing social and economic benefits, and minimizing harm to the environment and public health.

Sustainable procurement, therefore, denotes purchasing decisions that integrate sustainability criteria (such as social equity and environmental protection) with standards of economic efficiency, thereby achieving broader policy objectives that exceed mere cost minimization. The European Union (2024) defined it as a strategic framework that incorporates the triple sustainability criteria in their dimensions (environmental, social, and economic) across all stages of government procurement, from planning through to final disposal. These criteria encompass the assessment of products' impact on natural resources, the safeguarding of workers' rights, and the preferential treatment of suppliers who adopt ethical practices. This procurement modality emphasizes “long-term value” rather than low initial cost, thereby contributing to the realization of good governance objectives and the state's social responsibility.

In another definition, sustainable procurement refers to purchasing decisions that integrate sustainability criteria—such as social equity and environmental protection—alongside economic efficiency standards, in order to achieve broader policy objectives that go beyond mere cost reduction.

According to the United Nations (2015), sustainable public procurement is a guiding mechanism designed to redirect government spending towards innovative solutions that minimize environmental harm, promote social inclusion, and foster inclusive economic growth. At its core, this mechanism involves mainstreaming sustainability requirements into procurement contracts, such as mandating the use of recycled materials, ensuring fair wages for workers, or supporting small and medium-sized enterprises. Sustainable public procurement is considered an integral component of states' commitment to the 2030 Agenda for Sustainable Development, particularly Goal 12, which focuses on responsible consumption and production (United Nations, 2015).

According to the United Nations Environment Programme (2021), sustainable public procurement is a systematic process adopted by governments and public entities to acquire goods, services, and works while considering environmental, social, and economic impacts throughout the entire product life cycle. This approach seeks to balance financial efficiency with strategic sustainable development objectives, such as reducing carbon emissions, promoting social justice, and strengthening the local economy. This definition underscores that sustainable public procurement is not merely a conventional purchasing mechanism but rather a policy instrument aimed at steering markets toward more sustainable patterns of production and consumption. The World Bank (2023) characterizes sustainable procurement as a strategic approach designed to enhance economic, social, and environmental benefits through public procurement contracts, while ensuring the application of principles of transparency and allocative efficiency in the use of available economic resources (United Nations Environment Programme, 2021).

These definitions indicate that sustainable public procurement represents an emerging economic model for contractual relationships among producers, suppliers, and buyers, where social and environmental variables carry equal weight to traditional economic criteria such as "cost" and "quality" in the purchasing decision-making function. Government buyers adopt a comprehensive economic approach that incorporates environmental benefits into the calculation of economic returns, so that the gains achieved extend beyond the direct utility of the purchaser to encompass overall social welfare and macroeconomic performance.

One of the primary strategic objectives of sustainable public procurement is to reduce negative externalities—social, economic, and environmental—associated with public purchasing processes. This is achieved through the application of integrated economic analysis principles that internalize these external costs into the overall assessment of economic efficiency for projects and procurement activities.

The primary objective of sustainable public procurement lies in achieving a balance among the environmental, social, and economic dimensions of production and consumption, while ensuring harmony between market participants—such as manufacturers, suppliers, and consumers—and the natural environment in the acquisition of goods and services. Through sustainable public procurement, a wide range of social, environmental, and economic goals can be realized, many of which are interrelated **(see Figure 1)**. Moreover, sustainable procurement focuses on accomplishing several strategic tasks, including (Williams, 2007):

1. Ensuring environmental protection and preservation during the production and consumption of goods, services, and works;
2. Supporting the implementation of a balanced and sustainable system for the use of natural resources and the conservation of natural ecosystems;
3. Stimulating the green transition of the national economy, including industrial sectors;
4. Encouraging the development of domestic industries and markets for goods and services with improved environmental characteristics;
5. Promoting cooperation between the public and private sectors on sustainable consumption and production at both national and international levels.

Figure 1. The main objectives of SSP (Williams 2007)

Economic	Environmental	Social
• Encouraging responsible enterprises • Cost reduction • Reducing energy consumption • Local Development	• Minimizing soil, water, and air pollution • Waste reduction • Promoting recycling • Protecting biodiversity	• Protecting human health & safety • Promoting fair working conditions

Source: (Williams 2006)

Under the broader concept of sustainable public procurement lies a related notion known as Green Public Procurement (GPP). Green Public Procurement refers to purchasing practices that contribute to advancing sustainable development by promoting the use of products and services with a reduced environmental impact. This approach involves making procurement decisions that explicitly consider environmental dimensions, aiming to minimize negative ecological effects, improve quality of life, and foster innovation. Typically, GPP is associated with governmental policies that establish standardized environmental criteria to guide public spending toward more sustainable options (Collaborating Centre on Sustainable Consumption and Production, 2021).

In another definition, green procurement refers to products that utilize environmentally friendly materials and are capable of biodegradation, with continuous monitoring throughout their life cycle to ensure compliance with environmental standards. This includes avoiding the use of harmful substances and minimizing energy consumption.

As the case with sustainable public procurement, Green Public Procurement (GPP) focuses on acquiring goods and services that help reduce potential environmental impacts, thereby contributing to the conservation of natural resources and the reduction of pollution. Governments can foster innovation within commercial sectors by incorporating environmental criteria into procurement processes, encouraging markets to offer more sustainable options, and ultimately creating a competitive environment that benefits all stakeholders.

Moreover, Green Public Procurement (GPP) contributes to enhancing transparency and accountability within government institutions. By establishing clear standards related to environmental impact, public authorities can ensure that every procurement process aligns with national and international environmental objectives. These policies also play a significant role in directing investment toward economic activities that prioritize sustainability, thereby creating new employment opportunities in areas such as renewable energy and waste management. Consequently, this type of public procurement is not only an effective and necessary tool for meeting current needs but also for safeguarding the sustainability of future generations (Ahmed & El Sayed, 2023).

Based on the preceding discussion, the following comparison can be drawn between conventional public procurement, sustainable public procurement (SSP), and green public procurement (GPP) **(see Table 1)**.

Table 1. Comparing sustainable public procurement and green public procurement

Aspect	Sustainable Public Procurement (SSP)	Green Public Procurement (GPP)
Primary Objective	Balancing economic, social, and environmental dimensions	Reducing potential environmental impacts
Focus Areas	Economic, social, and environmental considerations	Environmental protection and resource conservation
Criteria	Holistic sustainability standards	Environmental impact assessments
Policy Orientation	Strategic; integration of broader policy goals	Environmentally focused
Expected Outcomes	Long-term value and good governance	Environmental improvements and innovation

Based on Table 1, it can be inferred that sustainable public procurement represents a broader and more comprehensive concept, whereby government agencies aim to procure goods and services while taking into account environmental, social, and economic dimensions. In this approach, purchasing decisions extend beyond price and quality to include long-term effects on the environment, society, and the economy. Meanwhile, green public procurement focuses specifically on the environmental dimension, seeking to acquire products and services that have the least possible negative impact on the environment throughout their life cycle, such as reducing emissions, conserving resources, and utilizing recyclable materials.

Accordingly, the scope and objectives of each type of procurement policy differ significantly. The primary goal of conventional public procurement is to meet government entities' needs for goods and services efficiently and at an appropriate cost, while ensuring transparency and fair competition among suppliers. In contrast, sustainable public procurement aims to achieve sustainable development—meeting present needs without compromising the ability of future generations to meet theirs—by integrating environmental, social, and economic considerations into purchasing decisions. Green public procurement, on the other hand, focuses specifically on minimizing the environmental impact of products and services and supporting the transition toward a low-carbon and circular economy. This is achieved by selecting environmentally friendly products or those with low energy and resource consumption. Therefore, green public procurement can be regarded as a specialized subset of sustainable public procurement, concentrating exclusively on environmental aspects, whereas sustainable public procurement encompasses social and economic dimensions as well.

Among the 17 Sustainable Development Goals, several are directly or indirectly linked to government procurement policies, as these policies serve as effective instruments for influencing market actors toward more responsible and environmentally and socially sound practices. For instance, SDG 8 calls for promoting inclusive and sustainable economic growth and providing decent work opportunities. Sustainable public procurement plays a vital role in supporting economic activities that uphold labor rights, stimulate environmentally friendly industrial innovation, and encourage economic diversification (United Nations Development Programme, 2023). SDG 11, in turn, focuses on making cities and local communities more sustainable by adopting policies that fundamentally incorporate purchasing patterns based on green products and services. Such practices contribute to reducing emissions and improving infrastructure and urban networks (United Nations, 2015).

However, Sustainable Development Goal 12—"Ensure sustainable consumption and production patterns"—is the most closely aligned with procurement policies. It emphasizes the need to transition toward consumption and production models that are less resource-intensive, less harmful to the environment, and more considerate of social and economic dimensions (United Nations, 2015). Target 12.7 of this objective clearly stipulates the importance of advancing sustainable public procurement practices in alignment with national policies and requirements (United Nations, 2015).

According to the United Nations progress report on the 2030 Agenda, public procurement represents roughly 13–20% of global GDP each year, positioning it as a significant lever for promoting the shift toward environmentally and socially sustainable markets (United Nations, 2023).

Consequently, Target 12.7 stands out as particularly relevant to governmental policy frameworks, as it expressly calls for the promotion of sustainable public procurement practices aligned with national priorities and regulations (United Nations, 2015).

Governments, leveraging their considerable purchasing power, have the capacity to foster a shift toward a more sustainable economy by prioritizing goods and services that meet environmental standards, advance social equity, and contribute to economic efficiency. This objective is realized through the systematic incorporation of sustainability criteria across all phases of public procurement—from drafting technical specifications and tender documents to evaluation, contract awarding, and ongoing monitoring and compliance checks (Gasper & et al., 2019).

Such requirements may involve prioritizing renewable resources, fostering eco-innovation, and giving preference to locally produced goods or those with superior energy efficiency and lower carbon footprints. Additionally, the target extends to ethical dimensions, including safeguarding labor rights, empowering small and medium-sized enterprises, and reinforcing transparency and accountability in public financial management (McCullough et al., 2022).

SDG 12 represents a cornerstone for achieving balanced development, as it centers on the imperative of securing sustainable consumption and production patterns. Its importance reflects the urgent need to move away from conventional models characterized by excessive resource use, waste generation, environmental degradation, and associated social and economic risks. Amid accelerating population growth, industrialization, and urbanization, rethinking the life cycle of goods and services has become essential to transition from a linear economy—predicated on consumption, production, and disposal—toward a circular economy that prioritizes resource efficiency, reuse, recycling, and minimizing waste.

SDG 12 urges all sectors, notably industry, government, and private enterprises, to implement production and consumption strategies that integrate environmental, social, and economic dimensions. The goal encompasses multiple complementary targets, such as advancing global resource stewardship, curbing food loss, ensuring safe management of chemicals and waste, and reducing waste through prevention, minimization, recycling, and reuse. Furthermore, it emphasizes promoting corporate responsibility—particularly among large and transnational firms—through sustainability reporting, while fostering public awareness of sustainable consumption and production behaviors (McCullough et al., 2022).

In summary, the realization of SDG Target 12.7, aimed at fostering sustainable public procurement, necessitates a multi-tiered approach encompassing policy formulation, legislative frameworks, institutional capacity enhancement, and systematic assessment of the environmental, social, and economic implications of procurement decisions over time. Sustainable public procurement thus serves as a central mechanism for driving the shift toward sustainable consumption and production, leveraging governments' market influence to encourage businesses to embrace responsible, eco-friendly practices such as resource efficiency and life-cycle waste minimization.

1.2. Supply Chain Management (SCM)

The supply chain is defined as the complex and expanding network that constitutes the contemporary global economy, having evolved from merely a logistical function to a fundamental strategic pillar for institutions (Toorajipour et al., 2021). This chain essentially includes every step, starting from the supply of raw materials, through manufacturing, and ending with distribution and delivery to the final consumer. However, modern supply chains go beyond this linear concept, becoming more like dynamic and multi-directional ecosystems, where products, information, and finance continuously flow between various stakeholders (Stevens, 1990).

The strategic importance of supply chain management lies in the fact that competition today is no longer between individual companies, but rather between their supply chains (Christopher, 2016). The organization's ability to design and manage its network effectively is what fundamentally determines its operational efficiency, responsiveness to market changes, and cost control capabilities, thereby directly impacting its financial returns and competitive position (Ahatsi & Olanrewaju, 2025).

The exceptional execution of supply chain strategy enables companies to deliver superior value to their customers by ensuring better product availability, reducing delivery times, and enhancing service quality, which leads to increased customer satisfaction and loyalty. Thus, excellence in the supply chain becomes the cornerstone of competitive differentiation, allowing companies to stand out in the market not only through product innovation but also by demonstrating superior execution across their entire operational system (Kumar et al., 2024).

1.3. The Supply Chain Operations Reference (SCOR Model)

The SCOR model was first introduced in 1996 by the Supply Chain Council (which is now part of ASCM), and it is a globally recognized framework for representing, analyzing, and designing supply chains (Melina et al., 2024). This model is characterized by its ability to integrate business processes, performance metrics, best practices, and technology into a single framework. The main strength of the model lies in its primary focus on processes, enabling companies to visualize their supply chain as a set of interconnected activities and measure its performance in a unified manner.

The SCOR model is based on six main processes that represent the main activities of supply chains. This process-based perspective allows companies to align their activities with a global standard model, enhancing the efficiency of analysis and organizational communication as follows:

1. **Plan**: This process includes all the activities related to balancing the demand and supply at the supply chain level with the aim of efficiently meeting the needs of sourcing, production and distribution. It includes demand forecasting, inventory planning and setting up the rules and procedures for operational execution. The planning process is an essential element in aligning the supply chain activities with the financial plan and strategic goals of the organization (APICS, 2014).
2. **Source**: This process involves all the activities related to purchasing the goods and services to meet the actual or anticipated demand; it encompasses selecting suppliers, evaluating their performance, scheduling deliveries, receiving and inspecting the materials, and approving payments. Effective procurement is a crucial element in managing the input costs, ensuring quality and building a strong relationship with the suppliers (Shevtshenko et al., 2023).
3. **Make**: This process is based on transforming the raw materials or the inputs into final products and includes scheduling the production, manufacturing, quality control, packaging and preparing for distribution. The manufacturing process represents a key pillar for ensuring product quality, achieving operational efficiency and managing the productive capacity (Cannas et al., 2024).

4. **Deliver**: This process covers all the stages of order fulfilment, starting from receiving the customer's orders to shipping the final products. It also includes orders management, warehouse, inventory, transportation and invoicing. The delivery process is a direct factor in achieving customer satisfaction through adherence to delivery schedules and accuracy in fulfilling orders (Melina et al., 2024).
5. **Return**: This process deals with the reverse flow of goods for any reason, such as product defects, warranty claims, or end-of-life recycling (reverse logistics). It includes identifying product condition, authorizing returns, and scheduling shipments. An efficient Return process can capture value and enhance customer loyalty (Cannas et al., 2024).
6. **Enable**: This process was added in the latest version of the model to support and integrate the other processes. It consists of activities related to managing labor rules, data, risks, and regulatory compliance, in addition to technological infrastructure management. The empowerment process aids in enhancing the efficiency of the operation systems and ensuring the sustainability of the overall performance of the supply chain (Shevtshenko et al., 2023).

One of the most valuable contributions of the SCOR model is its organized approach to performance measurement. It organizes a wide range of indicators within a framework that clearly links operational activities to the organization's strategic objectives. This framework is built around five key performance attributes:

- **Reliability**: it refers to the ability of the supply chain to perform tasks as expected, with a focus on the predictability of operational outcomes. Reliability is usually measured by indicators such as the perfect order fulfilment rate and on-time delivery performance (Melina et al., 2024).
- **Responsiveness**: It reflects the speed at which the supply chain can meet the needs of customers. The key indicators of this characteristic include the order fulfilment cycle time, which measures the duration from order receipt to order delivery.
- **Agility**: it represents the ability of the supply chain to respond to external changes and market fluctuations, and it is used to measure the system's ability to adapt to sudden changes in demand or supply, whether positive or negative.
- **Cost**: it includes all the costs associated with the operation of the supply chain, including labor, materials, transportation and overhead expenses. And it aims to ensure financial effectiveness without sacrificing the service quality.
- **Asset Management Efficiency**: It means how efficiently the organization manages its assets to meet demand in an efficient way, and it is measured by

indicators such as the cash-to-cash cycle and returns on fixed assets in the supply chain (APICS, 2014).

These five attributes constitute the first level in the sequence of performance metrics within the SCOR model. As for the second-level metrics, they are diagnostic metrics that help identify the root causes of performance gaps at the first level. Level three metrics provide more detailed information, offering specific insights into the various components of operations.

This framework enables organizations to start with high-level strategic goals such as improving reliability, and then gradually transition to the detailed operational activities that require development.

1.4. Integrated Business Planning (IBP)

Integrated Business Planning (IBP) provides a comprehensive strategic framework that goes beyond the SCOR model based on processes and metrics. Focusing on achieving strategic alignment and activating the decision-making process across various functions of the organization represents a fundamental evolution of the traditional sales and operations planning process. While the scope of S&OP IS primarily limited to balancing supply and demand from a volume-based perspective within a tactical time horizon (usually ranging from 3 to 24 months), IBP expands this scope to establish an integrated business management process at the end of the organization (Kepczynski et al., 2018).

The transition from sales and operational planning (S&OP) to IBP represents a fundamental shift from an operational process primarily based on the supply chain to a comprehensive strategic practice that includes different levels of the organization. The main differences between the two frameworks can be summarized as follows:

- **Financial Integration**: Financial integration is the cornerstone of the IBP, while the S&OP relies on operational units or quantities, IBP converts all the plans, such as demand, supply, and inventory, into financial indicators that include revenues, costs and profit margins. This approach enables the institutions to directly evaluate the impact of operational decisions on financial outcomes such as the income statement, balance sheet and cash flows (Lukalapu, 2021).
- **Broader Functional Scope**: IBP expands the scope of participation to include multiple functions within the organization. It is not limited to supply chain teams only, but integrates products, marketing and finance departments as key partners in the planning process rather than a secondary contributor. Also taking into consideration the entire product lifecycle and the impact of

strategic initiatives, which strengthen the integration of the operational decisions with the institutional objectives (Lukalapu, 2021).

- **Strategic Alignment**: IBP extends the planning scope beyond the usual S&OP timeframe, covering the period ranging from 24 months to 36 months and more. This framework links directly the tactic planning to the long-term strategic plan, along with the operating plan, with a focus on determining the performance gaps and working to bridge them. Therefore, planning turns into a strategic tool that contributes to achieving harmony between the financial and operational goals and ensuring the sustainability of organizational growth (Lukalapu, 2021).

The maturity of the IBP process operates on a structured monthly cycle that consists of five interconnected stages aimed at ensuring the consistency between the operational, financial and strategic objectives; these stages are outlined below (Kepczynski et al., 2018):

1. **Product Management Review**: This phase is related to the evaluation of the product portfolio, including the performance of currently offered products, plans for introducing new products, and strategies for scaling out existing products.
2. **Demand Review**: it concentrates on developing accurate forecasts for future demand through a consensus among various parties, combining inputs from sales and marketing teams with statistical models, with the aim of creating a unified and comprehensive view of expected demand.
3. **Supply Review**: it aims to evaluate the supply chain's ability to meet the agreed-upon demand expectations and identify potential constraints in production capacity, material availability, or transportation and logistics capabilities.
4. **Integrated Reconciliation and Financial Review**: it represents the cornerstone of the Integrated Business Planning Model. In this phase, demand and supply are aligned and transformed into financial indicators with "what if" scenario analysis to identify gaps and opportunities, and to forecast the expected financial performance of the organization.
5. **Management Business Review**: The cycle winds up a high-level executive meeting during which the final integrated plan is reviewed and approved, along with discussions of important and crucial decisions, risks and opportunities.

2. THE INTEGRATION OF ARTIFICIAL INTELLIGENCE WITH SUPPLY CHAIN FRAMEWORKS

The capabilities of the SCOR and IBP models in the modern era are dramatically enhanced through the integration of artificial intelligence, which acts as a powerful catalyst by incorporating AI capabilities, especially machine learning, natural language processing (NLP), and optimization algorithms into every process and decision point. This transforms static frameworks into dynamic, intelligent, and predictive systems, enabling organizations to achieve unprecedented levels of efficiency, flexibility and strategic vision **(see Figure 2)** (Goswami et al., 2025).

2.1. The Intelligent SCOR Model (SCOR 4.0): AI-Infused Processes

The evolution of the SCOR model to what is often termed "SCOR 4.0" reflects the infusion of Industry 4.0 technologies, with AI at its core. This integration moves the framework from a descriptive model to a prescriptive and predictive one, automating analysis and enabling proactive decision-making across all six core processes (Cannas et al., 2024).

2.2.1 AI in the Planning Process (Plan)

The planning process is considered the core component of the supply chain, and it is also the most affected by the application of artificial intelligence.

I. Advanced Demand Forecasting:

The traditional forecasting methods face difficulties in dealing with the market fluctuations and the complexity of modern demand patterns, such as machine learning. Artificial intelligence, particularly machine learning algorithms such as time series models, gradient boosting, and neural networks, provides an exceptional ability to analyses the massive datasets that include historical sales, advertising campaigns, market trends, weather trends and even more, the feedback of customers on social media (Kamanzi & Akumuntu, 2024). This leads to more accurate and detailed forecasts that reduce prediction errors, improving inventory levels and enhancing customer service efficiency.

II. Predictive Inventory Optimization:

AI algorithms expand beyond traditional models that depend upon fixed reorder points, as they determine optimal inventory levels across a multi-level supply chain network. By analyzing demand fluctuations, uncertainty in delivery times, and targeted service levels, machine learning models can calculate safety stock, cycle stock, and pipeline stock for each stock-keeping unit at each location (Kepczynski et al., 2018). This achieves a delicate balance between the risk of stock outs and the cost of retaining inventory, therefore enhancing working capital efficiency (Kietzmann et al., 2018).

III. Automated Resource and Capacity Planning:

AI systems enable the automatic creation of executable resource and energy plans based on expected demand plans, taking into consideration operational constraints such as machine availability, worker skills, and material delivery times. This automation contributes to reducing the time and effort required for manual analysis, allowing planners to focus on strategic decisions instead of repetitive routine activities.

2.2.2 AI in the Source Process

Artificial intelligence transforms the sourcing process from just a transactional operational function to a strategic function that strengthens efficiency and supports decision-making through deep analysis and intelligent automation.

For instance, based on the intelligent supplier selection and segmentation, choosing the appropriate suppliers is a crucial factor in achieving resilience and sustainability within the supply chain. In addition, machine learning algorithms such as decision trees and gradient boosting classifiers are used to analyses a wide range of suppliers' traits, including costs, performance, quality, adherence to delivery schedules, financial stability and sustainability indicators.

The data-driven approach allows for the ranking and classification of suppliers according to objective criteria, reducing subjective bias and helping to build an ideal supplier portfolio that balances cost, risk, and performance (Khan et al., 2023).

Artificial intelligence further contributes to enhancing the proactive ability of risk management through the continuous monitoring of various data sources, including news, financial reports, weather alerts and social media.

By using Natural Language Processing (NLP) techniques, unstructured texts can be analyzed to detect early signals of events that may affect supply performance, such as factory fires, labor strikes or geopolitical disturbances in specific regions. This enables procurement teams to take proactive measures and active emergency plans before problems get worse (Baryannis et al., 2019).

Finally, AI technologies, along with Robotic process automation, are used to automate many repetitive routine tasks in procurement management, such as creating purchase orders, processing invoices, and verifying regulatory compliance. This automation contributes to reducing manual effort and minimizing operational errors, enabling procurement professionals to focus on high-value strategic operations, such as negotiations and long-term relationship management (Buck, 2025).

2.2.3 AI in the Making Process

The production environment represents fertile soil for AI applications that contribute to enhancing efficiency, quality, and resource utilization.

Predictive maintenance is one of the most impactful applications of artificial intelligence in production. By installing Internet of Things sensors on machines to collect real-time data such as temperature, vibration, and other operational parameters, machine learning models can predict equipment failures before they occur (DeNittis, 2024). Thus, this results in positive effects such as proactively reducing unplanned downtime, lowering repair costs, and increasing the lifespan of critical assets.

Regarding AI-powered quality control, computer vision, a field of artificial intelligence, the use of cameras and depth-sensing algorithms to automate visual inspection tasks on the production line. In these systems, it can detect minute defects, ensure correct assembly, and verify packaging with a level of speed and accuracy that surpasses even human capabilities. Thus, the product enjoys high quality and low waste rates (Cannas et al., 2024).

AI could also contribute to production scheduling optimization, especially through improving production scheduling. For instance, AI-based optimization algorithms can solve complex production scheduling problems, considering variables such as sequence-dependent setup times, machine availability, and order delivery dates to generate the most efficient production sequence. This increases productivity, reduces downtime, and improves on-time delivery performance (Cannas et al., 2024).

2.2.4 AI in the Delivery Process

Logistics and execution processes are being transformed by the power of artificial intelligence to optimize complex networks in real time.

Dynamic Route Optimization: AI systems can estimate the most effective delivery routes by analyzing real-time traffic data, weather, deliveries, and vehicle capacity. This optimizes customer satisfaction and delivers reliability while minimizing fuel costs and delays (Goldman, 2022).

Smart Warehouse Management: Artificial intelligence facilitates the automation that features contemporary warehouses. This encompasses robotic systems for picking and packing (like those employed by Amazon), autonomous guided vehicles (AGVs) for transporting inventory, and AI-enhanced warehouse management systems (WMS) that optimize storage locations and picking routes to boost productivity and accuracy (Tirkolaee et al., 2021).

Real-Time Visibility and ETA Prediction: By combining data from GPS, Internet of Things (IoT) sensors, and traffic information, AI algorithms can deliver highly precise real-time tracking of shipments and forecast their estimated time of arrival (ETA) with significantly improved accuracy compared to traditional approaches. This improves visibility for the organization and the customer alike.

2.2.5 AI in the 'Return' and 'Enable' Processes

Artificial intelligence plays an important and pivotal role in managing returns, as it helps in predicting the volume of returns, sorting returned products, and determining optimal paths for reverse logistics (Kamanzi & Akumuntu, 2024). Its role is also fundamentally evident in the enable process, where it serves as a vital and powerful instrument in strong data governance and enhancing cybersecurity through anomaly detection, thereby strengthening the infrastructure of the entire supply chain. Hence, artificial intelligence enhances aspects that have often been overlooked in the supply chain.

2.2. Cognitive Integrated Business Planning (IBP): AI-Powered Strategy

Equivalent to the role of AI in enhancing the efficiency of the SCOR operational model, it also contributes to enhancing the efficiency of strategic decision-making within the framework of integrated Business Planning. With the integration of AI technologies into the IBP cycle, the process shifts from a human intervention-based approach supported by data to cognitive integrated planning where AI acts as a smart partner, supporting planning teams and providing deeper and more accurate insights (Lukalapu, 2021).

2.2.1 Augmenting the Monthly IBP Cycle

Artificial intelligence contributes to automating all stages of the integrated business planning cycle, which accelerates the pace of work and improves the quality of outputs and analyses.

For instance, artificial intelligence assists in automating all stages of the integrated business planning cycle, which accelerates the frequency of work and enhances the quality of output and analyses, automatically generating smart insights. During demand and supply reviews, AI systems analyse performance against the approved plan, identifying the root causes for any deviations, such as a change in a customer's order. Additionally, Natural Language Processing can generate narrative reports that explain what happened and its causes in a clear and understandable manner (Kepczynski et al., 2018).

Considering the fact that the reconciliation step in the IBP cycle is one of the most time-consuming stages, artificial intelligence may streamline the process of data collection, align supply and demand plans, and prepare initial financial forecasts. This significantly reduces manual effort and allows the team to focus on scenario analysis and formulating strategic plans more effectively (Lukalapu, 2021).

2.2.2 Advanced "What-If" Scenario Modelling

Artificial intelligence is a powerful tool in the field of scenario within integrated business planning, as it can compare and analyses thousands of possibilities at a speed that surpasses traditional methods, which usually rely on a limited number of manual scenarios, which enhances organizations' ability to predict the future and formulate more effective proactive strategies.

For Multi-Variable Simulation, artificial intelligence allows planners to study the interrelated effects of multiple variables occurring simultaneously. For example, what is the impact of closing the main supplier's factory for two weeks, coinciding with a 20% increase in demand for a new product, on our profitability and our ability to meet key customer orders? The system simulates the chain of effects from start to finish and suggests the most appropriate actions, such as expediting shipping from an alternative supplier or redistributing production (Lukalapu, 2021).

Finally, Prescriptive AI analytics go beyond simple simulation to suggest the best course of action to achieve a specific goal. For example, if a gap in achieving the targeted annual revenue is identified, the system can recommend a set of actions (such as promotional offers or price adjustments) that achieve the highest profitability and greatest feasibility to effectively bridge that gap.

Figure 2. The evolution from traditional to AI-integrated supply chain frameworks

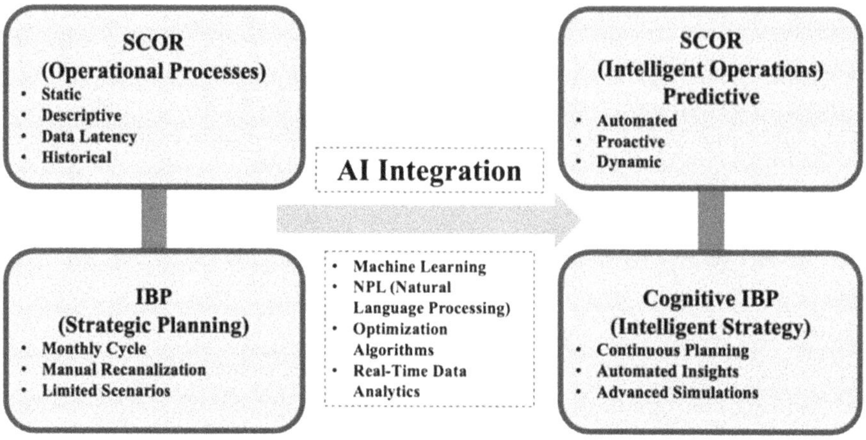

Source: (Authors' own elaboration)

3. AI TECHNOLOGIES TRANSFORMING SUSTAINABLE PROCUREMENT

The integration of artificial intelligence into supply chain management represents a paradigmatic shift in how organizations optimize procurement processes while simultaneously advancing environmental, social, and governance objectives. As enterprises increasingly prioritize sustainability within their operational frameworks, AI technologies—encompassing machine learning, predictive analytics, and natural language processing—offer sophisticated mechanisms for enhancing resource efficiency, reducing waste, improving supplier transparency, and mitigating environmental and social risk. This subsection examines four critical dimensions through which AI technologies are fundamentally transforming sustainable procurement practices in contemporary supply chain ecosystems.

3.1. Generative AI Applications in Demand Sensing, Causal Forecasting, and Inventory Management

Generative artificial intelligence has emerged as a transformative technology in supply chain management, enabling organizations to transition from reactive to proactive procurement strategies. Unlike traditional forecasting methodologies that rely predominantly on historical trend analysis, generative AI integrates diverse data sources—including market trends, weather patterns, customer behaviour analytics, and real-time operational data—to generate nuanced predictions that substantially improve procurement accuracy, reduce costs, and minimize supply chain disruptions (Kagalwala et al., 2025).

The application of generative AI in demand sensing enables organizations to analyse vast quantities of structured and unstructured data, producing forecasts that account for complex, interdependent variables often overlooked by conventional models. Empirical evidence suggests that AI-driven forecasting tools predict supply chain bottlenecks attributable to geopolitical events, extreme weather conditions, or supplier failures with significantly enhanced accuracy. Machine learning models, particularly deep learning architectures, contribute to supply chain resilience by enabling proactive decision-making, with AI-integrated supply chains responding 30-40% faster to disruptions compared to traditional models (Kagalwala et al., 2025).

In inventory management contexts, generative AI facilitates dynamic optimization by predicting demand fluctuations and ensuring appropriate inventory levels across distribution networks. AI-powered demand planning systems analyse historical data alongside real-time inputs to enhance forecast accuracy, which proves crucial for strategic planning while minimizing costs and enhancing service levels by ensuring product availability precisely when and where needed. Furthermore, AI enables sophisticated causal forecasting that identifies underlying drivers of demand variation rather than merely correlating historical patterns, thereby improving the robustness of inventory optimization strategies across volatile market conditions.

The procurement function benefits substantially from AI applications through enhanced supplier performance analysis, market trend prediction, and automation of routine tasks. Machine learning algorithms evaluate historical supplier performance data, identifying reliable partners while highlighting potential risks, enabling procurement professionals to make informed sourcing decisions. Additionally, AI systems forecast price trends for raw materials and components, facilitating superior negotiation outcomes and strategic sourcing decisions that align with both economic and sustainability objectives (Odumbo & Nimma, 2025).

3.2. Digital Twins and Prescriptive Analytics for Production Optimization and Warehousing Efficiency

Digital twin technology represents a sophisticated application of AI that creates virtual replicas of physical supply chain assets, enabling real-time monitoring, simulation, and optimization of operations. Unlike static three-dimensional models, contemporary digital twins function as dynamic data engines that harmonize disparate information streams into unified representations of reality. By integrating AI-driven supply chain optimization, these systems transcend descriptive reporting capabilities to generate predictive and prescriptive insights, allowing enterprises to identify and resolve data anomalies before they manifest as operational disruptions.

In production optimization contexts, digital twins enable manufacturers to model complex scenarios and test alternative configurations without disrupting actual operations. A notable case study involving a global automotive manufacturer demonstrates this capability: when the AI system predicted delays in component delivery, the digital twin automatically re-sequenced production tasks, prioritizing vehicles that did not require the delayed components, thereby maintaining throughput and minimizing idle capacity. This application of digital twin technology illustrates how AI enables adaptive production scheduling that responds dynamically to supply chain variability (Devi et al., 2023).

Warehousing operations benefit significantly from digital twin implementations, particularly in enhancing layout optimization, reducing congestion, and maintaining inventory accuracy. Digital twins improve warehouse management by simulating material flows, identifying bottlenecks, and testing alternative configurations in virtual environments before implementing physical changes. The technology provides early warnings through predictive maintenance algorithms, enabling organizations to address potential equipment failures before they cause operational disruptions. Each digital twin component models specific supply chain elements—warehouses, vehicles, production lines, and inventory flows—creating comprehensive visibility across the entire logistics network (Chen et al., 2024).

Prescriptive analytics, integrated within digital twin frameworks, advance beyond predictive capabilities to recommend specific actions that optimize operational outcomes. AI algorithms analyse thousands of variables simultaneously, including machine health indicators, workforce availability, material status, and environmental conditions, generating production schedules that maximize throughput while minimizing changeover processes. In inventory management applications, prescriptive analytics utilizing digital twin data eliminate "phantom inventory" discrepancies by providing real-time visibility across all storage locations, while AI models predict precise consumption rates, enabling dynamic safety stock calculations that reduce carrying costs while ensuring material availability (Choma, 2025).

3.3. Autonomous Operations Including Robotics, Drones, and Automated Storage/Retrieval Systems

Autonomous technologies are fundamentally transforming warehouse and supply chain operations, delivering unprecedented improvements in efficiency, accuracy, and operational resilience. Autonomous mobile robots (AMRs), distinguished from their predecessors—automated guided vehicles (AGVs)—by their capacity for independent decision-making without pre-installed infrastructure, have become increasingly viable due to recent technological developments in hardware and software systems (Keith & La, 2024).

In warehouse environments, AMRs collaborate with human operators in order-picking operations, carrying containers within picking areas and positioning themselves at locations where operators must retrieve items, then autonomously navigating to subsequent locations. This human-robot collaboration substantially reduces the time and physical effort associated with repetitive material handling tasks, improving performance while reducing worker fatigue. The operational advantages of AMRs are particularly pronounced in narrow-aisle, high-traffic environments where their superior manoeuvrability and safety features enable deeper penetration into operational areas compared to conventional AGVs (Torchio, 2023).

Autonomous aerial drones represent an innovative application in warehouse inventory management, leveraging their ability to navigate three-dimensional warehouse spaces and capture images of inventory storage locations at any height. Drone-based inventory systems employ artificial intelligence to process captured images, read barcodes or text, and detect empty locations, with information immediately reconciled into warehouse management systems, updating inventory records in real-time and enhancing fulfillment process efficiency. This autonomous data collection capability accelerates inventory audits and order processing activities that previously required extensive manual effort and time, making warehouses more agile and responsive to customer demands (Torchio, 2023).

Automated storage and retrieval systems (AS/RS), enhanced with AI capabilities, optimize warehouse space utilization and retrieval efficiency through intelligent algorithms that determine optimal storage locations based on product characteristics, retrieval frequency, and order patterns. Machine learning tools integrated into these autonomous systems analyse operational trends to optimize routes, minimize delays, and enhance task performance, contributing to long-term gains in accuracy, speed, and overall system reliability. The iterative improvements enabled by continuous data monitoring and performance analysis support ongoing operational excellence in increasingly complex warehouse environments.

3.4. AI-Enabled Innovations in Last-Mile Delivery

Last-mile delivery represents one of the most challenging and emission-intensive components of supply chains, accounting for a disproportionate share of logistics-related carbon emissions. AI technologies offer logistics providers and retailers unprecedented capabilities to reduce emissions while simultaneously improving efficiency and customer service through multiple complementary mechanisms (Guest Blogger, 2025).

Dynamic route optimization, powered by AI, addresses limitations of traditional static planning tools that cannot adapt to real-time variables including traffic congestion, weather conditions, or delivery constraints. AI-driven dynamic routing engines continuously recalculate optimal paths for each vehicle using real-time and historical data, substantially reducing unnecessary mileage and associated emissions. Walmart's implementation of AI-powered route optimization exemplifies this capability, eliminating 30 million unnecessary miles and bypassing 110,000 inefficient paths, thereby avoiding 94 million pounds of CO_2 emissions. Research indicates that optimized routing combined with autonomous fleet management can reduce fuel usage and carbon emissions by 18-25%, supporting corporate sustainability objectives (Guest Blogger, 2025).

Delivery slot optimization and demand forecasting represent another critical AI application in sustainable last-mile logistics. By analysing customer behaviour patterns, geographic factors, and historical demand data, AI systems recommend optimal delivery windows that encourage customers to select time slots clustered geographically or aligned with existing delivery routes. Ocado, a prominent online grocer in the United Kingdom, utilizes machine learning to recommend delivery slots aligned with local deliveries, achieving a six percent reduction in carbon intensity per 100,000 orders, from 489 to 458 metric tons of CO_2 equivalent (Guest Blogger, 2025).

Micro-fulfillment centre placement optimization leverages AI to determine ideal locations that minimize distances between inventory and end consumers. By analysing customer density, order frequency, and transportation patterns, AI guides strategic decisions regarding deployment of micro-fulfillment centres or dark stores, fundamentally restructuring last-mile networks to reduce transportation requirements. This network optimization capability enables organizations to shorten delivery distances while maintaining service quality, contributing to both environmental and operational objectives.

Autonomous delivery vehicles, including unmanned ground and aerial vehicles, represent an emerging frontier in sustainable last-mile logistics. Research on autonomous delivery vehicle routing problems demonstrates that these technologies, when optimized through sophisticated algorithms combining variable neighbourhood search and simulated annealing techniques, can substantially reduce carbon emissions in operational phases compared to conventional delivery methods. The integration of electric autonomous vehicles with AI-powered route optimization creates synergistic benefits, enabling logistics providers to reimagine last-mile operations not as emission bottlenecks but as benchmarks of sustainable innovation.

The convergence of AI technologies in demand forecasting, digital twin simulation, autonomous operations, and last-mile delivery optimization represents a fundamental transformation in sustainable procurement capabilities. Organizations that strategically integrate these AI applications can achieve simultaneous improvements in operational efficiency, cost performance, and environmental sustainability, positioning supply chains as drivers of both economic value and ecological responsibility.

4. LEGAL TRANSFORMATIONS AND REGULATORY FRAMEWORKS IN NORTH AFRICA

The integration of artificial intelligence into public procurement systems necessitates fundamental reconsideration of established legal frameworks that have traditionally governed governmental contracting processes. As North African countries pursue digital transformation agendas while modernizing their public sector operations, the intersection between legacy procurement regulations and emerging AI technologies creates both opportunities for enhanced efficiency and complex challenges requiring sophisticated legal responses. This subsection examines the existing legal landscape affecting procurement across five North African jurisdictions—Morocco, Tunisia, Algeria, Egypt, and Libya—before analysing AI-specific legal challenges including robotics regulation, computer vision analytics, and human-in-the-loop safety protocols.

4.1. Existing Legal Landscape Affecting Procurement in North African Countries

Public procurement governance in the Middle East and North Africa (MENA) region has undergone substantial transformation over the past two decades, driven by international development initiatives and domestic reform imperatives. The Deauville Partnership initiative, established following the Arab Spring, aimed to assist Arab countries in developing strong governance structures through domestic production of reforms supporting transparent national governance systems (Modaffari, 2023). Subsequently, the MENA-OECD Public Procurement Network was established in September to facilitate knowledge exchange and identify common interests directing regional procurement reform activities.

Institutional capacity varies significantly across North African countries, with only Morocco, Tunisia, and Egypt maintaining dedicated regulatory bodies or authorities overseeing public procurement. Algeria notably lacks a public procurement authority, creating potential governance gaps in oversight and compliance monitoring. Where regulatory authorities exist, their capacities differ substantially: in

Egypt, procurement authorities operate with autonomous budgets, enhancing their institutional independence and operational effectiveness (Modaffari, 2023).

4.1.1 Egypt

Egypt represents one of the most developed procurement legal frameworks in North Africa, having enacted Law No. 182 of 2018 to regulate contracts entered by public entities. This legislation replaced the Bids and Tenders Law No. 89 of 1998, introducing substantial modernizations aligned with international best practices as recognized by the World Bank. The New Public Procurement Law establishes principles of transparency, fairness, and equal opportunity while maintaining domestic preference mechanisms granting 15% price advantages to bidders supplying products fulfilling minimum local component percentages stipulated under Law No. 5 of 2015.

The Egyptian framework incorporates sophisticated provisions addressing contract security, including differentiated guarantee requirements based on contract types: for procurement or lease of movables, services, artworks, or consultancy contracts, contractors must pay 5% of contract value within 10 working days following bid acceptance notification (extended to 20 working days for contractors located outside Egypt). The law also permits Cabinet of Ministers authorization for administrative authorities to negotiate and conclude agreements directly with Egyptian or foreign entities providing fully funded investment projects that achieve economic and development objective.

Research examining the framework's applicability identified five dominant subjects requiring amendment to enhance equity and prevent unbalanced provisions that might deter international contractors: delay claims by contractors, contract termination procedures, compensation limits under performance guarantees, price adjustment mechanisms, and dispute resolution procedures. These considerations reflect ongoing efforts to balance domestic policy objectives with international competitiveness requirements (Helw, 2021).

Regarding the legal framework of AI, Egypt has established one of the most advanced AI governance frameworks in North Africa, anchored by the formation of the National Council for Artificial Intelligence (NCAI) in November 2019 following Egyptian Cabinet approval. The NCAI includes representatives from all relevant government entities as well as independent experts in artificial intelligence, with its primary mandate being to formalize and govern implementation of Egypt's National AI Strategy (Egyptian MCIT, 2021).

The initial National AI Strategy, launched in 2021, operated through 2024 and has been succeeded by a second edition covering 2025-2030. This updated strategy builds upon achievements from the first phase while addressing emerging technological developments and governance challenges. The NCAI oversees strategy implementation, establishes and tracks relevant key performance indicators (KPIs) to measure progress, and makes adjustments where necessary (Egyptian MCIT, 2025).

The strategy emphasizes ethical use of AI through a comprehensive regulatory framework embodied in the "Egyptian Charter for Responsible AI," launched by NCAI during its seventh meeting. This charter represents Egypt's first systematic attempt to interpret various international guidelines on ethical and responsible AI, adapted to the local context, with the objective of ensuring responsible use of AI systems. The charter addresses principles including transparency, accountability, fairness, privacy protection, and human oversight in AI deployment across public and private sectors (Egyptian NCHR, 2019).

4.1.2 Morocco

Morocco has developed a public procurement regime integrated with broader public-private partnership (PPP) frameworks, with specific PPP laws coexisting alongside public procurement regulations (ALSF, 2024). The country maintains a regulatory body overseeing public procurement operations, providing institutional oversight supporting transparency and accountability. Morocco's procurement framework incorporates preferential treatment for domestic enterprises, with offers submitted by Moroccan companies receiving price advantages relative to foreign competitors (Modaffari, 2023).

The legal landscape is currently experiencing significant expansion to address artificial intelligence governance, with Morocco's House of Representatives considering draft legislation to regulate AI applications. The proposed legislation outlines provisions for cybersecurity, data protection, and intellectual property protection, while proposing establishment of a national committee to oversee AI implementation and monitoring. Criminal liability provisions are included, with penalties ranging from fines to prison sentences for unlawful or harmful use of AI systems. Additionally, a bill proposed in the House of Councillors advocates for creating a dedicated national agency responsible for AI governance, implementing national AI strategy, monitoring applications, and promoting awareness across public and private sectors (LawGratis, 2025a).

4.1.3 Tunisia

Tunisia's public procurement system reflects the country's broader decentralization policies, with local governance structures playing increasingly important roles in procurement decisions. The country established decentralization laws following regional trends, though public spending on local governance averaged only five percent in the MENA region compared to 35 percent in OECD countries as of 2008

(Souissi-Kachouri & Guizani-Jelassi, 2022). Tunisia maintains a regulatory body overseeing public procurement, similar to Morocco and Egypt.

The Tunisian framework favours participation of national companies through preferential pricing mechanisms. State-owned enterprises (SOEs) receive advantages in the public procurement framework, raising competition concerns and potentially limiting private sector opportunities (Tunisia, 2014). Tunisia has developed a comprehensive National AI Strategy spanning 2021-2025, overseen by the Ministry of Industry, Mines, and Energy, the National Research and Innovation Programme, and the High Authority for Public Procurement. The strategy focuses on integrating AI into key sectors including health, education, environment, and transport, aiming to advance digital transformation and foster economic growth (Tunisia, 2022).

Tunisia has embarked on a comprehensive AI roadmap known as the National AI Strategy, spanning from 2021 to 2025. This strategy is overseen by the Ministry of Industry, Mines, and Energy, the National Research and Innovation Programme, and the High Authority for Public Procurement. It outlines ambitious objectives and proposes a detailed action plan for AI development across multiple sectors including health, education, transport, and environment (Trigui et al., 2024).

Tunisia's AI initiative sits squarely within a broader National Digital Strategy for 2021-2025 that positions digitalization as an engine of public-sector reform, infrastructure development, and digital inclusion. The strategy explicitly lists data governance, cybersecurity, and digital transformation of public administration as priority axes. This cross-ministerial National AI Roadmap prioritizes data governance, cybersecurity, cloud infrastructure, human-capital development, and sectoral pilots (Youssef, 2021).

While Tunisia currently lacks a comprehensive, standalone AI law, it enacted Decree-Law No. 54 in September 2022, addressing crimes related to information and communication systems. Although not specifically an AI law, this decree has significant implications for digital rights and AI applications, though critics argue its broad and vague terms could potentially suppress dissent and control online discourse, impacting AI technology development and deployment (LawGratis, 2025a).

4.1.4 Algeria

Algeria's public procurement framework operates without a dedicated regulatory authority, creating potential oversight challenges. The legal system mandates that certain contract shares must be awarded to national products or companies owned primarily by Algerian citizens, with additional requirements that needs or services satisfiable by micro-enterprises must be procured from such entities. SOEs receive preferential treatment in Algeria's procurement framework, similar to Tunisia and Morocco (Algeria, 2023).

Algeria launched its national strategy for artificial intelligence in December 2024 during the third African Startup Conference in Algiers. The initiative aims to develop local AI solutions and implement them across various sectors to reduce reliance on imported technologies. The strategy is designed to keep pace with technological innovation, focusing on six key areas: scientific research, creating a supportive environment for AI, building local expertise, assisting startups, providing solutions meeting business needs, and integrating AI across economic sectors.

The AI strategy follows Algeria's national digital transformation plan introduced in 2024, with these policies together aiming to accelerate the country's digital transition. According to the "Government AI Readiness Index 2023" by Oxford Insights, Algeria ranks 120th globally in readiness for large-scale AI adoption in the public sector, scoring 35.99 out of 100. The report highlights weaknesses across all evaluated areas, with scores below the 50-point average, indicating substantial capacity-building requirements (Oxford Insights, 2023).

Algeria has established foundational frameworks for data protection, cybersecurity, and ICT governance, including the 2018 Data Protection Law. However, implementation gaps persist, limiting innovation potential despite relatively solid regulatory foundations. Digital transformation maturity in Algeria faces challenges related to translating regulatory frameworks into operational effectiveness, a constraint affecting AI integration into public procurement systems (Oxford Insights, 2023).

Table 2. Comparing public procurement & AI frameworks in North Africa

Dimension	Egypt	Morocco	Tunisia	Algeria
Public Procurement Law	Law No. 182 of 2018	Public procurement regime integrated with a PPP framework	Decentralization-aligned public procurement system	National procurement framework
Procurement Regulatory Body	Yes – central regulatory body with significant autonomy	Yes – dedicated public procurement regulatory body	Yes – includes a High Authority for Public Procurement	No – no dedicated public procurement authority; oversight is more fragmented
Procurement Principles	Transparency, fairness, equal opportunity; domestic preference for locally produced content	Preferential treatment for domestic enterprises; integration with PPP mechanisms	Preferential pricing for national companies; advantages for state-owned enterprises	Quotas and preferences for national products and Algerian-owned companies; specific shares reserved for micro-enterprises

continued on following page

Table 2. Continued

Dimension	Egypt	Morocco	Tunisia	Algeria
AI Strategy/ Legislation	National AI Strategy 2025–2030); national charter on responsible AI	National AI strategy under development; draft AI law and "Digital X.0" framework to regulate AI and data	National AI Strategy 2021–2025; no standalone comprehensive AI statute yet	National AI Strategy launched; dedicated AI framework law (Law 22-01)
AI Governance Institution	National Council for Artificial Intelligence (NCAI)	Planned national AI committee/agency envisaged in draft legislation	AI governance coordinated by the Ministry of Industry, Mines and Energy and national research bodies	National AI Regulatory Authority and a Scientific Council for AI created under AI legislation
Data Protection Framework	General data protection, cybersecurity and fintech rules applied to AI; no single AI-specific data protection act	Personal data protection law supplemented by Digital X.0 rules on data governance and digital identity	Personal data protection law plus decree-law on ICT-related offences affecting digital and AI uses	Comprehensive personal data protection law with later amendments; national data protection authority with strong enforcement powers
AI Regulatory Approach	Principles-based, relying on strategy documents, ethical charter and alignment with international AI principles	Comprehensive, code-style framework in preparation, with emphasis on cybersecurity, data governance and consent	Strategy-driven approach; sectoral rules and digital laws form a patchwork rather than a unified AI code	Prescriptive, statute-based approach with clear obligations, risk assessment duties and administrative sanctions
Key AI Policy Priorities	Public services (health, education, transport), industry, agriculture, and digital government	Data governance, digital identity, interoperability, and development of multilingual AI models for Arabic, Amazigh and African languages	Use of AI in health, education, transport and environment; building data governance and human-capital capacity	Scientific research, training domestic experts, supporting startups and integrating AI across key economic sectors

4.2. AI-Specific Legal Challenges in North Africa

As of current assessments, no comprehensive regulatory framework guides AI development in the MENA region as a whole. While regulatory obligations remain minimal, general compliance with data protection laws and ethics principles continues to apply to AI implementations. Egypt, despite lacking AI-specific legislation, has developed elements supporting AI governance through existing laws and regulations addressing data protection, cybersecurity, and fintech. The Ministry of Communication and Information Technology (MCIT), as the lead ministry overseeing Egypt's National AI Strategy (NAIS), strives to provide AI governance elements through various strategies, soft laws, and hard laws, adhering to internationally recognized principles-based approaches such as the OECD AI Principles (OECD, 2024).

4.2.1 Robotics Regulation and Autonomous Systems Liability

The deployment of robotics and autonomous systems in public procurement contexts raises fundamental questions about legal personality, liability allocation, and regulatory oversight. Research examining civil liability for damage caused by autonomous and intelligent robots addresses whether AI systems and autonomous robots should possess legal entity status with legal rights and personal liability, or whether legal rights and liabilities should not extend to these technologies. Current practices have conferred legal personality to non-sentient entities such as maritime vessels, creating precedential frameworks potentially applicable to AI systems.

Liability frameworks for autonomous systems remain contentious across jurisdictions. Some jurisdictions have adopted risk-assessment approaches, while others apply product liability doctrines requiring proof of defectiveness rather than negligence. The challenge intensifies when AI systems employ self-learning algorithms, as unpredictability complicates traditional causation analyses. Courts may resolve this by reasoning that using self-learning algorithms in sensitive contexts constitutes a choice with foreseeable hazards, placing burden on developers or deployers to mitigate risks appropriately (Stanford, 2025).

4.2.2 Computer Vision Analytics and Data Protection Frameworks

Computer vision systems deployed in public procurement—for quality control, inventory management, or supplier verification—process visual data that may constitute personal information under data protection regulations. Under the General Data Protection Regulation (GDPR), which serves as a model for numerous jurisdictions including some North African countries developing data protection frameworks, personal data includes any information identifying an individual, such as video or image data where faces are visible (UnitX Labs, 2025).

Organizations implementing computer vision systems must ensure compliance with fundamental GDPR principles including lawfulness, fairness, transparency, purpose limitation, data minimization, accuracy, storage limitation, integrity, confidentiality, and accountability. Transparency requires informing individuals about camera use and data processing through clear privacy notices, workplace signage, and documentation of video capture events. Purpose limitation mandates using data only for specific, stated reasons—such as safety monitoring—restricting footage to stated purposes like hazard detection rather than unrelated investigations (UnitX Labs, 2025).

Machine vision systems must implement privacy by design, incorporating safeguards early in development processes. Strategies include data anonymization, pseudonymization, establishing lawful bases for data processing, and comprehensive accountability measures. Companies must document all data processing activities, maintain consent records, and report breaches within 72 hours. Risk assessments, encryption, and organizational and technical controls constitute essential data security measures (UnitX Labs, 2025).

4.2.3 Human-in-the-Loop Safety Protocols and Oversight Requirements

Human-in-the-loop (HITL) mechanisms represent critical governance strategies for mitigating AI risks in public procurement contexts. HITL approaches ensure that human intelligence and ethical judgment integrate at crucial stages of AI lifecycles, particularly for high-stakes decisions affecting public resource allocation, supplier selection, or contract award determinations (Peradze, 2025).

The European Union AI Act provides the most comprehensive regulatory framework addressing human oversight requirements for high-risk AI systems. Article 14 mandates that high-risk AI systems be designed and developed with appropriate human-machine interface tools enabling effective oversight by natural persons during operational periods (European Union, 2024). Human oversight aims to prevent or minimize risks to health, safety, or fundamental rights emerging when high-risk AI systems are used according to intended purposes or under reasonably foreseeable misuse conditions.

Regulatory frameworks require oversight measures commensurate with risks, autonomy levels, and contexts of use, implemented through measures identified and built into AI systems by providers before market placement, or measures identified by providers for implementation by deployers. High-risk AI systems must enable human overseers to fully understand AI system capacities and limitations, remain aware of potential automation bias tendencies, correctly interpret system outputs considering characteristics and interpretation tools, and decide not to use systems or disregard, override, or reverse outputs in particular situations.

For particularly sensitive applications—such as biometric identification systems referenced in Annex III of the EU AI Act—regulations mandate that no action or decision be taken by deployers based on system identifications unless separately verified and confirmed by at least two natural persons with necessary competence, training, and authority. This enhanced verification requirement reflects recognition that certain AI applications in public contexts demand heightened human oversight to protect fundamental rights and ensure accountability (European Union, 2024).

However, regulatory frameworks increasingly recognize that HITL is not a universal solution. The goal is not to slow systems but to apply human oversight where most impactful, as overuse can create workflow bottlenecks and automation complacency. Best practices emphasize risk-based design, where higher-risk AI outputs involve deeper human review, with structured review processes and diverse teams reducing overall error and bias rates.

Organizations using human-in-the-loop systems reported a 42% reduction in AI-driven errors compared to fully autonomous systems according to 2024 survey data (VerifyWise, 2025). These empirical findings support regulatory emphasis on human oversight as essential component of responsible AI governance in public procurement contexts, where transparency, accountability, and democratic oversight remain paramount values requiring legal protection.

5. ECONOMIC TRANSFORMATIONS AND IMPACTS

The economic implications of integrating artificial intelligence into sustainable procurement systems extend far beyond mere automation, fundamentally transforming cost structures, information flows, and environmental performance across supply chain networks. As organizations increasingly recognize procurement as a strategic lever for achieving both economic efficiency and sustainability objectives, AI technologies offer unprecedented capabilities to optimize complex trade-offs between cost minimization, performance enhancement, and environmental impact reduction. This subsection examines the economic transformations resulting from AI implementation in North African countries through four interconnected dimensions: cost-benefit analysis of AI adoption, impacts on transaction costs and information asymmetries, economic benefits of advanced analytical technologies, and improvements in environmental externalities through carbon-aware logistics.

5.1. Cost-Benefit Analysis of AI Implementation in Sustainable Procurement: North African Context

North African countries demonstrate varied investment trajectories in AI-enabled procurement systems, reflecting differential economic capacities and strategic priorities. Between 2016 and 2020, Egypt led the region with $241 million invested across 100 AI-related transactions, followed by Morocco with $57 million across seven deals (Oxford Business Group, 2020). These investments represent strategic commitments by North African governments and enterprises to harness AI for economic development and operational efficiency.

McKinsey analysis predicts that AI will contribute 7.7% to Egypt's GDP by 2030, reflecting substantial anticipated economic returns from AI deployment across sectors including public procurement and supply chain management. Morocco has positioned agriculture and logistics as priority sectors for AI application, where irrigation optimization and supply chain efficiency improvements can generate significant economic and environmental benefits. Tunisia, having launched its national AI strategy in 2018, has fostered AI startups such as Datavora, which raised $893,000 to develop market data platforms employing algorithms that consolidate e-commerce data, analyse market trends, and predict consumer behaviour—capabilities directly applicable to procurement optimization (Oxford Business Group, 2020).

Egypt, Morocco, and Tunisia have co-developed industrial and digital strategies recognizing digitalization as essential for supply chain modernization and procurement efficiency. Egypt has established Industry 4.0 Innovation Centres following memoranda of understanding between government agencies and multinational technology firms, creating infrastructure supporting AI-enabled manufacturing and procurement systems. Morocco's “Maroc Digital 2030” strategy emphasizes smart factory development, SME digitalization, and supply chain management technology adoption through initiatives like the Fez Smart Factory Consortium.

Tunisia's Programme de Modernisation Industrielle (PMN) successfully digitalized manufacturing companies, achieving 64% adoption of digital technologies across industrial firms and 70% among manufacturing SMEs, reducing the digital gap between small and large enterprises. These digitalization efforts create foundational infrastructure enabling AI deployment in procurement contexts, though adoption of advanced technologies including enterprise resource planning, customer relationship management, and supply chain management systems remains uneven.

Algeria, despite launching its national AI strategy in December 2024 and establishing an $11 million AI investment fund, ranks 120th globally in government AI readiness with a score of 35.99 out of 100, indicating substantial capacity-building requirements before realizing economic benefits from AI-enabled procurement. However, Algeria's construction of the region's largest data centre and establishment of the National School of Artificial Intelligence represent critical infrastructure investments supporting future AI deployment (Ecofin, 2024).

For North African countries confronting fiscal constraints, high youth unemployment rates, and inflation pressures—particularly acute in Egypt as the region's largest economy—AI-enabled procurement offers pathways to simultaneous cost reduction and service improvement. Digital transformation in MENA supply chains demonstrates heightened urgency, with 96% of Middle Eastern respondents in a

2020 Economist Intelligence Unit survey actively reconfiguring supply chains—the world's highest figure compared to a global average of 83% (Global Finance, 2025).

5.2. Impact on Transaction Costs, Information Asymmetry, and Regulatory Compliance in North Africa

5.2.1 Digital Infrastructure and Transaction Cost Reduction

North Africa's digital infrastructure development directly influences transaction cost reduction potential from AI-enabled procurement systems. Egypt, Morocco, and Tunisia have attempted to position themselves as major components of Europe-Mediterranean-Africa infrastructure and supply chains, necessitating investments in digital connectivity supporting efficient procurement processes. Global benchmarks rank Tunisia 62nd, Morocco 75th, Algeria 90th, and Egypt 34th in infrastructure quality, indicating varied foundations for digital transformation (United Nations Development Programme, 2023).

Digital infrastructure quality particularly impacts cross-border procurement transactions, where information asymmetries between buyers and suppliers are exacerbated by geographic distance, regulatory differences, and limited transparency. North African countries proximate to the European Union—including Algeria, Egypt, and Tunisia—possess better digital infrastructure than sub-Saharan African counterparts, yet still face connectivity constraints affecting real-time data exchange, supplier verification, and contract monitoring capabilities essential for AI-enabled procurement.

Transaction costs in North African procurement contexts include not only direct search, negotiation, and enforcement expenses but also indirect costs associated with bureaucratic processes, limited supplier databases, and fragmented regulatory frameworks. Digitalization reduces these costs by enabling electronic procurement platforms, automated compliance verification, and integrated supplier management systems accessible across decentralized governmental structures—particularly important in Tunisia's decentralized governance model where local authorities play significant procurement roles.

5.2.2 Information Asymmetry and Market Transparency

Information asymmetries in North African procurement markets stem from limited transparency regarding supplier capabilities, pricing benchmarks, and quality standards—challenges that AI technologies can substantially mitigate. The World Bank's procurement reform initiatives in the MENA region emphasize transparency and accountability as foundations for efficient public procurement, objectives directly supported by AI-powered information aggregation and analysis.

AI systems enable North African public entities to access comprehensive supplier information, analyse historical performance data, benchmark prices across regional and international markets, and assess compliance with sustainability criteria—capabilities historically limited by manual processes and fragmented information sources. Digital transformation drives cost reduction through better spend management, optimized supplier selection, and enhanced procurement visibility, enabling public sector entities to make informed decisions based on comprehensive data rather than limited information (IPCS MENA, 2025).

For small and medium-sized enterprises (SMEs) seeking public procurement opportunities in North Africa, AI-powered platforms reduce informational barriers by providing clear visibility into tender requirements, simplified application processes, and automated compliance checking—addressing longstanding challenges limiting SME participation in public contracting. Morocco, Tunisia, and Egypt's preferential treatment mechanisms for domestic SMEs gain effectiveness when combined with AI systems that match enterprise capabilities to procurement opportunities, reducing search costs and improving competitive dynamics.

5.2.3 Regulatory Compliance Cost Reduction

North African countries operate diverse regulatory frameworks governing public procurement, creating compliance complexities that AI technologies can address through automated monitoring and reporting. Egypt's Law No. 182 of 2018, Morocco's PPP-integrated framework, Tunisia's decentralized system coordinated by the High Authority for Public Procurement, and Algeria's fragmented oversight structure each impose distinct compliance requirements on procurement processes.

AI-enabled compliance systems reduce administrative burdens associated with verifying adherence to local content requirements, sustainability standards, and procedural regulations by automating documentation review, tracking contractual obligations, and generating audit trails. Algeria's prescriptive AI regulatory framework under Law No. 22-01, requiring risk assessments and transparency disclosures for AI systems, creates compliance obligations that paradoxically can be managed more efficiently through AI-powered compliance monitoring tools (LawGratis, 2025b).

5.3. Economic Benefits of Digital Twins, Scenario Planning, and Prescriptive Analytics in North Africa

5.3.1 Digital Twin Applications in Regional Supply Chains

North Africa's strategic positioning between European, Middle Eastern, and African markets creates complex supply chain optimization requirements that digital twin technologies can address. Egypt, Morocco, and Tunisia's integration into Europe-Mediterranean-Africa supply chains necessitates sophisticated modelling capabilities to optimize logistics networks, inventory positioning, and production scheduling across multiple jurisdictions with varying regulatory requirements.

Digital twins enable North African manufacturers and public procurement entities to simulate supply chain scenarios accounting for regional variables including seasonal agricultural production patterns in Morocco, Suez Canal logistics dynamics affecting Egyptian trade flows, and cross-border coordination challenges in the Maghreb region. Morocco's focus on agriculture as a priority AI application area reflects recognition that digital twin simulations of irrigation systems, crop yields, and distribution networks can substantially improve efficiency in a sector facing water scarcity and climate variability (AUC/OECD, 2025).

Egypt's attraction of over 91% of North Africa's private infrastructure investment between 2013 and recent years, alongside Morocco's significant foreign direct investment inflows, creates infrastructure foundations supporting digital twin deployment in logistics and manufacturing contexts (AUC/OECD, 2025). These investments in ports, industrial zones, and transportation networks generate data streams that digital twins integrate to optimize public procurement of infrastructure services, construction materials, and logistics contracts.

5.3.2 Scenario Planning for Economic Diversification

North African economies pursuing diversification away from hydrocarbon dependence (Algeria) or seeking to strengthen manufacturing competitiveness (Egypt, Morocco, Tunisia) require sophisticated scenario planning capabilities that prescriptive analytics provide (Medinilla, 2025). Algeria's target for AI to account for 7% of GDP by 2027 necessitates strategic planning regarding how AI deployment affects labour markets, industrial structures, and public service delivery—scenarios that AI-powered planning tools can model with greater sophistication than conventional approaches.

The triple clean energy opportunity facing North Africa—spanning electricity interconnections, hydrogen and clean fuels development, and energy-intensive manufacturing—requires prescriptive analytics to optimize procurement strategies for renewable energy infrastructure, low-carbon industrial inputs, and sustainable logistics services. Morocco, Egypt, and Tunisia's early momentum in green hydrogen development creates procurement requirements for electrolyzers, renewable energy generation equipment, and hydrogen transport infrastructure, where scenario planning tools model cost trajectories, technology evolution, and market demand (Medinilla, 2025).

Prescriptive analytics enable North African governments to balance competing objectives in public procurement including supporting domestic industries through preferential treatment mechanisms, achieving cost efficiency in resource-constrained fiscal environments, and advancing sustainability commitments under international climate agreements. These multi-objective optimization requirements exceed manual planning capabilities, particularly when considering dynamic variables including commodity price volatility, exchange rate fluctuations, and geopolitical supply chain disruptions affecting North African economies.

5.3.3 Infrastructure Optimization and Resilience

North Africa's infrastructure development priorities—including transportation networks, energy systems, water resources, and digital connectivity—generate substantial public procurement requirements where prescriptive analytics optimize project selection, contractor evaluation, and lifecycle cost management. The region's infrastructure quality rankings indicate significant investment needs, with prescriptive analytics supporting prioritization decisions that maximize economic returns while advancing sustainability and resilience objectives (AUC/OECD, 2025).

Digital twin simulations of infrastructure projects enable North African public entities to evaluate alternative designs, construction methodologies, and operational strategies before committing resources, reducing risks of cost overruns and performance failures that historically plague infrastructure procurement. Tunisia's relatively advanced infrastructure ranking (62nd globally) and Egypt's strong performance (34th) create foundations for digital twin deployment in infrastructure management, while Morocco and Algeria's lower rankings indicate opportunities for AI-enabled optimization to enhance infrastructure efficiency (Prakash, 2025).

5.4. Environmental Externalities and Carbon-Aware Logistics Improvements in North Africa

5.4.1 Regional Carbon Footprint and Logistics Challenges

North Africa's logistics and supply chain operations generate substantial carbon emissions through transportation, warehousing, and distribution activities, with environmental impacts exacerbated by the region's dependence on fossil fuel-powered transportation and limited adoption of renewable energy in logistics infrastructure. The region's role as a transit corridor linking European, Middle Eastern, and sub-Saharan African markets intensifies logistics activity and associated emissions, creating urgency for carbon-aware supply chain optimization (Sarioguz, 2025).

Carbon-aware logistics improvements leverage AI to optimize transportation routes, consolidate shipments, select low-emission transport modes, and schedule deliveries to minimize fuel consumption and emissions. These capabilities prove particularly valuable in North African contexts where transportation infrastructure constraints, including road quality variations and border crossing delays, create inefficiencies that AI-powered route optimization can address while simultaneously reducing environmental impacts (Sustainability Directory, 2025).

Research demonstrates that route optimization algorithms combined with real-time traffic data can reduce carbon emissions and fuel consumption by 18-25% in logistics operations—savings directly applicable to North African public sector supply chains procuring goods across dispersed geographic areas. Egypt's procurement of goods for public institutions across the Nile Delta and Valley, Morocco's distribution networks spanning Atlantic and Mediterranean coasts, and Tunisia's logistics connecting coastal and interior regions all benefit from AI-driven route optimization reducing both costs and emissions (AUC/OECD, 2025).

5.4.2 Green Logistics Integration and Renewable Energy

North Africa's exceptional renewable energy potential—particularly solar and wind resources—creates opportunities for integrating renewable energy into logistics and supply chain operations, reducing reliance on fossil fuels and lowering carbon footprints. The region's emergence as a potential green hydrogen and clean fuels hub positions North African countries to pioneer sustainable logistics powered by renewable energy, with public procurement playing a catalytic role through requirements for low-emission transport and warehousing.

Green logistics integration involves deploying renewable energy sources to power warehousing facilities, utilizing electric or hydrogen-powered vehicles for transportation, and optimizing supply chain configurations to minimize energy consumption. AI systems optimize renewable energy integration by forecasting energy generation from variable solar and wind sources, scheduling energy-intensive logistics activities during peak renewable generation periods, and coordinating charging or refuelling of electric vehicles to align with renewable energy availability.

Morocco's substantial investments in renewable energy infrastructure and Egypt's solar energy development initiatives create regional leadership in clean energy that can extend to sustainable logistics through public procurement requirements for renewable-powered transportation and distribution services. Tunisia's National AI Strategy's inclusion of environment as a priority sector reflects recognition that AI applications in environmental monitoring and resource optimization, including logistics sustainability, generate economic and ecological benefits.

5.4.3 Carbon Emission Reduction Through Supply Chain Optimization

Improving logistics performance through AI-driven optimization generates environmental benefits documented in empirical research examining relationships between logistics efficiency and carbon emissions. Studies analysing logistics performance indices (LPI) and CO_2 emissions reveal that logistics improvements result in significant environmental benefits, though the relationship varies based on how efficiency gains are achieved.

Efficient warehouse utilization, optimized distribution centre networks, and improved fleet management systems enabled by AI reduce overall energy consumption in logistics operations, contributing to lower greenhouse gas emissions and smaller carbon footprints. North African public procurement entities adopting AI-powered supply chain management can achieve dual objectives of cost reduction and emissions mitigation—particularly important for countries balancing fiscal constraints with environmental commitments under international climate frameworks.

The integration of carbon metrics into procurement decision-making, enabled by AI systems that calculate and compare carbon footprints of alternative suppliers, transportation modes, and sourcing strategies, transforms environmental considerations from peripheral concerns to core procurement criteria (Debales AI, 2025). Egypt's green economy transition under Vision 2030, Morocco's clean energy leadership, and Tunisia's environmental strategy all create policy contexts favouring carbon-aware procurement supported by AI analytics.

5.4.4 Circular Economy and Resource Efficiency

North Africa's resource constraints, including water scarcity and limited arable land, necessitate circular economy approaches in supply chain management where AI optimizes resource recovery, waste minimization, and material reuse. AI-enabled procurement systems identify suppliers employing circular economy practices, evaluate lifecycle environmental impacts of procured goods, and optimize reverse logistics for product returns, refurbishment, and recycling.

Algeria's emphasis on supporting 20,000 startups and integrating AI across economic sectors creates opportunities for circular economy innovations in supply chains, where AI coordinates material flows, matches waste streams with reuse opportunities, and optimizes collection and processing logistics. The economic benefits of circular economy approaches—including reduced raw material costs, new revenue streams from recovered materials, and enhanced resource security—align with environmental benefits of reduced extraction, lower emissions, and decreased waste generation (Bag et al., 2025).

North Africa's positioning as a future green industrial hub, particularly in energy-intensive manufacturing sectors including fertilizers, iron, steel, and aluminium, requires sustainable supply chain practices where AI optimizes energy consumption, minimizes emissions, and coordinates renewable energy utilization. Public procurement of industrial goods and services incorporating sustainability requirements, supported by AI systems verifying compliance and tracking performance, catalyses broader industrial transformation toward low-carbon, resource-efficient production models.

Table 3. Summary of Economic benefits of digital twins, scenario planning, and prescriptive analytics in North Africa

AI Technology	Application Area	Economic Benefits	Regional Focus	Impact	Strategic Value
Digital Twins	Supply Chain	15-25% inventory cost reduction; 10-15% service improvement	Egypt, Morocco, Tunisia	15-25% cost savings	Procurement optimization foundation
Digital Twins	Agriculture	Irrigation and crop yield optimization	Morocco priority sector	Major efficiency gains	Water scarcity solutions
Digital Twins	Infrastructure	Risk-adjusted value creation	Tunisia (62nd), Egypt (34th)	7-10% premium valuation	Investor confidence
Digital Twins	Manufacturing	20-30% operational performance gains	Egypt, Tunisia Industry 4.0	30% forecast accuracy	Export competitiveness
Digital Twins	Cross-Border Trade	Suez Canal and regional logistics modeling	All four countries	Integration efficiency	Regional cooperation
Prescriptive Analytics	Economic Diversification	GDP growth through AI adoption	Algeria hydrocarbon transition	7% GDP by 2027	Knowledge-based economy
Prescriptive Analytics	Renewable Energy	Solar/wind procurement optimization	Morocco, Egypt, Tunisia	Cost optimization	Green energy hub
Prescriptive Analytics	Multi-Objective Procurement	Balance cost, preference, sustainability	All countries (varied laws)	Multi-goal achievement	Policy balance

continued on following page

Table 3. Continued

AI Technology	Application Area	Economic Benefits	Regional Focus	Impact	Strategic Value
Prescriptive Analytics	Infrastructure	Project prioritization and selection	Egypt (91% investment share)	Maximized ROI	Development gaps
Prescriptive Analytics	Green Hydrogen	Technology cost modeling	Morocco, Egypt, Tunisia	Demand forecasting	New value chains
Integrated AI	Transaction Costs	Faster supply chain reconfiguration	Tunisia, Morocco, Egypt	7.4 vs 8.5 months	Digital transformation
Integrated AI	Compliance	Automated verification systems	Egypt Vision 2030, Algeria Law 22-01	Reduced admin costs	Transparency & anti-corruption
Integrated AI	Supplier Management	Enhanced SME participation	Morocco, Tunisia, Egypt preferences	Increased SME awards	Private sector innovation
Integrated AI	Carbon Logistics	Route and fuel optimization	Egypt, Morocco, Tunisia networks	18-25% emissions cut	Climate commitments

6. POLICY IMPLICATIONS AND RECOMMENDATIONS

6.1. Harmonization of AI Governance and Sustainable Procurement Regulations

The divergent regulatory approaches across North African countries—ranging from Egypt's principles-based governance through the NCAI and Responsible AI Charter to Algeria's prescriptive framework under Law No. 22-01, Morocco's pending comprehensive legislation, and Tunisia's strategy-driven patchwork regulation—create fragmentation that undermines regional integration and cross-border procurement efficiency. Harmonization of AI governance frameworks across Egypt, Morocco, Tunisia, and Algeria represents a critical policy priority for optimizing sustainable procurement systems while maintaining national sovereignty over strategic sectors.

6.1.1 Regional Regulatory Coordination Mechanisms

North African governments should establish a Maghreb AI Governance Forum modeled on the MENA-OECD Public Procurement Network, facilitating knowledge exchange, identifying common regulatory interests, and developing shared standards for AI deployment in public procurement. This forum would coordinate efforts to align fundamental principles including transparency, accountability, fairness, human oversight, and environmental sustainability while accommodating national variations in implementation approaches. The forum could develop model legislation for AI procurement systems, establish mutual recognition agreements for AI system certifications, create standardized data protection requirements for cross-border procurement, and coordinate enforcement mechanisms for AI-related violations.

Egypt's advanced institutional architecture through the NCAI, combined with Morocco's human rights-focused approach guided by the CNDH, Tunisia's multi-stakeholder consultation processes with organizations like The Future Society, and Algeria's regulatory authority with enforcement powers, offer complementary strengths that harmonization efforts should leverage. Regional coordination would reduce compliance costs for suppliers operating across multiple North African jurisdictions, enhance data sharing for supplier verification and performance monitoring, facilitate joint procurement initiatives for high-value contracts, and strengthen collective negotiating positions with multinational technology vendors.

6.1.2 Integration of Sustainability Criteria

Harmonized frameworks should systematically integrate environmental and social sustainability criteria into AI procurement regulations, moving beyond voluntary commitments to enforceable requirements. Egypt's Vision 2030 green economy objectives, Morocco's renewable energy leadership, Tunisia's environmental strategy priorities, and Algeria's economic diversification imperatives create convergent policy contexts favoring mandatory sustainability provisions in public procurement laws. Regional standards should require lifecycle carbon footprint assessments for procured goods and services, supplier adherence to circular economy principles and waste minimization, ethical sourcing standards addressing labor rights and community impacts, and biodiversity protection measures for supply chains affecting natural ecosystems.

6.2. Capacity-Building Strategies for Governments and Public Sector Stakeholders

The substantial capacity gaps identified across North African countries—most acutely reflected in Algeria's 120th global ranking in government AI readiness with a score of 35.99 out of 100, but present to varying degrees across all four countries—necessitate comprehensive, sustained capacity-building initiatives targeting technical skills, institutional capabilities, and organizational cultures.

6.2.1 Technical Skills Development

North African governments should establish AI Procurement Academies within existing public administration training institutions, offering specialized curricula for procurement professionals covering AI fundamentals and applications, data analytics and interpretation skills, supplier evaluation using AI-powered tools, contract management for AI-enabled services, cybersecurity and data protection requirements, and ethical considerations in algorithmic decision-making. Morocco's initiative to train 200,000 youth in digital and AI skills provides a model for scale, though public sector programs require specialized focus on procurement contexts.

Regional cooperation through the proposed Maghreb AI Governance Forum should facilitate exchange programs enabling procurement officials to observe AI implementation in partner countries, joint training initiatives sharing costs and expertise across jurisdictions, development of open-source training materials in Arabic and French, and certification programs establishing regional standards for AI procurement competency. Tunisia's relatively high manufacturing digitalization rate of 64% and advanced digital infrastructure create opportunities for Tunisia to serve as a regional training hub, while Egypt's Industry 4.0 Innovation Centers offer practical demonstration environments.

6.2.2 Institutional Capacity Enhancement

Beyond individual skills development, North African governments must strengthen institutional architectures supporting AI-enabled procurement through establishment of dedicated AI procurement units within central procurement authorities, creation of data analytics teams supporting procurement decision-making, development of AI ethics committees reviewing high-risk procurement applications, and integration of AI expertise into legal and compliance departments. Egypt's autonomous procurement authority budget and Morocco's dedicated regulatory body provide institutional foundations that Algeria—lacking a central procurement authority—must develop.

Institutional capacity building should emphasize organizational change management, as AI adoption requires transformation of established processes, workflows, and decision-making norms. Change management strategies should include stakeholder engagement processes addressing resistance and building buy-in, pilot projects demonstrating AI value before full-scale deployment, iterative implementation approaches allowing learning and adjustment, and performance measurement systems tracking AI adoption benefits and challenges.

6.2.3 Infrastructure Investment Priorities

Technical and institutional capacity building depends upon digital infrastructure investments creating foundational capabilities for AI deployment. Algeria's establishment of the region's largest data center and Morocco's digital infrastructure development under Maroc Digital 2030 represent critical enablers, but gaps remain particularly in rural and peripheral areas. Priority infrastructure investments should include high-speed internet connectivity across government facilities, secure data storage and processing capabilities meeting sovereignty requirements, interoperable IT systems enabling data sharing across agencies, and cybersecurity infrastructure protecting sensitive procurement information.

Public-private partnerships can accelerate infrastructure development while managing fiscal constraints, with procurement frameworks specifically designed to attract private investment in digital infrastructure through revenue-sharing arrangements, performance-based contracts, and risk mitigation mechanisms. Egypt's success in attracting 91% of North Africa's private infrastructure investment demonstrates potential for this approach, which Tunisia, Morocco, and Algeria should adapt to their contexts.

6.3. Frameworks for Maintaining Transparency, Trust, and Accountability While Adopting AI

The deployment of AI systems in public procurement raises fundamental governance challenges regarding algorithmic transparency, accountability for automated decisions, and maintenance of democratic oversight over resource allocation. North African countries must develop comprehensive frameworks balancing AI's efficiency benefits with essential accountability principles.

6.3.1 Algorithmic Transparency Requirements

Building on the EU AI Act's human oversight provisions and Egypt's Responsible AI Charter emphasizing transparency, North African regulatory frameworks should mandate explainability requirements for AI procurement systems, ensuring that algorithmic decision-making processes are comprehensible to affected stakeholders. Transparency frameworks should require disclosure of data sources, variables, and weighting used in AI algorithms, plain-language explanations of how AI systems generate procurement recommendations, documentation of algorithm training methodologies and validation procedures, and public reporting of AI system performance metrics and error rates.

For high-risk procurement decisions—including large infrastructure contracts, essential service delivery, or sensitive technology acquisitions—enhanced transparency requirements should apply, including mandatory external audits of AI systems by independent technical experts, publication of algorithm source code for open-source review, real-time monitoring dashboards showing AI system operations, and stakeholder consultation processes before AI deployment.

6.3.2 Human-in-the-Loop Governance

AI systems should augment rather than replace human judgment in procurement contexts, with human-in-the-loop mechanisms ensuring appropriate oversight. Following the EU AI Act's approach, North African frameworks should require that for particularly sensitive procurement decisions, no action be taken based solely on AI recommendations without verification by qualified human reviewers. Governance structures should establish clear decision rights specifying which procurement functions AI systems can perform autonomously versus requiring human approval, define competency requirements for personnel overseeing AI systems, create escalation procedures for cases where human reviewers disagree with AI recommendations, and implement safeguards against automation bias where reviewers rubber-stamp AI outputs without critical evaluation.

Tunisia's High Authority for Public Procurement, Egypt's central procurement authority, and Morocco's regulatory body should develop specialized oversight functions monitoring AI system performance, investigating complaints regarding algorithmic decisions, and ensuring compliance with transparency requirements. Algeria's development of such capacity represents a priority given the absence of a dedicated procurement authority.

6.3.3 Accountability Mechanisms

Clear accountability frameworks must address liability when AI systems generate flawed procurement decisions causing financial losses, supplier harm, or service delivery failures. Building on Algeria's administrative penalties under Law No. 22-01 and emerging liability frameworks in Morocco's draft legislation, regional standards should establish responsibility chains clarifying roles of AI system developers, procurement authority deployers, and individual officials, define circumstances warranting administrative sanctions, fines, or criminal liability, create indemnification mechanisms protecting public officials making good-faith decisions based on AI recommendations, and establish appeals processes enabling suppliers to challenge AI-driven procurement decisions.

Accountability mechanisms should include mandatory incident reporting requirements when AI systems malfunction or generate incorrect recommendations, regular performance audits assessing AI system accuracy and bias, sunset provisions requiring periodic review and reauthorization of AI procurement systems, and whistleblower protections for employees reporting AI system failures or misuse.

6.4. Recommendations to Optimize Economic and Environmental Benefits

Maximizing the economic and environmental returns from AI-enabled sustainable procurement requires strategic approaches addressing technology selection, implementation sequencing, and performance measurement.

6.4.1 Prioritization of High-Impact Applications

Given resource constraints and capacity limitations, North African governments should prioritize AI applications generating substantial economic and environmental benefits relative to implementation costs. Priority areas identified through the economic analysis include carbon-aware logistics optimization achieving 18-25% emissions reductions while lowering fuel costs, particularly valuable for Egypt's Nile Delta distribution networks, Morocco's Atlantic-Mediterranean corridors, and Tunisia's coastal-interior logistics; digital twin modelling for infrastructure projects reducing the 15-25% inventory costs while improving service levels by 10-15%; supplier performance management systems reducing transaction costs and information asymmetries, accelerating supply chain reconfiguration from the North African average of 7.4 months to even faster timelines; and renewable energy procurement optimization supporting Morocco, Egypt, and Tunisia's clean energy transitions and positioning the region as a green industrial hub.

Agricultural applications deserve particular priority in Morocco given water scarcity challenges and the sector's economic importance, where digital twins optimizing irrigation systems and crop distribution generate food security benefits alongside resource efficiency gains. Similarly, Algeria's focus on AI contributing 7% to GDP by 2027 requires strategic concentration on applications supporting economic diversification from hydrocarbon dependence.

6.4.2 Phased Implementation Strategies

Rather than attempting comprehensive AI transformation simultaneously across all procurement functions, North African governments should adopt phased approaches beginning with pilot projects demonstrating value, building capacity, and refining systems before scaling. Implementation phases should progress from low-risk applications including spend analysis and market research to moderate-risk functions such as supplier discovery and preliminary screening, then to high-value applications including contract award recommendations and performance monitoring, with continuous evaluation informing advancement decisions.

Pilot projects should target specific procurement categories amenable to AI optimization—for example, standardized goods where supplier comparisons are straightforward, repetitive service contracts where pattern recognition generates efficiency gains, or logistics optimization where route planning algorithms deliver measurable benefits. Egypt's Industry 4.0 Innovation Centres and Tunisia's relatively high manufacturing digitalization provide testing environments for pilot initiatives before wider deployment.

6.4.3 Performance Measurement and Continuous Improvement

Optimizing AI benefits requires robust measurement frameworks tracking both economic and environmental outcomes. Performance measurement systems should establish baseline metrics before AI implementation enabling comparison, define key performance indicators across cost reduction, service improvement, and sustainability dimensions, implement real-time monitoring dashboards providing visibility into AI system impacts, and conduct regular evaluations assessing whether anticipated benefits materialize.

Recommended KPIs synthesizing the economic analysis include procurement cycle time reductions from baseline durations, total cost of ownership improvements compared to conventional procurement, supplier diversity metrics tracking SME participation facilitated by AI platforms, carbon footprint reductions measured across supply chains, regulatory compliance rates for sustainability criteria, and stakeholder satisfaction assessments from procurement staff and suppliers.

Continuous improvement mechanisms should create feedback loops where performance data informs algorithm refinement, establish mechanisms for incorporating user suggestions and complaints, benchmark performance against international best practices and peer countries, and update systems to reflect technological advances and evolving policy priorities.

6.5. Addressing Challenges Related to Water Scarcity, Energy, and Climate Adaptation via AI Procurement

North Africa faces distinctive environmental challenges requiring AI procurement systems specifically designed to address water scarcity, energy constraints, and climate adaptation imperatives.

6.5.1 Water-Aware Procurement Strategies

The region's status as experiencing the world's highest water stress rates necessitates integration of water consumption metrics into procurement decision-making. AI systems should evaluate supplier water footprints across production processes, prioritize water-efficient technologies and practices in procurement specifications, optimize supply chain configurations to minimize water-intensive transportation and storage, and model climate scenarios affecting water availability and supply chain resilience.

Morocco's agricultural AI applications should incorporate precision irrigation technologies reducing water consumption while maintaining productivity, with public procurement serving as demand aggregation mechanisms enabling smallholder farmer access to these technologies. Egypt's Nile-dependent agriculture and urban water systems require AI-optimized procurement of water infrastructure, treatment technologies, and conservation equipment. Tunisia and Algeria's water challenges in arid interior regions necessitate procurement strategies emphasizing water recycling systems, drought-resistant inputs, and efficient distribution networks.

6.5.2 Energy-Conscious Supply Chain Optimization

North Africa's dual challenge of growing electricity demands and renewable energy transition opportunities requires AI procurement systems optimizing energy consumption while accelerating clean energy adoption. AI applications should prioritize energy-efficient products and services in procurement scoring, schedule energy-intensive logistics activities during renewable energy generation peaks, model energy demands from data centres and computing infrastructure supporting AI systems themselves, and coordinate procurement of renewable energy generation and storage technologies.

The region's exceptional solar and wind potential enables ambitious renewable energy procurement strategies where AI optimizes technology selection, site location, and grid integration. Morocco's clean energy leadership, Egypt's solar energy development, and Tunisia's environmental strategy create policy contexts where public procurement catalyses renewable energy adoption through demand aggregation, long-term offtake agreements, and risk-sharing mechanisms.

6.5.3 Climate Adaptation Procurement

Climate change impacts including temperature increases, rainfall variability, sea level rise, and extreme weather events require AI-enhanced procurement strategies building supply chain resilience. AI systems should conduct climate risk assessments for suppliers and supply chains, diversify sourcing to reduce vulnerability to climate-related disruptions, prioritize climate-resilient infrastructure and technologies in procurement decisions, and model long-term climate scenarios informing strategic procurement planning.

North Africa's positioning as a transit corridor linking Europe, Middle East, and sub-Saharan Africa creates responsibilities for climate-resilient logistics infrastructure supporting regional trade. Public procurement of port facilities, transportation networks, and warehousing should incorporate climate adaptation measures including flood protection, heat-resistant materials, and backup systems for climate-disrupted operations. AI-powered scenario planning enables evaluation of alternative adaptation investments, optimization of limited resources across competing priorities, and coordination of adaptation efforts across jurisdictions.

The green hydrogen opportunity positioning Morocco, Egypt, and Tunisia as potential clean fuel exporters requires strategic procurement of hydrogen production equipment, storage infrastructure, and transport systems where AI optimizes technology pathways, cost structures, and market development strategies. Public procurement serving as anchor demand creates market signals encouraging private investment in hydrogen value chains, accelerating industrial transformation toward low-carbon production models.

CONCLUSION

The integration of artificial intelligence into sustainable procurement systems across North African public sectors represents a transformative opportunity to simultaneously advance economic efficiency, environmental sustainability, and governance effectiveness. This research has examined how generative AI, digital twins, autonomous operations, and prescriptive analytics fundamentally reshape procurement practices through enhanced demand forecasting, optimized supply chain configurations, reduced transaction costs, and improved environmental performance. The analysis has demonstrated that AI-enabled procurement can generate inventory cost reductions of 15-25%, operational performance improvements of 20-

30%, and carbon emissions reductions of 18-25%—benefits particularly valuable for resource-constrained governments balancing fiscal pressures with developmental and environmental commitments.

The legal and regulatory landscape across Egypt, Morocco, Tunisia, and Algeria reveals divergent approaches to AI governance that both reflect national priorities and create coordination challenges. Egypt's principles-based framework anchored by the National Council for Artificial Intelligence and Responsible AI Charter, Morocco's comprehensive legislative development through the Digital X.0 Law, Tunisia's strategy-driven approach integrating AI priorities across sectors, and Algeria's prescriptive regulatory framework under Law No. 22-01 demonstrate varied pathways toward AI governance. These differences create opportunities for mutual learning and best practice exchange while necessitating harmonization efforts to facilitate regional integration, reduce compliance fragmentation, and strengthen collective capabilities.

The economic transformations enabled by AI in North African sustainable procurement extend beyond direct cost savings to encompass strategic value creation through enhanced supply chain resilience, improved investor confidence, accelerated digital transformation, and strengthened competitive positioning in global markets. Digital twins provide foundations for sophisticated supply chain modelling addressing the region's distinctive challenges including cross-border trade complexities, infrastructure constraints, and agricultural optimization in water-scarce environments. Prescriptive analytics support critical policy objectives including economic diversification in Algeria, renewable energy transitions across all four countries, and infrastructure development prioritization balancing competing demands with limited resources.

Environmental externalities represent both challenges and opportunities in North African AI-enabled procurement. The region's severe water stress, growing energy demands, and climate vulnerability necessitate procurement strategies explicitly addressing environmental constraints through water-aware supplier selection, energy-conscious logistics optimization, and climate adaptation investments. Simultaneously, North Africa's exceptional renewable energy potential and emerging positioning as a green industrial hub create opportunities for AI procurement systems to catalyse low-carbon transformations by optimizing clean energy adoption, supporting hydrogen value chain development, and coordinating circular economy initiatives.

The policy recommendations emerging from this analysis emphasize harmonization of regulatory frameworks through regional coordination mechanisms, comprehensive capacity-building addressing technical skills and institutional capabilities, robust transparency and accountability frameworks maintaining democratic oversight of algorithmic decision-making, strategic prioritization of high-impact AI applications generating measurable economic and environmental benefits, and targeted strategies addressing water scarcity, energy transitions, and climate adaptation through procurement innovation.

Implementation challenges persist across technical infrastructure constraints, human capital limitations, institutional fragmentation, and the fundamental tension between rapid AI advancement and deliberate governance development. Yet the convergence of digital transformation imperatives, sustainability commitments, and fiscal pressures creates powerful incentives for North African governments to embrace AI-enabled sustainable procurement as a strategic priority. The region's strong innovation capacity, educated youth populations, dynamic startup ecosystems, and engaged diaspora communities provide human capital foundations supporting successful AI adoption when complemented by sustained political commitment, adequate resource allocation, and inclusive stakeholder engagement.

The transformation of North African public sector supply chains through AI integration will unfold over years rather than months, requiring patience, persistence, and continuous learning. Early movers establishing robust governance frameworks, investing in capacity development, and demonstrating measurable benefits will position themselves advantageously in an increasingly AI-enabled global economy. Regional cooperation amplifies national efforts by sharing costs and expertise, establishing common standards, and creating economies of scale attracting technology vendors and investors.

Ultimately, the success of AI-enabled sustainable procurement in North Africa depends not merely on technological sophistication but on the alignment of AI deployment with fundamental values of transparency, accountability, equity, and environmental stewardship. AI systems must serve as tools amplifying human judgment rather than replacing democratic decision-making, enhancing rather than undermining public trust, and advancing inclusive prosperity rather than concentrating benefits narrowly. By maintaining this values-centred approach while harnessing AI's transformative capabilities, North African countries can pioneer models of sustainable procurement that generate economic prosperity, environmental sustainability, and good governance—demonstrating pathways valuable not only regionally but for developing economies worldwide confronting similar challenges in an era of rapid technological change and urgent environmental imperatives.

REFERENCES

African Union Commission. (2020). *Digital transformation strategy for Africa (2020–2030).* African Union Commission. https://au.int/sites/default/files/documents/38507-doc-dts-english.pdf

Ahatsi, E., & Olanrewaju, O. A. (2025). Enhancing humanitarian supply chain resilience: Evaluating artificial intelligence and big data analytics in two nations. *Logistics (Basel)*, *9*(2), 1–28. DOI: 10.3390/logistics9020064

Ahmed, E., & El Sayed, K. (2023). Studying the relationship between green supply chain management dimensions and improve healthcare quality service: An empirical study. *The Arab Journal of Administration*, *43*(3), 43–56. DOI: 10.21608/aja.2022.139386.1247

APICS. (2014). *SCOR quick reference guide* (Version 12.0). APICS. https://www.apics.org/docs/default-source/scor-p-toolkits/apics-scc-scor-quick-reference-guide.pdf

Bag, S., Rahman, M. S., Gupta, S., & Jabbour, A. B. L. de S. (2025). Artificial intelligence driven ethical procurement systems, circular economy and governance: A supplier performance analysis. *Journal of Purchasing and Supply Management.* Advance online publication. Article ID 101075. .DOI: 10.1016/j.pursup.2025.101075

Baryannis, G., Validi, S., Dani, S., & Antoniou, G. (2019). Supply chain risk management and artificial intelligence: State of the art and future research directions. *International Journal of Production Research*, *57*(7), 2179–2202. DOI: 10.1080/00207543.2018.1530476

Buck, S. (2025, November 16). Designing for supply chain resilience with Nestlé. *Coupa Blog.* https://www.coupa.com/blog/designing-for-supply-chain-resilience-with-nestle

Cannas, V. G., Ciano, M. P., Saltalamacchia, M., & Secchi, R. (2024). Artificial intelligence in supply chain and operations management: A multiple case study research. *International Journal of Production Research*, *62*(9), 3333–3360. DOI: 10.1080/00207543.2023.2232050

Chen, H., Chu, T., Yang, L., Wang, Z., & Xue, L. (2024). Digital twin warehouse management platform developed based on Unity3D. In *Proceedings of the 4th International Conference on Internet of Things and Machine Learning.* https://doi.org/DOI: 10.1145/3697467.3697667

Choma, K. (2025). How digital twins drive production scheduling & supply chain optimization. *Nomtek Blog.* https://www.nomtek.com/blog/digital-twins-and-supply-chain-optimization

Christopher, M. (2016). *Logistics & supply chain management.* Pearson.

Collaborating Centre on Sustainable Consumption and Production. (2021). *Green public procurement for sustainable horticulture: A policy brief.* https://www.cscp.org/wp-content/uploads/2021/07/GOALAN_GPP_Policy_Brief.pdf

DeNittis, N. (2024, February 5). Artificial intelligence at Procter & Gamble. *Emerj.* https://emerj.com/ai-sector-overviews/artificial-intelligence-at-procter-gamble/

Devi, D. P., Allur, N. S., Dondapati, K., Chetlapalli, H., Kodadi, S., & Perumal, T. (2023). Digital twin technology and IoT enabled AI using real-time analytics for smart warehouse management and predictive inventory optimization. *International Journal of Marketing Management, 11*(4). https://ijmm.in/index.php/ijmm/article/view/208

European Commission. (2008). *Public procurement for a better environment.* https://eur-lex.europa.eu/LexUriServ/LexUriServ.do?uri=COM:2008:0400:FIN:EN:pdf

European Union. (2024). *Artificial Intelligence Act: Article 14 – Human oversight* (Regulation (EU) 2024/1689). https://artificialintelligenceact.eu/article/14/

Gasper, D., Shah, A., & Tankha, S. (2019). The framing of sustainable consumption and production in SDG 12. *Global Policy, 10*(Suppl. 1), 83–95. DOI: 10.1111/1758-5899.12592

Goldman, S. (2022, June 6). How AI helps Coca Cola boost supply chain procurement. *VentureBeat.* https://venturebeat.com/business/how-ai-helps-coca-cola-boost-supply-chain-procurement/

Goswami, S. S., Mondal, S., Sarkar, S., Gupta, K. K., Sahoo, S. K., & Halder, R. (2025). Artificial intelligence enabled supply chain management: Unlocking new opportunities and challenges. *Artificial Intelligence and Applications (Commerce, Calif.), 3*(1). https://elibrary.ru/item.asp?id=74126909

Guest Blogger. (2025, September 15). AI in last mile delivery: Smarter, faster, greener 2025. *Last Mile TMS.* https://lastmiletms.com/ai-in-last-mile-delivery-smarter-faster-greener-2025/

Helw, A. M. A. (2021). *Framework for enhanced applicability of the Egyptian public procurement law to international administrative construction contracts* (Master's thesis). The American University in Cairo. https://fount.aucegypt.edu/cgi/viewcontent.cgi?article=2914&context=etds

Kagalwala, H., Radhakrishnan, G. V., Mohammed, I. A., Kothinti, R. R., & Kulkarni, N. (2025). Predictive analytics in supply chain management: The role of AI and machine learning in demand forecasting. *Advances in Consumer Research. Association for Consumer Research (U. S.)*, *2*(1), 142–149.

Kamanzi, E., & Akumuntu, J. (2024). Effect of machine learning model on supply chain performance: A case of Dubai Port (DP) World/Kigali Rwanda. *Journal of Procurement & Supply Chain*, *8*(1). Advance online publication. DOI: 10.53819/81018102t2311

Keith, R., & La, H. M. (2024). Review of autonomous mobile robots for the warehouse environment. *arXiv preprint arXiv:2406.08333.* /arXiv.2406.08333DOI: 10.48550

Kepczynski, R., Jandhyala, R., Sankaran, G., & Dimofte, A. (2018). *Integrated business planning.* Springer. https://link.springer.com/content/pdf/10.1007/978-3-319-75665-3.pdf

Khan, M. M., Bashar, I., Minhaj, G. M., Wasi, A. I., & Hossain, N. U. I. (2023). Resilient and sustainable supplier selection: An integration of SCOR 4.0 and machine learning approach. *Sustainable and Resilient Infrastructure*, *8*(5). Advance online publication. DOI: 10.1080/23789689.2023.2165782

Kietzmann, J., Paschen, J., & Treen, E. (2018). Artificial intelligence in advertising: How marketers can leverage artificial intelligence along the consumer journey. *Journal of Advertising Research*, *58*(3). Advance online publication. DOI: 10.2501/JAR-2018-035

Kumar, A., Kashyap, D. R., Kataria, P., & Kumar, A. (2024). The expected contribution of artificial intelligence (AI) adoption in supply chain management. *American Journal of Artificial Intelligence*, *8*(2). Advance online publication. DOI: 10.11648/j.ajai.20240802.15

Law, No. (2018). *182 of 2018 Regulating Contracts Concluded by Public Entities.* Official Gazette of Egypt.

LawGratis. (2025a). Artificial intelligence law at Morocco. https://www.lawgratis.com/blog-detail/artificial-intelligence-law-at-morocco

LawGratis. (2025b). Artificial intelligence law at Algeria. https://www.lawgratis.com/blog-detail/artificial-intelligence-law-at-algeria

Lukalapu, D. R. (2021). *Advancement of sales and operations planning for effective demand management with IBP* (Master's thesis). Politecnico di Milano. https://www.politesi.polimi.it/handle/10589/182167

McCullough, B., Kellison, T., & Melton, E. N. (Eds.). (2022). *The Routledge handbook of sport and sustainable development*. Taylor & Francis.

Medinilla, A. (2025, November 12). Seizing the moment for North African green industrialisation. *ECDPM*. https://ecdpm.org/work/seizing-moment-north-african-green-industrialisation

Melina, D. R., Yunani, A., & Hidayat, A. M. (2024). Measuring supply chain performance using the SCOR model: A case study of CV. XYZ. *International Journal for Multidisciplinary Research*, *6*(6). Advance online publication. DOI: 10.1007/s43069-024-00314-y

Modaffari, F. G. (2023). The procurement law in the Middle East. *Scholars International Journal of Law. Crime and Justice*, *6*(9). Advance online publication. DOI: 10.36348/sijlcj.2023.v06i09.001

Odumbo, O. R., & Nimma, S. Z. (2025). Leveraging artificial intelligence to maximize efficiency in supply chain process optimization. *International Journal of Research Publication and Reviews*, *6*(1). Advance online publication. DOI: 10.55248/gengpi.6.0125.0508

OECD. (2024). *Artificial Intelligence Review of Egypt.* OECD Publishing. https://www.oecd.org/content/dam/oecd/en/publications/reports/2024/05/oecd-artificial-intelligence-review-of-egypt_3c437131/2a282726-en.pdf

OECD. (2025a). *Governing with artificial intelligence: The state of play and way forward in core government functions.* OECD Publishing. https://www.oecd.org/content/dam/oecd/en/publications/reports/2025/06/governing-with-artificial-intelligence_398fa287/795de142-en.pdf

OECD. (2025b). *Implementing the OECD recommendation on public procurement in OECD and partner countries: 2020–2024 report.* OECD Publishing. https://www.oecd.org/content/dam/oecd/en/publications/reports/2025/06/implementing-the-oecd-recommendation-on-public-procurement-in-oecd-and-partner-countries_dbc4aca7/02a46a58-en.pdf

Oxford Business Group. (2020). *Infinite potential: Emerging markets are beginning to unlock the wide-ranging benefits of artificial intelligence.* Egypt 2020 Report. https://oxfordbusinessgroup.com/reports/egypt/2020-report/economy/infinite-potential-emerging-markets-are-beginning-to-unlock-the-wide-ranging-benefits-of-artificial-intelligence

Oxford Insights. (2023). *Government AI readiness index 2023.* https://oxfordinsights.com/wp-content/uploads/2023/12/2023-Government-AI-Readiness-Index-1.pdf

Peradze, E. (2025, July 30). How humans in the loop powers responsible AI through data annotation. *Humans in the Loop.* https://humansintheloop.org/how-humans-in-the-loop-powers-responsible-ai-through-data-annotation/

Prakash, O. (2025). How digital twin technology can revolutionize a supply chain. *Supply Chain Management Review.* https://www.scmr.com/article/how-digital-twin-technology-can-revolutionize-a-supply-chain

Sarioguz, O. (2025). Artificial intelligence for sustainable logistics: Reducing carbon emissions and fuel consumption through route optimization. *Journal of International Scientific Research Archive*, *15*(3). Advance online publication. DOI: 10.30574/ijsra.2025.15.3.1933

Shevtshenko, E.. (2023). Development of SCOR database for digitalisation of supply chain customer feedback analysis. *Inzinerine Ekonomika–Engineering Economics*, *34*(4). Advance online publication. DOI: 10.5755/j01.ee.34.4.31618

Stanford, E. (2025). Autonomous AI: Who is responsible when AI acts autonomously and things go wrong? In *AI, machine learning & big data laws and regulations.* Global Legal Insights. https://www.globallegalinsights.com/practice-areas/ai-machine-learning-and-big-data-laws-and-regulations/autonomous-ai-who-is-responsible-when-ai-acts-autonomously-and-things-go-wrong/

Stevens, G. C. (1990). Successful supply chain management. *Management Decision*, *28*(8). Advance online publication. DOI: 10.1108/00251749010140790

Tirkolaee, E. B., Sadeghi, S., Mansoori Mooseloo, F., Rezaei Vandchali, H., & Aeini, S. (2021). Application of machine learning in supply chain management: A comprehensive overview of the main areas. *Mathematical Problems in Engineering. Article ID, 1476043.* Advance online publication. DOI: 10.1155/2021/1476043

Toorajipour, R., Sohrabpour, V., Nazarpour, A., Oghazi, P., & Fischl, M. (2021). Artificial intelligence in supply chain management: A systematic literature review. *Journal of Business Research*, *122*, 502–517. DOI: 10.1016/j.jbusres.2020.09.009

Torchio, F. (2023). *Survey on automated systems for smart warehouses* (PhD thesis). Politecnico di Torino. https://webthesis.biblio.polito.it/secure/29879/1/tesi.pdf

Tunisia. (2014). *Decree No. 2014-1039 organizing public procurement procedures.* Official Gazette of the Republic of Tunisia.

Tunisia (Various Ministries). (2022). *National artificial intelligence strategy: Unlocking Tunisia's capabilities potential.*

Unit, X. Labs. (2025). Defining GDPR machine vision systems for today's businesses. https://www.unitxlabs.com/resources/general-data-protection-regulation-gdpr-machine-vision-system/

United Nations. (2015). *Transforming our world: The 2030 Agenda for Sustainable Development* (A/RES/70/1). https://sdgs.un.org/2030agenda

United Nations. (2023). *The Sustainable Development Goals report 2023.* UN DESA. https://unstats.un.org/sdgs/report/2023/The-Sustainable-Development-Goals-Report-2023.pdf

United Nations Development Programme. (2023). *Procurement for sustainable development strategy 2022–2025.* https://www.undp.org/sites/g/files/zskgke326/files/2025-05/undp_procurement_for_sust_dev_strategy_2022-25.pdf

United Nations Environment Programme. (2021). *Sustainable public procurement: A global review.* https://wedocs.unep.org/handle/20.500.11822/8522

VerifyWise. (2025). Human in the loop safeguards. https://verifywise.ai/lexicon/human-in-the-loop-safeguards

Williams, S. (2007). *Buying a better world: Sustainable public procurement.* Forum for the Future. https://www.oneplanetnetwork.org/sites/default/files/sustainable_procurement_manual_-_resource_book.pdf

World Bank. (2023). *Sustainable procurement.* World Bank Group. https://thedocs.worldbank.org/en/doc/01802d374f64ff681613cff8ccad3576-0290012023/original/Sustainable-Procurement-August-2023.pdf

Chapter 9
Insurance of Goods Under the Provisions of the UAE Maritime Law: Legal Framework, Practice, and Comparative Analysis

Ahmed Moustafa Aldabousi
https://orcid.org/0000-0002-9073-7254
Umm Al Quwain University, UAE

ABSTRACT

Considering the UAE Maritime Law No. (43) of 2023, this study examines cargo insurance as a fundamental mechanism ensuring legal and financial protection against maritime risks. It explores the legislative development of marine insurance in the UAE, the obligations of the insurer and the insured, and the principles of utmost good faith, insurable interest, and subrogation. The research analyzes the scope of covered risks, total and partial loss, and the evidentiary value of insurance documents in proving rights and obligations. A comparative analysis with international instruments such as the York–Antwerp Rules and the UK Marine Insurance Act highlights the alignment of UAE law with global standards. The findings demonstrate that the 2023 law modernizes the legal framework, strengthens cargo owners' protection, balances the interests of insurers and carriers, and enhances confidence in maritime transactions, contributing to the UAE's vision of a competitive global maritime hub

DOI: 10.4018/979-8-3373-8841-0.ch009

INTRODUCTION

The insurance of goods under UAE Maritime law is governed by Federal Maritime Law No. 43/2023, which updates and aligns insurance provisions with international maritime practices. The framework integrates both conventional and Sharia-compliant (takaful) insurance, but faces challenges in judicial interpretation, enforcement of disclosure and seaworthiness warranties, and harmonization with international standards. Coverage typically includes bulk, containerized, and manufactured goods, with valuation clauses influenced by global standards such as the Institute Cargo Clauses. Regulatory gaps and lack of recent case law highlight the need for further empirical research and legislative refinement to ensure effective risk management and compliance in the UAE maritime sector.

1.1 Study Scope

1.1.1. Time Period: Focus on legislative reforms and insurance practice from 2020–2024, with historical context from prior statutes.
1.1.2. Disciplines: Maritime law, insurance law, comparative law, risk management.
1.1.3. Methods: Doctrinal legal analysis, comparative review, synthesis of secondary literature, meta-analysis of regulatory and case law trends.
1.1.4. Assumptions & Limitations
1.1.5. Assumptions: The report assumes the effective implementation of Federal Maritime Law No. 43/2023 and ongoing integration of Sharia principles in insurance practice.
1.1.6. Limitations: Lack of recent judicial decisions interpreting the new law; limited empirical data on underwriting criteria for different goods; reliance on secondary sources and literature reviews.

1.2 Suggested Further Research

1.2.1 Empirical analysis of judicial/arbitration decisions under Federal Maritime Law No. 43/2023
1.2.2 Differentiation of underwriting criteria for bulk vs. containerized goods in the UAE context.
1.2.3 Development and testing of blockchain-based compliance frameworks for maritime insurance.
1.2.4 Comparative studies on harmonization of Sharia-compliant and conventional insurance in maritime sectors.

1.3 Scope and Significance

1.3.1 The insurance of goods under UAE maritime law is a cornerstone of the nation's commercial infrastructure, supporting its role as a global logistics and shipping hub. Recent legislative reforms, notably Federal Maritime Law No. 43/2023, have modernized the regulatory environment, aiming to align local practices with international standards while integrating Islamic jurisprudence. This evolution reflects the UAE's ambition to balance global best practices with local legal and cultural imperatives, particularly in the context of risk management, liability, and contract enforcement in maritime insurance (Madi, 2025).

1.3.2 The UAE's maritime insurance sector is in transition, with new laws and regulatory frameworks seeking to address historical gaps and future challenges. The integration of Sharia principles and the adoption of international conventions signal a commitment to both innovation and compliance, though practical and judicial clarity remains a work in progress.

1.4. Research Problem

1.4.1. The central problem of this research can be summarized in the following question:

1.4.5. To what extent has UAE Maritime Law No. (43) of 2023 achieved a fair balance between the rights of the insurer and the insured in cargo insurance contracts? And are its provisions sufficiently comprehensive to align with international standards governing marine insurance?

1.5. Future Research Directions

Empirical Case Law Analysis: Systematic review of judicial and arbitration decisions under Federal Maritime Law No. 43/2023.

Underwriting Criteria Differentiation: Research into risk assessment standards for bulk versus containerized goods in the UAE.

Blockchain-based Compliance Frameworks: Development and pilot testing of integrated technological solutions for insurance transparency.

Comparative Harmonization Studies: In-depth analysis of Sharia-compliant and conventional insurance integration in maritime sectors. Addressing current research gaps will require mixed-method approaches, combining doctrinal analysis with empirical data and technological innovation. Future studies should focus on judicial interpretation, underwriting practices, and the practical integration of Sharia and international standards

2. THEORETICAL FRAMEWORKS

The theoretical foundation of marine cargo insurance under UAE law is anchored in a multifaceted legal environment that brings together international maritime conventions, federal civil and commercial legislation, and Islamic jurisprudence. The enactment of Federal Maritime Law No. 43 of 2023, effective from March 2024, represents a fundamental restructuring of the maritime legislative framework. By repealing Commercial Maritime Law No. 26 of 1981, the new statute modernizes the rules governing ship registration, ownership, chartering, and the carriage of goods under the Emirati flag.

These amendments carry profound implications for the insurance of goods, particularly with respect to the liability of carriers, delay in delivery, and resulting economic loss (Naboush, 2020). The law seeks to harmonize UAE practice with international maritime instruments and align it with the broader Federal Civil Transactions Law, thus embedding maritime insurance within a unified legal system that balances domestic needs with global standards (Fayyad & Hayajneh, 2022).

2.1 The Regulatory Environment

The regulatory landscape governing maritime insurance in the UAE is structured around three interrelated dimensions:

1. Integration with International Conventions

The UAE's commitment to international maritime norms is reflected in the incorporation of standards governing carrier liability, delay, and compensation. This alignment promotes legal predictability and fosters confidence among foreign investors and trading partners.

2. Federal Civil Transaction Laws

These laws provide the contractual foundation for insurance relations, addressing key elements such as formation, consent, fraud, duress, and remedies for contractual defects (Sarhan, 2024). They ensure that maritime insurance contracts adhere to the principles of fairness and enforceability embedded in civil law.

3. Technological and Environmental Standards Recent developments emphasize environmental sustainability, safety, and the integration of digital technologies in maritime operations and insurance risk assessment, The inclusion of such standards highlights the UAE's transition toward an innovative-driven legal

system that integrates global sustainability priorities (Al Abdouli & Sipos, 2024).

The current framework is both robust and transitional comprehensive in its design yet evolving in its application. While it aligns with international practice, the absence of extensive judicial interpretation underscores the need for continuous scholarly engagement and judicial refinement to ensure legal coherence and certainty.

2.2 Integration with Federal Civil Transaction Law

The relationship between maritime insurance and the Federal Civil Transactions Law reveals the UAE's distinctive approach to legal harmonization. Civil law governs the general principles of contracts, including formation, validity, consent, and remedies in cases of defect or coercion (Sarhan, 2024). This integration ensures that maritime insurance contracts are enforceable, equitable, and consistent with national legal values.

The Civil Transactions Law also determines the extent to which foreign law may apply in contracts with international elements, permitting its use only when it does not contravene Islamic law or public policy. This careful balance allows contractual flexibility while preserving the integrity of the Emirati legal order.

Additionally, the doctrines of res judicata and functus officio, derived from procedural law, play an important role in ensuring the finality of arbitral awards and judicial decisions in maritime insurance disputes (Daradkeh, 2015). These principles reflect the UAE's commitment to procedural fairness and the efficient administration of justice.

The interaction between maritime insurance and civil transaction law guarantees that contracts are both legally binding and ethically defensible. It creates a legal system where commercial certainty coexists with moral accountability, reinforcing the legitimacy and predictability of insurance relations.

2.3 Influence of Islamic Jurisprudence

Islamic jurisprudence (Fiqh al-Muʿāmalāt) continues to exert a defining influence on the interpretation and ethical foundation of maritime insurance in the UAE, its principles ensure that contractual relations respect both commercial fairness and moral legitimacy, embedding an ethical dimension within the economic transaction.

Islamic law mandates that contracts be concluded with mutual consent and in good faith, prohibiting elements of deceit (gharar) and fraud that undermine transparency and trust (Hidayat & Ahmad, 2023). The prohibition of usury (riba) and excessive uncertainty shapes the architecture of insurance agreements, compelling insurers to avoid speculative or exploitative structures (Alkhan & Hassan, 2024).

Moreover, the doctrine of contractual options (khiyārāt) grants parties a limited right to withdraw before full contractual commitment, protecting genuine consent and ensuring that obligations are undertaken with informed intention. This principle strengthens the moral foundation of maritime insurance contracts and reflects the fusion of Sharia ethics with civil law formality.

Islamic jurisprudence thus functions as a normative and corrective layer within the UAE's maritime insurance framework. It guides contract formation and interpretation, ensuring that risk allocation and compensation mechanisms comply with Sharia principles while remaining consistent with international commercial norms.

3. METHODOLOGICAL FRAMEWORK

This research adopts a multi-layered qualitative methodology designed to examine the statutory, doctrinal, and comparative dimensions of maritime insurance regulation in the United Arab Emirates. The methodological structure combines doctrinal legal analysis, comparative review, and meta-analysis, providing a comprehensive foundation for analyzing both the theoretical constructions and the practical applications of UAE maritime insurance law.

3.1 Doctrinal Legal Analysis

A doctrinal analytical approach is utilized to investigate the statutory and regulatory texts governing maritime insurance, alongside authoritative legal commentaries and interpretative materials. The analysis focuses on Federal Maritime Law No. 43 of 2023, its executive regulations, and related provisions of the Federal Civil Transactions Law, which collectively define the contractual rights and liabilities of parties engaged in maritime insurance. This approach allows for a systematic interpretation of the legislative intent and its implications for risk allocation and carrier responsibility within the UAE's legal framework.

3.2 Comparative Review

Complementing the doctrinal approach, a comparative legal perspective is employed to analyse international maritime instruments—particularly the Institute Cargo Clauses, Hague-Visby Rules, and IMO Conventions—to assess their influence on the UAE's evolving maritime insurance regime. This comparative analysis reveals both points of convergence and divergence between Emirati law and international norms, particularly concerning the principles governing carrier liability, delay, and compensation for loss or damage. Through this lens, the study identifies how UAE legislation integrates international standards while preserving national legal and economic priorities.

3.3 Meta-Analysis

A meta-analytical approach is also incorporated, synthesizing secondary academic and professional sources, including peer-reviewed legal research, industry reports, and bibliometric data in maritime and insurance law. This layer of analysis enables the identification of major academic trends, policy shifts, and recurring regulatory challenges affecting the insurance of goods under UAE maritime law. The meta-analysis supports the doctrinal and comparative findings by situating the UAE's framework within a broader global and scholarly context.

3.4 Research Limitations

While methodological design ensures analytical depth and theoretical diversity, the study recognizes several limitations. Chief among them is the lack of recent judicial rulings interpreting Federal Maritime Law No. 43 of 2023, given its relatively recent implementation. As a result, the research relies primarily on secondary sources and comparative materials rather than empirical case law (Abu Al-Haija & Houcine, 2024). Despite this constraint, the integration of doctrinal and comparative methodologies provides a solid analytical framework that supports a nuanced understanding of the law's practical and theoretical dimensions (Obeidat, Alfil, Aldabousi, & Dganni, 2024).

The methodological framework thus provides a structured and coherent foundation for analyzing the UAE's maritime insurance regime. It integrates doctrinal precision, comparative breadth, and analytical synthesis, allowing for a balanced examination of both the legislative framework and its practical implications. Nevertheless, it highlights the ongoing need for empirical research and judicial interpretation to substantiate the evolving understanding of enforcement and implementation in practice.

4. CRITICAL ANALYSIS OF FINDINGS

4.1 Types of Goods Insured and Coverage Criteria

Within the UAE's maritime insurance practice, the classification of insured goods and the scope of coverage are determined by nature, packaging, and mode of transportation. The analysis identifies several key categories of insured goods commonly covered under marine cargo policies in the UAE:

4.2 Bulk Goods

This category includes commodities such as ore, sand, grain, fertilizers, and other unpackaged raw materials transported in bulk quantities. The insurance of such goods typically emphasizes risks related to spillage, contamination, and handling losses during loading and discharge operations (Awad & Aldabousi, 2024).

4.3 Containerized Goods

These refer to manufactured or semi-finished goods transported via containers across international routes. Policies covering containerized goods often include clauses addressing partial loss, mixed consignments, and multimodal transportation, providing flexibility in cross-border trade arrangements.

4.4 Warehouse-to-Warehouse Coverage

A distinctive feature of UAE maritime insurance is the warehouse-to-warehouse clause, which ensures continuous protection from the point of dispatch at the factory to the final delivery location. This coverage extends to interim storage and customs clearance phases, reflecting international practice under the Institute Cargo Clauses (A) and guaranteeing seamless protection throughout the transit chain (Alper, 2008).

The range of insured goods underscores the adaptability and comprehensiveness of the UAE's maritime insurance regime. However, the scope and adequacy of coverage largely depend on the precision of policy drafting, the definition of insured perils, and the interaction between contractual terms and statutory obligations. These dynamics reveal the importance of aligning domestic insurance practices with international standards while ensuring that regulatory adaptation remains responsive to local commercial realities.

5. CRITERIA FOR INSURABILITY AND COVERAGE

The determination of insurability and coverage under UAE maritime insurance law is guided by established international principles that define when and how goods may qualify for protection within a marine adventure.

5.1 Insurable Interest

For insurance coverage to be valid, the insured must possess a demonstrable financial interest in the goods forming part of a marine adventure. This principle ensures that the insured stands to suffer a genuine economic loss should the insured event occur, reinforcing the distinction between legitimate insurance and speculative arrangements (Li, 2023).

Marine insurance applies exclusively to fortuitous events, those that are unforeseen and accidental in nature. Losses that are inevitable, expected, or attributable to the insured's negligence fall outside the ambit of indemnifiable perils, preserving the foundational element of uncertainty essential to insurance contracts.

In accordance with established maritime practice, consignees must provide prompt notice of any damage or loss within a specified time frame. UAE law, in harmony with international precedent, requires such notice to be given at the time of delivery or within three days thereafter; failure to comply relieves the carrier of liability (*Consignee Must Give Notice of His Claim*, 1995). This procedural safeguard ensures the timely verification of damage and prevents fraudulent claims.

An unjustified deviation from the contractual voyage route constitutes a serious breach under marine insurance law and may discharge the insurer from liability for subsequent sea perils. Such deviations alter the degree of risk originally contemplated in the policy and undermine the doctrine of utmost good faith (Aldabousi, 2022).

These principles collectively establish the boundaries of insurability within the UAE's maritime framework. They ensure that only lawful, transparent, and fortuitous risks are covered, thereby maintaining the integrity of the insurance system and aligning Emirati practice with well-recognised standards in international marine insurance law.

5.2 Valuation Clauses and International Standards

The valuation of insured goods forms a cornerstone of marine insurance, determining the quantum of compensation and reflecting the contractual understanding between insurer and insured. UAE maritime insurance practice increasingly draws upon international standards to regulate these valuation mechanisms.

5.3 Institute Cargo Clauses

The Institute Cargo Clauses promulgated by the London insurance market serve as the principal reference for defining the scope of coverage, exclusions, and risk allocation in marine cargo policies. Their global acceptance provides predictability and uniformity, which the UAE market has progressively embraced (Asgarian, 2021).

5.4 Landed Cost vs. Selling Price

Valuation clauses often specify whether indemnity is calculated based on the landed cost (i.e., cost, freight, and insurance value at the port of arrival) or the selling price of the goods. The distinction has practical significance: while the landed cost reflects the insured's immediate financial exposure, valuation at the selling price accounts for anticipated profit margins, offering broader protection to traders (Aldabousi, 2025).

5.5 Jurisdictional Preferences

English law and London market customs continue to exert a strong influence over the drafting of marine insurance contracts(Baatz, 2020), However, their applicability in the UAE remains limited by jurisdictional considerations and public policy constraints . Courts in the UAE may recognize English precedents as persuasive authority but not as binding, ensuring that local legal sovereignty and Sharia-based principles prevail where conflicts arise.

The valuation structure of UAE marine insurance contracts demonstrates a clear convergence with international best practices, particularly in relation to coverage definition, indemnity calculation, and risk assessment. Nonetheless, further research is required to clarify the underwriting criteria applied to bulk and containerized goods, which remain areas of practical and doctrinal uncertainty(Asgarian, 2021).

6. ROLES AND RESPONSIBILITIES OF INSURERS AND INSURED PARTIES

6.1 Duties and Liabilities

The allocation of duties and liabilities between insurers and insured parties under UAE maritime insurance law reflects a deliberate legislative balance aimed at promoting fairness, transparency, and efficient risk management.

Insurers are primarily responsible for indemnifying covered losses, managing and accessing risks, and ensuring the enforcement of policy terms and limitations. Their role extends beyond mere compensation, encompassing the evaluation of seaworthiness, underwriting compliance, and the enforcement of preventive measures to minimize exposure.

Insured parties, on the other hand, are legally obligated to disclose all material facts, pay insurance premiums promptly, mitigate potential damages, and notify insurers immediately upon the occurrence of any loss or incident. Failure to comply with these obligations can result in a denial of claims, particularly where delivery procedures or notification protocols are violated (*Carrier Will Be Liable for Damages to Goods If Delivery Was at the Port's Warehouse and Not to the Consignee*, 1995).

6.2 Disclosure Obligations and Warranty of Seaworthiness

The duty of disclosure is a cornerstone of maritime insurance, derived from the doctrine of *utmost good faith (uberrimae fidei)*. The insured must disclose all material information that may affect the insurer's assessment of risk especially matters concerning the vessel's seaworthiness. Failure to meet this duty may entitle the insurer to avoid the policy altogether, even if the loss is unrelated to the undisclosed fact (Aldabousi, 2022).

The warranty of seaworthiness, though rooted in traditional maritime law, has evolved into a context-dependent obligation shaped by the nature of the voyage, the type of vessel, and the applicable international standards. In modern practice, it operates as a relative rather than absolute concept, acknowledging that a vessel's condition must be reasonably fit for the intended voyage. Nonetheless, breach of this warranty—particularly through non-disclosure—may render a policy void or bar recovery under the terms of UAE maritime insurance (Aldabousi, 2024).

6.3 Claims Handling and Risk Management

Claims handling within the UAE maritime insurance framework adheres to strict procedural and evidentiary requirements. Consignees and insured parties must comply with delivery and notification protocols to preserve their right to indemnity. Insurers may justifiably reject claims arising from unjustified deviations, breaches of voyage conditions, or late reporting of loss (*Carrier Will Be Liable for Damages to Goods If Delivery Was at the Port's Warehouse and Not to the Consignee*, 1995).

From a risk management perspective, insurers mitigate exposure through policy warranties, mandatory surveys, and safety compliance measures, ensuring that vessels meet operational and regulatory standards prior to and during coverage (Pijaca, Bulum, & Primorac, 2023). These mechanisms support proactive risk control rather than post-incident compensation.

Equally, insured parties bear responsibility for proper cargo handling, storage, and documentation, as negligent or fraudulent management practices may invalidate coverage or trigger liability claims (Whiteman, 1984).

The allocation of responsibilities under UAE maritime insurance law is designed to achieve a delicate equilibrium between contractual freedom and legal accountability. The intertwined duties of disclosure, seaworthiness, and compliance form the structural foundation of insurance validity. Their rigorous enforcement by insurers and courts alike not only preserves the integrity of contractual relations but also strengthens confidence in the UAE's maritime insurance regime as a fair, transparent, and internationally aligned system.

7. THE LEGAL CONDITIONS AND CASES PERMITTING CARGO ABANDONMENT UNDER UAE MARITIME LAW NO. (43) OF 2023

Marine cargo insurance is a type of insurance designed to protect both the goods and the vessel during maritime transport. This form of insurance is specifically intended to cover potential risks that may affect goods during shipment, storage, unloading, and even during intermodal transport (such as between ships, trains, and trucks), The marine cargo insurance contract aims to guarantee compensation for the loss or damage of the insured goods during the sea voyage because of any unforeseen maritime incident, whether the loss is total or partial, with the insurer bearing responsibility for any damages sustained by the insured cargo.

The coverage of marine cargo insurance includes various risks such as sinking, fire, theft, damage, or delays in delivery due to environmental conditions or natural events such as sea storms. Cargo owners or consignees may either insure the goods themselves or rely on insurance provided by the carrier or the manufacturing company.

The cost of marine cargo insurance varies depending on several factors, including the type and value of the goods, the method of packaging, shipping conditions, the maritime route, and the potential risks along that route.

The UAE legislator has regulated marine cargo insurance under Articles (325–332) of the UAE Maritime Law No. (43) of 2023. Cargo may be insured under a single voyage policy or a floating/open cover policy that applies to multiple voyages or for a specific period defined in the policy. The objective is to protect the owner or carrier of the goods from potential losses during maritime transport, whether arising from marine accidents, natural events, or other factors that could cause damage or loss of the cargo.

The insurance policy refers to the contract whereby the insurer undertakes to cover all damages arising from insured marine risks affecting the goods shipped on behalf of the insured during a specified period and within the agreed limits of coverage. An open cover policy does not, at the time of its conclusion, specify the goods insured, the premium, the voyage, or the name of the carrying vessel, since these details are unknown to both parties at that stage. They are determined later by a notification from the insured to the insurer for each shipment, within the timeframe stipulated in the policy. Once the notification is made, the insurance coverage automatically takes effect without the need to issue a separate policy for each shipment.

This type of policy is also known as a floating policy, open policy, or open cover agreement, as it does not specify, at the time of its conclusion, the goods insured, the premium, the voyage, or the carrying vessel. These details are unknown to both parties when the policy is issued and are determined only through a notice submitted by the insured to the insurance company for each shipment, within the time frame specified in the policy. Upon such notification, the shipment is automatically covered by insurance without the need to issue a separate policy for it.

Accordingly, the subscription policy, floating policy, open policy, or open cover agreement does not, by itself, oblige the insurer to compensate for losses unless the insurer has been duly notified of the specific goods to be insured, the amount of insurance, and such notification occurs before the insured takes place.

Insurance for a single voyage means that coverage applies solely during one specific sea voyage in which the goods are transported. For instance, if a trader ships a container of goods from one port to another, the insurance covers only that single voyage.

Conversely, a subscription policy for several voyages provides coverage for multiple sea voyages undertaken by the vessel within a certain period. For example, if a company regularly imports goods from various sources, it may purchase a subscription policy covering all its shipments over a month or a longer period.

In both cases, the policy sets forth the terms and conditions of insurance, including the insured amount, covered risks, exclusions, and any additional coverage available. The purpose of such a policy is to provide financial protection to cargo owners and carriers during maritime shipping operations and to minimize the associated risks. The insured goods remain continuously covered throughout the entire voyage, regardless of their location, if that location is included within the contractual agreement between the parties.

For example, if the vessel stops at an intermediate port to load or unload cargo, the insurance remains valid during the stopover. If, during the voyage, the goods are subject to complementary land, river, or air transport, the provisions of marine insurance continue to apply to all stages of the journey unless otherwise agreed. This means that marine insurance coverage extends to these supplementary transport stages unless specific exclusions or different agreements are established between the contracting parties.

Accordingly, if the policy stipulates that marine insurance coverage shall extend to non-marine risks, such as a *"warehouse-to-warehouse"* clause whereby the insurer guarantees all risks to which the goods are exposed from the moment they leave the consignor's warehouse until they reach the consignee's warehouse then the insurance shall cover not only maritime perils during the voyage but also the risks occurring during land transport from the shipper's warehouse to the port of loading, while the goods are at the dock, and during the post-discharge transport from the port of arrival to the consignee's warehouse. Such an agreement results in the application of the rules of marine insurance to cover land-based risks that are part of the overall transport of goods, as defined in the insurance policy.

The UAE legislator has set a maximum limit for insurance that may be fixed for goods, which cannot be exceeded under any circumstances. In other words, compensation payable to the insured for damage resulting from the occurrence of an insured peril is limited to the actual loss sustained; the insured cannot claim an amount exceeding the real damage. Thus, the insured may not demand payment of the insured sum if the actual damage is less than that amount. Consequently, the value of the insured goods may not exceed the higher of the following amounts:

The purchase price of the goods at the time and place of shipment, or their current market value at that time and place if they were not purchased, plus the costs of transport to the port of destination and the expected profit. This means that the insurance amount must not exceed the actual value of the goods at the time of shipment, including their purchase price, transport expenses, and anticipated profit.

The value of the goods at the time and place of arrival, or at the date when they ought to have arrived in the event of loss. This ensures that the compensation corresponds to the real value of the goods at the time of arrival or their expected arrival date in case of damage or loss during transport.

The sale price of the goods, if they were sold by the insured, plus any additional amounts agreed upon in the sales contract. Thus, the insurance value cannot exceed the actual selling price of the goods upon arrival, together with any supplementary amounts stipulated in the sale agreement.

The damage to goods is assessed by comparing their value in a damaged condition with their sound value at the same time and place, and the percentage of depreciation is applied to the insured amount. For instance, if the sound value of the goods at a given time and place is USD 10,000, and their value after damage decreases to USD 8,000, the depreciation rate is 20%. Based on this rate, the compensation due from the insurer is calculated as 80% of the agreed insured amount. This mechanism ensures fair compensation to the owner for the actual losses likely sustained because of damage occurring during maritime transport.

The UAE legislator has defined specific cases in which the insured is permitted to abandon the goods to the insurer, thereby transferring ownership and claiming the full insurance amount. These cases are as follows:

1. Loss of communication with the vessel for 90 days:

If no news is received from the vessel for ninety (90) days after the last report, the goods are presumed to have perished as of the date of the last known communication. For example, if a vessel carrying food supplies loses contact for 90 days after the last message, the cargo is presumed destroyed or lost, and the insured may abandon the goods and claim compensation from the insurer.

2. Unseaworthiness of the vessel:

If the vessel becomes unfit for navigation and the transportation of goods by any means has not commenced within ninety (90) days from the date on which the insured notified the insurer of the vessel's unseaworthiness, the insured may abandon the goods. For instance, if maritime authorities declare a vessel unfit for sailing due to a severe technical issue and no steps are taken to transport the goods within 90 days, the insured may abandon the cargo without further liability.

3. Destruction or damage of goods equal to three-fourths of their value:

If the goods are destroyed or damaged to an extent of at least three-quarters of their insured value, the insured may abandon the goods. For example, if a shipment insured for USD 10,000 suffers damage valued at USD 7,500 or more, the insured has the right to abandon the cargo and claim compensation.

4. Sale of goods during the voyage due to material damage:

If the goods are sold during the voyage because of material damage, the insured may abandon them. For example, if furniture cargo is damaged during marine transport and sold as a result, the insured may abandon the goods to the insurer.

In cases (3) and (4) above, if the insurance is limited to specific perils, abandonment is accepted only if the damage arises from one of those covered perils, ensuring that the insurer is not held liable for risks outside the agreed coverage.

Furthermore, if war risks are covered, the insured may exercise the right of abandonment in cases of capture, detention, or immobilization of the vessel by public authorities, provided that the goods have not been placed at the disposal of the insured within four (4) months from the date of notifying the insurer of the incident. In other words, if the vessel is seized or detained due to war-related circumstances and the cargo is not recovered or released within four months of notice, the insured has the right to abandon the goods and claim full indemnity under the marine insurance policy.

The subscription policy for cargo insurance, when issued as a single document, must include the terms and conditions binding upon both the insurer and the insured. Among the essential provisions that must be included are the following:

A. Duration of insurance:

The period of insurance coverage must be clearly defined, specifying the time-frame during which the goods are protected. For example, if the insurance period is six months, the goods remain covered throughout that duration.

B. The insurance amount:

The policy must specify the total amount that the insurer undertakes to compensate in the event of loss or damage.

C. The amount of insurance premiums:

The policy should state the premiums payable by the insured, which are determined based on the value of the goods and the level of risk associated with their transport. For instance, if the goods are of high value or subject to significant transport risks, the insurance premium will naturally be higher.

D. Specification of the insured goods, voyages, and vessel name(s):

Each shipment must be reported individually through notifications specifying the insured goods, voyage details, and the vessel's name. For example, if the insured goods are garments to be shipped aboard the vessel *"Ocean Voyager,"* this information must be disclosed to the insurer in advance.

In emphasizing the importance of information exchange between the insurer and the insured during the cargo insurance process, the UAE legislator requires the insured to notify the insurer of subsequent shipments, and obliges the insurer to accept coverage for them, under the following conditions:

1. Shipments executed on behalf of the insured or under contracts of sale or purchase:

The insured must notify the insurer of all such shipments within the period specified in the insurance contract. For example, if company (A) ships goods under a purchase contract, it must notify its insurer of the shipment details within the agreed notification period.

2. Shipments executed on behalf of third parties for which the insured undertake insurance:

The insured must also notify the insurer of all shipments that they have agreed to insure on behalf of others, provided they have a direct interest in such shipments (as an agent, trustee, or in any other capacity). For instance, if a shipping company undertakes to insure goods for company (B) as its agent, it must immediately notify the insurer of these shipments upon concluding the shipping contract.

Including such provisions in the subscription policy ensures a continuous flow of information between both parties, establishes mutual obligations for the proper and effective execution of insurance coverage, safeguards the financial interests of both the insurer and the insured, and clearly defines their respective responsibilities and liabilities within the framework of the insurance contract.

The Dubai Court of Cassation ruled that, according to the established jurisprudence of the Court, cargo insurance under a subscription policy constitutes "an agreement whereby the insurer undertakes to cover all damages arising from insured marine risks affecting all goods shipped on behalf of the insured during a specified period and within the agreed limits of coverage(Dubai Court of Cassation – Civil Judgments, Appeal No. 248 of 2008 (Commercial Circuit), judgment dated April 20, 2009, Technical Office, Vol. 20, Part 2, Rule No. 128(2), p. 1121).

This type of policy is referred to as a floating policy or an open policy because, at the time of its conclusion, it does not specify the goods insured, the insurance premium, the voyage, or the name of the carrying vessel. These details are unknown to both parties when the policy is executed and are later determined through a notification from the insured to the insurance company for each shipment separately, within the time frame stipulated in the policy or from the time the insured is notified if the insurance is taken out on behalf of another party.

If, however, the insured intentionally breaches any of these obligations mentioned above, the insurer has the right to request the termination of the contract, recover any amounts paid for incidents related to shipments occurring after the violation, and claim, by way of compensation, the premiums corresponding to the shipments that were not duly reported.

8. CHALLENGES, GAPS, AND COMPARATIVE ANALYSIS

8.1 Current Challenges and Recent Developments

The implementation of Federal Maritime Law No. 43 of 2023 marks a substantial reform in the UAE's maritime legal system, modernizing the framework governing ship operations, liability, and cargo insurance. Nevertheless, effective enforcement remains a pressing challenge. The new provisions, though progressive, require institutional alignment, judicial consistency, and administrative efficiency to achieve their intended impact.

Enforcement gaps persist due to overlapping regulatory jurisdictions and the interpretative interplay between Sharia principles and civil law procedures. These complexities often result in procedural bottlenecks and inconsistent judicial reasoning in the enforcement of maritime contracts and insurance disputes (Alhadhrami, 2025).

Emerging environmental and technological risks including marine pollution, cyberattacks, and the advent of autonomous maritime vehicles have also exposed gaps in existing liability regimes. Such developments call for updated regulatory and insurance models capable of addressing both operational risks and civil liability arising from automation and environmental harm (Ishii, 2024).

8.2 Sharia Compliance and Takaful Integration

The Takaful model offers a distinct approach to maritime insurance, rooted in Islamic principles of cooperation (ta'awun), solidarity, and shared risk, while explicitly prohibiting *riba* (interest), *gharar* (excessive uncertainty), and *maisir* (gambling) (Awad & Aldabousi, 2024). These principles ensure that financial arrangements in maritime insurance conform to moral and legal expectations derived from Sharia.

To institutionalize compliance, regulatory authorities have developed Shariah governance frameworks encompassing internal control mechanisms, independent supervisory boards, and Shariah audit functions to oversee operational integrity (Puad, 2024).

In parallel, technological innovations notably blockchain applications—are being explored to enhance transparency, traceability, and compliance verification in Takaful operations (Al-Sherman & Aldabousi, 2024). Furthermore, the equitable management of Takaful surplus remains guided by the principles of fairness and mutual benefit, reinforcing the cooperative nature of Islamic insurance schemes.

8.3 Comparison with International Maritime Insurance Standards

From a comparative perspective, the UAE's maritime insurance system demonstrates growing alignment with international conventions while maintaining its legal and cultural identity. The adoption of standards consistent with IMO conventions including those governing marine pollution, civil liability, and compensation mechanisms illustrates the UAE's commitment to global maritime governance (El Yanboiy, 2024).

Similarly, the influence of the Institute Cargo Clauses on Emirati insurance contracts is evident in the harmonization of coverage definitions, valuation methods, and risk classifications. However, regulatory divergence remains a defining feature of the UAE framework. The requirement for Sharia compliance, coupled with local governance constraints, generates unique interpretive and practical challenges when harmonizing domestic insurance law with international maritime standards (de Faria, 2024).

The UAE's maritime insurance sector stands at a critical juncture between reform and consolidation. Persistent challenges in enforcement, regulatory harmonization, and technological adaptation underscore the complexity of aligning Sharia-based insurance models with international maritime norms. Yet, technological innovation and Takaful integration represent promising avenues for enhancing transparency, accountability, and compliance—paving the way for a more resilient and globally compatible maritime insurance regime.

9. REAL-WORLD IMPLICATIONS

The practical implications of the UAE's maritime insurance framework extend far beyond the legal domain, influencing the operational stability and global competitiveness of the shipping, logistics, and financial sectors.

9.1 Risk Management

Enhanced levels of insurance adequacy and sophisticated risk management practices play a vital role in strengthening supply chain resilience within the UAE. By integrating insurance mechanisms into logistics planning, firms can mitigate exposure to unforeseen disruptions and maintain trade continuity (Alsheikh & Morshed, 2025).

9.2 Contractual Clarity

The emphasis on clear contractual drafting particularly regarding disclosure obligations and seaworthiness warranties serves to protect both insurers and insured parties. This transparency reduces the likelihood of disputes, minimizes claim denials, and promotes confidence in the enforcement of maritime insurance contracts (Zheng, 2022).

9.3 Regulatory Compliance

The UAE's adoption of international conventions and its integration of Sharia-compliant insurance frameworks ensure alignment with global trade standards while maintaining legal coherence with national values. Such dual compliance fosters investor confidence and facilitates cross-border commercial operations in a regulated and predictable environment.

9.4 Technological Integration

Innovations such as blockchain technology and smart contracts are reshaping the operational landscape of the insurance sector. These technologies enhance transparency, traceability, and enforcement efficiency, though they also require continuous regulatory adaptation to ensure security and compatibility with existing legal frameworks (Sharma, Ajmani, & Iwendi, 2023).

In practice, the effectiveness of UAE maritime insurance law depends on its ability to balance risk mitigation, contractual integrity, and technological advancement. The system's evolving interaction between regulatory precision and market innovation positions the UAE as a regional benchmark for maritime insurance governance—one that combines legal certainty with strategic flexibility in a rapidly globalising maritime economy.

CONCLUSION

The Federal Maritime Law No. 43 of 2023 represents a significant milestone in the evolution of maritime legislation within the United Arab Emirates. It has redefined the philosophy of marine insurance by establishing a coherent and balanced framework that integrates international principles with the economic and legal particularities of the UAE. Through its comprehensive provisions, the law provides clarity, consistency, and adaptability in addressing the complexities of contemporary maritime trade and transport.

The analysis reveals that marine insurance under this new legislation transcends its traditional contractual nature; it now operates as a strategic legal mechanism to safeguard the national maritime economy and ensure the continuity of global supply chains. The Emirati legislator successfully resolved many of the ambiguities that previously led to inconsistent practice, particularly regarding the scope of the insurer's liability, the right of abandonment, the assessment of compensation, and the disclosure obligations of the insured. Moreover, the law enshrines the principles of good faith, transparency, and fairness as the cornerstones of the contractual relationship, thus enhancing trust and efficiency in the insurance market.

While these reforms constitute a major step forward, the principal challenge lies in consistent judicial interpretation and effective institutional enforcement. Achieving full alignment between insurance authorities, maritime regulators, and the judiciary remains essential to realize the law's objectives. Furthermore, the integration of digital technologies into marine insurance such as electronic policies, automated claims assessment, and AI-based risk analysis has become indispensable for ensuring competitiveness in an era of digital transformation across global shipping industries.

The UAE's maritime insurance framework is not merely a product of legislative modernization; it symbolizes a paradigm shift in the governance of maritime risk. By combining legal sophistication with economic pragmatism, the law positions the UAE as a regional leader in maritime governance, one that seeks equilibrium between legal protection, market efficiency, and sustainable development.

The law's success will ultimately depend on how effectively it is implemented in practice. This requires continuous legal refinement, empirical research, and the incorporation of technological innovation in insurance operations. It also necessitates an active dialogue between policymakers, insurers, traders, and the judiciary to ensure that the statutory framework evolves in step with international standards and the realities of maritime commerce.

In essence, the Federal Maritime Law No. 43 of 2023 demonstrates a legislative vision that views marine insurance not only as an instrument of risk transfer but as a pillar of economic security and commercial resilience, underpinning the UAE's ambition to remain a global maritime hub founded on justice, transparency, and sustainability.

Recommendations

1. Issuance of a detailed executive regulation to clarify procedural aspects of marine insurance, including claims settlement, disclosure obligations, and compensation criteria, ensuring uniform application and judicial consistency.
2. Revision of standard marine insurance policies to cover emerging risks such as cyberattacks, marine pollution, and damage arising from the operation of autonomous and smart vessels.
3. Strengthening of institutional coordination between the Insurance Authority, maritime regulators, and judicial bodies to guarantee transparency and expedite dispute resolution.
4. Creation of a unified national digital database recording all marine insurance contracts and incidents of loss or damage, enabling accurate risk assessment and fair premium calculation.
5. Expansion of specialized maritime arbitration frameworks to include insurance-related disputes, supported by expert arbitrators with combined legal and technical competence.

6. Capacity-building of specialized judicial chambers in maritime and insurance law, accompanied by professional training for judges and practitioners on contemporary developments in maritime risk and insurance practice.
7. Promotion of international and regional cooperation with maritime and insurance organizations to exchange data, harmonize professional standards, and maintain the UAE's leading role in maritime commercial insurance.

REFERENCES

Abu Al-Haija, E., & Houcine, A. (2024). Risk management efficiency of takaful and conventional insurance sectors in UAE and KSA. *Journal of Islamic Accounting and Business Research*. Advance online publication. DOI: 10.1108/JIABR-03-2022-0065

Al Abdouli, J., & Sipos, A. (2024). An overview of the dynamic and complex regulatory landscape of cargo transportation in the United Arab Emirates. Journal of Infrastructure. *Policy and Development*, *8*(9). Advance online publication. DOI: 10.24294/jipd.v8i9.6586

Al-Sherman, N., & Aldabousi, A. M. (2024). The complementary penalties enforced to combat corporate crimes in UAE law. *Pakistan Journal of Criminology*, *16*(3), 635–648. DOI: 10.62271/pjc.16.3.635.648

Aldabousi, A. M. (2022). Legal problems of electronic pollution according to UAE and Egyptian law. *Arab World Geographer*, *25*(2–3), 154–168. DOI: 10.5555/1480-6800-25.2.154

Aldabousi, A. M. (2024). The joint responsibility of the air carrier established in accordance with international conventions on the status of air terrorism. *Pakistan Journal of Criminology*, *16*(2), 133–144. DOI: 10.62271/pjc.16.2.133.144

Aldabousi, A. M. (2025). Managing commercial space activities: Legal and regulatory challenges in UAE's space sector. *Problems and Perspectives in Management*, *23*(2). Advance online publication. DOI: 10.21511/ppm.23(2).2025.30

Alhadhrami, K. A. (2025). Challenges and solutions in enforcing foreign arbitral awards: A case study of the UAE. *Arbitration*, *2025*(1), 45–62. DOI: 10.54648/amdm2025007

Alkhan, A. M., & Hassan, M. K. (2024). *From revelation to modern Islamic finance: Islamic commercial law in the UAE as a case study. International Journal of Law and Management*. Advance online publication. DOI: 10.1108/IJLMA-06-2024-0206

Alper, E. (2008). *Marine insurance: Insuring your imports*. Canadian Apparel.

Alsheikh, M., & Morshed, A. (2025). Insurance adequacy and supply chain resilience: Risk management mediation and complexity moderation in UAE firms. Journal of Logistics. *Informatics and Service Science*, *12*(6), 315–334. DOI: 10.33168/JLISS.2025.0615

Asgarian, H. (2021). *The doctrine of deviation, its historical and legal roots*. Baku State University Law Review.

Awad, A., & Aldabousi, A. M. (2024). Analyzing the impact of viral marketing on brand equity dimensions in Egypt's home appliances sector: A customer and legal perspective. *Innovative Marketing*, *20*(4), 82–94. DOI: 10.21511/im.20(4).2024.09

Baatz, Y. (2020). Choice of jurisdiction in bills of lading and cargo insurance. In *Research Handbook on Maritime Law and Regulation* (pp. 345–364). Edward Elgar Publishing., DOI: 10.4337/9781786438799.00020

Consignee must give notice of his claim during delivery of goods or within three days from date of delivery, otherwise carrier is not liable. (1995). *Arab Law Quarterly, 10*(3), 300–302. DOI: 10.1163/157302595X00300

Daradkeh, L. (2015). *The applicability of res judicata and functus officio on enforcing foreign arbitral awards under UAE civil procedural law* [Conference paper]. *International Journal of Public Law and Policy*. DOI: 10.1504/IJPLAP.2015.071038

de Faria, D. L. (2024). *The liability emerging from the maritime safety law and the importance of the I.S.M. Code: The MSC Patricia oil spill court case in Sines (Portugal) [A responsabilidade emergente da Lei sobre a Segurança Marítima e a importância do Código I.S.M. - o caso do derrame de hidrocarbonetos do MSC Patrícia em Sines (Portugal)]. Revista Jurídica Portucalense, 35,* 415–432. DOI: 10.34625/issn.2183-2705(35)2024.ic-25

El Yanboiy, L. (2024). Managing surplus in takaful insurance companies: The Moroccan experience as a model. *Journal of King Abdulaziz University: Islamic Economics*, *37*(3), 65–88. DOI: 10.4197/Islec.37-3.3

Fayyad, M. I., & Hayajneh, A. M. (2022). Reconsidering the special rules of mitigation of damages for breach of contract for the sale of goods in UAE law. *Arab Law Quarterly*, *36*, 1–30. DOI: 10.1163/15730255-bja10101

Hidayat, E., & Ahmad, A. U. F. (2023). Legal maxims of Ba'i Ibn Al-Arabi's contract and their relevance to contemporary muamalah māliyah issues. *Jurnal Hukum Islam*, *21*(1). Advance online publication. DOI: 10.28918/jhi_v21i1_01

Ishii, Y. (2024). *Environmental and maritime security, civil liability regimes, and maritime autonomous vehicles*. In *Maritime Autonomous Vehicles and International Law: Maritime Security Perspectives* (pp. 245–262). Routledge. DOI: 10.4324/9781032724072-17

Li, X. (2023). The insurable interest in the stoppage in transit under English and Chinese marine insurance law: A comparative analysis. In Brown, T. (Ed.), *Maritime Law Perspectives Old and New* (pp. 115–132).

Madi, R. (2025). Sailing through changes: A close look at the latest UAE maritime law updates. [Sweet & Maxwell.]. *Journal of Business Law*, *2025*(1), 49–53.

Naboush, E. (2020). The carrier's liability for delay under UAE maritime law: A comparative study. *Arab Law Quarterly*. Advance online publication. DOI: 10.1163/15730255-14030068

Obeidat, M. A., Alfil, N. Z., Aldabousi, A. M., & Dganni, K. M. (2024). Criminal protection for the merchants from the crimes of electronic publishing about invasion of privacy in UAE legislation. *Pakistan Journal of Criminology*, *16*(3), 779–792. DOI: 10.62271/pjc.16.3.779.792

Pijaca, M., Bulum, B., & Primorac, Ž. (2023). Duties of the ship's master in the event of a maritime accident as a type of insured loss. TransNav. *The International Journal on Marine Navigation and Safety of Sea Transportation*, *17*(2), 353–358. DOI: 10.12716/1001.17.02.06

Puad, N. A. M. (2024). Future directions of Shariah audit for takaful industry: Perceptions of Shariah committee. In *Springer Proceedings in Business and Economics*. Springer., DOI: 10.1007/978-3-031-67511-9_13

Sarhan, A. I. (2024). *Options that impair the binding effect of contract and their role in protecting contractual consent: An analysis of how Arab civil laws are influenced by Islamic jurisprudence. Manchester Journal of Transnational Islamic Law and Practice.*

Sharma, V., Ajmani, P., & Iwendi, C. (2023). *Blockchain application with specific reference to smart contracts in the insurance sector.* In *The Application of Emerging Technology and Blockchain in the Insurance Industry. Dubai Court of Cassation – Civil Judgments, Appeal No. 248 of 2008 (Commercial Circuit), judgment dated April 20, 2009, Technical Office, Vol. 20, Part 2, Rule No. 128(2), p. 1121*

Whiteman, T. (1984). Supervision necessary? *Bulk Syst. Int.*, *4*(2), 45–47.

Zheng, R. (2022). *Marine insurance law reform in China: Experiences from the UK.* In *Commercial and Maritime Law in China and Europe* (pp. 123–140). Routledge. DOI: 10.4324/9781003160298-7

Compilation of References

3rd Partner Logistics. (n.d.). *Drug track and trace system (RSD) revolutionizing security*. Retrieved from https://3rd-partner.com/en/drug-track-and-trace-system-rsd/

About, U. P. S. (2022). *UPS invests millions in advanced training for on-the-road drivers*. Retrieved from https://about.ups.com/us/en/newsroom/press-releases/people-led/ups-invests-millions-in-advanced-training-for-on-the-road-driver.html

About, U. P. S. (n.d.). *Virtual reality helping train safe drivers*. Retrieved from https://about.ups.com/us/en/our-stories/innovation-driven/virtual-reality-helping-to-create-safety-for-ups-drivers.html

Abu Al-Haija, E., & Houcine, A. (2024). Risk management efficiency of takaful and conventional insurance sectors in UAE and KSA. *Journal of Islamic Accounting and Business Research*. Advance online publication. DOI: 10.1108/JIABR-03-2022-0065

Adadi, A., & Berrada, M. (2018). Peeking inside the black-box: A survey on explainable artificial intelligence (xai). *IEEE Access : Practical Innovations, Open Solutions*, *6*, 52138–52160. DOI: 10.1109/ACCESS.2018.2870052

Aem-on, K., Setamanit, S.-O., Chandrachai, A., & Sinthupinyo, S. (2024). Empowering Supply Chain Resilience in High-Growth of Small and Medium Enterprises (SMEs) Through the Integration of the SCOR Model Paradigm. *TEM Journal, 13*(2), 1331–1344. https://doi.org/DOI: 10.18421/TEM132-47

African Union Commission. (2020). *Digital transformation strategy for Africa (2020–2030)*. African Union Commission. https://au.int/sites/default/files/documents/38507-doc-dts-english.pdf

Ahatsi, E., & Olanrewaju, O. A. (2025). Enhancing humanitarian supply chain resilience: Evaluating artificial intelligence and big data analytics in two nations. *Logistics (Basel)*, *9*(2), 1–28. DOI: 10.3390/logistics9020064

Ahmed, E., & El Sayed, K. (2023). Studying the relationship between green supply chain management dimensions and improve healthcare quality service: An empirical study. *The Arab Journal of Administration*, *43*(3), 43–56. DOI: 10.21608/aja.2022.139386.1247

Al Abdouli, J., & Sipos, A. (2024). An overview of the dynamic and complex regulatory landscape of cargo transportation in the United Arab Emirates. Journal of Infrastructure. *Policy and Development*, *8*(9). Advance online publication. DOI: 10.24294/jipd.v8i9.6586

Alahmari, D., & Awad, A. (2025). Strategic integration of marketing and supply chain functions for superior customer experience: Insights from logistics startups under Saudi Vision 2030. *PLoS One*, *20*(11), e0336132. DOI: 10.1371/journal.pone.0336132 PMID: 41270081

Aldabousi, A. M. (2022). Legal problems of electronic pollution according to UAE and Egyptian law. *Arab World Geographer*, *25*(2–3), 154–168. DOI: 10.5555/1480-6800-25.2.154

Aldabousi, A. M. (2024). The joint responsibility of the air carrier established in accordance with international conventions on the status of air terrorism. *Pakistan Journal of Criminology*, *16*(2), 133–144. DOI: 10.62271/pjc.16.2.133.144

Aldabousi, A. M. (2025). Managing commercial space activities: Legal and regulatory challenges in UAE's space sector. *Problems and Perspectives in Management*, *23*(2). Advance online publication. DOI: 10.21511/ppm.23(2).2025.30

Aldabousi, A. M., Awad, A., Hassan, H. E. M., Abdullah, S. S., & Ghonim, A. (2025). Arbitration in Islamic banking: Exploring legal and practical implications for dispute resolution. *Banks and Bank Systems*, *20*(2), 15–26. DOI: 10.21511/bbs.20(2).2025.02

Alhadhrami, K. A. (2025). Challenges and solutions in enforcing foreign arbitral awards: A case study of the UAE. *Arbitration*, *2025*(1), 45–62. DOI: 10.54648/amdm2025007

Ali, A. S., ... (2025). *Advancing cybersecurity in ASEAN: Current trends and challenges. International Journal of Information Security.* https://link.springer.com/article/10.1007/s10207-025-01111-2

Alkhan, A. M., & Hassan, M. K. (2024). *From revelation to modern Islamic finance: Islamic commercial law in the UAE as a case study. International Journal of Law and Management.* Advance online publication. DOI: 10.1108/IJLMA-06-2024-0206

Alper, E. (2008). *Marine insurance: Insuring your imports*. Canadian Apparel.

Al-Rodhan, N. (2013). *Cybersecurity and cyberwarfare: The need for a new UN convention*. Geneva Centre for Security Policy.

Alsheikh, M., & Morshed, A. (2025). Insurance adequacy and supply chain resilience: Risk management mediation and complexity moderation in UAE firms. Journal of Logistics. *Informatics and Service Science*, *12*(6), 315–334. DOI: 10.33168/JLISS.2025.0615

Al-Sherman, N., & Aldabousi, A. M. (2024). The complementary penalties enforced to combat corporate crimes in UAE law. *Pakistan Journal of Criminology*, *16*(3), 635–648. DOI: 10.62271/pjc.16.3.635.648

Analysis, R. (n.d.). *Metaverse in healthcare use cases revealing benefits of this next generation technology*. Retrieved from https://www.rootsanalysis.com/key-insights/metaverse-in-healthcare-use-cases.html

Anderson, J. R., Bothell, D., Byrne, M. D., Douglass, S., Lebiere, C., & Qin, Y. (2004). An integrated theory of the mind. *Psychological Review*, *111*(4), 1036–1060. DOI: 10.1037/0033-295X.111.4.1036

APICS. (2014). *SCOR quick reference guide* (Version 12.0). APICS. https://www.apics.org/docs/default-source/scor-p-toolkits/apics-scc-scor-quick-reference-guide.pdf

ASEAN. (2022, January 28). *ASEAN Cybersecurity Cooperation Strategy 2021–2025*. https://asean.org/wp-content/uploads/2022/02/01-ASEAN-Cybersecurity-Cooperation-Paper-2021-2025_final-23-0122.pdf

Asgarian, H. (2021). *The doctrine of deviation, its historical and legal roots*. Baku State University Law Review.

Assembly Magazine. (n.d.). *BMW scales virtual factory with accelerated computing, digital twins, and AI*. Retrieved from https://www.assemblymag.com/articles/99322-bmw-scales-virtual-factory-with-accelerated-computing-digital-twins-and-ai

Awad, A. (2025). The role of universities' social responsibility in enhancing business sustainability: Mediating role of entrepreneurial culture. *Problems and Perspectives in Management*, *23*(1), 181–192. DOI: 10.21511/ppm.23(1).2025.14

Awad, A., & Aldabousi, A. M. (2024). Analyzing the impact of viral marketing on brand equity dimensions in Egypt's home appliances sector: A customer and legal perspective. *Innovative Marketing*, *20*(4), 100–111. DOI: 10.21511/im.20(4).2024.09

Awad, A., Al-fil, N. Z., Dganni, K. M., Aldabousi, A. M., & Obeidat, M. A. (2024). Optimizing dormant account management in UAE banking: Legal gaps and proposed reforms. *Banks and Bank Systems*, *19*(4), 124–135. DOI: 10.21511/bbs.19(4).2024.10

Awad, A., & Mahmoud, M. (2024). Impact of electronic customer relationship management on competitive advantage: Mediating role of customer satisfaction in EgyptAir. *Problems and Perspectives in Management*, *22*(3), 276–286. DOI: 10.21511/ppm.22(3).2024.22

Baatz, Y. (2020). Choice of jurisdiction in bills of lading and cargo insurance. In *Research Handbook on Maritime Law and Regulation* (pp. 345–364). Edward Elgar Publishing., DOI: 10.4337/9781786438799.00020

Bag, S., Rahman, M. S., Gupta, S., & Jabbour, A. B. L. de S. (2025). Artificial intelligence driven ethical procurement systems, circular economy and governance: A supplier performance analysis. *Journal of Purchasing and Supply Management*. Advance online publication. Article ID 101075. .DOI: 10.1016/j.pursup.2025.101075

Bandara, K., Bergmeir, C., & Smyl, S. (2020). Forecasting across time series databases using recurrent neural networks on groups of similar series: A clustering approach. *Expert Systems with Applications*, *140*, 112896. DOI: 10.1016/j.eswa.2019.112896

Barbosa, J., Leitão, P., Adam, E., & Trentesaux, D. (2020). Dynamic self-organization in holonic multi-agent manufacturing systems: The ADACOR evolution. *Computers in Industry*, *66*, 99–111. DOI: 10.1016/j.compind.2014.10.011

Barredo Arrieta, A., Díaz-Rodríguez, N., Del Ser, J., Bennetot, A., Tabik, S., Barbado, A., & Herrera, F. (2020). Explainable Artificial Intelligence (XAI): Concepts, taxonomies, opportunities and challenges toward responsible AI. *Information Fusion*, *58*, 82–115. DOI: 10.1016/j.inffus.2019.12.012

Baryannis, G., Dani, S., & Antoniou, G. (2019). Predicting supply chain risks using machine learning: The trade-off between performance and interpretability. *Future Generation Computer Systems*, *101*, 993–1004. DOI: 10.1016/j.future.2019.07.059

Baryannis, G., Validi, S., Dani, S., & Antoniou, G. (2020). Supply chain risk management and artificial intelligence: State of the art and future research directions. *International Journal of Production Research*, *57*(7), 2179–2202. DOI: 10.1080/00207543.2018.1530476

Beltrán, M. (2025). AI algorithms under scrutiny: GDPR, DSA, AI Act and CRA as pillars for algorithmic security and privacy in the European Union. *Computers & Security*, *158*. Advance online publication. DOI: 10.1016/j.cose.2025.104628

Ben-Daya, M., Hassini, E., & Bahroun, Z. (2019). Internet of things and supply chain management: A literature review. *International Journal of Production Research*, *57*(15–16), 4719–4742. DOI: 10.1080/00207543.2017.1402140

Bhide, P. (n.d.). *Digital twins: Revolutionizing fashion from concept to closet*. Retrieved from https://www.jprutha.com/digital-twins-revolutionizing-fashion-from-concept-to-closet/

BlueVoyant. (n.d.). Supply chain security: Why it's important & 7 best practices [[https://www.bluevoyant.com/knowledge-center/supply-chain-security-why-its- important-7-b](https://www.bluevoyant.com/knowledge-center/supply-chain - security-why-its-important-7-b) [Accessed: 2025-10-07]].

Bode, C., & Wagner, S. M. (2015). Structural drivers of upstream supply chain complexity and the frequency of supply chain disruptions. *Journal of Operations Management*, *36*(1), 215–228.

Bodendorf, F., & Franke, J. (2021). A machine learning approach to estimate missing values in procurement data. *Decision Support Systems*, *150*, 113565. DOI: 10.1016/j.dss.2021.113565

Boone, T., Ganeshan, R., Jain, A., & Sanders, N. R. (2019). Forecasting sales in the supply chain: Consumer analytics in the big data era. *International Journal of Forecasting*, *35*(1), 170–180. DOI: 10.1016/j.ijforecast.2018.09.003

Bostrom, N., & Yudkowsky, E. (2014). The ethics of artificial intelligence. In Frankish, K., & Ramsey, W. M. (Eds.), *The Cambridge handbook of artificial intelligence* (pp. 316–334). Cambridge University Press., DOI: 10.1017/CBO9781139046855.020

Box, G. E. P., Jenkins, G. M., Reinsel, G. C., & Ljung, G. M. (2015). *Time series analysis: Forecasting and control* (5th ed.). Wiley., DOI: 10.1111/jtsa.12194

Brandenburg, M., Govindan, K., Sarkis, J., & Seuring, S. (2014). Quantitative models for sustainable supply chain management: Developments and directions. *European Journal of Operational Research*, *233*(2), 299–312. DOI: 10.1016/j.ejor.2013.09.032

Brewster, T. (2022). *Cyberattacks on supply chains: The hidden threat to global trade. Forbes*. https://www.forbes.com

Brownlee, J. (2018). *Deep learning for time series forecasting: Predict the future with MLPs, CNNs and LSTMs in Python*. Machine Learning Mastery.

Buck, S. (2025, November 16). Designing for supply chain resilience with Nestlé. *Coupa Blog*. https://www.coupa.com/blog/designing-for-supply-chain-resilience-with-nestle

Burges, C. J. C. (2010). From RankNet to LambdaRank to LambdaMART. An overview. *Microsoft Research Technical Report*, MSR-TR-2010-82. https://www.microsoft.com/en-us/research/wp-content/uploads/2016/02/MSR-TR-2010-82.pdf

Cannas, V. G., Ciano, M. P., Saltalamacchia, M., & Secchi, R. (2024). Artificial intelligence in supply chain and operations management: A multiple case study research. *International Journal of Production Research, 62*(9), 3333–3360. DOI: 10.1080/00207543.2023.2232050

Cart.com. (2024, June). Secure fulfillment: Navigating physical and cybersecurity in logistics [https://cart.com/blog/navigating-fulfillment-logistics-security [Accessed: 2025-10-07]].

Carter, C. R., & Rogers, D. S. (2008). A framework of sustainable supply chain management: Moving toward new theory. *International Journal of Physical Distribution & Logistics Management, 38*(5), 360–387. DOI: 10.1108/09600030810882816

Charmet, F., Tanuwidjaja, H. C., Ayoubi, S., Gimenez, P. F., Han, Y., Jmila, H., & Zhang, Z. (2022). Explainable artificial intelligence for cybersecurity: A literature survey. *Annales des Télécommunications, 77*(11), 789–812.

Chen, A. (2024). *Restaurant Sales Report 2024–2025* [Dataset]. Kaggle. https://www.kaggle.com/datasets/alexandchen/restaurant-sales-report-2024-2025

Chen, H., Chu, T., Yang, L., Wang, Z., & Xue, L. (2024). Digital twin warehouse management platform developed based on Unity3D. In *Proceedings of the 4th International Conference on Internet of Things and Machine Learning*. https://doi.org/DOI: 10.1145/3697467.3697667

Chen, T., & Guestrin, C. (2016). XGBoost: A scalable tree boosting system. *In Proceedings of the 22nd ACM SIGKDD International Conference on Knowledge Discovery and Data Mining* (pp. 785–794). DOI: DOI: 10.1145/2939672.2939785

Chen, W., Men, Y., Fuster, N., Osorio, C., & Juan, A. A. (2024). Artificial intelligence in logistics optimization with sustainable criteria: A review. *Sustainability, 16*(21), 9145. DOI: 10.3390/su16219145

Choma, K. (2025). How digital twins drive production scheduling & supply chain optimization. *Nomtek Blog*. https://www.nomtek.com/blog/digital-twins-and-supply-chain-optimization

Christopher, M. (1992). *Logistics and supply chain management*. Pitman Publishing.

Christopher, M. (2016). *Logistics & supply chain management*. Pearson.

Christopher, M., & Holweg, M. (2017). Supply chain 2.0 revisited: A framework for managing volatility-induced risk in the supply chain. *International Journal of Physical Distribution & Logistics Management, 47*(1), 2–17. DOI: 10.1108/IJPDLM-09-2016-0245

CIPS. (n.d.). *How Nike transformed supply chains to survive Covid*. Retrieved from https://www.cips.org/knowledge-and-insight/how-nike-transformed-supply-chains-to-survive-covid

Cobalt.io. (2025, July). A CISO's view of AI and supply chain risks [[https://www.cobalt.io/blog/the-new-supply-chain-is-intelligent-a-cisos-view-on-ai-risk](https://www.cobalt.io/blog/the-new-supply-chain-is-intelligent-a-cisos-view- on-ai-risk) [Accessed: 2025-10-07]].

Collaborating Centre on Sustainable Consumption and Production. (2021). *Green public procurement for sustainable horticulture: A policy brief.* https://www.cscp.org/wp-content/uploads/2021/07/GOALAN_GPP_Policy_Brief.pdf

Common Share News. (n.d.). *EU's game-changing move: Introducing digital product passports for sustainable textiles*. Retrieved from https://news.commonshare.com/blog/eu-s-game-changing-move-introducing-digital-product-passports-for-sustainable-textiles

Consignee must give notice of his claim during delivery of goods or within three days from date of delivery, otherwise carrier is not liable. (1995). *Arab Law Quarterly, 10*(3), 300–302. DOI: 10.1163/157302595X00300

Council of Europe. (2001). *Convention on Cybercrime (Budapest Convention)*. Council of Europe.

Craighead, C. W., Ketchen, D. J.Jr, & Darby, J. L. (2020). Pandemics and supply chain management research: Toward a theoretical toolbox. *Decision Sciences, 51*(4), 838–866. PMID: 34234384

Daradkeh, L. (2015). *The applicability of res judicata and functus officio on enforcing foreign arbitral awards under UAE civil procedural law* [Conference paper]. *International Journal of Public Law and Policy*. DOI: 10.1504/IJPLAP.2015.071038

Datadog. (2023, September). Abusing supply chains: How poisoned models, data, and third-party libraries compromise AI systems [[https://www.datadoghq.com/blog/detect-abuse-ai-supply-chains](https: //www.datadoghq.com/blog/detect-abuse-ai-supply-chains) [Accessed: 2025-10-07]].

Davis, F. D. (1989). Perceived usefulness, perceived ease of use, and user acceptance of information technology. *Management Information Systems Quarterly, 13*(3), 319–340. DOI: 10.2307/249008 de Faria, D. L. (2024). *The liability emerging from the maritime safety law and the importance of the I.S.M. Code: The MSC Patricia oil spill court case in Sines (Portugal) [A responsabilidade emergente da Lei sobre a Segurança Marítima e a importância do Código I.S.M. - o caso do derrame de hidrocarbonetos do MSC Patrícia em Sines (Portugal)]. Revista Jurídica Portucalense, 35,* 415–432. DOI: 10.34625/issn.2183-2705(35)2024.ic-25

DeNittis, N. (2024, February 5). Artificial intelligence at Procter & Gamble. *Emerj.* https://emerj.com/ai-sector-overviews/artificial-intelligence-at-procter-gamble/

Devi, D. P., Allur, N. S., Dondapati, K., Chetlapalli, H., Kodadi, S., & Perumal, T. (2023). Digital twin technology and IoT enabled AI using real-time analytics for smart warehouse management and predictive inventory optimization. *International Journal of Marketing Management, 11*(4). https://ijmm.in/index.php/ijmm/article/view/208

DHL. (n.d.). *Extended reality - DHL - United States of America.* Retrieved from https://www.dhl.com/us-en/home/innovation-in-logistics/logistics-trend-radar/augmented-and-extended-reality.html

Dive, T. (n.d.). *UPS takes driver safety to the next level with virtual reality.* Retrieved from https://www.truckingdive.com/news/UPS-driver-training-virtual-augmented-reality-AR-VR/596831/

Doshi-Velez, F., & Kim, B. (2017). Towards a rigorous science of interpretable machine learning. *arXiv preprint arXiv:1702.08608.* /arXiv.1702.08608DOI: 10.48550

Dragos. (2023). *OT cybersecurity breach disrupts operations at the Port of Nagoya, Japan.*

DuBravac, S. (n.d.). *Augmented reality is changing the supply chain workforce and improving operational efficiency and profitability.* Retrieved from https://shawndubravac.com/augmented-reality-is-changing-the-supply-chain-workforce-and-improving-operational-efficiency-and-profitability/2/

El Yanboiy, L. (2024). Managing surplus in takaful insurance companies: The Moroccan experience as a model. *Journal of King Abdulaziz University: Islamic Economics, 37*(3), 65–88. DOI: 10.4197/Islec.37-3.3

Endsley, M. R. (1995). Toward a theory of situation awareness in dynamic systems. *Human Factors, 37*(1), 32–64. DOI: 10.1518/001872095779049543

ENISA. (2022). *Cybersecurity in ports and maritime logistics.* European Union Agency for Cybersecurity.

ENISA. (2023, June 13). *Good practices for supply chain cybersecurity.* European Union Agency for Cybersecurity. https://www.enisa.europa.eu/publications/good-practices-for-supply-chain-cybersecurity

ENISA. (n.d.-a). *Threat landscape for supply chain attacks.* European Union Agency for Cybersecurity. https://www.enisa.europa.eu/publications/threat-landscape-for-supply-chain-attacks

ENISA. (n.d.-b). *NIS2 technical implementation guidance.* European Union Agency for Cybersecurity. https://www.enisa.europa.eu/publications/nis2-technical-implementation-guidance#contentList

European Commission. (2008). *Public procurement for a better environment.* https://eur-lex.europa.eu/LexUriServ/LexUriServ.do?uri=COM:2008:0400:FIN:EN:pdf

European Union. (2022). *Directive (EU) 2022/2555 (NIS2) on measures for a high common level of cybersecurity across the Union. Official Journal of the European Union, L333*, 80–152.

European Union. (2024). *Artificial Intelligence Act: Article 14 – Human oversight* (Regulation (EU) 2024/1689). https://artificialintelligenceact.eu/article/14/

Fayyad, M. I., & Hayajneh, A. M. (2022). Reconsidering the special rules of mitigation of damages for breach of contract for the sale of goods in UAE law. *Arab Law Quarterly*, *36*, 1–30. DOI: 10.1163/15730255-bja10101

Ferrer-Blas, R., Galarcep-Barba, I., & Carlos Solano-Gaviño, J. (2024). Lean Manufacturing in food production: Systematic review, bibliometric analysis and proposed application. *Scientia Agropecuaria*, *15*(4). Advance online publication. DOI: 10.17268/sci.agropecu.2024.042

Fiddler. (n.d.). Accelerate financial AI adoption with Fiddler [[https://www.fiddler.ai/ai- in-financial-services](https://www.fiddler.ai/ai-in-financial-services) [Accessed: 2025-10-08]].

Friedman, J. H. (2001). Greedy function approximation: A gradient boosting machine. *Annals of Statistics*, *29*(5). Advance online publication. DOI: 10.1214/aos/1013203451

Frontiers in Virtual Reality. (2025). *Metaverse in industrial contexts - a comprehensive review*. Retrieved from https://www.frontiersin.org/journals/virtual-reality/articles/10.3389/frvir.2025.1488926/full

Gasper, D., Shah, A., & Tankha, S. (2019). The framing of sustainable consumption and production in SDG 12. *Global Policy, 10*(Suppl. 1), 83–95. DOI: 10.1111/1758-5899.12592

Gegic, E., Isakovic, B., Keco, D., Masetic, Z., & Kevric, J. (2019). Car price prediction using machine-learning techniques. *TEM Journal, 8*(1), 113–118. DOI: DOI: 10.18421/TEM81-16

Ghonim, A., & Awad, A. (2025). Shaping customer insights through e-marketing: An applied study in the banking sector. *International Journal of Advanced and Applied Sciences, 12*(4), 88–98. DOI: 10.21833/ijaas.2025.04.011

Gijsbrechts, J., Boute, R. N., Van Mieghem, J. A., & Zhang, D. (2022). Can deep reinforcement learning improve inventory management? Performance on lost sales, dual-sourcing, and multi-echelon problems. *Manufacturing & Service Operations Management, 24*(3), 1349–1368. DOI: 10.1287/msom.2021.1064

Goldman, S. (2022, June 6). How AI helps Coca Cola boost supply chain procurement. *VentureBeat.* https://venturebeat.com/business/how-ai-helps-coca-cola-boost-supply-chain-procurement/

Goswami, S. S., Mondal, S., Sarkar, S., Gupta, K. K., Sahoo, S. K., & Halder, R. (2025). Artificial intelligence enabled supply chain management: Unlocking new opportunities and challenges. *Artificial Intelligence and Applications (Commerce, Calif.), 3*(1). https://elibrary.ru/item.asp?id=74126909

GovInsider Asia. (2025, July 14). *Tackling supply chain cybersecurity in Southeast Asia.* https://govinsider.asia/intl-en/article/tackling-supply-chain-cybersecurity-in-southeast-asia

Green Threads, D. P. P. (n.d.). *The role of digital twins in product lifecycle management.* Retrieved from https://greenthreadsdpp.com/post/digital-twins-product-lifecycle-management

Greenberg, A. (2018). *Sandworm: A new era of cyberwar and the hunt for the Kremlin's most dangerous hackers*. Doubleday.

Grieves, M., & Vickers, J. (2017). Digital twin: Mitigating unpredictable, undesirable emergent behavior in complex systems. In Kahlen, F. J., Flumerfelt, S., & Alves, A. (Eds.), *Transdisciplinary perspectives on complex systems* (pp. 85–113). Springer., DOI: 10.1007/978-3-319-38756-7_4

Guest Blogger. (2025, September 15). AI in last mile delivery: Smarter, faster, greener 2025. *Last Mile TMS.* https://lastmiletms.com/ai-in-last-mile-delivery-smarter-faster-greener-2025/

Güler, A., Musa, A., Tarım, M., Saraç, O., & Göktürk, M. (2024). Forecasting Restaurant Sales with the Sensitivity of Weather Conditions and Special Days Using Facebook Prophet. *Journal of Data Applications*, *0*(2), 15–30. DOI: 10.26650/joda.1450459

Gunning, D., & Aha, D. (2019). Darpa's explainable artificial intelligence (xai) program. *AI Magazine*, *40*(2), 44–58. DOI: 10.1609/aimag.v40i2.2850

Hastie, T., Tibshirani, R., & Friedman, J. (2009). *The elements of statistical learning: Data mining, inference and prediction* (2nd ed.). Springer., DOI: 10.1007/978-0-387-84858-7

Healey, J. (2019). *A fierce domain: Conflict in cyberspace, 1986 to 2012*. Cyber Conflict Studies Association.

Helw, A. M. A. (2021). *Framework for enhanced applicability of the Egyptian public procurement law to international administrative construction contracts* (Master's thesis). The American University in Cairo. https://fount.aucegypt.edu/cgi/viewcontent.cgi?article=2914&context=etds

Hidayat, E., & Ahmad, A. U. F. (2023). Legal maxims of Ba'i Ibn Al-Arabi's contract and their relevance to contemporary muamalah māliyah issues. *Jurnal Hukum Islam*, *21*(1). Advance online publication. DOI: 10.28918/jhi_v21i1_01

Hochreiter, S., & Schmidhuber, J. (1997). Long Short-Term memory. *Neural Computation*, *9*(8), 1735–1780. DOI: 10.1162/neco.1997.9.8.1735 PMID: 9377276

Hofmann, E., & Rüsch, M. (2017). Industry 4.0 and the current status as well as future prospects on logistics. *Computers in Industry*, *89*, 23–34. DOI: 10.1016/j.compind.2017.04.002

Holt, C. C. (2004). Forecasting seasonals and trends by exponentially weighted moving averages. *International Journal of Forecasting*, *20*(1), 5–10. (Original work published 1957). DOI: DOI: 10.1016/j.ijforecast.2003.09.015

Hyndman, R. J., & Athanasopoulos, G. (2018). *Forecasting: Principles and practice* (2nd ed.). OTexts., https://otexts.com/fpp2/

ICG. (2025). *Innovating the future: The role of the metaverse in Saudi Arabia's Vision 2030*. Retrieved from https://icg.co/wp-content/uploads/2025/02/Innovating-the-Future_-The-Role-of-the-Metaverse-in-Saudi-Arabias-Vision-2030.pdf

ICRC. (2019). *International humanitarian law and cyber operations during armed conflicts (Position paper).*

IEEE-USA. (2023). *Effective and ethical governance of artificial intelligence systems* (Position Statement) ([Accessed: 2025-10-07]). IEEE-USA. %5Bhttps://ieeeusa.org/assets/public-policy/positions/ai/EffectiveGovernanceofAI1123.pdf%5D(https: //ieeeusa.org/assets/public-policy/positions/ai/EffectiveGovernanceofAI1123.pdf)
IEEE-USA. (2024). *Public interest policy priorities for artificial intelligence* (tech. rep.) ([Accessed: 2025-10-07]). IEEE-USA. %5Bhttps://ieeeusa.org/assets/public-policy/policy-log/2024/090924.pdf%5D(https://ieeeusa.org/assets/public- policy/policy-log/2024/090924.pdf)

IMO. (2017). *Resolution MSC.428(98): Maritime cyber risk management in safety management systems.*

International Law Commission (ILC). (2001). *Responsibility of States for internationally wrongful acts*. United Nations.

International Telecommunication Union (ITU). (2020). *Arab States cyber drill report*. ITU.

Ishii, Y. (2024). *Environmental and maritime security, civil liability regimes, and maritime autonomous vehicles.* In *Maritime Autonomous Vehicles and International Law: Maritime Security Perspectives* (pp. 245–262). Routledge. DOI: 10.4324/9781032724072-17

Ivanov, D., & Dolgui, A. (2020). Viability of intertwined supply networks: Extending the supply chain resilience angles towards survivability. A position paper motivated by COVID-19 outbreak. *International Journal of Production Research*, *58*(10), 2904–2915. DOI: 10.1080/00207543.2020.1750727

Ivanov, D., Dolgui, A., & Sokolov, B. (2021). Cloud supply chain: Integrating Industry 4.0 and digital platforms in the "Supply Chain-as-a-Service.". *Transportation Research Part E, Logistics and Transportation Review*, *160*, 102676. DOI: 10.1016/j.tre.2022.102676

Jacyna-Gołda, I., Shmygol, N., Sembiyeva, L., Cherniavska, O., Burtebayeva, A., Uskenbayeva, A., & Salwin, M. (2025). Modeling Sustainable Development of Transport Logistics Under Climate Change, Ecosystem Dynamics, and Digitalization. *Applied Sciences (Switzerland)*, *15*(13). Advance online publication. DOI: 10.3390/app15137593

Japan, E. Y. (n.d.). *Leveraging the industrial metaverse for digital transformation in manufacturing*. Retrieved from https://www.ey.com/en_jp/insights/technology/industrial-metaverse-unlocks-the-future-realizing-next-generation-factories-through-digital-transformation

Jarrahi, M. H. (2018). Artificial intelligence and the future of work: Human-AI symbiosis in organizational decision making. *Business Horizons*, *61*(4), 577–586. DOI: 10.1016/j.bushor.2018.03.007

Jethva, B., Traoré, I., Ghaleb, A., Ganame, K., & Ahmed, S. (2020). Multilayer ransomware detection using grouped registry key operations, file entropy and file signature monitoring. *Journal of Computer Security*, *28*(3), 337–373. DOI: 10.3233/JCS-191346

Jobin, A., Ienca, M., & Vayena, E. (2019). The global landscape of ai ethics guidelines.

Journal of Minimally Invasive Surgery. (n.d.). *Research trends in virtual reality surgical simulation for education: A systematic review*. Retrieved from https://www.e-jmis.org/journal/view.html?uid=764&vmd=Full

Julka, N., Srinivasan, R., & Karimi, I. (2002). Agent-based supply chain management—1: Framework. *Computers & Chemical Engineering*, *26*(12), 1755–1769. DOI: 10.1016/S0098-1354(02)00150-3

Kagalwala, H., Radhakrishnan, G. V., Mohammed, I. A., Kothinti, R. R., & Kulkarni, N. (2025). Predictive analytics in supply chain management: The role of AI and machine learning in demand forecasting. *Advances in Consumer Research. Association for Consumer Research (U. S.)*, *2*(1), 142–149.

Kagermann, H., Wahlster, W., & Helbig, J. (2013). *Recommendations for implementing the strategic initiative INDUSTRIE 4.0*. Final report of the Industrie 4.0 Working Group. Forschungsunion.

Kamanzi, E., & Akumuntu, J. (2024). Effect of machine learning model on supply chain performance: A case of Dubai Port (DP) World/Kigali Rwanda. *Journal of Procurement & Supply Chain*, *8*(1). Advance online publication. DOI: 10.53819/81018102t2311

Kaur, H., & Singh, S. P. (2021). Multi-stage hybrid model for supplier selection and order allocation considering disruption risks and disruptive technologies. *International Journal of Production Economics*, *231*, 107830. DOI: 10.1016/j.ijpe.2020.107830

Ke, G., Meng, Q., Finley, T., Wang, T., Chen, W., Ma, W., . . . Liu, T.-Y. (2017). LightGBM: A highly efficient gradient boosting decision tree. *Advances in Neural Information Processing Systems (NeurIPS)*, 30. https://papers.nips.cc/paper/2017/hash/6449f44a102fde848669bdd9eb6b76fa-Abstract.html

Kepczynski, R., Jandhyala, R., Sankaran, G., & Dimofte, A. (2018). *Integrated business planning*. Springer. https://link.springer.com/content/pdf/10.1007/978-3-319-75665-3.pdf

Khan, M. M., Bashar, I., Minhaj, G. M., Wasi, A. I., & Hossain, N. U. I. (2023). Resilient and sustainable supplier selection: An integration of SCOR 4.0 and machine learning approach. *Sustainable and Resilient Infrastructure*, *8*(5). Advance online publication. DOI: 10.1080/23789689.2023.2165782

Kietzmann, J., Paschen, J., & Treen, E. (2018). Artificial intelligence in advertising: How marketers can leverage artificial intelligence along the consumer journey. *Journal of Advertising Research*, *58*(3). Advance online publication. DOI: 10.2501/JAR-2018-035

Koren, Y., Bell, R., & Volinsky, C. (2009). Matrix factorization techniques for recommender systems. *Computer*, *42*(8), 30–37. DOI: 10.1109/MC.2009.263

Kranthi, P., Geeta, M., Shankar, C. N. U., Ranjith, P. V., Thoti, K. K., & Mishra, N. (2025). Comparative Efficiency Analysis of High-Speed Cross-Belt Sorters Using The SCOR Model: A Case Study from India's Courier Network. *International Journal of Basic and Applied Sciences*, *14*(4), 786–794. DOI: 10.14419/7bnz2v49

Kritzinger, W., Karner, M., Traar, G., Henjes, J., & Sihn, W. (2018). Digital Twin in manufacturing: A categorical literature review and classification. *IFAC-PapersOnLine*, *51*(11), 1016–1022. DOI: 10.1016/j.ifacol.2018.08.474

Kuerbis, B., & Badiei, F. (2021). Cyber capacity building: A development agenda for cybersecurity. *Journal of Cyber Policy*, *6*(1), 1–20.

Kumar, A., Kashyap, D. R., Kataria, P., & Kumar, A. (2024). The expected contribution of artificial intelligence (AI) adoption in supply chain management. *American Journal of Artificial Intelligence*, *8*(2). Advance online publication. DOI: 10.11648/j.ajai.20240802.15

Laird, J. E., Lebiere, C., & Rosenbloom, P. S. (2017). A standard model of the mind: Toward a common computational framework across artificial intelligence, cognitive science, neuroscience, and robotics. *AI Magazine*, *38*(4), 13–26. DOI: 10.1609/aimag.v38i4.2744

Laksono, M. N. G., Tiaraputri, Z. A., Sekti, B. A., & Laksono, M. I. A. (2025). Cyber-physical systems security in space. In *Advanced Cyber Defense for Space Missions and Operations* (pp. 85–113). Concepts and Applications., DOI: 10.4018/979-8-3693-7939-4.ch004

LawGratis. (2025a). Artificial intelligence law at Morocco. https://www.lawgratis.com/blog-detail/artificial-intelligence-law-at-morocco

LawGratis. (2025b). Artificial intelligence law at Algeria. https://www.lawgratis.com/blog-detail/artificial-intelligence-law-at-algeria

Law, No. (2018). *182 of 2018 Regulating Contracts Concluded by Public Entities*. Official Gazette of Egypt.

Lee, H. L. (2004). The triple-A supply chain. *Harvard Business Review*, *82*(10), 102–113.

Lee, J. D., & See, K. A. (2004). Trust in automation: Designing for appropriate reliance. *Human Factors*, *46*(1), 50–80. DOI: 10.1518/hfes.46.1.50_30392

Leng, J., Wang, D., Shen, W., Li, X., Liu, Q., & Chen, X. (2020). Digital twins-based smart manufacturing system design in Industry 4.0: A review. *Journal of Manufacturing Systems*, *60*, 119–137. DOI: 10.1016/j.jmsy.2021.05.011

Li, C., Gao, X., Chu, J., & Tang, J. (2025). Research on a Robust Traceability Method for the Assembly Manufacturing Supply Chain Based on Blockchain. *Applied Sciences (Switzerland)*, *15*(21). Advance online publication. DOI: 10.3390/app152111598

Li, S., Ma, M., Han, Y., & Xu, C. (2025). Towards subversion-resistant password-protected encryption for deduplicated cloud storage. *Journal of Information Security and Applications*, *94*. Advance online publication. DOI: 10.1016/j.jisa.2025.104233

Little, A. D. (n.d.). *The industrial metaverse*. Retrieved from https://www.adlittle.com/en/insights/report/industrial-metaverse

Liu, M., Fang, S., Dong, H., & Xu, C. (2021). Review of digital twin about concepts, technologies, and industrial applications. *Journal of Manufacturing Systems*, *58*, 346–361. DOI: 10.1016/j.jmsy.2020.06.017

Liu, Y., Tao, X., Li, X., Colombo, A. W., & Hu, S. (2023). Artificial intelligence in smart logistics cyber-physical systems: State-of-the-arts and potential applications. *IEEE Transactions on Industrial Cyber-Physical Systems*, *1*, 1–20. DOI: 10.1109/TICPS.2023.3283230

Li, X. (2023). The insurable interest in the stoppage in transit under English and Chinese marine insurance law: A comparative analysis. In Brown, T. (Ed.), *Maritime Law Perspectives Old and New* (pp. 115–132).

Llorca, D. F., Hamon, R., Junklewitz, H., Grosse, K., Kunze, L., Seiniger, P., & Kriston, A. (2025). Testing autonomous vehicles and AI: Perspectives and challenges from cybersecurity, transparency, robustness and fairness. *European Transport Research Review*, *17*(1), 38. DOI: 10.1186/s12544-025-00732-x

Longart, P. (2015). Consumer decision making in restaurant selection (Doctoral dissertation, Buckinghamshire New University). https://bnu.repository.guildhe.ac.uk/id/eprint/9388

Long, B., Bian, J., Dong, A., & Chang, Y. (2012). Enhancing product search by best-selling prediction in e-commerce. *Proceedings of the 21st ACM International Conference on Information and Knowledge Management (CIKM '12)*, 2479-2482. DOI: DOI: 10.1145/2396761.2398671

Lukalapu, D. R. (2021). *Advancement of sales and operations planning for effective demand management with IBP* (Master's thesis). Politecnico di Milano. https://www.politesi.polimi.it/handle/10589/182167

Lu, Z., Zhao, Z., & Huang, G. Q. (2026). STAR: Spatial–Temporal Attention Reasoning model for dynamic logistics network routing in Cyber–Physical Internet. *Advanced Engineering Informatics*, *69*. Advance online publication. DOI: 10.1016/j.aei.2025.103830

Maalouf, A., Jadhav, N., Jatavallabhula, K. M., Chahine, M., Vogt, D. M., Wood, R. J., & Rus, D. (2024). Follow Anything: Open-Set Detection, Tracking, and Following in Real-Time. *IEEE Robotics and Automation Letters*, *9*(4), 3283–3290. DOI: 10.1109/LRA.2024.3366013

Madi, R. (2025). Sailing through changes: A close look at the latest UAE maritime law updates. [Sweet & Maxwell.]. *Journal of Business Law*, *2025*(1), 49–53.

Maersk. (2018). *Annual report 2018: Learning from the NotPetya cyberattack.* Copenhagen: A.P. Moller–Maersk Group.

Mahir, S. H., Tashrif, M. T. A., Shathe, A. S., Karim, M. A., Rahman, A., Kundu, D., & Muhammad, G. (2026). PriFL-XAI: Hybrid privacy-preserving federated learning models for monkeypox detection through GAN augmentation and explainable AI. *Biomedical Signal Processing and Control*, *112*. Advance online publication. DOI: 10.1016/j.bspc.2025.108426

Mahmoud, M., Shma, T., Aziz, A., & Awad, A. (2025). Integrating knowledge management with smart technologies in public pharmaceutical organizations. *Knowledge and Performance Management*, *9*(1), 31–44. DOI: 10.21511/kpm.09(1).2025.03

Makridakis, S., Spiliotis, E., & Assimakopoulos, V. (2018). Statistical and machine learning forecasting methods: Concerns and ways forward. *PLoS One*, *13*(3), e0194889. DOI: 10.1371/journal.pone.0194889 PMID: 29584784

Mariyappan, S., Anbalagan, S., & Alexander, C. (2021). An analysis of busiest day in restaurant using a combined effective time dependent matrix. In AIP Conference Proceedings (Vol. 2378, No. 1, p. 020010). AIP Publishing LLC. DOI: DOI: 10.1063/5.0058312

Mashaile, A. (2025, March). Securing the future: Cybersecurity imperatives in automated transport and logistics [[https://www.transportevolution.com/securing-the-future- cybersecurity-imperatives-in-automated-transport-and-logistics](https://www.transportevolution.com/securing-the-future-cybersecurity-imperatives-in - automated-transport-and-logistics) [Accessed: 2025-10-07]].

McCullough, B., Kellison, T., & Melton, E. N. (Eds.). (2022). *The Routledge handbook of sport and sustainable development*. Taylor & Francis.

MDPI. (2024). *The use of virtual reality in surgical training: Implications for education, patient safety, and global health equity*. Retrieved from https://www.mdpi.com/2673-4095/4/4/61

Medinilla, A. (2025, November 12). Seizing the moment for North African green industrialisation. *ECDPM*. https://ecdpm.org/work/seizing-moment-north-african-green-industrialisation

Melina, D. R., Yunani, A., & Hidayat, A. M. (2024). Measuring supply chain performance using the SCOR model: A case study of CV. XYZ. *International Journal for Multidisciplinary Research*, *6*(6). Advance online publication. DOI: 10.1007/s43069-024-00314-y

Mentzer, J. T., DeWitt, W., Keebler, J. S., Min, S., Nix, N. W., Smith, C. D., & Zacharia, Z. G. (2001). Defining supply chain management. *Journal of Business Logistics*, *22*(2), 1–25. DOI: 10.1002/j.2158-1592.2001.tb00001.x

Metaverse Reality, I. E. E. E. (n.d.). *What is industrial metaverse and why it is important*. Retrieved from https://metaversereality.ieee.org/publications/articles/what-is-industrial-metaverse-and-why-it-is-important/

Microsoft. (2025, August). AI red teaming agent [[https://learn.microsoft.com/en - us/azure/ai-foundry/concepts/ai-red-teaming-agent](https: //learn.microsoft.com/en-us/azure/ai-foundry/concepts/ai-red-teaming-agent) [Accessed: 2025-10-08]].

Min, Q., Lu, Y., Liu, Z., Su, C., & Wang, B. (2019). Machine learning based digital twin framework for production optimization in petrochemical industry. *International Journal of Information Management*, *49*, 502–519. DOI: 10.1016/j.ijinfomgt.2019.05.020

Modaffari, F. G. (2023). The procurement law in the Middle East. *Scholars International Journal of Law. Crime and Justice*, *6*(9). Advance online publication. DOI: 10.36348/sijlcj.2023.v06i09.001

Mohapatra, H. (2025). The Fine-Tuning Journey of ChatGPT in Industry Applications: Domains From Generic to Specific. In Zhao, J., Kumar, V. V., Katina, P. F., & Richards, J. (Eds.), *Humans and Generative AI Tools for Collaborative Intelligence* (pp. 263–284). IGI Global., DOI: 10.4018/979-8-3693-8332-2.ch011

Mohapatra, H. (2025). The Role of 6G in Empowering Smart Cities Enabling Ubiquitous Connectivity and Intelligent Infrastructure. In Nwajana, A. O. (Ed.), *RFID, Microwave Circuit, and Wireless Power Transfer Enabling 5/6G Communication* (pp. 231–254). IGI Global., DOI: 10.4018/979-8-3693-8799-3.ch008

Moica, S., Lucian, T., Kostopoulos, V., Gligor, A., & Mostafa, N. A. (2025). GenAI Technology Approach for Sustainable Warehouse Management Operations: A Case Study from the Automative Sector. *Sustainability (Switzerland)*, *17*(20). Advance online publication. DOI: 10.3390/su17209081

Monostori, L., Váncza, J., & Kumara, S. R. (2006). Agent-based systems for manufacturing. *CIRP Annals*, *55*(2), 697–720. DOI: 10.1016/j.cirp.2006.10.004

Mourtzis, D., Angelopoulos, J., & Panopoulos, N. (2022). A literature review of the challenges and opportunities of the transition from Industry 4.0 to Society 5.0. *Energies*, *15*(17), 6276. DOI: 10.3390/en15176276

Naboush, E. (2020). The carrier's liability for delay under UAE maritime law: A comparative study. *Arab Law Quarterly*. Advance online publication. DOI: 10.1163/15730255-14030068

NAIC. (n.d.). *The impact of motor vehicle simulator training on law enforcement officer driving behavior: Empirical evidence from accident frequency and severity*. Retrieved from https://content.naic.org/sites/default/files/jir-za-38-03-el-vehicle-simulation-training.pdf

NATO Cooperative Cyber Defence Centre of Excellence (NATO CCDCOE). (2019). *Case study: NotPetya and the lessons for national cybersecurity*. NATO CCDCOE.

Negri, E., Fumagalli, L., & Macchi, M. (2017). A review of the roles of digital twin in CPS-based production systems. *Procedia Manufacturing*, *11*, 939–948. DOI: 10.1016/j.promfg.2017.07.198

NEOM. (n.d.). *Oxagon | A reimagined industrial city in NEOM*. Retrieved from https://www.neom.com/en-us/regions/oxagon

Nicoletti, B., & Appolloni, A. (2025). The Impact of AI Foundation models on the future of digital engineering for logistics and supply Chain. *Digital Engineering*, *7*. Advance online publication. DOI: 10.1016/j.dte.2025.100058

Nike, A. (n.d.). *Sustainability — NIKE, Inc.* Retrieved from https://about.nike.com/en/mission/focus-areas/sustainability

Norton Rose Fulbright. (n.d.). Preparing for change: How businesses can thrive under the EU's AI act [https: //www.nortonrosefulbright.com/en/knowledge/publications/228538a2/preparing- for-change-how-businesses-can-thrive-under-the-eus-ai-act [Accessed: 2025-10-08]].

NTT Security. (2023). *Cyber security reports – July 2023.*

NUPCO. (n.d.). *Logistics services - Riyadh.* Retrieved from https://www.nupco.com/en/services/logistics-service/

NVIDIA. (n.d.). *BMW Group starts global rollout of NVIDIA Omniverse.* Retrieved from https://resources.nvidia.com/en-us-industrial-sector-resources/bmw-group-nvidia-omn

Obeidat, M. A., Alfil, N. Z., Aldabousi, A. M., & Dganni, K. M. (2024). Criminal protection for the merchants from the crimes of electronic publishing about invasion of privacy in UAE legislation. *Pakistan Journal of Criminology*, *16*(3), 779–792. DOI: 10.62271/pjc.16.3.779.792

Odumbo, O. R., & Nimma, S. Z. (2025). Leveraging artificial intelligence to maximize efficiency in supply chain process optimization. *International Journal of Research Publication and Reviews*, *6*(1). Advance online publication. DOI: 10.55248/gengpi.6.0125.0508

OECD. (2024). *Artificial Intelligence Review of Egypt.* OECD Publishing. https://www.oecd.org/content/dam/oecd/en/publications/reports/2024/05/oecd-artificial-intelligence-review-of-egypt_3c437131/2a282726-en.pdf

OECD. (2025a). *Governing with artificial intelligence: The state of play and way forward in core government functions.* OECD Publishing. https://www.oecd.org/content/dam/oecd/en/publications/reports/2025/06/governing-with-artificial-intelligence_398fa287/795de142-en.pdf

OECD. (2025b). *Implementing the OECD recommendation on public procurement in OECD and partner countries: 2020–2024 report.* OECD Publishing. https://www.oecd.org/content/dam/oecd/en/publications/reports/2025/06/implementing-the-oecd-recommendation-on-public-procurement-in-oecd-and-partner-countries_dbc4aca7/02a46a58-en.pdf

Ogunde, F. (2025). Legal large language models (LLMs): Legal dynamos or "fancifully packaged ChatGPT"? *Discover Artificial Intelligence*, *5*(1). Advance online publication. DOI: 10.1007/s44163-024-00167-8

Oliveira, A., & Fiser, D. (2025, September). AI-powered app exposes user data, creates risk of supply chain attacks [[https://www.trendmicro.com/en_us/research/25/i/ai-powered-app-exposes-user- data.html](https://www.trendmicro.com/en_us/research/25/i/ai-powered-app- exposes-user-data.html) [Accessed: 2025-10-07]].

Owens, E., Sheehan, B., Mullins, M., Cunneen, M., Ressel, J., & Castignani, G. (2022). Explainable artificial intelligence (xai) in insurance. *Risks*, *10*(12). Advance online publication. DOI: 10.3390/risks10120230

Oxford Business Group. (2020). *Infinite potential: Emerging markets are beginning to unlock the wide-ranging benefits of artificial intelligence.* Egypt 2020 Report. https://oxfordbusinessgroup.com/reports/egypt/2020-report/economy/infinite-potential-emerging-markets-are-beginning-to-unlock-the-wide-ranging-benefits-of-artificial-intelligence

Oxford Insights. (2023). *Government AI readiness index 2023.* https://oxfordinsights.com/wp-content/uploads/2023/12/2023-Government-AI-Readiness-Index-1.pdf

Palo Alto Networks. (n.d.). What is AI red teaming? [[https://www.paloaltonetworks.com/cyberpedia/what-is-ai-red-teaming](https: //www.paloaltonetworks.com/cyberpedia/what-is-ai-red-teaming) [Accessed: 2025-10-08]].

Parasuraman, R., Sheridan, T. B., & Wickens, C. D. (2000). A model for types and levels of human interaction with automation. *IEEE Transactions on Systems, Man, and Cybernetics. Part A, Systems and Humans*, *30*(3), 286–297. DOI: 10.1109/3468.844354

Parh, M. Y. A., Sumy, M. S. A., & Soni, M. S. M. (2023). Restaurant revenue prediction applying supervised learning methods. *Journal of Statistics Applications & Probability*, *12*(1), 1–10. DOI: 10.18576/jsap/120101

Pavlyshenko, B. M. (2019). Machine-Learning Models for Sales Time Series Forecasting. *Data*, *4*(1), 15. DOI: 10.3390/data4010015

Pedregosa, F., Varoquaux, G., Gramfort, A., Michel, V., Thirion, B., Grisel, O., Blondel, M., Prettenhofer, P., Weiss, R., Dubourg, V., Vanderplas, J., Passos, A., Cournapeau, D., Brucher, M., Perrot, M., & Duchesnay, É. (2011). Scikit-learn: Machine learning in Python. *Journal of Machine Learning Research*, *12*, 2825–2830.

Peradze, E. (2025, July 30). How humans in the loop powers responsible AI through data annotation. *Humans in the Loop*. https://humansintheloop.org/how-humans-in-the-loop-powers-responsible-ai-through-data-annotation/

Pettit, T. J., Croxton, K. L., & Fiksel, J. (2013). Ensuring supply chain resilience: Development and implementation of an assessment tool. *Journal of Business Logistics*, *34*(1), 46–76. DOI: 10.1111/jbl.12009

Pijaca, M., Bulum, B., & Primorac, Ž. (2023). Duties of the ship's master in the event of a maritime accident as a type of insured loss. TransNav. *The International Journal on Marine Navigation and Safety of Sea Transportation*, *17*(2), 353–358. DOI: 10.12716/1001.17.02.06

PixelPlex. (n.d.). *Industrial metaverse guide: The future of manufacturing*. Retrieved from https://pixelplex.io/blog/industrial-metaverse-guide/

Place North West. (n.d.). *CASE STUDY | BMW enjoys 'vast efficiency' of digital twin factories*. Retrieved from https://www.placenorthwest.co.uk/case-study-bmw-enjoys-vast-efficiency-of-digital-twin-factories/

Pournader, M., Ghaderi, H., Hassanzadegan, A., & Fahimnia, B. (2021). Artificial intelligence applications in supply chain management. *International Journal of Production Economics*, *241*, 108250. DOI: 10.1016/j.ijpe.2021.108250

Prakash, O. (2025). How digital twin technology can revolutionize a supply chain. *Supply Chain Management Review*. https://www.scmr.com/article/how-digital-twin-technology-can-revolutionize-a-supply-chain

Puad, N. A. M. (2024). Future directions of Shariah audit for takaful industry: Perceptions of Shariah committee. In *Springer Proceedings in Business and Economics*. Springer., DOI: 10.1007/978-3-031-67511-9_13

Qadeer, A., & Awad, A. (2025). AI-powered ChatGPT in branding: Benefits, challenges, and future directions. In *Impacts of AI generated content on brand reputation* (pp. 1–26). IGI Global., DOI: 10.4018/979-8-3373-4327-3.ch001

Qi, Q., Tao, F., Hu, T., Anwer, N., Liu, A., Wei, Y., Wang, L., & Nee, A. Y. C. (2021). Enabling technologies and tools for digital twin. *Journal of Manufacturing Systems*, *58*, 3–21. DOI: 10.1016/j.jmsy.2019.10.001

Rasheed, A., San, O., & Kvamsdal, T. (2020). Digital twin: Values, challenges and enablers from a modeling perspective. *IEEE Access : Practical Innovations, Open Solutions*, *8*, 21980–22012. DOI: 10.1109/ACCESS.2020.2970143

ResearchGate. (2024). *Metaverse healthcare supply chain: Conceptual framework and barrier identification*. Retrieved from https://www.researchgate.net/publication/378265130_Metaverse_Healthcare_Supply_Chain_Conceptual_Framework_and_Barrier_Identification

Ribeiro, M., Singh, S., & Guestrin, C. (2016). "why should i trust you?": Explaining the predictions of any classifier, 1135–1144. https://doi.org/DOI: 10.1145/2939672.2939778

RocketMeUpCybersecurity. (2024, October). Cybersecurity for autonomous systems – Cars, drones, and beyond [[https://medium.com/@RocketMeUpCybersecurity/cybersecurity-for-autonomous- systems-cars-drones-and-beyond-8d32b1d92d5b] (https: //medium.com/@RocketMeUpCybersecurity/cybersecurity-for-autonomous - systems-cars-drones-and-beyond-8d32b1d92d5b) [Accessed: 2025-10-07]].

Roscoe, S., Aktas, E., Petersen, K. J., Skipworth, H. D., Handfield, R. B., & Habib, F. (2022). Redesigning global supply chains during compounding geopolitical disruptions: The role of supply chain logics. *International Journal of Operations & Production Management*, *42*(9), 1407–1434. DOI: 10.1108/IJOPM-12-2021-0777

SABIC. (2021). *Supply chain*. Retrieved from https://www.sabic.com/en/reports/annual-2021/corporate/supply-chain

SABIC. (n.d.). *SABIC's digital transformation journey*. Retrieved from https://www.sabic.com/en/newsandmedia/stories/our-future/sabic-digital-transformation-journey

Saccomanno, F. P., Trivella, A., & Guerriero, F. (2026). Integrated sales planning for in-store retail: A multi-stage stochastic optimization approach. *European Journal of Operational Research*, *329*(2), 669–686. DOI: 10.1016/j.ejor.2025.07.015

Sadeghi, K., Ojha, D., Kaur, P., Mahto, R. V., & Dhir, A. (2024). Explainable artificial intelligence and agile decision-making in supply chain cyber resilience. *Decision Support Systems*, *180*, 114194. DOI: 10.1016/j.dss.2024.114194

Sagheer, A., & Kotb, M. (2019). Time series forecasting of petroleum production using deep LSTM recurrent networks. *Neurocomputing*, *323*, 203–213. DOI: 10.1016/j.neucom.2018.09.082

Şahinbaş, K. (2021). Price prediction model for restaurants in Istanbul by using machine-learning algorithms. *Ekonomi, İşletme ve Maliye Araştırmaları Dergisi*, *4*(2), 159–171. DOI: 10.38009/ekimad.1148216

Sarhan, A. I. (2024). *Options that impair the binding effect of contract and their role in protecting contractual consent: An analysis of how Arab civil laws are influenced by Islamic jurisprudence. Manchester Journal of Transnational Islamic Law and Practice.*

Sarioguz, O. (2025). Artificial intelligence for sustainable logistics: Reducing carbon emissions and fuel consumption through route optimization. *Journal of International Scientific Research Archive*, *15*(3). Advance online publication. DOI: 10.30574/ijsra.2025.15.3.1933

Sarker, I. H., Janicke, H., Mohsin, A., Gill, A., & Maglaras, L. (2024). Explainable AI for cybersecurity automation, intelligence and trustworthiness in digital twin: Methods, taxonomy, challenges and prospects. *ICT Express*, *10*(4), 935–958. DOI: 10.1016/j.icte.2024.05.007

Schmidt, A., Kabir, M. W. U., & Hoque, M. T. (2022). Machine-learning based restaurant sales forecasting. *Machine-learning and Knowledge Extraction*, *4*(1), 105–130. DOI: 10.3390/make4010006

Schmitt, M. N. (Ed.). (2017). *Tallinn Manual 2.0 on the international law applicable to cyber operations.* Cambridge University Press.

Secretariat, A. S. E. A. N. (2021). *ASEAN Cybersecurity Cooperation Strategy.* ASEAN Secretariat.

SecuriThings. (n.d.). Physical security & cybersecurity in the logistics industry [[https://securithings.com/cybersecurity-in-the-logistics-industry](https: // securithings.com/cybersecurity-in-the-logistics-industry) [Accessed: 2025-10-07]].

Seuring, S., & Müller, M. (2008). From a literature review to a conceptual framework for sustainable supply chain management. *Journal of Cleaner Production*, *16*(15), 1699–1710. DOI: 10.1016/j.jclepro.2008.04.020

SFDA. (n.d.). *Home - RSD.* Retrieved from https://rsd.sfda.gov.sa/index-en.html

Shaheen, A., Khataan, A., Awad, A., Shams Eldin, A. Y., & Elnour, A. (2025). The role of influencer content value and credibility in purchase intention. *Innovative Marketing*, *21*(3), 14–30. DOI: 10.21511/im.21(3).2025.02

Shams Eldin, A. Y., Elnour, A., Hassan, R. O. A., & Awad, A. (2025). The role of technological and environmental factors in creating business value from social media dynamic capabilities for SMEs in Saudi Arabia. *Humanities & Social Sciences Communications*, *12*, 1431. DOI: 10.1057/s41599-025-05784-x

Shao, S., Gu, T., Yang, Q., Du, H., Liang, W., Sun, Z., & Ji, Y. (2025). Master-slave multi-chain with risk assessment based access control model for zero trust network. *Peer-to-Peer Networking and Applications, 18*(6). Advance online publication. DOI: 10.1007/s12083-024-01853-1

Sharma, V., Ajmani, P., & Iwendi, C. (2023). *Blockchain application with specific reference to smart contracts in the insurance sector.* In *The Application of Emerging Technology and Blockchain in the Insurance Industry. Dubai Court of Cassation – Civil Judgments, Appeal No. 248 of 2008 (Commercial Circuit), judgment dated April 20, 2009, Technical Office, Vol. 20, Part 2, Rule No. 128(2), p. 1121*

Shevtshenko, E.. (2023). Development of SCOR database for digitalisation of supply chain customer feedback analysis. *Inzinerine Ekonomika–Engineering Economics, 34*(4). Advance online publication. DOI: 10.5755/j01.ee.34.4.31618

Shi, H., Xia, Y., Zong, Z., Hua, Y., Sun, J., & Chen, X. (2025). Does Data Asset Information Disclosure Mitigate Supply Chain Risk? Causal Evidence from Double-Debiased Machine Learning. *Systems, 13*(10). Advance online publication. DOI: 10.3390/systems13100844

Shrestha, Y. R., Ben-Menahem, S. M., & von Krogh, G. (2019). Organizational decision-making structures in the age of artificial intelligence. *California Management Review, 61*(4), 66–83. DOI: 10.1177/0008125619862257

Siemens. (n.d.). *The state of the industrial metaverse.* Retrieved from https://www.siemens.com/global/en/company/insights/the-state-of-the-industrial-metaverse.html

Simchi-Levi, D., Kaminsky, P., & Simchi-Levi, E. (2000). *Designing and managing the supply chain: Concepts, strategies, and case studies.* McGraw-Hill.

Singapore, C. S. A. (2021, October 11). *16th iteration of ASEAN CERT incident drill tests responding to supply chain attacks.* https://www.csa.gov.sg/news-events/news-articles/csa-hosts-16th-iteration-of-asean-cert-incident-drill

Singh, S., Khanna, T., & Verma, D. K. (2025). A hybrid ensemble model for ransomware detection using feature engineering and deep learning. *International Journal of Information Technology (Singapore), 17*(8), 5095–5104. DOI: 10.1007/s41870-025-02681-z

Sloan, M. I. T. (n.d.). *Solve real-world problems with the industrial metaverse.* Retrieved from https://mitsloan.mit.edu/ideas-made-to-matter/solve-real-world-problems-industrial-metaverse

Soumpenioti, V., & Panagopoulos, A. (2023, September). AI Technology in the Field of Logistics. In *2023 18th International Workshop on Semantic and Social Media Adaptation & Personalization (SMAP) 18th International Workshop on Semantic and Social Media Adaptation & Personalization (SMAP 2023)* (pp. 1-6). IEEE. DOI: 10.1109/SMAP59435.2023.10255203

Stanford, E. (2025). Autonomous AI: Who is responsible when AI acts autonomously and things go wrong? In *AI, machine learning & big data laws and regulations*. Global Legal Insights. https://www.globallegalinsights.com/practice-areas/ai-machine-learning-and-big-data-laws-and-regulations/autonomous-ai-who-is-responsible-when-ai-acts-autonomously-and-things-go-wrong/

Stevens, G. C. (1990). Successful supply chain management. *Management Decision*, *28*(8). Advance online publication. DOI: 10.1108/00251749010140790

Supply Chain Digital. (n.d.). *DHL Supply Chain to roll out 'Vision Picking' smart glasses across the globe*. Retrieved from https://supplychaindigital.com/technology/dhl-supply-chain-roll-out-vision-picking-smart-glasses-across-globe

Supply Chain, N. H. S. (n.d.). *Transforming NHS inventory management – A blueprint for success*. Retrieved from https://www.supplychain.nhs.uk/news-article/transforming-nhs-inventory-management-a-blueprint-for-success/

Syntetos, A. A., Babai, Z., Boylan, J. E., Kolassa, S., & Nikolopoulos, K. (2016). Supply chain forecasting: Theory, practice, their gap and the future. *European Journal of Operational Research*, *252*(1), 1–26. DOI: 10.1016/j.ejor.2015.11.010

Taeihagh, A. (2021). Governance of artificial intelligence. *Policy and Society*, *40*(2), 137–157. DOI: 10.1080/14494035.2021.1928377

Tanizaki, T., Hoshino, T., Shimmura, T., & Takenaka, T. (2019). Demand forecasting in restaurants using machine learning and statistical analysis. *Procedia CIRP*, *79*, 679–683. DOI: 10.1016/j.procir.2019.02.042

Tao, F., Zhang, H., Liu, A., & Nee, A. Y. C. (2018). Digital twin in industry: State-of-the-art. *IEEE Transactions on Industrial Informatics*, *15*(4), 2405–2415. DOI: 10.1109/TII.2018.2873186

Telecommunications and Digital Government Regulatory Authority (TDRA). (2020). *Annual cybersecurity report*. UAE Government.

Tirkolaee, E. B., Sadeghi, S., Mansoori Mooseloo, F., Rezaei Vandchali, H., & Aeini, S. (2021). Application of machine learning in supply chain management: A comprehensive overview of the main areas. *Mathematical Problems in Engineering. Article ID, 1476043*. Advance online publication. DOI: 10.1155/2021/1476043

Toorajipour, R., Sohrabpour, V., Nazarpour, A., Oghazi, P., & Fischl, M. (2021). Artificial intelligence in supply chain management: A systematic literature review. *Journal of Business Research, 122*, 502–517. DOI: 10.1016/j.jbusres.2020.09.009

Torchio, F. (2023). *Survey on automated systems for smart warehouses* (PhD thesis). Politecnico di Torino. https://webthesis.biblio.polito.it/secure/29879/1/tesi.pdf

Tornatzky, L. G., & Fleischer, M. (1990). *The processes of technological innovation.* Lexington Books.

Traxtech. (2025, August). AI supply chain risks: The hidden vulnerabilities in your third-party network [[https://www.traxtech.com/ai-in-supply-chain/ai-supply - chain-risks-the-hidden-vulnerabilities-in-your-third-party-network](https: //www .traxtech.com/ai-in-supply-chain/ai-supply-chain-risks-the-hidden- vulnerabilities-in-your-third-party-network) [Accessed: 2025-10-07]].

TrustPath. (n.d.). AI compliance as a service: Navigating the new regulatory landscape [[https://www.trustpath.ai/blog/ai-compliance-as-a-service-navigating-the-new - regulatory-landscape](https://www.trustpath.ai/blog/ai-compliance-as-a-service - navigating-the-new-regulatory-landscape) [Accessed: 2025-10-08]].

Tsagourias, N., & Buchan, R. (2015). *Research handbook on international law and cyberspace*. Edward Elgar Publishing.

Tsagourias, N., & Buchan, R. (2021). *Cyber interventions and international law.* Cambridge University Press.

Tunisia (Various Ministries). (2022). *National artificial intelligence strategy: Unlocking Tunisia's capabilities potential.*

Tunisia. (2014). *Decree No. 2014-1039 organizing public procurement procedures.* Official Gazette of the Republic of Tunisia.

UK Foreign and Commonwealth Office. (2018, February 15). *UK condemns Russia for NotPetya cyber-attack.* https://www.gov.uk/government/news/foreign-office -minister-condemns-russia-for-notpetya-attacks

Ulmer, M. W., Goodson, J. C., Mattfeld, D. C., & Thomas, B. W. (2020). On modeling stochastic dynamic vehicle routing problems. *EURO Journal on Transportation and Logistics, 9*(2), 100008. DOI: 10.1016/j.ejtl.2020.100008

UN GGE. (2015). *Report of the Group of Governmental Experts on developments in the field of information and telecommunications in the context of international security (A/70/174).*

UN GGE. (2021). *Advancing responsible state behaviour in cyberspace in the context of international security (A/76/135).*

UN OEWG. (2021). *Final substantive report (A/75/816).*

UNGA. (2015). *Developments in the field of information and telecommunications in the context of international security (A/RES/70/237).*

UNGA. (2023). *Second annual progress report of the OEWG 2021–2025 (A/RES/78/237).*

Unit, X. Labs. (2025). Defining GDPR machine vision systems for today's businesses. https://www.unitxlabs.com/resources/general-data-protection-regulation-gdpr-machine-vision-system/

United Nations Development Programme. (2023). *Procurement for sustainable development strategy 2022–2025.* https://www.undp.org/sites/g/files/zskgke326/files/2025-05/undp_procurement_for_sust_dev_strategy_2022-25.pdf

United Nations Environment Programme. (2021). *Sustainable public procurement: A global review.* https://wedocs.unep.org/handle/20.500.11822/8522

United Nations. (2015). *Transforming our world: The 2030 Agenda for Sustainable Development* (A/RES/70/1). https://sdgs.un.org/2030agenda

United Nations. (2023). *The Sustainable Development Goals report 2023.* UN DESA. https://unstats.un.org/sdgs/report/2023/The-Sustainable-Development-Goals-Report-2023.pdf

Unyer. (n.d.). *How metaverse technology is revolutionizing healthcare & life science supply chains.* Retrieved from https://www.unyer.com/revolutionizing-healthcare-and-life-science-supply-chains-with-metaverse-technology/

Varga, L. Z. (2022). Solutions to the routing problem: Towards trustworthy autonomous vehicles. *Artificial Intelligence Review*, *55*, 5445–5484. DOI: 10.1007/s10462-021-10131-y

Venkatesh, V., & Davis, F. D. (2000). A theoretical extension of the technology acceptance model: Four longitudinal field studies. *Management Science*, *46*(2), 186–204. DOI: 10.1287/mnsc.46.2.186.11926

VerifyWise. (2025). Human in the loop safeguards. https://verifywise.ai/lexicon/human-in-the-loop-safeguards

Villareal, M. A., & Fergusson, I. F. (2020). *The United States-Mexico-Canada Agreement (USMCA).* Congressional Research Service.

Wang, J., Ma, Y., Zhang, L., Gao, R. X., & Wu, D. (2020). Deep learning for smart manufacturing: Methods and applications. *Journal of Manufacturing Systems*, *48*, 144–156. DOI: 10.1016/j.jmsy.2018.01.003

WCO. (2021/2025). *SAFE Framework of Standards to Secure and Facilitate Global Trade*. World Customs Organization.

Webelight Solutions Pvt. Ltd. (2025). Digital twins vs. AI logistics twins: Which will define the future of supply chain management? [[https://medium.com/@webelightsolutions/digital-twins-vs-ai-logistics-twins- which-will-define-the-future-of-supply-chain-management-c08a78512abf](https: //medium.com/@webelightsolutions/digital-twins-vs-ai-logistics-twins-which-will- define-the-future-of-supply-chain-management-c08a78512abf) [Accessed: 2025-10-07]].

Weimer, D., Scholz-Reiter, B., & Shpitalni, M. (2016). Design of deep convolutional neural network architectures for automated feature extraction in industrial inspection. *CIRP Annals*, *65*(1), 417–420. DOI: 10.1016/j.cirp.2016.04.072

Wen, S. F., Shukla, A., & Katt, B. (2025). Artificial intelligence for system security assurance: A systematic literature review. *International Journal of Information Security*, *24*, 43. DOI: 10.1007/s10207-024-00959-0

Whiteman, T. (1984). Supervision necessary? *Bulk Syst. Int.*, *4*(2), 45–47.

Williams, S. (2007). *Buying a better world: Sustainable public procurement.* Forum for the Future. https://www.oneplanetnetwork.org/sites/default/files/sustainable_procurement_manual_-_resource_book.pdf

World Bank. (2022). *Cybersecurity capacity building in critical infrastructure: Transport and customs*. World Bank.

World Bank. (2023). *Sustainable procurement.* World Bank Group. https://thedocs.worldbank.org/en/doc/01802d374f64ff681613cff8ccad3576-0290012023/original/Sustainable-Procurement-August-2023.pdf

Xpert.Digital. (n.d.). *Industrial metaverse factory planning from BMW iFactory: Digital twin & virtual factory & planning with the NVIDIA Omniverse*. Retrieved from https://xpert.digital/en/bmw-metaverse

Xu, L. D., Xu, E. L., & Li, L. (2018). Industry 4.0: State of the art and future trends. *International Journal of Production Research*, *56*(8), 2941–2962. DOI: 10.1080/00207543.2018.1444806

Yin, R. K. (2018). *Case study research and applications: Design and methods* (6th ed.). SAGE Publications.

Zhang, D., Kabuka, M. R., & Yu, N. (2021). Real-time vehicle dispatching using deep reinforcement learning. In *Proceedings of the 2021 IEEE International Conference on Big Data* (pp. 4187-4192). IEEE. DOI: 10.1109/BigData52589.2021.9671579

Zhang, X., & Wu, X. (2026). Collaborative scheduling for heterogeneous robots with simultaneous pickup and delivery tasks in order-picking systems. *Expert Systems with Applications, 297*. Advance online publication. DOI: 10.1016/j.eswa.2025.129457

Zheng, R. (2022). *Marine insurance law reform in China: Experiences from the UK.* In *Commercial and Maritime Law in China and Europe* (pp. 123–140). Routledge. DOI: 10.4324/9781003160298-7

About the Contributors

Abdelrehim Awad is an Associate Professor, Researcher in digital marketing, AI applications in business, and supply chain innovation; multiple Scopus/WoS publications; supervises graduate research and contributes to editorial activities at the University of Bisha.

Dhafer Al Ahmari is an Assistant professor, Academic–practitioner in public procurement and supply chain management; leads procurement transformation initiatives and supervises theses; also serves as a logistics consultant.

***

Ahmed Moustafa Aldabousi is an Associate Professor of Commercial Law and Maritime Umm Al Quwain University, umm al-Quwain, United Arab Emirates.

Abrar Alharbi is a Medical Laboratory Specialist with academic, research, and administrative experience across university laboratories and BSL-3 research units. Background spans internship/co-op coordination, accreditation self-study contributions, and day-to-day laboratory operations with strict biosafety compliance. Skilled in SOP development, records and inventory control, scheduling, and cross-functional coordination with clinical, academic, and research teams.

Nawaf Alharbi is a Laboratory Specialist and Researcher specialized in Medical Laboratory with extensive experience in managing and operating clinical and research laboratories. Skilled in implementing advanced laboratory techniques, scientific data analysis, and preparing precise technical reports. Proficient in technical supervision, team organization, coordinating volunteer activities, and training technical staff to ensure compliance with quality standards and academic accreditation.

Duggirala Aravind is currently associated with the Department of Aviation, bearing the registration number 249207990030, at ASET Institute of Science and Technology, Chennai, India. He previously completed his Bachelor's degree in Electrical and Electronics Engineering at MITS University. His research interests include aircraft maintenance engineering, aviation safety management, renewable energy technologies in air transport, and sustainable energy systems. (aravindaset.edu@gmail.com).

Suzan Bakr is a Professor of Business Administration and the Director of the Quality Assurance Unit at Al-Azhar University's Faculty of Commerce in Cairo, I have dedicated my career to academia and institutional development. I am a proud alumna of Al-Azhar, where I graduated first in my class with a Bachelor's degree in Business Administration. My entire professional journey has been with the university, starting as a Demonstrator and progressing through the academic ranks to become an Associate Professor in December 2018 and then Professor in January 2024. I hold a Master's degree and a PhD in Business Administration, which I earned in 2012. My work focuses on contemporary management issues, and I am an active researcher and author with numerous publications on topics like strategic intelligence, digital transformation, and organizational behavior. Beyond my research, I am passionate about teaching and mentoring the next generation of scholars, having taught extensively at both the undergraduate and postgraduate levels and supervised many master's and doctoral theses. In my administrative role, I am committed to advancing our faculty's standards by leading curriculum development and spearheading key quality assurance initiatives.

Amer Fakhoury is a Professor of Public International Law and Human Rights at the College of Law, American University in the Emirates (AUE), Dubai. He holds a Ph.D. in International Law with extensive experience in teaching, research, and graduate supervision. His main research areas include international humanitarian and criminal law, state responsibility for cross-border cyberattacks, territorial disputes and sovereignty (notably the Russia–Ukraine case), space law and artificial intelligence, maritime security and piracy, and intellectual property protection in the digital era. He teaches advanced courses such as Public International Law, International Organizations, International Humanitarian Law, International Crimes, Cybercrime Law, and Enforcement Law. Known for linking legal theory with practical political analysis, he employs real-world case studies and simulations to enhance students' analytical skills. Institutionally, Dr. Fakhoury contributes to accreditation processes, program design (Master's and Ph.D.), and serves on thesis committees and international conference panels. A frequent media commentator, he appears on regional and international TV networks

Roba Gamal is a Senior Algorithm Engineer at Valeo, I specialize in developing innovative machine learning solutions for the automotive industry. My work has resulted in four patents for a radar-based seat occupancy detection system using advanced deep learning techniques. Prior to Valeo, I worked as a Data Scientist at Orange Labs, where I led diverse projects in computer vision, NLP, and data analysis. My experience ranges from image classification and segmentation to building recommendation systems. I am currently a PhD candidate in Computer Engineering at Cairo University, holding Master's degrees from both Cairo University and Arizona State University. I also share my passion for the field as a Teaching Assistant at Zewail University. I am an AWS Certified Machine Learning Engineer with strong proficiency in PyTorch, TensorFlow, Python, and C++.

Abdelrhman A. Gami is an AI Engineer with three years of experience at a leading French automotive supplier, I specialize in deploying real-time deep learning models. My work focuses on creating innovative in-cabin solutions, blending computer vision with generative AI to enhance vehicle safety and user experience. I have successfully led computer vision features from concept to production, including a seat occupancy detection (SOD) system for a publicly funded project with leading OEMs. My experience spans the full project lifecycle, from data collection to model deployment using Libtorch. Furthermore, I have engineered systems for 3D hand pose estimation and integrated advanced models, including LLMs, VLMs, and real-time speech-to-speech technologies, to build interactive conversational agents for ADAS demonstrations. Proficient in MLOps, I use ClearML for experiment tracking and Docker for training on GPU clusters. My commitment to innovation is evidenced by my contributions as an inventor on multiple patent applications for driver monitoring and safety. I am passionate about solving real-world problems with cutting-edge AI.

Bhoomi Gupta is an undergraduate student pursuing a Bachelor of Technology (B.Tech.) in Computer Science and Engineering at Jaypee University of Engineering and Technology (JUET), Guna, India. Her research interests include AI, Machine Learning, and their applications in various domains.

Geet Madnani is an undergraduate student pursuing a Bachelor of Technology (B.Tech.) in Computer Science and Engineering at Jaypee University of Engineering and Technology (JUET), Guna, India. His research interests include AI, Machine Learning, and their applications in various domains.

Kunj Bihari Meena is a faculty member and researcher in Computer Science and Engineering at Jaypee University and Engineering Technology Guna. Dr. Meena has published multiple papers in reputed international journals and conferences, including SCI and Scopus-indexed publications. He has received Best Paper Awards for his research contributions and serves as a reviewer for prestigious SCI/Scopus journals and conferences. His areas of research include image processing, digital image forensics, deep learning, and blockchain.

Yash Pathak is an undergraduate student pursuing a Bachelor of Technology (B.Tech.) in Computer Science and Engineering at Jaypee University of Engineering and Technology (JUET), Guna, India. His research interests include AI, Machine Learning, and their applications in various domains.

Binastya Anggara Sekti has been a lecturer at the Faculty of Computer Science, Esa Unggul University, Jakarta, since 2016. He is actively involved in the Artificial Intelligence and Information Security Study Group. He holds a Bachelor's degree in Informatics Engineering from the Bandung Institute of Technology and a Master's degree in Information Systems Management from Trisakti University, Jakarta. Prior to entering academia, he accumulated over 25 years of professional experience as an IT practitioner in various companies across Jakarta. His work focused on developing data centers for internet service providers and delivering IT solutions for the manufacturing and oil & gas sectors. His research interests include artificial intelligence, cybersecurity, and the development of IT infrastructure.

N.V. Suresh is a renowned academician from Chennai, Tamil Nadu. He completed his schooling in Chennai. He obtained his BA degree (2012) from D.G.Vaishnav College, Madras University. He joined the Bharathiar University received an MBA degree and PGDM. He Awarded Ph.D. in Management from University of Madras. Dr.N.V.Suresh joined then IIKM in June 2014 as an Assistant Professor (2014 to 2016). He moved to Remo International College in June, 2019 as an Assistant Professor and rose through the ranks to the position of Head of the Department in Aug 2020 to July 2021 then Shifted to Working Academy of Maritime Education and Training (Deemed to be University) Presently Working as Associate Professor and Vice-Principal in ASET College of Science and Technology from March 2022 to Till Date. He is the Visiting Faculty for Institute of Distance Education, University of Madras, Tamil Nadu Open University, Anna University and Directorate of Online Education SRM University for MBA from 2015 to till date. Dr.N.V. Suresh has carried out all his research work entirely in India and has published 30 research papers in international journals.

Vipin Tyagi is a distinguished academician, researcher and author, currently serving as Dean (Academic and Research) at Jaypee University of Engineering and Technology in Guna, Madhya Pradesh. With a rich background in Computer Science, his expertise spans across Image Processing, Cyber Forensics, and Speech

Recognition. Prof. Tyagi has a prolific publication record, contributing significantly to his fields of interest. His scholarly work includes numerous journal articles, conference papers, and books. Some of his notable publications are in the areas of image forgery detection, image denoising, and content-based image retrieval. He has authored and edited several books and papers in the field of computing and data sciences, such as “Digital Image Forgery Detection: Techniques, Challenges and Applications”, “Predictive Computing and Information Security” and “Content-Based Image Retrieval: Ideas, Influences, and Current Trends” published by Springer Singapore. His book “Understanding Digital Image Processing” using MATLAB, published by Taylor and Francis is highlighted by Mathworks at: https://in.mathworks.com/academia/books/understanding-digital-image-processing-tyagi.html His scholarly work has earned him a respectable h-index and numerous citations in the academic community.

Index

A

C

D

S

T

V

Z

www.ingramcontent.com/pod-product-compliance
Ingram Content Group UK Ltd.
Pitfield, Milton Keynes, MK11 3LW, UK
UKHW052001051026
15624UKWH00003B/495

9 798337 388410